GRAMMAR
Form and Function
3

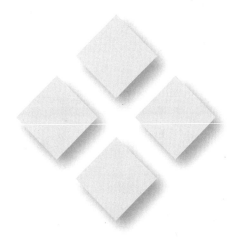

Milada Broukal
and
Ingrid Wisniewska, Contributing Author

McGraw-Hill

Grammar Form and Function 3

Published by McGraw-Hill ESL/ELT, a business unit of The McGraw-Hill Companies, Inc., 1221 Avenue of the Americas, New York, NY 10020. Copyright © 2005 by The McGraw-Hill Companies, Inc.

ISBN: 0-07-008313-4

Editorial director: Tina B. Carver
Senior managing editor: Erik Gundersen
Developmental editors: Arley Gray, Annie Sullivan
Editorial assistants: David Averbach, Kasey Williamson
Production manager: Juanita Thompson
Cover design: AcentoVisual
Interior design: AcentoVisual
Art: Eldon Doty

Photo credits:
All photos are courtesy of Getty Images Royalty-Free Collection with the exception of the following: *Page 44* © Bettmann/CORBIS; *Page 95* © Bettmann/CORBIS; *Page 111, top* © Jade Albert Studio Inc./Getty Images; *Page 111, bottom* © David Zelick/Getty Images; *Page 132* © Bettmann/CORBIS; *Page 182* © David Katzenstein/CORBIS; *Page 190* © Bettmann/CORBIS; *Page 224* © Reuters/CORBIS; *Page 305, top* © CP/JACQUES NADEAU; *Page 327* © Bettmann/CORBIS; *Page 328* © Michael Nicholson/CORBIS; *Page 357* © CORBIS; *Page 369* © Hulton-Deutsch Collection/CORBIS; *Page 381* © Helen Thayer; *Page 414* © Hulton-Deutsch Collection/CORBIS.

The *McGraw-Hill* Companies

Contents

UNIT 7 MODALS II

UNIT 8 THE PASSIVE VOICE, CAUSATIVES, AND PHRASAL VERBS

UNIT 9 GERUNDS AND INFINITIVES

UNIT 10 AGREEMENT AND PARALLEL STRUCTURE

UNIT 11 NOUN CLAUSES AND REPORTED SPEECH

UNIT 12 ADJECTIVE CLAUSES

UNIT 13 ADVERB CLAUSES

UNIT 14 CONDITIONAL SENTENCES

APPENDICES

INDEX

Acknowledgements

The publisher and author would like to thank the following individuals who reviewed **Grammar Form and Function** during the development of the series and whose comments and suggestions were invaluable in creating this project.

- Tony Albert, *Jewish Vocational Services, San Francisco, CA*
- Leslie A. Biaggi, *Miami–Dade Community College, Miami, FL*
- Gerry Boyd, *Northern Virginia Community College, VA*
- Marcia M. Captan, *Miami–Dade Community College, Miami, FL*
- Yongjae Paul Choe, *Dongguk University, Seoul, Korea*
- Sally Gearhart, *Santa Rosa Junior College, Santa Rosa, CA*
- Mary Gross, *Miramar College, San Diego, CA*
- Martin Guerin, *Miami–Dade Community College, Miami, FL*
- Patty Heiser, *University of Washington, Seattle, WA*
- Susan Kasten, *University of North Texas, Denton, TX*
- Sarah Kegley, *Georgia State University, Atlanta, GA*
- Kelly Kennedy-Isern, *Miami–Dade Community College, Miami, FL*
- Grace Low, *Germantown, TN*
- Irene Maksymjuk, *Boston University, Boston, MA*
- Christina Michaud, *Bunker Hill Community College, Boston, MA*
- Cristi Mitchell, *Miami–Dade Community College-Kendall Campus, Miami, FL*
- Carol Piñeiro, *Boston University, Boston, MA*
- Michelle Remaud, *Roxbury Community College, Boston, MA*
- Diana Renn, *Wentworth Institute of Technology, Boston, MA*
- Alice Savage, *North Harris College, Houston, TX*
- Karen Stanley, *Central Piedmont Community College, Charlotte, NC*
- Roberta Steinberg, *Mt. Ida College, Newton, MA*

The author would like to thank everyone at McGraw-Hill who participated in this project's development, especially Arley Gray, Erik Gundersen, Annie Sullivan, Jennifer Monaghan, David Averbach, Kasey Williamson, and Tina Carver.

Welcome to Grammar Form and Function!

In **Grammar Form and Function 3**, high-interest photos bring high intermediate to advanced grammar to life, providing visual contexts for learning and retaining new structures and vocabulary.

Welcome to **Grammar Form and Function 3**. This visual tour will provide you with an overview of the key features of a unit.

❖ *Form* **presentations** teach grammar structures through complete charts and high-interest, memorable photos that facilitate students' recall of grammar structures.

❖ *Form* **presentations** also include related information such as punctuation rules.

11b Noun Clauses Beginning with Wh- Words (Indirect Wh- Questions)

Form

I don't know **why he takes his computer on camping trips.**

Main Clause	Noun Clause (Indirect Question)*
She wanted to know	who I was.
	where they came from.
	why he called.
I don't know	when he arrives.
	what she said.
	how they did it so fast.

Indirect question is the name of this type of noun clause.

1. Noun clauses may also begin with wh- words. Sentences with noun clauses beginning with wh- words are also called indirect questions.

   Direct Question: Why did he call?
   Indirect Question: I don't know why he called.

2. Although wh- clauses begin with a question word, they do not follow question word order. Instead, they use statement word order.

   CORRECT: I know where **she is**.
   INCORRECT: I know where ~~is she~~.

3. We use a question mark at the end of a sentence if the main clause is a direct question and a period at the end of a sentence if the main clause is a statement.

	Main Clause	Noun Clause (Indirect Question)
Main clause is a question	Can you tell me	where the elevators are?
Main clause is a statement	I wonder	where the elevators are.

321
Noun Clauses and Reported Speech

❖ *Function* **presentations** clarify when to use grammar structures.

Function

1. We usually use an indirect question to express something we do not know or to express uncertainty.

   I don't know **how much it is.**

2. We often use indirect questions to ask politely for information.

   Direct Question: What time does the train leave?
   Indirect Question: Can you tell me what time the train leaves?

❖ *Extensive* **practice** guides students from accurate production to fluent use of the grammar.

4 Practice

Rewrite each question as a main clause + a wh- noun clause. Be sure to use correct punctuation at the end of the sentences.

You are going to a job interview. What questions will you ask?

1. How many people does your company employ?

   Can you tell me _how many people the company employs?_

2. When did the company first get started?

   I'd like to know _____

3. Where is the head office?

   Can you tell me _____

4. What are the job benefits?

   Can you tell me _____

5. How many vacation days do people get?

   I wonder _____

6. What is the salary?

   Can you tell me _____

7. Who will my manager be?

   I'd like to know _____

8. When does the job start?

   Can you tell me _____

❖ *Topical* **exercises** provide opportunities for students to use language naturally.

9. How many people are you going to interview for this job?

   Can you tell me _____

10. When can you tell me the results of this interview?

    If you don't mind, I'd like to know _____

5 Practice

Rewrite each direct question as an indirect question (a main clause + a wh- noun clause). Be sure to use correct punctuation at the end of the sentences.

You have a job interview tomorrow, and you are asking a friend to help you prepare. Your friend is telling you about the questions that they will probably ask you.

1. They will probably ask _what your current job title is._
   (What is your current job title?)

2. They will want to know _____
   (What are your job duties?)

3. They will ask _____
   (What qualifications do you have?)

4. They will want to know _____
   (Who was your previous employer?)

5. They will ask _____
   (How long did you work in your last job?)

6. They will want to know _____
   (Why did you leave your last job?)

7. They will ask _____
   (What was your salary?)

8. They will want to know _____
   (Why do you want the job?)

9. They will ask _____
   (How did you find out about the job?)

❖ *Your Turn* activities guide students to practice grammar in personally meaningful conversations.

6 Your Turn

Work with a partner. Think of an unusual job. Imagine that you went to a job interview for this job and write five wh- questions the interviewer asked you. Tell the class about the questions using a main clause + a wh- noun clause. Your classmates should guess the job.

Example:
(The unusual job was a lion tamer.)
They asked (me) why I was interested in lions.

REVIEW:

1 Review

Rewrite the quotes and questions.

1. Cindy said, "Matthew, get out of bed, or you'll be late for your interview."

   Cindy told *Matthew to get out of bed or he'd be late for*

   his interview.

2. Matthew said, "Why didn't you get me up earlier?"

   Matthew wanted to know _____

3. Cindy said, "I was at the gym, and I expected you to be gone by now."

   Cindy said that _____

4. Matthew said, "Did I set my alarm clock or not?"

   Mathew couldn't remember _____

5. Cindy suggested, "Matthew, you'd better hurry if you want to get that job."

   Cindy suggested that _____

6. The interviewer had said, "Be here on time."

   The interviewer had insisted _____

7. Cindy said, "Why did you sleep so late?"

   Cindy said she didn't understand _____

8. Matthew explained, "I was preparing for the interview until 2:00 A.M."

   Matthew explained that _____

9. Cindy asked, "How do expect to get there, Matthew?"

   Cindy asked _____

10. Matthew asked, "Can you drive me there?"

    Matthew wondered if _____

11. Cindy asked, "How far is it to the office?"

    Cindy wanted to know _____

12. Matthew said, "It's about 20 miles."

    Matthew explained that _____

14. Susan warned, "We'll miss the bus."

    Susan warned Michael that _____

3 Review

Read the following fable from West Africa. Find and correct the errors in noun clauses and quoted and reported speech.

Ananse lived with his family. One year there was no rain, so the crops did not grow.
Ananse ~~that~~ knew ^*that* there would not be enough food to feed everyone. One day his wife
asked Will it rain at all this summer?

I don't believe so he replied. You know, I prefer to die than to see my children starve.
Therefore, I will allow myself to die so there is enough food for the family. Ananse then
told to his wife that he wants the family to bury me on the farm and to put into my coffin
all the things I would need for my journey into the next world. He said, "It's critical that
you left my grave open. I want my soul to be free to wander. And I insist that no one
should visit the farm for three months after my death.

The next morning, Ananse's family found him dead. But Ananse was only pretending.
At night he would lift the lid of his coffin and take food from the farm. One day his son,
Ntikuma, realized that food was going scarce and that he must visit the farm to get some.
He said he needed to go today to get what little food the farm had to feed the family.
Where is all the corn and millet? he said to himself when he got to the farm. His mother
told him the food was disappearing at night. It's a thief, exclaimed Ntikuma. I want to
know who is he.

Ntikuma carved a statue from wood and covered it with tar*. Then he placed the
figure in the field. That evening, Ananse came out of his coffin and saw the figure. Good
evening he said. I don't know you. Please tell me who are you? The figure did not reply.
Ananse got angry, so he slapped the figure. His hand stuck fast. Ananse shouted If you
don't let go of his right hand, he'll hit you with his left! He hit the figure with his left
hand. He hit with his right leg, then the left. Ananse struggled as the figure fell. He was
stuck was very clear.

❖ *Review* Four review pages in each unit bring key grammar points together for consolidated practice and review.

❖ *Writing* **assignments** build composition skills such as narrating and describing through real-life step-by-step tasks.

WRITING: Write a Fable or a Legend

All cultures have stories. A fable is a story that teaches a lesson, which is called a "moral." The moral is usually stated at the end of the fable. In many fables, animals speak and act as humans do. A legend is a story, usually about famous people or events, that is handed down from generation to generation. It may be based in historical reality.

Step 1. Think of a legend or fable that you know. Tell it to your partner. Discuss its meaning to the culture it comes from.

Step 2. Write the events of your story in order.

Step 3. Write the story. Include quoted and reported speech from the characters. Write a title for your story. Here is an example of a fable.

The Fox and the Crow

One day a fox was walking through the forest when he noticed a crow up in a tree. The crow had a piece of cheese in its beak, and the fox was hungry. "That cheese looks delicious," the fox said to himself. He wondered how he could get the cheese. He thought, and he said,

❖ *Self*-**tests** at the end of each unit allow students to evaluate their mastery of the grammar while providing informal practice of standardized test taking.

SELF-TEST

A Choose the best answer, A, B, C, or D, to complete the sentence. Mark your answer by darkening the oval with the same letter.

1. I wondered where _____.

A. he came from Ⓐ Ⓑ Ⓒ Ⓓ
B. did he come from
C. came he from
D. he did come from

2. My mother said, "Don't come in with your dirty shoes."
My mother warned me _____ in with my dirty shoes.

A. to come Ⓐ Ⓑ Ⓒ Ⓓ
B. not come
C. not come

6. "Don't drive too fast."

He told _____ drive fast.
A. not to Ⓐ Ⓑ Ⓒ Ⓓ
B. to
C. us not to
D. to us not to

7. He asked, "Where do you want to go?"
He asked where _____.

A. did I want to go Ⓐ Ⓑ Ⓒ Ⓓ
B. I want to go
C. I wanted to go
D. I want to go

B Find the underlined word or phrase, A, B, C, or D, that is incorrect. Mark your answer by darkening the oval with the same letter.

1. The teacher <u>warned</u> <u>us</u> <u>that</u> <u>not to</u> cheat
           A   B   C   D
during the test.

Ⓐ Ⓑ Ⓒ Ⓓ

2. The interviewer <u>asked</u> <u>to me</u> when
               A   B
<u>I wanted</u> to start <u>working</u>.
 C   D

Ⓐ Ⓑ Ⓒ Ⓓ

3. <u>Can you tell me</u> where <u>can I</u> get
      A   B
information about trains and where

6. Ted <u>said that</u> he <u>hadn't</u> <u>fill out</u> the
      A   B   C
application form <u>yet</u>.
             D

Ⓐ Ⓑ Ⓒ Ⓓ

7. <u>It is</u> <u>imperative that</u> <u>I fail not</u> any of
   A   B   C
my courses this year <u>if</u> I want to apply
                 D
to a university.

Ⓐ Ⓑ Ⓒ Ⓓ

8. _____ called from Boston yesterday and

To the Teacher

Grammar Form and Function is a three-level series designed to ensure students' success in learning grammar. The series features interesting photos to help students accurately recall grammar points, meaningful contexts, and a clear, easy-to-understand format that integrates practice of the rules of essential English grammar (form) with information about when to apply them and what they mean (function).

Features

❖ **Flexible approach to grammar instruction** integrates study of structures (form) with information on how to use them and what they mean (function).

❖ **High-interest photos** contextualize new grammar and vocabulary.

❖ **Comprehensive grammar coverage** targets all basic structures.

❖ **Extensive practice** ensures accurate production and fluent use of grammar.

❖ **Your Turn activities** guide students to practice grammar in personally meaningful conversations.

❖ **Review sections** bring key grammar points together for consolidated practice.

❖ **Writing assignments** build composition skills like narrating and describing through step-by-step tasks.

❖ **Self-Tests and Unit Quizzes** offer multiple assessment tools for student and teacher use, in print and Web formats.

❖ **Companion Website activities** develop real-world listening and reading skills.

Components

❖ **Student Book** has 14 units with abundant practice in both form and function of each grammar structure. Each unit also features communicative *Your Turn* activities, a *Review* section, a step-by-step *Writing* assignment, and a *Self-Test*.

❖ **Teacher's Manual** provides the following:
   ◆ Teaching tips and techniques
   ◆ Overview of each unit
   ◆ Answer keys for the Student Book and Workbook
   ◆ Expansion activities
   ◆ Culture, usage, and vocabulary notes
   ◆ Answers to frequently asked questions about the grammar structures
   ◆ Unit quizzes in a standardized test format and answer keys for each unit.

❖ **Workbook** features additional exercises for each grammar structure, plus an extra student Self-Test at the end of each unit.

❖ **Website** provides further practice, as well as additional assessments.

Overview of the Series

Pedagogical Approach

What is *form*?

Form is the structure of a grammar point and what it looks like. Practice of the form builds students' accuracy and helps them recognize the grammar point in authentic situations, so they are better prepared to understand what they are reading or what other people are saying.

What is *function*?

Function is when and how we use a grammar point. Practice of the function builds students' fluency and helps them apply the grammar point in their real lives.

Why does **Grammar Form and Function** incorporate both form and function into its approach to teaching grammar?

Mastery of grammar relies on students knowing the rules of English (form) and correctly understanding how to apply them (function). Providing abundant practice in both form and function is key to student success.

How does **Grammar Form and Function** incorporate form and function into its approach to teaching grammar?

For each grammar point, the text follows a consistent format:

- ❖ **Presentation of Form.** The text presents the complete form, or formal rule, along with several examples for students to clearly see the model. There are also relevant photos to help illustrate the grammar point.
- ❖ **Presentation of Function.** The text explains the function of the grammar point, or how it is used, along with additional examples for reinforcement.
- ❖ **Practice.** Diverse exercises practice the form and function together. Practice moves logically from more controlled to less controlled activities.
- ❖ **Application.** Students apply the grammar point in open-ended communicative activities. **Your Turn** requires students to draw from and speak about personal experiences, and **Review** provides consolidated practice of key grammar points. **Writing** provides a variety of writing assignments that rely on communicative group and pair discussions, and **Expansion** activities in the Teacher's Manual provide additional creative, fun practice for students.

What is the purpose of the photos in the book?

Most people have a visual memory. When you see a photo aligned with a grammar point, the photo helps you remember and contextualize the grammar. The photo reinforces the learning and retention. If there were no visual image, you'd be more likely to forget the grammar point. For example, let's say you are learning the present progressive. You read the example "She is drinking a glass of water." At the same time, you are shown a photo of a girl drinking a glass of water. Later, you are more likely to recall the form of the present progressive because your mind has made a mental picture that helps you remember.

Practice

How were the grammar points selected?

We did a comprehensive review of courses at this level to ensure that all of the grammar points taught were included.

Does **Grammar Form and Function** have controlled or communicative practice?

It has both. Students practice each grammar point through controlled exercises and then move on to tackle open-ended communicative activities.

Do students have a chance to personalize the grammar?

Yes. There are opportunities to personalize the grammar in **Your Turn** and **Writing**. **Your Turn** requires students to draw from and speak about personal experiences, and **Writing** provides a variety of writing assignments that rely on communicative group and pair discussions.

Does **Grammar Form and Function** help students work toward fluency or accuracy?

Both. The exercises are purposefully designed to increase students' accuracy and enhance their fluency by practicing both form and function. Students' confidence in their accuracy helps boost their fluency.

Why does the text feature writing practice?

Grammar and writing are linked in a natural way. Specific grammar structures lend themselves to specific writing genres. In *Grammar Form and Function*, carefully devised practice helps students keep these structures in mind as they are writing.

In addition to the grammar charts, what other learning aids are in the book?

The book includes 38 pages of appendices that are designed to help the students as they complete the exercises. In addition to grammar resourses such as lists of irregular verbs and spelling rules for endings, the appendices also feature useful and interesting information, including grammar terms, verb form charts, rules for capitalization and punctuation, and writing basics. In effect, the appendices constitute a handbook that students can use not only in grammar class, but in other classes as well.

Are there any additional practice opportunities?

Yes, there are additional exercises in the Workbook and on the Website. There are also **Expansion** activities in the Teacher's Manual that provide more open-ended (and fun!) practice for students.

Assessment

What is the role of student self-assessment in **Grammar Form and Function?**

Every opportunity for student self-assessment is valuable! *Grammar Form and Function* provides two Self-Tests for each unit – one at the end of each Student Book unit and another at the end of each Workbook unit. The Self-Tests build student confidence, encourage student independence as learners, and increase student competence in following standardized test formats. In addition, the Self-Tests serve as important tools for the teacher in measuring student mastery of grammar structures.

Does **Grammar Form and Function** offer students practice in standardized test formats?

Yes, the two Self-Tests and the Unit Quiz for each unit all utilize standardized test formats. Teachers may use the three tests in the way that best meets student, teacher, and institutional needs. For example, teachers may first assign the Self-Test in the Workbook as an untimed practice test to be taken at home. Then in the classroom, teachers may administer the Self-Test in the Student Book for a more realistic, but still informal, test-taking experience. Finally, teachers may administer the Unit Quiz from the Teacher's Manual as a more standardized timed test.

How long should each Self-Test or Unit Quiz take?

Since there is flexibility in implementing the Self-Tests and Unit Quizzes, there is also flexibility in the timing of the tests. When used for informal test-taking practice at home or in class, they may be administered as untimed tests. When administered as timed tests in class, they should take no more than 20 minutes.

How can I be sure students have mastered the grammar?

Grammar Form and Function provides a variety of tools to evaluate student mastery of the grammar. Traditional evaluation tools include the practice exercises, Self-Tests, and Unit Quizzes. To present a more complete picture of student mastery, the series also includes **Your Turn** activities and **Writing**, which illustrate how well students have internalized the grammar structures and are able to apply them in realistic tasks. Teachers can use these activities to monitor and assess students' ability to incorporate new grammatical structures into their spoken and written discourse.

Unit Format

What is the unit structure of **Grammar Form and Function**?

Consult the guide to **Grammar Form and Function** on pages X–XIII. This walk-through provides a visual tour of a Student Book unit.

How many hours of instruction are in **Grammar Form and Function 3**?

The key to **Grammar Form and Function** is flexibility! The grammar structures in the Student Book may be taught in order, or teachers may rearrange units into an order that best meets their students' needs. To shorten the number of hours of instruction, teachers may choose not to teach all of the grammar structures, or use all of the exercises provided. On the other hand, teachers may add additional hours by assigning exercises in the Workbook or on the Website. In addition, the Teacher's Manual provides teaching suggestions and expansion activities that would add extra hours of instruction.

Ancillary Components

What can I find in the Teacher's Manual?

- ❖ Teaching tips and techniques
- ❖ Overview of each unit
- ❖ Answer keys for the Student Book and Workbook
- ❖ Expansion activities
- ❖ Culture, usage, and vocabulary notes
- ❖ Answers to frequently asked questions about the grammar structures
- ❖ Unit quizzes in a standardized test format and quiz answer keys.

How do I supplement classroom instruction with the Workbook?

The Workbook exercises can be used to add instructional hours to the course, to provide homework practice, and to reinforce and refresh the skills of students who have mastered the grammar structures. It also provides additional standardized test-taking practice.

What can students find on the Website?

Students and teachers will find a wealth of engaging reading and listening activities on the **Grammar Form and Function** Website. As with the Workbook, the Website exercises can be used to add instructional hours to the course, to provide homework practice, and to reinforce and refresh the skills of students who have mastered the grammar structures.

UNIT 1

THE PRESENT TENSES

The Simple Present Tense and
The Present Progressive Tense

'The king of animals is very lazy
and **sleeps** a lot.
He **sleeps** 20 hours a day.
In this photo, he **isn't sleeping.**

THE SIMPLE PRESENT TENSE

See page 441 for charts showing statements and questions in the simple present tense.

1. We form affirmative statements in the simple present tense with a subject + a verb
   or a verb + -s or -es. We form negative statements with a subject + *do not/don't*
   or *does not/doesn't* + a verb.

   > I **like** football.
   > Tom **likes** football.
   > We **don't like** tennis.
   > Tom **doesn't** like baseball.

   See page 439 for spelling rules for verbs + -s or -es.

2. We form yes/no questions in the simple present tense with *do* or *does* + a subject +
   a verb. In short answers, we use a pronoun subject + *do/don't* or *does/doesn't.*

   > A: **Do** you **like** soccer?
   > B: Yes, I **do.**/No, I **don't.**

   > A: **Does** Sue **like** tennis?
   > B: Yes, she **does.**/No, she **doesn't.**

3. We use the wh- words *what, where, when, how, which, why, who,* and *whom* to form
   wh- questions in the simple present tense. We form these questions in two ways.

   a. If the wh- word is the subject of the question, we do not use the auxiliary verbs
      do or *does,* and we do not change the word order of the subject and the verb.

      Who wants to play basketball?

b. If the wh- word is not the subject of the question, we use the wh- word + *do* or *does* + the subject + the base verb.

Why do you **like** baseball?
What does the catcher **do** in baseball?

THE PRESENT PROGRESSIVE TENSE

See page 442 for charts showing statements and questions in the present progressive tense.

4. We form affirmative statements in the present progressive tense with a subject + the present tense of *be* + a verb + *-ing*. We form negative statements with the present tense of *be* + *not* + a verb + *-ing*.

The players **are trying** to score.
They **aren't succeeding**.

See page 440 for spelling rules for verbs ending in -ing.

5. We form yes/no questions with the present tense of *be* + a subject + a verb + *-ing*. In affirmative short answers, we use a pronoun subject + the present tense of *be*. In negative short answers, we use a pronoun subject + the present tense of *be* + *not*. We usually contract negative short answers.

A: **Is** our team **winning**?
B: Yes, it **is**./No, it **isn't**.

A: **Are** you **enjoying** the game?
B: Yes, I **am**./No, I'm **not**.

Note: There is no contraction for *am* + *not*.

CORRECT: No, I'm not.
INCORRECT: No, I ~~amn't~~.

6. We form wh- questions in the present progressive tense in the same two ways as in the simple present tense, but we use present progressive verb forms.

Who is winning?
Why is that player **running** now?

In speech and in informal writing, we often contract *is* with the wh- word. In speech, we also contract *are* with the wh- word, but we do not usually write this form.

Who**'s** speaking?
Where**'s** he going?
How**'s** your car running?

1. Here are the uses of the simple present and the present progressive tenses when we are referring to present time.

The Simple Present Tense	The Present Progressive Tense
a. To describe repeated actions or habits. I **get up** at seven every morning.	a. To talk about something which is in progress at the moment of speaking. It **is raining** right now.
b. To talk about things that are always or generally true. The sun **sets** in the west. It **snows** a lot in the winter here.	b. To talk about something which is in progress around the present, but not exactly at the time of speaking. Tony **is looking** for a new job these days.
c. To describe a permanent situation or a condition with no definite start or finish but that is true now. They **live** in Mexico City.	c. To talk about situations which are developing or temporary. Computers **are becoming** more and more important in our lives.
d. With adverbs of frequency such as *always, usually, often, sometimes, seldom/rarely,* and *never* to say how often we do something. If the verb is *be,* we put the adverb after the verb. If the verb is not *be,* we put the adverb before the verb. They are **seldom** late. She **often** studies in the library.	d. With adverbs such as *always* or *constantly* to express complaints or annoyance. He is **always** calling me late at night.
e. With time expressions such as *every day/week/year, in the morning/afternoon/ evening,* and *at night.* We can put these time expressions at the beginning or the end of a sentence. I go to the store **once a week**. **On weekends**, we have dinner at seven.	e. With time expressions such as *now, at the moment, at present, these days, nowadays,* and *today.* We can put these time expressions at the beginning or the end of a sentence. I'm writing an e-mail message **right now.** **These days**, I'm using e-mail to keep in touch with my friends.

2. We also use the simple present and the present progressive tenses to refer to future time. See page 67 for information on these meanings.

Practice

Complete the sentences with the simple present or the present progressive tense. Use the words in parentheses.

Karen: Hi, Dan! What (you/do) ___*are you doing*___ these days?
                                                  1

Dan: Hi, Karen. I (take) _____ a course in computer
                                       2

       programming. What about you?

Karen: Oh, I (work) _____ at the library until July.
                                       3

Dan: (you/like) _____ it?
                             4

Karen: Yes, I _____. Right now, they (give)
                             5

       _____ me a lot of training. Every morning, they
                       6

       (train) _____ me for an hour.
                           7

       I (work) _____ long hours, and
                       8

       I (not/get) _____ home until seven. But that's OK
                       9

       because I (learn) _____ a lot.
                           10

Dan: I (look) _____ for a job, too. It (become)
                        11

       _____ harder and harder to find a job. Companies
                12

       (look) _____ for people who are familiar with new
                    13

       computer software.

Karen: (you/learn) _____ about all the new software in
                        14

       your course?

Dan: Yes, I (be) _am_____.
                       15

Karen: How long (the course/run) _____?
                           16

Dan: It usually (run) _____ for eight weeks, but
                     17

       I (do) _____ it in six.
                   18

Karen: (they/give) _____ you a certificate at the end?
                       19

Dan: Yes, they _____. They also
                   20

       (give) _____ students a list of companies to apply for a job.
                21

Karen: Well, good luck!

Dan: Thanks.

Practice

Complete the sentences with the simple present or the present progressive tense. Use the words in parentheses.

I have a guest at my house. She is a friend, and she (stay) ___*is staying*___ with

<u>1</u>

me for a few weeks. I (sleep) _____ on the sofa in the living room

<u>2</u>

while she's here, and she (stay) _____ in my bedroom. I always

<u>3</u>

(get up) _____ at six, have breakfast, and then (go) _____

<u>4</u>   <u>5</u>

to work. She (not/get up) _____ before ten, and then she

<u>6</u>

(eat) _____ breakfast. She only (drink) _____ fresh juice. She

<u>7</u>   <u>8</u>

usually (make) _____ oatmeal for breakfast. She (not/eat) _____

<u>9</u>   <u>10</u>

meat, and she (not/drink) _____ tea or coffee.

<u>11</u>

    She (use) _____ my computer, and she (drive) _____ my

<u>12</u>   <u>13</u>

car while she's here. That's OK. But she (always/make) _____ long distance

<u>14</u>

phone calls on my phone. That's not OK. She (constantly/take) _____ clothes

<u>15</u>

from my closet and never (ask) _____ me first. That's not OK. She

<u>16</u>

(become) _____ a problem. I'm glad she (not/stay) _____ long!

<u>17</u>   <u>18</u>

3 Practice

Work with a partner or the class. Match the sentences with the uses of the simple present tense and the present progressive tense.

Simple Present Tense	Present Progressive Tense
a. permanent situation	d. action in progress
b. repeated action	e. changing situation
c. general truth	f. action in progress around the present

___*a*___ **1.** My parents **live** in Mexico City.

_____ **2.** My brother **is looking for** a new car these days.

_____ **3.** Look at that car! It**'s driving** through a red light.

_____ **4.** I usually **walk** to school every morning.

_____ **5.** My English compositions **are getting** better.

_____ **6.** Water **freezes** at 32 degrees Fahrenheit or 0 degrees centigrade.

4 Practice

The following sentences are about what people generally do or how life is changing. Write G (what happens in general) or C (changing situation) next to each sentence. Then rewrite the sentences with the correct form of the verb.

_G_ **1.** People (watch) a lot of television.

People watch a lot of television.

_C_ **2.** People (go) to the movies a lot these days.

People are going to the movies a lot these days.

_____ **3.** The seasons (change) four times a year.

_____

_____ **4.** The weather (change) these days.

_____

_____ **5.** Wild animals (live) in the forests.

_____

_____ **6.** Many wild animals (become) extinct.

_____

_____ **7.** Men (work) to take care of their families.

_____

_____ **8.** Women (work) to take care of their families.

_____

_____ **9.** Men and women (live) longer.

_____

_____ **10.** Computers (make) our lives easier these days.

_____

5 Your Turn

What changes are taking place right now in your country? Discuss with a partner or the class.

Example:
In my country, more and more people are moving to the cities, so the cities are getting larger.

1b Stative Verbs and Action Verbs

He **seems** very worried.

Most verbs describe actions, but there are some English verbs that describe states and not actions. We call these verbs *stative verbs*. Sometimes we call them *nonprogressive verbs*. Here are some types of stative verbs.

Types of Stative Verbs and Examples	Verbs	
1. Verbs of the senses and perception **Do** you **smell** the coffee?	feel hear see	smell sound taste
2. Verbs of mental states I **remember** him.	believe doubt forget know mean realize	recognize remember suppose think understand
3. Verbs of possession My boss **owns** this building.	belong have	own possess
4. Verbs of feeling or emotion I **love** chocolate.	adore astonish enjoy envy fear hate like	love mind please prefer surprise wish

5. Verbs of measurement This watch is nice, but it **costs** too much.	contain	measure
	cost	weigh
	equal	
6. Other verbs that express states You **seem** sad today.	be	require
	exist	seem
	owe	

Function

1. Stative verbs and action verbs have different uses.

Stative Verbs	Action Verbs
a. A stative verb describes a state. A state means that something is and stays the same. The school **is** big. I **have** a watch. We **own** our apartment.	a. An action verb describes an action. An action means that something happens. I **am reading**. She **is sitting** in her favorite chair. He **goes** to work every morning.
b. Stative verbs cannot be in the progressive form. CORRECT: We have two dogs. INCORRECT: We ~~are having~~ two dogs.	b. Action verbs can be in the progressive form. I **read** a book every week. This week, I **am reading** Moby Dick.

2. Some verbs have both a stative meaning and an active meaning.

Verb	Stative Meaning	Active Meaning
appear	She **appears** happy. (appears = seems)	She **is appearing** in a new movie. (is appearing = is starring in)
smell	The milk **smells** strange. (smells strange = has a strange smell)	He **is smelling** the milk. (is smelling = is sniffing)
taste	This food **tastes** delicious. (tastes delicious = has a delicious flavor)	She **is tasting** the food. (is tasting = checking to see if she likes it)
think	I **think** it is a good idea. (think = believe)	I **am thinking** about the problem. (am thinking = am considering)

3. *Be* + an adjective usually expresses a stative meaning.

    She **is tall**.

However, when we use *be* + an adjective with a progressive tense, it has a temporary meaning. To use the progressive, the adjective that follows the verb *be* must describe a behavior that the subject can control.

    He is polite. (character—permanent state)
    He is being polite because his father is in the room. (behavior—temporary state)

    CORRECT: She is beautiful. (permanent state)
    INCORRECT: She ~~is being~~ beautiful. (The subject cannot control this.)

6 | Practice

Complete the sentences with the simple present or the present progressive of the verbs in parentheses.

Ken: You (have) _____*have*_____ a nice apartment.
                                  1

Maria: Thank you. It is small, but it (have) _____ a nice view.
                                  2

        You can see the lake from here.

Ken: Yes, I (see) _____ it. Your apartment
                            3

        (be) _____ very sunny, and I
                    4

        (love) _____ your furniture.
                  5

Maria: Thank you. I (know) _____ a very good furniture
                      6

        store that (have) _____ great things, and they
                    7

        (not, cost) _____ much.
                  8

        I (go) _____ there today with a friend.
                9

        You can come with us if you want.

Ken: That (sound) _____ great!
                  10

        I (think) _____ about buying a new sofa,
                11

        but I (not, know) _____ where to go. Mmm.
                12

        Something (smell) _____ good! What
                13

        (you, cook) _____?
                14

Maria: I (make) _____ an apple pie.
                15

        Look, it (turn) _____ golden brown.
                16

        I (think) _____ it's done.
                17

        (you, want) _____ to have some?
                18

Ken: Yes, of course.

Choose verbs from the following list to make the sentences below true for you. Read your sentences to a partner.

Example:
I expect to have a large family.

believe	dislike	expect	know	love	think
deserve	doubt	have	like	prefer	wonder

1. I _____ a large family.

2. I _____ I will be rich.

3. I _____ cooking.

4. I _____ to be lucky.

5. I _____ how I will look in 20 years.

1c The Present Perfect Tense and The Present Perfect Progressive Tense

Form

He **has run** six miles.
He **has been running** for two hours.

THE PRESENT PERFECT TENSE

See page 443 for charts showing statements and questions in the present perfect tense.

1. We form affirmative statements in the present perfect tense with a subject + the present tense of *have* + a past participle. We form negative statements with a subject + the present tense of *have* + *not* + a past participle.

   I**'ve played** tennis for many years.
   Our team **hasn't won** any games this year.

   We form regular past participles by adding -*d* or -*ed* to a base verb. Sometimes the spelling changes when we add -*d* or -*ed*. See page 440 for spelling rules.

   Some verbs have irregular past participles. See page 438 for a list of common ones.

2. We form yes/no questions in the present perfect tense with the present tense of *have* + a subject + a past participle. In affirmative short answers, we use a pronoun subject + the present tense of *have*. In negative short answers, we use a pronoun subject + the present tense of *have* + *not*. We usually contract negative short answers.

> A: **Have** you ever **played** squash?
> B: Yes, I **have**./No, I **haven't**.

3. We use the wh- words *what, where, when, how, which, why, who,* and *whom* to form wh- questions in the present perfect tense.

> **Who has won** the most games?
> **How many** games **have** they **won**?

4. In speech and in informal writing, we often contract *has* (*'s*) with the wh- word. In speech, we also contract *have* with the wh- word, but we do not usually write this form.

> Who**'s** finished?
> Where**'s** she traveled?

5. We often use adverbs such as *ever, never, already, yet, still,* and *so far* with the present perfect tense. They have the following positions in a sentence:

Position	Adverb	Examples
Beginning of the Sentence	so far*	**So far**, he hasn't said anything.
Before the Auxiliary	still	He **still** hasn't said anything.
Before the Past Participle	ever	Have you **ever** been to India?
		I haven't **ever** been to Beijing.
	never	He has **never** been to India.
	already	Have you **already** eaten?
	just	I've **just** returned from Morocco.
End of the Sentence	already	He has left **already**.
	yet	Has he left **yet**?
		He hasn't left **yet**.
	so far	He hasn't said anything **so far**.

*When *so far* comes at the beginning of a sentence, we put a comma after it.

THE PRESENT PERFECT PROGRESSIVE TENSE

See page 444 for charts showing statements and questions in the present perfect progressive tense.

6. We form affirmative statements in the present perfect progressive tense with a subject + the present tense of *have* + *been* + a verb + *-ing*. We form negative statements with a subject + the present tense of *have* + *not* + *been* + a verb + *-ing*.

> They**'ve been practicing** all morning, so they're tired.
> She **hasn't been playing** basketball very long.

See page 440 for the spelling of verbs ending in *-ing*.

7. We form yes/no questions in the present perfect progressive tense with *have* or *has* + a subject + *been* + a verb + *-ing*. In affirmative short answers, we use a pronoun subject + *have* or *has*. In negative short answers, we use a pronoun subject + *'s not/hasn't* or *'ve not/haven't*.

> A: **Have** they **been winning** a lot of games?
> B: Yes, they **have.**/No, they **haven't.**

8. We use the wh- words *what, where, when, how, which, why, who,* and *whom* to form wh- questions in the present perfect progressive tense.

> **Who has been scoring** the most goals?
> **Why have** they **been losing** so much?

9. In speech and in informal writing, we often contract *has* (*'s*) with the wh- word. In speech, we also contract *have* with the wh- word, but we do not usually write this form.

> Who**'s** been trying hard?
> Where**'s** she been living?

Function

1. Here are the uses of the present perfect and present perfect progressive tenses.

The Present Perfect Tense	The Present Perfect Progressive Tense
a. To talk about something that started in the past and that continues up to the present. I **have been** here for 30 minutes. (I came here 30 minutes ago, and I am still here.)	a. To emphasize the continuation of an action that started in the past and continues into the present. I **have been waiting** for your call all morning. (I have been waiting all morning, and I am still waiting.)

The Present Perfect Tense	The Present Perfect Progressive Tense
b. To talk about a completed action that has an importance in the present. She **has done** her homework. (Therefore, she can watch television *now*.)	b. To talk about an action that may or may not be completed. She**'s been doing** her homework. (Maybe she has finished it, maybe she has not.)
c. To talk about what has been achieved in a period of time. He **has written** three letters this morning.	c. To talk about how long something has been in progress. He **has been writing** all morning.
d. To describe a situation that is more permanent and that continues into the present. She **has always** worked here.	d. To describe a situation that is more temporary and that continues into the present. She**'s been working** here for a couple of weeks.
	e. To talk about evidence in the present that shows that an action was happening in the recent past. A: What smells so good? B: Oh, I**'ve been making** cookies.

2. We can use the present perfect tense or the present perfect progressive tense with action verbs.

> We**'ve finished** our work.
> We**'ve been finishing** our work.

But we do not use the present perfect progressive with stative verbs.

> CORRECT: I've had this car for five years.
> INCORRECT: I've ~~been having~~ this car for five years.

3. We often use *for* or *since* with the present perfect and the present perfect progressive tenses. We use *for* to talk about a length of time. We use *since* to talk about a point in time.

> I've been waiting here **for an hour.**
> I've been waiting here **since 2:00 P.M.**

4. With certain verbs used with *for* and *since,* there is little or no difference between the present perfect and the present perfect progressive. These verbs include *work, live, study, teach, stay, feel,* and *wear.*

> We **have lived/have been living** in this house for fifteen years.

5. We often use adverbs such as *ever, never, already, yet, still, just,* and *so far* with the present perfect tense.

Adverb	Meaning and Common Uses	Examples
so far	At any time up to now. Use in all types of sentences.	**So far**, I've been to three countries. I haven't been to Argentina **so far**. Have you been only to Argentina **so far**? How many cities have you visited **so far**?
still	Expected at some time before now. Use in negative statements.	He **still** hasn't visited Egypt.
ever	At any time up to the present. Use in negative statements and yes/no questions.	I haven't **ever** traveled in Vietnam. Have you **ever** been to Thailand?
never	At no time up to the present. Use in affirmative statements.	I have **never** sailed on a ship.
already	At some time sooner than expected. Use in affirmative statements, yes/no questions, and wh- questions.	They have **already** packed. Have you **already** bought your ticket? What have they **already** done?
just	Very recently. Use in all types of sentences.	We've **just** landed. The bus hasn't **just** arrived. It's **just** left. Has the bus **just** arrived? Where have they **just** gone?
yet	Expected at some time before now. Use in negative statements and yes/no questions.	They haven't called for a taxi **yet**. Have you left **yet**?

8 Practice

Complete the sentences with the present perfect or the present perfect progressive tense of the verbs in parentheses. Sometimes both tenses are possible.

A.

1. Soccer (be) _____ *has been* _____ the most popular sport in the world for a long time.

2. People (play) _____ soccer in England for hundreds of years.

3. Since 1870, there (be) _____ 11 players on one side.

4. Women (compete) _____ in the Olympic games since 1900.

B.

1. Parachuting (be) _____ an official sport only since 1951.

2. Women (compete) _____ in singles matches at Wimbledon since 1884.

3. In the United States, baseball (become) _____ the country's favorite sport.

4. Our basketball team (practice) _____ all morning.

5. Our team (win) _____ three games so far.

6. My friends (watch) _____ that baseball game for the last two hours!

9 | Practice

A. Read about Barbara Bates.

> Barbara Bates is an actor who has made over 20 movies in her career. She started acting when she was 13 years old, and she has traveled to many parts of the world. She has finished a romantic comedy with the famous actor Jason James. Although she has done lots of comedies, she hasn't acted in a drama. But has she won an Oscar? Not yet, but she has not given up. She says that she has not had the right part that could win an Oscar for her.

B. Choose the correct adverb from the choices in parentheses and put it in the correct position in the sentences. Only one adverb is correct.

just
1. She's ^ finished a romantic comedy. (still/just/ever)

2. She's traveled to many parts of the world. (yet/already)

3. She's done lots of comedies over the years. (already/just/yet)

4. She hasn't acted in a drama. (never/still)

5. Has she won an Oscar? (still/yet)

6. She's not won an Oscar. (so far/never)

7. She hasn't given up. (never/still)

8. She's not had the right part. (still/never)

10 Practice

A. Read about J.K. Rowling.

J.K. Rowling is an author. She has written a series of books about a boy named Harry Potter. Harry Potter is a wizard—he has magical powers. The Harry Potter books are very popular among children.

Rowling was born in the United Kingdom in 1965. In 1990, she went to Portugal to teach English. There, she married a Portuguese man and had a daughter. She wasn't happy in her marriage, so she came back to the U.K. She had no job and very little money. She started to write the first Harry Potter book. Five years later she finished the book and sent it to publishers. The publishers did not like her book. Finally, one publisher liked it, and soon the book was in the bookstores. The book quickly became a best seller in England, and Rowling wrote more Harry Potter books.

By now, publishers have translated the Harry Potter books into 42 languages, and the books are bestsellers all over the world. In fact, Rowling has sold over 100 million books. Hollywood has made movies of the books, and Rowling has made a lot of money. But the most important thing she has done is to write books that children love to read.

B. You are a newspaper reporter who is interviewing J.K. Rowling. Write wh- or yes/no questions that go with her answers. Use the simple present or the present perfect tense.

1. QUESTION: *What have you written?* _____

   ANSWER: I've written a series of books about a very special boy named Harry Potter.

2. QUESTION: _____

   ANSWER: He's special because he has magical powers.

3. QUESTION: _____

   ANSWER: I live in the U.K.

4. QUESTION: _____ in other countries?

   ANSWER: Yes. I've lived in Portugal, too.

5. QUESTION: _____

   ANSWER: Up to now, they've been translated into 42 languages.

6. QUESTION: _____

   ANSWER: Up to now, over 100 million have been sold.

7. QUESTION: _____

   ANSWER: Hmm. I think it's to write books that children love to read.

Practice

Write sentences about the people using the prompts. Use the present perfect or present perfect progressive tense. If both tenses are possible, use the present perfect progressive.

A.

James is a mountain climber.

1. climb/many mountains in the Himalayas/ in his career

   <u>He has climbed many mountains</u>

   <u>in the Himalayas in his career.</u>

2. climb/Mount Everest

   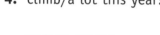
   _____

   _____

3. be/in the hospital many times?

   _____

4. climb/a lot this year?

   _____

B.

Mike Manners is a singer.

1. be/on tour in the United States and Europe

   _____

   _____

2. sell/two million CDs a year/for five years

   _____

   _____

3. win/any Grammy awards?

   _____

4. appear/on television yet?

   _____

C.

Jenny Thomas is a television journalist.

1. interview/many famous people/since she
   became a journalist

   _____

   _____

2. travel/all over the world in her career

   _____

   _____

3. meet/the president

   _____

   _____

4. ever/have/her own show on television?

   _____

---

12 **Your Turn**

**Work with a partner. Look at the photo.
Say or write three sentences about the
man using the present progressive,
present perfect, or the present perfect
progressive tense.**

Example:
The man is looking into the sun. Maybe
he's been waiting for someone.

REVIEW

1 Review (1a–1c)

Complete the sentences with a
correct present tense of the verbs
in parentheses. If there are
other words in parentheses,
include them.

Untitled - Message

Send   Save   Insert File...   Priority ▾   Options...

To...

Cc...

Subject:

Hi, Alex.

I (have) _____ `ve had` _____ a great summer! Right now, I (sail)
                 1

_____ on a big sailing ship. There (be) _____
         2   **3**

14 other students, three teachers, and the people who work on the ship. We (sail)

_____ for almost three weeks now. We (wake) _____
         4   **5**

up at 5:00 in the morning every day. At 6:00, we (sit) _____ at a
                                                               6

long table and (eat) _____ breakfast together. At 6:45, a bell (ring)
                          7

_____ , and we (know) _____ it (be)
         8   **9**

_____ time to put our dishes away and (go) _____
         10   **11**

up to the deck. I (be) _____ always there first. I (love)
                            12

_____ to smell the sea air and (listen) _____
         13   **14**

to the waves.

I (have) _____ a job on the ship. I (take) _____
              15   **16**

care of the safety equipment. I (know) _____ what to do in an emergency.
                                            17

We (not, have) _____ any problems so far, but you (know, never)
                    18

_____. The captain says there (be, always) _____
                19   20
storms this time of year. I (not, think) _____ about that right now.
                                                        21

We (work) _____ hard on the ship, but I (love)
                        22
_____ it. Since the first day that we (come) _____
                23   24
on board ship, we (take) _____ sailing lessons. Also, we (study)
                                        25
_____ the ocean. Today is our day off. Right now, I (sit)
                26
_____ at the front of the ship. Dolphins (ride) _____
                27   28
the waves next to me. Everything (be) _____ peaceful, for now, but a light
                                                        29
wind (blow) _____ all morning, and now it (seem)
                        30
_____ stronger. Uh, oh! I (see) _____ dark
                31   32
clouds. The waves (get) _____ bigger. I think a storm (come)
                                        33
_____. I (need) _____ to send this message
                34   35
now. Things (get) _____ exciting. Don't forget to feed my goldfish!
                        36
Pete

2 | Review (1a–1b)

Review of verb tenses. Complete the sentences with a correct present tense of the verbs in parentheses. If there are other words in parentheses, include them.

One morning, Paul and Julie meet in a store.

Paul: Hi, Julie. How (be) _____*are*_____ you?
                                        1

Julie: Not so well. I (have) _____ a problem.
                                        2

Paul: Well, that (be) _____ nothing new.
                                3

Julie: Something (always, go) _____ wrong.
                                                4

Paul: What (be) _____ it this time? Maybe it (not/be)
                                5
        _____ your fault.
                        6

Julie: This time, it (be) _____ my fault. This morning, I took
                                                7
        out the shoe polish to shine my brown shoes. I went into the living room ...

Paul: I'll bet I know! You got shoe polish on your parents' new white carpet. And you
        (try) _____ to get it out all morning.
                                8

Julie: No, not exactly. Anyway, it was a big brown spot at first, but it (not, be)

_____ a brown spot any more. It (be) _____
          9   10

an orange spot. I put bleach on it.

Paul: Bleach! On the new carpet? Oh no! So, what (you, do) _____
                                                                         11

here at the store?

Julie: I (buy) _____ some new towels.
                       12

Paul: Why (you, buy) _____ towels?
                              13

Julie: Because I used towels to clean the carpet this morning, and now they (have)

_____ big orange spots on them, too!
          14

Paul: You know. I (worry) _____ about you sometimes.
                                      15

Julie: That (be) _____ very nice of you, Paul, but I
                        16

(need) _____ help now. My parents (come)
             17

_____ home this minute!
          18

Paul: Poor Julie. By the way, I (look) _____ at your hair while
                                                    19

we (talk) _____. (you, know) _____
                 20   21

that it (be) _____ green?
                   22

Julie: Of course. But that (be) _____ just another long story
                                          23

you (not/want) _____ to hear!
                      24

3 | Review (1a–1c)

A. Read about the Hubble telescope.

The Hubble is a telescope. It travels in space 375 miles
(600 kilometers) above Earth. It has been in space since 1990.
The Hubble has powerful instruments and sends us pictures every
day. The pictures show us amazing views of stars and planets.
Astronauts often go to the Hubble and repair it. New equipment
has been added to the telescope. The Hubble has had many
successes. It has taken over 330,000 pictures. It has answered
many questions for scientists all over the world.

B. Use the prompts to write questions about the Hubble.

1. Where/Hubble/travel

   Where does the Hubble travel?

2. How far/Hubble/travel/above Earth

   _____

3. How long/Hubble/be/in space

   _____

4. What/Hubble/do every day

   _____

5. What/pictures/show/us

   _____

6. How many pictures/Hubble/take

   _____

7. What/Hubble/do/for scientists and astronomers all over the world

   _____

---

4 Review (Ia–Ic)

Complete the sentences with a correct present tense of the verbs in parentheses. If there are other words in parentheses, include them.

David: Hi, Martha. This (be) ___is___ David.
            1

I (call) _____ to ask if you
          2

(enjoy) _____ your vacation.
          3

Martha: Oh, yes, very much. Right now, I (look)

_____ at the ocean outside my window. It (be)
               4

_____ very beautiful here.
               5

David: That (sound) _____ great! (you, be) _____
                            6   7

to the Kilauea volcano yet?

Martha: Yes, we (be, already) _____ there. (you, be, ever)
                                          8

_____ there?
               9

David: No, I haven't, but I want to go.

Martha: I, (love) _____ it here. I (already, think) _____
                       10   11

about my next trip!

WRITING: Write an Informal Letter

Write an informal letter to someone you haven't seen for a long
time. See page 470 for general
writing guidelines.

**Step 1. Notice the parts of a
letter in this model.**

**Step 2. Write paragraphs to tell
your friend about the following.**

1. Your present situation and what
you are doing in your life. For
example:

*I am still working for the
same company, but right
now I am in Los Angeles for
a week. . .*

Opening	Your address *1860 N. Adams St.* *Santa Monica, CA 91307* Date *March 17, 20XX*
	Dear Ken,
Body	*I'm still working for . . .* _____
Closing	*Your friend,*
Signature	*Jill*

2. What you do every day. For example:

The exhibit hall opens at 9:00 in the morning, and. . .

3. What is happening while you are writing this letter. For example:

*I'm writing this letter from my hotel room. The hotel is right on the beach, and I
can see surfers in the ocean. . .*

Step 3. Write a your letter using the model in step 1.

Step 4. Evaluate your letter.

Checklist

_____ Did you put the address and date at the top of the letter?

_____ Did you start your letter with "Dear" and the person's name?

_____ Did you end your letter with an ending such as "Your friend," and your signature?

**Step 5. Work with a partner or a teacher to edit your letter. Check spelling, vocabulary, and
grammar.**

Step 6. Write your final copy.

SELF-TEST

A   **Choose the best answer, A, B, C, or D, to complete the sentence. Mark your answer by darkening the oval with the same letter.**

1. For thousands of years, bread _____ a staple food for many people.

   A. is   Ⓐ Ⓑ Ⓒ Ⓓ
   B. has
   C. has been
   D. been

2. The earth's climate _____ warmer.

   A. gets   Ⓐ Ⓑ Ⓒ Ⓓ
   B. is getting
   C. have gotten
   D. have been getting

3. A person's nose and ears _____ to grow throughout his or her life.

   A. continues   Ⓐ Ⓑ Ⓒ Ⓓ
   B. are continuing
   C. continue
   D. is continuing

4. What _____ these days?

   A. are girls wearing   Ⓐ Ⓑ Ⓒ Ⓓ
   B. girls wear
   C. girls are wearing
   D. are girls wear

5. In Toronto, it _____ without stopping everyday for two weeks.

   A. is raining   Ⓐ Ⓑ Ⓒ Ⓓ
   B. raining
   C. has been raining
   D. rains

6. It _____ 17 muscles to smile.

   A. takes   Ⓐ Ⓑ Ⓒ Ⓓ
   B. has been taking
   C. is taking
   D. has taken

7. Potato chips _____ popular since 1865.

   A. have been   Ⓐ Ⓑ Ⓒ Ⓓ
   B. are
   C. are being
   D. been

8. More women _____ in universities now than in the past.

   A. is studying   Ⓐ Ⓑ Ⓒ Ⓓ
   B. have studied
   C. studies
   D. are studying

9. How much _____ at birth?

   Ⓐ Ⓑ Ⓒ Ⓓ
   A. is a baby usually weighing
   B. a baby usually weighs
   C. does a baby usually weigh
   D. usually a baby weigh

10. We _____ New York City many times.

    A. have been visiting   Ⓐ Ⓑ Ⓒ Ⓓ
    B. visiting
    C. visit
    D. have visited

B **Find the underlined word or phrase, A, B, C, or D, that is incorrect. Mark your answer by darkening the oval with the same letter.**

1. Many people <u>are</u> <u>been</u> <u>exercising</u> in the
            A   B   C

   United States <u>since</u> the start of the
                D

   fitness craze.

   Ⓐ Ⓑ Ⓒ Ⓓ

2. The cures <u>for</u> many diseases <u>has</u> <u>advanced</u>
           A   B   C

   greatly <u>since</u> the discovery of antibiotics.
         D

   Ⓐ Ⓑ Ⓒ Ⓓ

3. It is warm <u>usually</u> <u>in June</u>, but this year
             A   B

   it <u>is</u> <u>still</u> cool.
      C D

   Ⓐ Ⓑ Ⓒ Ⓓ

4. What <u>people</u> <u>are</u> <u>doing</u> <u>these</u> <u>days</u>?
         A   B   C   D

   Ⓐ Ⓑ Ⓒ Ⓓ

5. People in the U.S. and Britain <u>usually</u>
                              A

   <u>have</u> turkey for Christmas, but other
    B

   countries <u>have</u> <u>not</u>.
           C   D

   Ⓐ Ⓑ Ⓒ Ⓓ

6. Some <u>scientists</u> <u>thinks</u> the earth <u>is</u>
          A   B   C

   <u>getting</u> colder.
    D

   Ⓐ Ⓑ Ⓒ Ⓓ

7. Some roses <u>are</u> <u>not</u> <u>smell</u>. They <u>have</u> no
            A   B   C   D

   scent at all.

   Ⓐ Ⓑ Ⓒ Ⓓ

8. People <u>have</u> <u>grown</u> the potato in Europe
          A   B

   <u>since</u> hundreds of <u>years</u>.
     C   D

   Ⓐ Ⓑ Ⓒ Ⓓ

9. Many <u>people</u> are <u>buy</u> DVDs instead of CDs
           A   B

   <u>these</u> <u>days</u>.
     C   D

   Ⓐ Ⓑ Ⓒ Ⓓ

10. Some people relax <u>never</u>. <u>They</u> <u>worry</u>
                      A   B   C

    <u>all the time</u>.
       D

    Ⓐ Ⓑ Ⓒ Ⓓ

UNIT 2

THE PAST TENSES

Form

Jenny **was watching** television when I **came** home.

THE SIMPLE PAST TENSE

See page 445 for charts showing statements and questions in the simple past tense.

1. We form affirmative statements in the simple past tense with a subject + the past form of a verb. We form negative statements with a subject + *did not* + a base verb.

   > I **enjoyed** the movie last night.
   > I **liked** the story, but I **didn't like** the photography.

   Exception: The negative of *be* is the past form of *be* + *not*.

   > I **was not/wasn't** happy with the ending.
   > We **were not/weren't** disappointed.

2. We form the past form of regular verbs with a base verb + *-d* or *-ed*. See page 440 for spelling rules for regular verbs.

3. Irregular verbs form their past forms in different ways. Here are some examples.

Base Form	Past Form
be*	I/He/She/It was We/You/They were
fall	fell
feel	felt
run	ran
see	saw
sit	sat

   Be is the only verb that has two past forms.

See page 438 for additional irregular past verb forms.

4. We form yes/no questions with *did* + a subject + a base verb. In short answers, we use a pronoun subject + *did* or *didn't*.

> A: **Did** you **hear** the concert last night?
> B: Yes, I **did.**/No, I **didn't.**

5. We use the wh- words *what, where, when, how, which, why, who,* and *whom* to form wh- questions.

> **Who watched** "Police Story" on television last night?
> **What did** you **watch** on television last night?

THE PAST PROGRESSIVE TENSE

See page 445 for charts showing statements and questions in the past progressive tense.

6. We form affirmative statements in the past progressive tense with a subject + the past tense of *be* + a verb + *-ing*. We form negative statements with a subject + the past tense of *be* + *not* + a verb + *-ing*.

> When I turned on the television, someone **was singing** the national anthem of my country.
> The people in the crowd **weren't singing.** They **were cheering.**

See page 440 for spelling rules for verbs that end in *-ing*.

7. We form yes/no questions with *was* or *were* + a subject + a verb + *-ing*. In short answers, we use a pronoun subject + *was/wasn't* or *were/weren't*.

> A: **Were** you **listening** to the radio at 9:00 last night?
> B: Yes, I **was.**/No, I **wasn't.**

8. We use the wh- words *what, where, when, how, which, why, who,* and *whom* to form wh- questions in the past progressive tense.

> **Who was playing** that loud music when I called you?
> **Why was** the audience **laughing** at the end of the movie?

1. Here are the main uses of the simple past and the past progressive tenses.

The Simple Past Tense	The Past Progressive Tense
a. To describe an action that happened at a definite time in the past. We can state the time. Edmund Hillary and Tenzing Norgay **climbed** Mount Everest (in 1953).	a. To describe an action that was in progress at a specific time in the past. The action began before the specific time and might continue after that time. Mary **was working** at ten o'clock yesterday morning.
b. To talk about actions that happened in a sequence in the past. I **came** home, **picked** up my mail, and **left**.	b. To talk about two actions in the past when one action began first and was in progress when the second action happened. I **was studying** when the electricity **went** off.
c. With time expressions such as *yesterday, last night/week/month/year, Wednesday, four days/weeks/months/years ago,* and *in 2004*. I saw a great movie **last night.**	c. To talk about two actions in the past that were in progress at the same time. The workers **were demanding** more money while the management **was asking** for layoffs.
	d. To give background information in a story. We use the simple past tense for the main actions and events. It **was getting** dark. I **was walking** down a country road. I **looked** down the road and **saw** a car coming towards me.
	e. With time expressions such as *while, when,* and *all morning/day/evening*. I was working **all day.**

2. We do not use the progressive form if the verb has a stative meaning.

   CORRECT: I had an exam yesterday.
   INCORRECT: I ~~was having~~ an exam yesterday.

3. We use *when* or *while* in sentences with two actions in the past.

   When I **came** home, I **picked up** my mail.
   I was sleeping **when** the fire alarm **went** off.
   They were watching TV **while** I was sleeping.

4. Clauses with *when* or *while* can come at the beginning or at the end of a sentence. If the clause comes at the beginning, we put a comma after it.

   When the phone rang, I was watching television.
   I was watching television **when the phone rang.**

1 Practice

Complete the sentences with the simple past tense or past progressive tense of the verbs in parentheses.

A.

I (wait) _____was waiting_____ (1) at the bus stop this morning when

I (see) _____ (2) an accident, or almost an accident. A man

(talk) _____ (3) on his cell phone while he

(drive) _____ (4). He (not/pay) _____ (5) attention

to the road when suddenly the traffic light (turn) _____ (6) red.

A woman (cross) _____ (7) the street at that moment. The driver

(stop) _____ (8) the car just in time. The woman wasn't hurt, but she

was certainly lucky.

B.

There was a dangerous accident at the river yesterday. A five-year-old boy

(fall) _____ (1) into the water while he

(run) _____ (2) after a ball. The boy

(scream) _____ (3) for help. Luckily, a man

(notice) _____ (4) him. He (jump) _____ (5)

into the river and (pull) _____ (6) the boy out. A jogger

(stop) _____ (7) when she saw the two very wet people by the side of

the river, and she (call) _____ (8) for an ambulance.

C.

A few months ago, I (sit) _____ (1) at home alone.

I (watch) _____ (2) a boring show on TV, and

I (feel) _____ (3) a little tired. I (think) _____ (4)

about going to bed early when I (hear) _____ (5) a strange noise.

The noise (seem) _____ (6) to be coming from upstairs.

I was scared—very scared. I (turn) _____ (7) off the TV,

(take) _____ the cordless phone in my hand, and
        8

(start) _____ to walk up the stairs. Then
         9

I (hear) _____ the same noise again.
           10

I (freeze) _____. My hands (shake) _____.
             11   12

I (call) _____ the police.
            13

2 | What Do You Think?

What do you think happened next? Continue and complete the story from Practice 1C. Use the simple past and past progressive tenses.

3 | Practice

Complete the sentences with the simple past or the past progressive tense of the words in parentheses.

Joshua Slocum (be) _____*was*_____ a sea captain, but he
                            1

couldn't swim. At the age of 51, he (decide) _____ to sail
                                                2

around the world alone. He (buy) _____ an old fishing boat.
                                       3

He (call) _____ the boat the *Spray*. It
            4

(need) _____ repairs, so he (cut down) _____
          5   6

a tree and (use) _____ the wood to repair the boat.
                    7

He (leave) _____ Boston in 1895. While he
             8

(sail) _____ around the world, he (stop) _____
          9   10

at many different ports. He (give) _____ lectures in
                                      11

the ports. While he (travel) _____ around the world, he
                                12

(meet) _____ important people. He finally (return)
          13

_____ three years later and (write) _____
        14   15

a book about his travels. At age 65, Slocum (start) _____
                                                         16

a new journey on the *Spray*. It was November, 1909. During this trip,

he (disappear) _____, and nobody
                     17

(hear) _____ from him again.
          18

4 | Practice

Complete the sentences with the simple past or past progressive tense of the verbs in parentheses.

Ludwig van Beethoven was born in Germany in 1770. His father, who was a musician,

(give) _____*gave*_____ his son piano lessons when he was four. Ludwig
₁

(stand) _____ on the piano seat while he (play) _____
₂   ₃

because he was so small. When his father (see) _____ how quickly his son
₄

(learn) _____, he (know) _____ his son was talented.
₅   ₆

His father was a difficult man. He (hit) _____ Ludwig's hand when he
₇

(make) _____ a mistake. He often (wake) _____ Ludwig up
₈   ₉

in the middle of the night while he (sleep) _____ because he wanted
₁₀

Ludwig to play for him.

When he was 16, Beethoven (go) _____ to Vienna to study. While
₁₁

he (study) _____, he (performed) _____ for important
₁₂   ₁₃

people. One day he (play) _____ for Wolfgang Mozart. When Mozart
₁₄

(hear) _____ him, he was amazed at his talent.
₁₅

In his twenties, Beethoven (begin) _____ to lose his hearing. By the time
₁₆

he was 50, he was almost completely deaf, so he couldn't hear the music while the orchestra

(play) _____. In his last performance, he (continue) _____ to
₁₇   ₁₈

conduct while the audience (applaud) _____. Then, one of the musicians turned
₁₉

Beethoven around so he could see the audience. When Beethoven (see) _____
₂₀

how much they loved his music, he (start) _____ to cry.
₂₁

5 Practice

Write yes/no questions and answers about Beethoven or a composer of your choice. Use the prompts in parentheses.

1. QUESTION: *Did his father teach him to play the piano?*
   (father/teach/to play the piano)

   ANSWER: *Yes, he did.*

2. QUESTION: _____
   (study/Vienna)

   ANSWER: _____

3. QUESTION: _____
   (meet/Mozart one day)

   ANSWER: _____

4. QUESTION: _____
   (hear/the music/in his last performance)

   ANSWER: _____

5. QUESTION: _____
   (cry/when he saw the audience)

   ANSWER: _____

6 Practice

Use the question words to write questions for the answers that follow.

1. QUESTION: Why _____?

   ANSWER: Beethoven went to Vienna to study.

2. QUESTION: Who _____?

   ANSWER: He entertained important people.

3. QUESTION: When _____?

   ANSWER: He began to lose his hearing when he was in his 20s.

4. QUESTION: What _____?

   ANSWER: He continued to conduct while the audience was applauding.

5. QUESTION: How many _____?

   ANSWER: Over 20,000 people went to his funeral.

7 Practice

Combine the sentences about Beethoven into one using *while* or *when*. Use correct punctuation.

1. Beethoven didn't like an audience. He didn't perform.

   When *Beethoven didn't like an audience, he didn't perform.*

2. Beethoven ate in restaurants. He sometimes didn't pay the bill.

   When _____

3. He worked. He didn't eat or sleep.

   _____ while _____

4. Beethoven wrote his music. He didn't bathe or clean his room.

   While _____

5. Beethoven conducted the orchestra. He couldn't hear the music.

   While _____

6. People cried because his music was beautiful. He laughed at them.

   When _____

7. He died at age 57. Over 20,000 people went to Beethoven's funeral.

   _____ when _____

8 Practice

Complete the sentences with the simple past or present perfect tense of the verbs in parentheses.

Tiger Woods was born in California in 1975. His father (name)

_____*named*_____ him after a friend who saved his life in the Vietnam War.
$_1$

His father (teach) _____ him how to play golf. Tiger (start)
$_2$

_____ to play golf when he was nine months old, and he (play)
$_3$

_____ his first game when he was one and a half years old. At the age
$_4$

of eight, he (win) _____ his first tournament in the same year. In
$_5$

recent years, Tiger (help) _____ to make golf a popular sport for
$_6$

young and old. He also (earn) _____ a lot of money! He says the
$_7$

best advice he (get) _____ was from his father: "Always be yourself."
$_8$

Work with a partner. Think of a composer, popular or classical, that you like. Tell your partner some interesting facts about his or her life.

Example:
Elton John was born in England in 1947. He could play the piano by ear at the age of four. Early in his career, he was writing the music for songs such as "Rocket Man."

2b The Past Perfect Tense and The Past Perfect Progressive Tense

Form

Sue took off her shoe. She **had been wearing** her new shoes all day.

THE PAST PERFECT TENSE

See page 446 for charts showing statements and questions in the past perfect tense.

1. We form affirmative statements with a subject + *had* + a past participle. We form negative statements with a subject + *had not* + a past participle.

   I **had seen** that play before, so I didn't want to go again.
   She didn't do well on the quiz because she **hadn't studied** for it.

   We form regular past participles by adding *-d* or *-ed* to a base verb. Sometimes the spelling changes when we add *-d* or *-ed*. See page 440 for spelling rules.

   Some verbs have irregular past participles. See page 438 for a list of common ones.

2. We form yes/no questions in the past perfect tense with *had* + a subject + a past participle. In short answers, we use a pronoun subject + *had* or *had not*. We usually contract negative short answers.

   A: **Had** he **finished** by 2:00?
   B: Yes, he **had.** / No, he **hadn't.**

3. We use the wh- words *what, where, when, how, which, why, who,* and *whom* to form wh- questions in the past perfect tense.

> **Where had** Kelly **traveled** by the time she finished her trip?

THE PAST PERFECT PROGRESSIVE TENSE

See page 447 for charts showing statements and questions in the past perfect progressive tense.

4. We form affirmative statements with a subject + *had* + *been* + a verb + *-ing*.
   We form negative statements with a subject + *had not* + *been* + a verb + *-ing*.

> Susan **had been studying** the violin for only a month when she quit.
> She **hadn't been studying** it very long.

5. We form yes/no questions with *had* + a subject + *been* + a verb + *-ing*. In short answers, we use a pronoun subject + *had* or *had not*. We usually contract negative short answers.

6. We use the wh- words *what, where, when, how, which, why, who,* and *whom* to make wh- questions in the past perfect progressive tense.

Function

1. Here are the main uses of the past perfect and the past perfect progressive tenses.

The Past Perfect Tense:	The Past Perfect Progressive Tense:
a. To talk about a past action that ended before another action or time in the past The movie **had started** before we arrived. It is not usually necessary to use the past perfect tense when we use *before* or *after* in a sentence. *Before* and *after* tell us the order of the actions, so we may use the simple past tense. The movie **started** before we arrived.	a. To emphasize the continuation of an action that was in progress before another action or time in the past. Sara **had been working** here for two weeks when she got called away on family business.
b. To show the cause of a past action. I was tired on Monday. I **hadn't slept** well the night before.	b. To show the cause of a past action. I **had been traveling** all night, so I was tired on Monday.
c. With time expressions such as *when, after, before, as soon as, by the time, by,* and *until.* Kasey had already eaten **when** Francie stopped by to get her.	c. With time expressions such as *when, before, by the time, for, since,* and *how long.* He had been working **for** two hours when you interrupted him.

2. We do not use the progressive form with verbs that have a stative meaning.

    CORRECT: She had been tired all day.
    INCORRECT: She ~~had been being~~ tired all day.

3. We often use adverbs such as *ever, never, already, yet, so far,* and *still* with the past perfect tense. See page 15 for more information.

    Ellen had **never** eaten a fresh mango.
    At the end of my trip to Texas, I **still** hadn't eaten barbeque.

10 Practice

Complete the sentences with the simple past or the past perfect tense of the verbs in parentheses.

Janet had a bad day last Friday. She was late for class because her bus

(arrive) _____*had arrived*_____ late. When she (get) _____
                          1   2

to school, classes (already, begin) _____. Friday
                                                   3

(be) _____ the day of the grammar test. The test (already, start)
                  4

_____ when Janet (walk) _____
                   5   6

into the classroom. She (take) _____ the test, but she
                                  7

(not, finish) _____ because she (start)
                    8

_____ late. It was a shame because she (study)
          9

_____ very hard for it the night before.
          10

That evening, she (want) _____ to go out with her
                                11

roommate, but her roommate (leave) _____ a note for her saying
                                    12

that she was at the gym. So Janet (decide) _____ to go to
                                        13

a movie, but she (not, like) _____ to go to the movies alone. It was
                              14

a movie she (want) _____ to see for a long time, but she
                      15

(never, have) _____ the chance. She
                16

(call) _____ her mother, but her mother
           17

(see) _____ it before and (not, want) _____
         18   19

to see it again. She (call) _____ her friend Linda, but Linda
                              20

(read) _____ the book and (not, like) _____
    21   22

it. So, she (call) _____ me, but I
                        23

(already, make) _____ plans to go out of town.
                        24

I (hear) _____ later that Janet (do) _____
            25   26

something she (never, do) _____ before—she
                                27

(go) _____ to see a movie alone.
        28

II Practice

Look at the photo of Julia. This is how she looked when you saw her yesterday. Why did she look tired? Complete the sentences using the prompts and the past perfect or the past perfect progressive tense.

1. She looked tired because ____*she had*____

   ____*been working too much.*____
       (work, too much)

2. She looked tired because _____

   _____
       (sleep, badly)

3. She looked tired because _____
                                    (not, eat, well lately)

4. She looked tired because _____
                                    (worry, about her parents)

5. She looked tired because _____
                                    (your idea)

6. She looked tired because _____
                                    (your idea)

**A. Read this well-known story.
It is one of Aesop's fables.**

The Shepherd Boy and the Wolf

Once, there was a shepherd boy who took care of sheep for his master. His job wasn't very exciting, and he soon got bored. One day he thought of a plan to have fun because he'd been getting so bored.

His master had told him to call for help when he saw a wolf near the sheep. Then the people in the village would come and scare the wolf away. So one day, the shepherd boy ran toward the village and shouted, "Wolf! Wolf!" although he hadn't seen a wolf.

As his master had told him, the villagers left their work and ran to the field. When they got there, they found the boy laughing because he'd played a trick on them.

A few days later, the boy did what he'd done before. He shouted, "Wolf! Wolf!" Again, the villagers ran to help him, and again he laughed at them.

Then one evening a wolf really came and attacked the sheep. This time the boy was scared and ran toward the village. He shouted, "Wolf! Wolf!" The villagers heard him, but they didn't run to help him as they'd done before.

The wolf killed many of the sheep and disappeared into the forest.

B. Use the prompts to write questions and answers. Write complete sentences using the past perfect or the simple past tense.

1. Why/the shepherd boy/think/of a plan to have fun

QUESTION: _Why did the shepherd boy think of a plan to have fun?_

ANSWER: _He thought of a plan because he was bored._

2. What/his master/tell/him

QUESTION: _____

ANSWER: _____

3. What/he/decide/to do one day

QUESTION: _____

ANSWER: _____

4. he/see/a wolf

QUESTION: _____

ANSWER: _____

5. What/the villagers/do

QUESTION: _____

ANSWER: _____

6. Why/the boy/laugh

QUESTION: _____

ANSWER: _____

7. What/the boy/do/a few days later

QUESTION: _____

ANSWER: _____

8. he/laugh/at the villagers again

QUESTION: _____

ANSWER: _____

9. What/the boy/do/when the wolf really came

QUESTION: _____

ANSWER: _____

10. What/the villagers/do/this time

QUESTION: _____

ANSWER: _____

13 | What Do You Think?

A fable is a story that has a moral, or a lesson about life. What do you think the moral of the fable about the boy and the wolf is?

14 Practice

Complete the sentences with the present perfect progressive or the past perfect progressive tense of the words in parentheses.

1. I am at the dentist's office now. I (wait) _____ *'ve been waiting* _____ for forty-five minutes.

2. I was at the dentist's office yesterday. I (wait) _____ *'d been waiting* _____ for two hours before the receptionist called my name.

3. I feel terrible because my tooth (hurt) _____ for days.

4. I felt terrible yesterday because my tooth (hurt) _____ for several days before I went to the dentist.

5. I (take) _____ aspirin for several days for the pain, but it doesn't help.

6. I (take) _____ aspirin for several days before I went to the dentist, but it didn't help.

7. I (hope) _____ that the pain would go away, but it didn't.

8. I (go) _____ to the same dentist since I was a child, so I trust him.

9. The dentist (work) _____ on my tooth for ten minutes now.

10. He (work) _____ for five minutes when I couldn't stand it any more and . . .

15 What Do You Think?

What happened to the patient in the dentist's chair?

16 Your Turn

Tell a partner what had already happened or hadn't happened in class by the time you got there. Use ideas from the list or think of your own.

Example:
By the time I got to class, the teacher hadn't arrived.

1. the teacher/arrive
2. the teacher/take attendance
3. the class/begin
4. the teacher/collect the homework
5. all the students/arrive

17 Your Turn

Think about your life. Choose a particular age and list four experiences you had had by that age. Think about these kinds of experiences:

1. people you had met
2. places you had visited
3. things you had learned to do
4. things you had done

Example:
By age twelve, I had learned to swim and ride a bicycle.

2c *Used To* + Base Verb and *Would* + Base Verb

The Beatles **used to be** the most popular group in the world.
We **would listen** to their songs on the radio all the time.

USED TO + BASE VERB

1. We form affirmative statements with a subject + *used to* + a verb. We form negative statements with a subject + *did not* + *use to* + a verb.

    CORRECT: I **used to like** rock music.
                  I **didn't use to like** rock music.
    INCORRECT: I didn't ~~used~~ to like rock music.

2. We form yes/no questions with *did* + a subject + *use to* + a verb. We form short answers with a pronoun subject and *did* or *didn't*.

    CORRECT: Did you use to work there?
                  Yes, I **did**./No, I **didn't**.
    INCORRECT: Did you ~~used~~ to work there?

3. We use the wh- words *what, where, when, how, which, why, who*, and *whom* to form questions with *used to* + base verb when the wh- word is the subject. When the wh- word is not the subject, we form questions with *did* + a subject + *use to* + base verb.

    CORRECT: **Where did** you **use** to work?
    INCORRECT: Where did you ~~used~~ to work?

WOULD + BASE VERB

4. We form affirmative statements with a subject + *would* + a verb.
   We form negative statements with a subject + *would not* + a verb.

   When Tom lived in New York, he **would take** the subway. He **wouldn't take** taxis.

5. We form yes/no questions with *would* + a subject + a verb. We form short answers
   with a pronoun subject + *would* or *wouldn't*.

   A: **Would** he **go** to museums a lot?
   B: Yes, he **would.** No, he **wouldn't.**

6. We use the wh- words *what, where, when, how, which, why, who*, and *whom* to
   form questions with *would* + base verb.

   A: Where **would** he **eat** dinner?
   B: He**'d** usually **eat** in his apartment.

Function

1. We use *used to* to talk about a past habit which does not exist any longer.
   We can also use the simple past in this case with no difference in meaning.

   We **used to go** to the beach every week, but now we don't.
   OR We **went** to the beach every week, but now we don't.

   When we give a specific time, we do not use *used to*.

   CORRECT: We went to the beach every week in 20XX.
   INCORRECT: We ~~used to go~~ to the beach every week in 20XX.

2. We can also use *would* instead of *used to* for a past habit.

   I **used to visit** my grandmother on weekends.
   OR I **would visit** my grandmother on weekends.

   But in this meaning, we cannot use *would* with stative verbs.

   CORRECT: I used to have a red bicycle.
   INCORRECT: I ~~would have~~ a red bicycle.

3. We use *used to* to talk about a past situation that no longer exists.

   We **used to live** in a small apartment.

   But we cannot use *would* to talk about these situations.

   CORRECT: We used to live in Poland before we moved here.
   INCORRECT: We ~~would~~ live in Poland before we moved here.

4. We often start a story about the past with *used to* and then use *would* to talk about the rest of the story.

> When I was a child, I **used to do** my homework first, and then I **would go out** and **play** with my friends.

5. We often use *would* to show stubbornness and that the speaker disapproves of this.

> He **would come** home whenever he wanted, and nobody could do anything about it.

6. In the negative, *would* shows refusal. We cannot replace *didn't use to* with *wouldn't* because the meaning will change.

> She **didn't use to work** late. (neutral)
> She **wouldn't work** late. (She refused to work late. Maybe she didn't want to get caught in bad traffic.)

7. Do not confuse *used to* + a base verb with *be used to* + a base verb + *-ing*. *Be used to* + a base verb + *-ing* means "to be accustomed to."

> He **used to work** long hours. (He did this in the past, but he does not do it any more.)
> He **is used to working** long hours. (He is accustomed to this.)

18 Practice

Underline the correct form in parentheses.

1. People (<u>used to watch</u> / would watch) black and white television in the 1960s.
2. Women (used to wear / used to wearing) mini-skirts in the 60s.
3. Some young men (would not fight / didn't use to fight) in the Vietnam War.
4. Many young men (would have / used to have) long hair in the 1960s.
5. The Beatles (used to become / became) the most popular group in England in the 1960s.
6. The Beatles (used to come / came) to the United States in 1965.
7. Girls (used to scream / used to be screaming) when they saw the Beatles.
8. Other groups like the Rolling Stones, the Beach Boys, and the Bee Gees also (used to be / would be) popular in the 1960s and 1970s.
9. I (used to listen / am used to listening) to the radio when I drive to work. I hear many of my favorite songs from the 1960s.
10. People (used to be / would be) afraid of the atom bomb in the 1960s.

Practice

Look at the chart of information about Bruno Martin in the year 2000 and now.
Write sentences about him that say what he *used to do* or *would do,* and what he
is doing now. Use the verbs in the chart.

	Verb	2000	Now
Home	live	Brazil	Canada
Marital Status	be	single	married
Job	be	student	architect
Sports	play	soccer	hockey
Weight	weigh	160 pounds/72.5 kilos	200 pounds/90.7 kilos
Hobbies	like	movies and dancing	watching TV
Languages	speak	Portuguese	Portuguese and English
Personality	(your ideas)	(your ideas)	(your ideas)

1. *Bruno used to live in Brazil, but now he lives in Canada.*

2. _____

3. _____

4. _____

5. _____

6. _____

7. _____

8. _____

What Do You Think?

What other things happened in the 1960s? What did people use to do then?

21 Your Turn

Work with a partner. Complete the chart with information about your partner. Use the chart to ask and answer questions about your lives now and when you were children.

Example:

You: What TV shows did you use to like as a child?
Your partner: I used to like cartoons.
You: What shows do you like now?
Your partner: I like comedies.

	As a Child	Now
TV shows/like		
newspapers and books/read		
food/like		
sports/play		
go on vacation		
do on the weekends		

REVIEW

1 Review (2a–2b)

Complete the sentences with a correct past tense of the verbs in parentheses. Sometimes more than one tense is possible. If there are other words in parentheses, include them.

When I (see) _____ *saw* _____ my friends, I (know)
                              1

_____ they (not, be) _____ happy. It (be)
         2   3

_____ already 10:00 in the morning, and I (oversleep)
         4

_____ . By the time I (arrive) _____ , they
         5   6

(wait) _____ for me almost an hour. They (want)
                     7

_____ to leave without me, but Ann (not, let)
         8

_____ them. I thanked her. I told her that she (be)
         9

_____ a good friend.
        10

Soon we (hike) _____ up the mountain. It (be)
                          11

_____ fun for a while. Everyone (be) _____
         12   13

happy. I (look) _____ forward to this trip all week. But now I (be)
                         14

_____ very tired. I (not, sleep) _____ well
         15   16

the night before.

We (come) _____ to a place where two paths crossed. No one
                     17

(know) _____ which way to go. None of us (hike)
                  18

_____ this mountain before. That is, no one except me. They all (expect)
         19

_____ me to know the way. After all, I (be) _____
         20   21

there before. But I (not, hike) _____ there since I was a teenager.
                                          22

Everything (change) _____ . Meanwhile, everyone (wait)
                                23

_____ . Finally I (tell) _____ them to turn
         24   25

right. We (walk) _____ and (walk) _____ .
                          26   27

Suddenly the path (end) _____ at the edge of a cliff. We (have)
                                    28

_____ no idea where we were.
         29

By this time, we (walk) _____ for six hours. We (be)
                                30
_____ all very tired. The sun (go) _____
       31   32
down. It (get) _____ dark. Why (I, tell) _____
                      33   34
them to take the path to the right? I (be) _____ so angry at myself.
                                                    35
I (not, feel) _____ so upset for a long time.
                    36

Suddenly we (hear) _____ a noise. Everyone (be)
                          37
_____ scared! Then we (laugh) _____.
       38   39
As we (look) _____ up the path, a park ranger (walk)
                    40
_____ toward us. He had seen us from his lookout. We
       41
(be) _____ very happy that he (come) _____
          42   43
to rescue us.

2 | Review (2a)

**Complete the sentences with a correct past tense of the verbs in parentheses.
Sometimes more than one tense is possible. If there are other words in parentheses,
include them.**

The Maori (be) _____*were*_____ the first people in New Zealand. They first
                            1
(come) _____from Polynesia in small boats as long ago as 700 C.E.
                    2
While these original people (live) _____ there, other Polynesians
                                              3
(come) _____ to their islands. In the 14th century, another
                4
large group (arrive) _____ from the Society Islands. They
                              5
(be) _____ hungry and at war for many years before they (decide)
            6
_____ to leave their islands. Later, the stories of their voyages
       7
across the Pacific Ocean (pass) _____ from one generation to another.
                                            8
When they (land) _____ in New Zealand, the original people (live)
                          9
_____ there for centuries. But the culture of the new people
       10
(replace) _____ the old. The new people (be)_____
                      11   12
warriors*. They (build) _____ their villages on top of hills or
                                13
near a river or the sea because they (need) _____ protection. It
                                                          14
(be) _____ easy for one group to insult another, so they (have)
            15

_____ wars all the time. They (fight) _____

among themselves.

    The Maoris (not, have) _____ a written language. How (they, teach)

_____ their children? They (tell) _____ them

stories. The Maoris (be) _____ also great artists and craftsmen. The

Maoris (respect) _____ nature. They (care)_____

for the land. They (not, destroy) _____ anything natural. They

(have)_____ many gods. They (believe) _____

these gods protected the sea, forest, and the crops they planted. The Maoris (have)

_____ strong families, religious beliefs, and traditions.

    Several years ago, New Zealanders (begin) _____ to show a great

interest in the Maori way of life. They (decide) _____ to teach

Maori language, art, song and dance in their schools. They (realize)

_____ that Maori culture is part of New Zealand's culture.

warriors: people who make war

3 | Review (2a–2b)

Write wh- questions about the information in Review 2.

1. _Where did the first Maoris come from?_ _____

2. _____

3. _____

4. _____

5. _____

6. _____

7. _____

8. _____

9. _____

10. _____

4 Review (2a–2c)

Complete the sentences with a correct past tense of the verbs in parentheses. Sometimes more than one tense is possible.

When I (be) ___*was*___ a child, my grandparents
                  1
(live) ___*lived*___ with us. Every night our grand-
              2
mother (tell) _____ us
                          3
stories about the 1950s. She (not, let) _____ us go to bed until we
                                                        4
(hear) _____a story. We (be) _____ very
                5   6
sleepy by the time she (finish) _____ her story. Until a few years
                                              7
ago, I (not, think) _____ about my grandmother's stories for a long
                              8
time. I (start) _____ writing them down, and now I have a
                        9
collection of stories for my own children.

Grandma also taught us dances from the 1950s. One night I (be) _____
                                                                                  10
late. Grandma (already, start) _____ a dance by the time I came in.
                                              11
She (show) _____ my sisters how to do the "hokey pokey" dance as
                        12
I (walk) _____ into the room. Grandma (put) _____
              13   14
one foot in and one foot out of the circle of dancers. Then she (shake) _____
                                                                                  15
it all around. Grandma (not, let) _____ me go to bed until I (dance)
                                            16
_____ too. I (not, believe) _____ her when
          17   18
she said that the "hokey pokey" (be) _____ very popular in the 50s.
                                                19
By 1952, people (drive) _____ a lot more. The cars then (be)
                                  20
_____ more comfortable than the cars of the past. In those days,
          21
more men (drive) _____ than women, but more and more women
                              22
(learn) _____ to drive during those years. Every summer, my grand-
                  23
parents (pack up) _____ their car with bags and children and drive
                              24
hundreds of miles to a vacation spot. Over the years, they (go) _____
                                                                              25
to the Grand Canyon, to New York City, to Florida, and to the mountains in Colorado. On the
trips, the children (ask) _____, "Are we there yet?" over and over.
                                  26
My children still ask this question today. Some things never change.

WRITING: Write a Narrative

Write a paragraph or an essay about a person's life in the order of events. We call this type of writing a narrative. Narrative is another word for "story." See page 470 for general writing guidelines. See page 471 for information on writing an essay.

Step 1. Choose one of the following topics.

1. A Person I Admire
2. My Life
3. The Life of (a famous person)

Step 2. Make notes to answer these questions.

1. When and where was the person born?
2. Where did the person study, work, etc. Note all the most important events in the person's life up to the present or until the person died.

Step 3. Arrange the events in correct time order using time expressions such as the following.

after	in 1989	one day	when
finally	next	then	

Step 4. Write your narrative in the form of a paragraph or an essay. Make sure your paragraph or essay has a beginning, a middle, and an end. If you write an essay, each paragraph should be about a major time period in the person's life, for example, school, work, and achievements. Remember to indent your paragraph(s).

Step 5. Evaluate your paragraph or essay.

Checklist

_____ Did you write a title and put it in the right place?

_____ Did you indent the paragraph(s)?

_____ Did you use time expressions to show the correct order of events?

Step 6. Work with a partner or a teacher to edit your paragraph or essay. Check spelling, vocabulary, and grammar.

Step 7. Write your final copy.

SELF-TEST

A **Choose the best answer, A, B, C, or D, to complete the sentence. Mark your answer by darkening the oval with the same letter.**

1. By 10:00 yesterday, John _____ his test.

   A. has finished   Ⓐ Ⓑ Ⓒ Ⓓ
   B. had finished
   C. had been finishing
   D. finishing

2. When John was a boy, he _____ in the Philippines.

   A. would live   Ⓐ Ⓑ Ⓒ Ⓓ
   B. has lived
   C. used to live
   D. living

3. I didn't hear the phone. I _____.

   A. was sleeping   Ⓐ Ⓑ Ⓒ Ⓓ
   B. slept
   C. used to sleep
   D. had been sleeping

4. Tom: Did you watch the concert on TV last night?
   Sue: _____. I was reading.

   A. No, I wasn't   Ⓐ Ⓑ Ⓒ Ⓓ
   B. No, I didn't
   C. Yes, I was
   D. Yes, I did

5. They _____ TV when the fire alarm rang.

   A. was watching   Ⓐ Ⓑ Ⓒ Ⓓ
   B. were watching
   C. watched
   D. would watch

6. Bob: I _____ a strange e-mail message yesterday.
   Jan: Really? Who was it from?

   A. did get   Ⓐ Ⓑ Ⓒ Ⓓ
   B. was getting
   C. got
   D. have got

7. Ted _____ two hours to work, but now he lives closer to his job.

   A. used to drive   Ⓐ Ⓑ Ⓒ Ⓓ
   B. is used to driving
   C. has driven
   D. use to drive

8. How long _____ for him when he arrived?

   A. have you been waiting   Ⓐ Ⓑ Ⓒ Ⓓ
   B. had you been waiting
   C. did you wait
   D. you waited

9. Which movie _____ yesterday?

   A. you saw   Ⓐ Ⓑ Ⓒ Ⓓ
   B. did you see
   C. you did see
   D. you see

10. I _____ a test yesterday.

   A. have had   Ⓐ Ⓑ Ⓒ Ⓓ
   B. was having
   C. would have
   D. had

B Find the underlined word or phrase, A, B, C, or D, that is incorrect. Mark your answer by darkening the oval with the same letter.

1. <u>Before</u> he <u>became</u> an artist, Steven <u>has</u>
       A   B   C

    <u>been</u> a teacher.
     D

    Ⓐ Ⓑ Ⓒ Ⓓ

2. <u>As soon as</u> the alarm <u>rang</u>, he <u>got up</u> and
       A   B   C

    <u>was putting</u> on his clothes.
      D

    Ⓐ Ⓑ Ⓒ Ⓓ

3. I <u>was</u> <u>driving</u> to work <u>when</u> I <u>was seeing</u>
       A   B   C   D

    the accident.

    Ⓐ Ⓑ Ⓒ Ⓓ

4. What <u>do</u> people <u>use to</u> <u>do</u> when they
          A   B   C

    <u>got</u> sick?
     D

    Ⓐ Ⓑ Ⓒ Ⓓ

5. The mail carrier <u>delivered</u> this package
                   A

    <u>this morning</u> <u>while</u> you <u>were slept</u>.
      B   C   D

    Ⓐ Ⓑ Ⓒ Ⓓ

6. <u>When</u> Sally <u>were</u> young, she <u>practiced</u> the
      A   B   C

    piano <u>every day</u>.
          D

    Ⓐ Ⓑ Ⓒ Ⓓ

7. Rob <u>have</u> <u>been training</u> <u>for</u> three years
        A   B   C

    <u>when</u> he entered the tournament.
     D

    Ⓐ Ⓑ Ⓒ Ⓓ

8. <u>When</u> <u>did</u> you <u>called</u> me last <u>night</u>?
      A   B   C   D

    Ⓐ Ⓑ Ⓒ Ⓓ

9. <u>When</u> I <u>was</u> a child, I <u>would like</u> to <u>do</u>
      A   B   C   D

    things with my father.

    Ⓐ Ⓑ Ⓒ Ⓓ

10. They <u>have lived</u> here <u>for</u> four years <u>before</u>
        A   B   C

    they <u>moved</u>.
        D

    Ⓐ Ⓑ Ⓒ Ⓓ

UNIT 3

THE FUTURE TENSES

3a *Be Going To* and *Will*

Are you going to show me your report card?

BE GOING TO

See page 448 for charts showing statements and questions with *be going to*.

1. We form affirmative statements with a subject + the present tense of *be* + *going to* + a verb. We form negative statements with a subject + the present tense of *be* + *not* + *going to* + a verb.

   I'm going to have a party for my roommate's birthday this weekend.
   I'm not going to tell him because I want it to be a surprise.

2. We form yes/no questions with the present tense of *be* + a subject + *going to* + a verb. In short answers, we use a pronoun subject + the present tense of *be* (+ *not* for negatives). We usually contract negative short answers.

   A: **Are** your friends **going to make** all of the food?
   B: Yes, they are.
   A: **Are** they **going to make** American food?
   B: No, they**'re not**./No, they **aren't**. They're going to make Mexican food.

3. We use the wh- words *what, where, when, how, which, why, who,* and *whom* to form wh- questions.

   Who is going to make the food?
   Where are they **going to make** it?

4. In speech and in informal writing, we often contract *is* with the wh- word. In speech, we also contract *are* with the wh- word, but we do not usually write this form.

WILL

See page 449 for charts showing statements and questions with *will*.

5. We form affirmative statements with a subject + *will* + a verb. We form negative statements with a subject + *will not* + a verb.

> A: I need a big pot to make the chili in.
> B: I have one. **I'll lend** it to you.
> A: Thanks. Could you bring it to me by 9:00 Saturday morning?
> B: Sure. Don't worry. I **won't be** late.

6. We form yes/no questions with *will* + a subject + a base verb. In short answers, we use a pronoun subject + *will* or *will not*. We usually contract negative short answers.

> A: **Will** your roommate **like** the surprise?
> B: Yes, he **will**. He loves parties.
> A: **Will** he **guess** that there's going to be a party?
> B: No, he **won't**. I'm going to hide everything.

7. We use the wh- words *what, where, when, how, which, why, who,* and *whom* to form wh- questions.

> I need some help. **Who will set** the table for me?
> **When will** the food **be** ready?

8. In speech, we often contract *will* with the wh- word, but we do not usually write this form.

1. Here are the main uses of *be going to* + base verb and *will* + base verb.

Will + Base Verb	Be Going To + Base Verb
a. To talk about something we decide to do at the moment of speaking. A: Oh no! I've spilled some coffee on the rug. B: Don't worry. **I'll clean** it up for you.	a. To talk about plans or something we have already decided to do. **I'm going to have** lunch with my brother today.
b. To say what we think or believe will happen in the future, usually with verbs such as *think*, *believe*, and *expect*, with adverbs such as *probably*, *perhaps*, *maybe*, and *certainly*, and with expressions such as *I'm sure* and *I'm afraid*. They**'ll** probably **get** here late. I'm sure he**'ll be** there.	b. To talk about something in the future that we can see as a result of something in the present. There isn't a cloud in the sky. It**'s going to be** a beautiful day.
c. To talk about actions and events that will definitely happen in the future. I **will be** twenty next Monday. The sun **will rise** again tomorrow.	c. To talk about plans, intentions, or ambitions for the future. She's **going to be** a doctor some day.

2. We often use *be going to* to talk about an intention and *will* to give details and comments.

   I **am going to have** a surprise birthday party for Ken. I**'ll invite** all his friends.

3. We can use either *will* or *be going to* to make predictions.

   They**'ll win** the game.
   They**'re going to win** the game.

4. We use *will* and *be going to* with time expressions such as *soon, tonight, tomorrow,* and *next Monday/week/month/year.*

5. You might occasionally notice the use of *shall* instead of *will* with the pronouns I or we to express future time. This use is more common in British English than in American English. However, in American English we do use *shall* to make polite suggestions.

   Shall we go? It's getting late.

1 Practice

Complete the sentences with the *be going to* or the *will* form of the verbs in parentheses.

Tim: What (you, do) _____*are you going to do*_____ tonight?
                                                          1

Mike: I (see) _____ the new Spielberg movie with
                                    2

Melissa. How about you?

Tim: Oh, I think I (stay) _____ home tonight.
                                              3

Mike: Why don't you come with us? It (be) _____ fun.
                                                                    4

Tim: OK. I (go) _____ with you.
                                  5

Mike: We (leave) _____ at seven, and we probably
                                  6

(get) _____ there by seven thirty.
                    7

Tim: OK. I (see) _____ you in front of the movie
                                  8

theater at 7:30 then.

2 Practice

A. Read about the city of the future.

> In the future, cities like Tokyo in Japan are going to be even more crowded than they are today. Japan does not have a lot of land, so where are people going to live? Japanese architects have a plan for a city in the sky. At the moment, the architects do not have enough money to start their plan, but maybe they will get the money soon. They are going to find a place near Tokyo to build this city.
>
> This city in the sky will be a glass pyramid over 2,000 meters high. The pyramid will be 500 floors high. It will have residential areas with apartments, parks, and leisure centers. It will also have offices, restaurants, schools, hospitals, post offices, and everything else that a city has, but it won't have cars. The city will be climate-controlled so the weather will always be nice. Imagine. You will be able to go out for a relaxing run in the middle of winter and take the elevator to your job. People will travel in elevators, on walkways, and on special trains.
>
> The architects hope that one day they will get the money to build this city.

B. Write yes/no and wh- questions for the answers. The underlined words in the answers are prompts for the questions.

1. QUESTION: *Are cities like Tokyo going to be very crowded in the future?*

   ANSWER: <u>Yes,</u> cities like Tokyo are going to be very crowded.

2. QUESTION: _____

   ANSWER: They are going to build this city <u>near Tokyo</u>.

3. QUESTION: _____

   ANSWER: The shape of this city will be <u>a pyramid</u>.

4. QUESTION: _____

   ANSWER: The pyramid will be <u>2,000 meters high</u>.

5. QUESTION: _____

   ANSWER: The pyramid will be made of <u>glass</u>.

6. QUESTION: _____

   ANSWER: <u>Yes,</u> it will have apartments for people to live in.

7. QUESTION: _____

   ANSWER: <u>No,</u> it won't have cars.

8. QUESTION: _____

   ANSWER: People will travel <u>in elevators, on walkways, and on special trains</u>.

9. QUESTION: _____

   ANSWER: <u>Yes,</u> the weather will always be nice.

10. QUESTION: _____

    ANSWER: The architects hope <u>that one day they will get the money to build this city</u>.

---

3 | Your Turn

What will your town be like 100 years from now? Work with a partner to answer this question. Then exchange your ideas with the rest of the class.

Example:
There will be no cars in the center of the city. People will travel on special chairs with wheels.

3b Time Clauses and Conditional Sentences in the Future

When we grow up, we'll fly in one of those planes and go all over the world.

1. All clauses have a subject and a verb. Main clauses can stand alone as complete sentences. Dependent clauses cannot. We must use them with a main clause. There are several kinds of dependent clauses. One of them is the time clause.

2. Time clauses begin with words such as *when, while, as soon as, before, after,* and *until.* Conditional clauses begin with words such as *if* and *unless.*

Main Clause	Time/Conditional Clause
I'll buy a car	as soon as I have enough money.
I'll get a bigger apartment	if I have enough money next year.

3. A time clause gives information about when something happens in the main clause.

Time Clause	**Main Clause**
When you get here,	we'll start the game.

A future conditional sentence expresses a possible situation in the conditional clause and a result in the main clause.

Conditional Clause	**Main Clause**
If you're late,	we'll start without you.

4. The time or conditional clause can come either at the beginning or end of the sentence. When the time or conditional clause comes at the beginning of a sentence, we put a comma after it.

Time/Conditional Clause	Main Clause
As soon as I have enough money,	I'll buy a car.
If I have enough money next year,	I'll get a bigger apartment.

5. We do not use *will* or *be going to* in a time clause even though we are talking about the future. We usually use the simple present tense.

Time Clause—Present Tense	Main Clause—Future Tense
When I **see** him,	I**'ll give** him the message.
If the weather **is** nice,	we**'ll go** to the beach.

6. We can also use the present perfect in a time clause to show that the first action will be finished before the second action.

> I'll talk with her when she **arrives**.
> OR I'll talk with her when she **has arrived**.

7. In some cases we can use the present progressive (instead of the simple present) to talk about an action that will be in progress at a future time.

> While we **are traveling** around Mexico next summer, we will visit all the famous colonial cities.

4 Practice

A. Matt is 16 years old. His teacher asked him to write about his future. Read what he wrote.

> Matthew Richards
> English 4
> October 20, 20XX
>
>   I want to be rich and famous in the future. I will be a famous rock singer and guitarist before I am 25. When I'm 30, I'll have a lot of money. As soon as I become a millionaire, I'll retire.
>   After I leave school, I'll travel all over the world. Before I travel, I'll save some money. As soon as I have enough money, I'll go to Africa. After I have seen the main cities and been on a safari, I'll go to Asia. When I go there, I'll visit my friend Hong in China. If he has time, he'll show me around. Before I come back home, I'll visit Japan. I'll see all these places if I have the money, of course.
>   When I come back home, I'll go back to my hometown. I'll go to college if my parents want me to.

B. Answer the following questions about Matt's plans for the future. Write complete sentences.

1. What does Matt want to be in the future?

   Matt wants to be a famous rock singer in the future.

2. When will he become a famous rock star?

   _____

3. When will he have a lot of money?

   _____

4. What will he do as soon as he becomes a millionaire?

   _____

5. What does he want to do after he leaves school?

   _____

6. What will he do before he travels?

   _____

7. Where will he go as soon as he has enough money?

   _____

8. When will he leave Africa?

   _____

9. Who will he visit when he goes to Asia?

   _____

10. When will he visit Japan?

    _____

11. What will he do when he comes home?

    _____

12. What will he do if his parents want him to?

    _____

5 Your Turn

Complete the sentences with a time clause.

Example:
I'll get a job as soon as I can.

1. I'll get a job as soon as _____

2. I'll live with my parents until _____

3. I'll get to travel a lot _____

4. I'll buy a house or an apartment _____

6 Your Turn

Work with a partner. One of you is going hiking in the mountains for the first time. Say and write questions and answers using the prompts.

Example:
What/do/if/hurt yourself
You: What will you do if you hurt yourself?
Your partner: I'll call for help on my cell phone.

1. What/do/if/hurt yourself

   Your Question: _____

   Your Partner's Answer: _____

2. What/do/if/rains

   Your Question: _____

   Your Partner's Answer: _____

3. What/do/if/get/hungry

   Your Question: _____

   Your Partner's Answer: _____

4. What/do/if/gets dark

   Your Question: _____

   Your Partner's Answer: _____

5. What/do/if/get lost

   Your Question: _____

   Your Partner's Answer: _____

3c Present Tenses with Future Meaning

I'm really excited! The train **leaves** at 8:15, and I**'m meeting** Mr. Sharp for an interview at 9:00.

THE PRESENT PROGRESSIVE TENSE

1. We use the present progressive tense for actions that we have already arranged or planned for in the future.

   A: What are you doing on Sunday morning?
   B: I**'m meeting** Susan.

   We**'re flying** to New York tomorrow morning.

   When we use the present progressive tense in this way, we often use a time expression such as *on Monday, tonight,* or *next week.*

2. We use the present progressive tense more often than *be going to* with the verbs *go* and *come.*

   We**'re going** camping on Saturday, and we**'re coming** back on Sunday evening.

   I**'m going** to Toronto soon.

THE SIMPLE PRESENT TENSE

3. We use the simple present tense to talk about actions or events that are part of a fixed schedule.

   The train **arrives** at 8:10 in the morning.
   The movie **starts** at 9:00 in the evening, and it **ends** at 10:45.

7 | Practice

Christina Lang is a famous tennis player. Complete the sentences about her trip to London next week. Use the present progressive tense or the simple present tense.

1. Christina's flight from Rio (arrive) _____*arrives*_____ in London at 1:30 P.M.
   on Monday.

2. After she rests a little, she (have) _____ dinner with some sports
   reporters.

3. The next morning, she (meet) _____ with her coach at 9:00, and she
   (see) _____ her doctor at 11:00.

4. In the afternoon, she (practice) _____ for two hours.

5. On Wednesday morning, she (meet) _____ some of the other players. The
   meeting (start) _____ at 9:00 and (end) _____ at 10:30.

6. After that, she (go) _____ for a medical check-up. She
   (have) _____ an appointment with the doctor at 2:00.

7. On Thursday morning, she (rest) _____.

8. On Thursday afternoon, she (play) _____ her match. The game
   (start) _____ at 2:00.

9. She (fly) _____ home on Friday morning. The plane
   (take off) _____ at 11:30.

8 | Your Turn

Write about three arrangements or plans you have made for the future.

Example:
I am meeting my friend downtown tomorrow afternoon.

9 Your Turn

A. Read this schedule of college classes. Describe the schedule using the simple present tense of verbs from the list.

begin   end   start

Example:
Classes begin on September 4.

Schedule	
September 4	First day of class
October 18–22	Fall vacation
November 24–28	Thanksgiving vacation
December 9	Last day of class
December 12–17	Final exams

B. Now write a schedule of classes for your school and describe it as you did in Part A using the simple present tense.

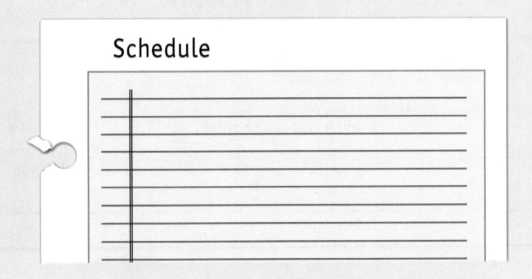

3d The Future Progressive Tense

At this time tomorrow, I'll be walking on a sandy beach.

See page 450 for charts showing statements and questions in the future progressive tense.

1. We form affirmative statements in the future progressive tense with a subject + *will* + *be* + a verb + *-ing*. We form negative statements with a subject + *will not* + *be* + a verb + *-ing*.

    I can't talk to you at 10:00 this morning. **I'll be meeting** with my boss.

2. We form yes/no questions with *will* + a subject + *be* + a verb + *-ing*. In short answers, we use a pronoun subject + *will (not)*. We usually contract negative short answers.

    A: **Will** you **be working** when I get to your office?
    B: Yes, I **will**. Don't interrupt me if I'm on the phone.
       OR No, I **won't**. I'll be at lunch.

3. We use the wh- words *what, where, when, how, which, why, who,* and *whom* to form wh- questions in the future progressive tense.

    Who will be taking the day off tomorrow?
    If I need to find you, **where will** you **be sitting**?

4. In speech, we often contract *will* with the wh- word, but we do not usually write this form.

1. We use *will be* + a verb + *-ing* to talk about something which will be in progress at a specific time in the future.

   At this time next week, I **will be walking** on a beach.

2. We also use *will be* + a verb + *-ing* to talk about something which has already been arranged or is part of a routine.

   I**'ll be having** lunch with my boss tomorrow. (arrangement)
   I**'ll be doing** the laundry tomorrow morning. (routine)

3. We often use *will be* + a verb + *-ing* as a polite way of asking about someone's plans in the near future, especially when those plans affect us. When we use this form, it means that we do not want the other person to change their plans for us.

   Will you **be using** the copy machine soon?
   No. Why?
   I have to make a copy of this report.

10 Practice

Susan Brooks is a manager. Read her schedule for Monday. Write complete sentences using the future progressive tense about what she will be doing at these times.

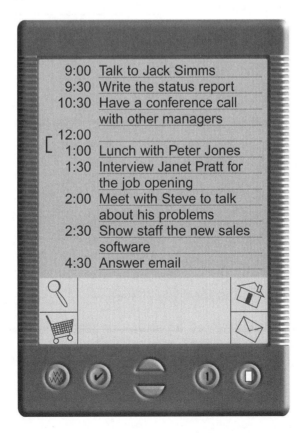

9:00 Talk to Jack Simms
9:30 Write the status report
10:30 Have a conference call with other managers
12:00
1:00 Lunch with Peter Jones
1:30 Interview Janet Pratt for the job opening
2:00 Meet with Steve to talk about his problems
2:30 Show staff the new sales software
4:30 Answer email

1. _At 9:00, she will be talking to Jack Simms._

2. _____

3. _____

4. _____

5. _____

6. _____

7. _____

8. _____

II Practice

Complete the conversation with *will* + base verb or the future progressive (*will* + *be* + verb + *-ing*) of the verbs in parentheses.

Isabel is talking to her friend Susan about going on a vacation to Barcelona, Spain. Susan's family lives there, and Isabel is going to stay with them.

Susan: When you arrive at the airport in Barcelona, my sister

(wait) _____*will be waiting*_____ for you.
            1

Isabel: How (I/recognize) _____ her? I don't know her.
                                    2

Susan: Don't worry, she (recognize) _____ you. She has a
                                             3

photo of you. Anyway, you (not/miss) _____ her.
                                           4

She looks like me, and she (wear) _____ a red dress
                                       5

or jacket. She always wears red.

Isabel: OK. I (not/worry) _____. I still can't believe it.
                                  6

This time tomorrow, I (sit) _____ on a plane on my
                                7

way to Spain.

Susan: I'm sure you (enjoy) _____ your flight.
                                   8

And at one o'clock the next day, you (eat) _____
                                                9

lunch with my family, and then you (have) _____
                                                10

a siesta, which is what we call an afternoon rest. Oh, by the way,

(you/do) _____ me a favor?
              11

(you/buy) _____ a purse similar to this

                     12

one for me? I (pay) _____ for it. It

                     13

(not/cost) _____ more than twenty dollars.

                 14

Isabel: Sure. I (be) _____ happy to do it.

                 15

Susan: That (be) _____ great!

                 16

Isabel: No problem. I think I (get) _____ one for myself, too.

                 17

Susan: I (work) _____ tomorrow, so I can't take you to the

                 18

airport. What time (you/leave) _____?

                 19

Isabel: At 5:00 in the afternoon. I (call) _____ you

                 20

tomorrow at about 3:00 your time. Is that OK?

Susan: Of course. I (wait) _____ for your call at 3:00.

                 21

12 Your Turn

What will you be doing at these times tomorrow? Write and say one sentence for each time.

Example:
At 7:05, I'll be drinking a cup of coffee.

7:05 A.M.	7:30 A.M.	8:00 A.M.	8:55 A.M.
9:15 A.M.	1:20 P.M.	4:00 P.M.	6:15 P.M.

1. _____

2. _____

3. _____

4. _____

5. _____

6. _____

7. _____

8. _____

3e Other Expressions of the Future; The Future in the Past

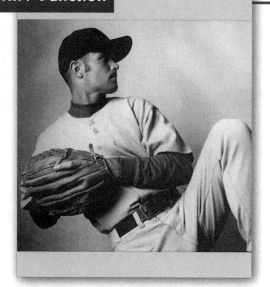

He**'s about to throw** the ball.

1. We can also express the future in these ways.

Form	Function
a. *be about to* + a base verb	We use *be about to* to talk about the very near future. The movie **is about to start**.
b. *be to* + a base verb	We use *be to* + base verb to refer to a future plan. This form is mainly used in formal English. The president **is to visit** Japan next week.
c. a present tense of verbs like *plan, intend, decide,* or *mean* + an infinitive	We use these verbs + infinitive to express a future plan or intention. We **plan to buy** a house next year. He **has decided to take** the job in Baltimore.

2. We use *was/were going to* + a base verb to say that we planned something for the future at a past time. We sometimes call this "the future in the past." When we use this structure, it often means that the planned future action did not happen.

   They **were going to buy** the house, but they changed their minds at the last minute.
   We **were going to eat** at a Chinese restaurant, but it was too crowded, so we went to an Italian restaurant instead.

13 Practice

The following famous people intended to be one thing but became something else instead. Write a sentence about each one using *was going to be* in the first part of the sentence, and *became* in the other.

PERSON	GOING TO BE	BECAME
1. Albert Einstein	violinist	he/physicist
2. Mahatma Gandhi	lawyer	he/great political leader
3. George Washington Carver	artist	he/chemist and botanist
4. Hans Christian Anderson	actor	he/fairy tale writer
5. Frida Kahlo	doctor	she/artist
6. Sigmund Freud	doctor	he/psychoanalyst

1. *Albert Einstein was going to be a violinist, but instead he became a physicist.*

2. _____

_____

3. _____

_____

4. _____

_____

5. _____

_____

6. _____

_____

14 Practice

Jane and her husband, Jim, had planned to do a lot of things on their day off because Jane's family was coming for a visit. Unfortunately, everything went wrong. Complete the sentences using *was/were about to* + the verbs in parentheses.

1. Jane (do) _____ *was about to do* _____ the laundry when she

realized she didn't have enough detergent.

2. She and Jim (drive) _____ to the

supermarket when the phone rang.

3. She (make) _____ a cake when she

realized she didn't have enough butter.

4. She and Jim (do) _____ some housework

when the doorbell rang.

5. Her relatives (ring) _____ the doorbell

when they realized they had left their gift in the car.

6. She (tell) _____ them that they were too

early, but she changed her mind.

7. She (give) _____ her aunt a cup of coffee

when she dropped it on the floor.

8. She (scream) _____, but she didn't. She

just laughed.

15 Practice

Complete the sentences with *be to* or *be about to* + the verbs in parentheses.

1. The president (visit) _____*is to visit*_____ the university today.

2. The ceremony (begin) _____. The students are very excited.

3. He (enter) _____ the auditorium any minute.

4. The newspaper says that he (give) _____ a speech about more

money for education.

5. This speech (help) _____ him get elected again. The next

election is six months away.

6. The president of our university is standing on the stage. She

(introduce) _____ the nation's president.

16 Your Turn

Tell your partner three things about you or other people that were going to happen but didn't.

Example:
My sister was going to get married last month, but she didn't.

3f The Future Perfect Tense and The Future Perfect Progressive Tense

By this time next year, Mr. Yamasaki **will have been working** for his company for 45 years.

THE FUTURE PERFECT TENSE

See page 451 for charts showing statements and questions in the future perfect tense.

1. We form affirmative statements with a subject + *will* + *have* + a past participle. We form negative statements with a subject + *will not* + *have* + a past participle.

    By this time next year, the people **will have chosen** a new president.

2. We form yes/no questions with *will* + a subject + *have* + a past participle. In short answers, we use a pronoun subject + *will/won't (have)*.

    A: **Will** the candidates **have visited** every state before the election?
    B: Yes, they **will (have)**./No, they **won't (have)**.

    The use of *have* in short answers is optional.

3. We use the wh- *words what, where, when, how, which, why, who,* and *whom* to form wh- questions in the future perfect tense.

    Which candidate **will have spent** the most money?
    Why will they **have spent** so much?

THE FUTURE PERFECT PROGRESSIVE TENSE

See page 452 for charts showing statements and questions in the future perfect progressive tense.

4. We form affirmative statements with a subject + *will* + *have* + *been* + a verb + *-ing*. We form negative statements with a subject + *will not* + *have* + *been* + a verb + *-ing*.

> By the time the election is over, the candidates **will have been running** for four months.

5. We form yes/no questions with *will* + a subject + *have* + *been* + a verb + *-ing*. In short answers, we use a pronoun subject + *will/won't (have)*. In negative short answers, we use a pronoun subject + *will not/won't (have)*.

> A: **Will** they **have been running** for six months?
> B: Yes, they **will (have)**./No, t hey **won't (have)**.

The use of *have* in short answers is optional.

6. We use the wh- words *what, where, when, how, which, why, who,* and *whom* to form wh- questions in the future perfect progressive tense.

> **Which** candidates **will have been traveling** the most?
> In **which** states **will** they **have been traveling** the most?

Function

1. Here are the main uses of the future perfect tense and the future perfect progressive tense.

The Future Perfect Tense	The Future Perfect Progressive Tense
a. To say that a future action will be completed before another action or stated time in the future. My computer at work is broken, but the technology department **will have repaired** it when I **get** to the office tomorrow.	a. To emphasize the continuation of an action that will be in progress up to a certain time in the future. By the end of this year, he **will have been working** for the company for twenty years.
b. With time expressions such as *by the time, by* + time, and *before*. They will have repaired it **before** 8:00 tomorrow morning.	b. With time expressions such as *by the time, by* + time, and *before*. By the time I finish my degree, I'll have been living here **for** three years.

2. When expressions such as *by the time* and *before* introduce time clauses that refer to the future, we use a present tense in the clause. The main clause, with the future perfect tense or the future perfect progressive tense, can go either before or after the time clause.

Time Clause **Main Clause**
By the time I **get** there, I **will have flown** for nine hours.

17 Practice

Complete the sentences about the people in this family. Then write four sentences about them with your ideas. Use the future perfect tense and the verbs in parentheses.

1. By next year, Carlos Sanchez (drive) ___will have driven___ 10,000 miles on his way to and from work.

2. By next year, Rosa Sanchez (help) _____ hundreds of people in her job as a nurse.

3. By next year, their daughter (play) _____ soccer for five years.

4. By next year, their son (finish) _____ college.

5. By then, he (study) _____ at that college for four years.

6. By next year, their daughter (start) _____ college.

7. She (decide) _____ what to study for her major.

8. Carlos Sanchez (spend) _____ more of his savings on his children.

9. (*your idea*) _____

10. (*your idea*) _____

11. (*your idea*) _____

12. (*your idea*) _____

18 Practice

In each sentence, underline the correct form of the future tense of the words in parentheses.

1. Scientists (<u>are planning</u> / will plan) a mission to the moon.

2. They (are going to send / are sending) some astronauts to the moon.

3. There (will be / is being) a press conference tomorrow at 9:00 to announce the mission.

4. As usual, some people (are going to be / will have been) happy about such an announcement, but others (are not / will have not).

5. The astronauts (will be preparing / will have prepared) to go to the moon for the next three years.

6. The astronauts (will have been leaving / are leaving) the earth on March 20.

7. While they are on the moon, they (will be doing / are doing) experiments.

8. They (will be looking / are looking) for signs of life.

9. They (will be collecting / are collecting) samples.

10. By the end of their stay on the moon, the astronauts (will be living / will have been living) there for four weeks.

11. By the time they get back, they (will have taken / will be taking) 5,000 photos.

12. When they get back, they (are being / will have been) part of the space program for over three years.

13. After this mission, we (will have learned / are learning) many things we do not know right now.

14. This mission (will be / is being) one more step for humankind.

19 Your Turn

Choose an age in your future. For example, if you are 25 years old, you might choose 30. What do you think you will have done by that age? Say or write four things using the future perfect tense.

Example:
By the time I am XX, I will have gotten married.

20 Your Turn

Answer these questions with complete sentences. Use the future perfect progressive + *for* + length of time.

1. How long will you have been attending this school by the end of the year?

   _____

   _____

2. How long will you have been living in your house or apartment by next July?

   _____

   _____

3. How long will you have been studying English by the end of the school year?

   _____

   _____

4. How long will you have been wearing your present shoes by the end of the year?

   _____

   _____

5. How long will you have been studying with your present teacher by the end of this school year?

   _____

   _____

6. How long will you have been using this book by the end of the year?

   _____

   _____

REVIEW

1 **Review (3a, 3f)**

Complete the sentences with a correct future tense of the verbs in parentheses. Sometimes more than one tense is possible. If there are other words in parentheses, include them.

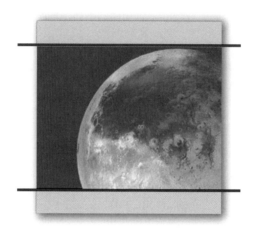

(humans, ever, go) _Will human beings ever go_ to Mars? I feel sure that
                                    1

humans (achieve) _____ this goal. Here's what I think (happen)
                              2

_____.
                3

The International Space Station (help) _____ to make travel to
                                                    4

Mars possible. At the same time that some astronauts (travel) _____
                                                                              5

to Mars, others (work) _____ in the space station. By then,
                                  6

scientists in the space station (find) _____ ways to keep humans
                                              7

healthy in space for a long time. By that time, they (prepare) _____
                                                                              8

people for the long and difficult trip to Mars, and many nations (join) _____
                                                                                      9

together to prepare for the first human travel to Mars.

By the time humans land on Mars, robots (be) _____ there for
                                                        10

many years. By then, they (give) _____ us all the information we
                                          11

need about living on Mars. How (the first travelers, find) _____
                                                                      12

life on Mars? Eventually, we (know) _____ the answer to that
                                              13

question. Future missions to Mars (give) _____ us much more information
                                                    14

about this interesting planet. Eventually, robots (put) _____ 15 special equipment in places all around Mars. Humans (know) _____ 16 a lot about the planet before they get there. Maybe the robots (discover) _____ 17 water on Mars by then. Surely by the time humans land on Mars, we (create)

_____ 18 detailed maps of the planet. Most likely scientists (discovered)

_____ 19 ways to make air on Mars that humans can breathe.

Soon, exploring distant planets (no longer, be) _____ 20 a dream. It (be) _____ 21 real. (you, be) _____ 22 one of the first people to travel to Mars? How far do you think humans (travel) _____ 23 by the year 2025? What planets (they, visit) _____ 24 ? How (they, get) _____ 25 there?

2 | Review (3a, 3c–3d)

Complete the sentences with a correct future tense of the verbs in parentheses. Sometimes more than one tense is possible.

☐	Untitled - Message	回回

| Send | Save | Insert File... | Priority ▾ | Options... |

To...	
Cc...	
Subject:	

Tom,

I (fly) ___*'m flying*___ 1 to Johannesburg tomorrow. I (be) _____ 2 in South Africa for a month. At this time tomorrow, I (fly) _____ 3 over the coast of Africa. I'm so excited. While I (travel) _____ 4 around South Africa, I (see) _____ 5 game parks, mountains, and beautiful cities. By this time next week, I (visit) _____ 6 the Transvaal and Kruger National Park. I (take) _____ 7 pictures of all the animals with my new digital camera. On Wednesday, I (be) _____ 8 in the park looking for giraffes, elephants, and zebras!

I was going to work this summer, but I changed my mind. After all, I (work) _____ for the rest of my life. Well, one day I (get) _____ out of school. By the end of next year, I (study) _____ to be a doctor for six years! That's a long time. My plane (leave) _____ very early tomorrow morning. I (go) _____ to bed now.

Emma.

<table>
<tr><td>9</td></tr>
<tr><td>10</td></tr>
<tr><td>11</td></tr>
<tr><td>12</td></tr>
<tr><td>13</td></tr>
</table>

3 Review (3a, 3c)

Complete the sentences with a correct future tense, including *going to, be about to,* and the simple present tense, of the verbs in parentheses. If there are other words in the parentheses, include them.

Charlene is calling Maria on the phone.

Charlene: Hi, Maria. What are you doing?

Maria: Oh, I (start) *was about to start* working on my psychology paper
when you called.

Charlene: What are your plans for Saturday?

Maria: I (not, do) _____ anything special. What about you?

Charlene: I (go) _____ to the beach. Why don't you come with me?

Maria: I (ask) _____ if I could go with you, but I remembered
that I don't have a bathing suit. What (I, do) _____ at
the beach if I (not, have) _____ a bathing suit?

Charlene: You (sit) _____ on the sand and not go into
the water! No, I'm just joking. By this time tomorrow, we (buy)
_____ you a bathing suit.

Maria: But I don't know where to buy one here.

Charlene: Don't worry. I (help) _____ you find the perfect suit.

Maria: Oh, thanks. While I (be) _____ at the store, I
(buy) _____ a beach towel, too. By the way, when
(we, leave) _____ tomorrow morning?

Charlene: At 9:30. We (get) _____ 13 to the beach by 10:00.

According to the radio, it (be) _____ 14 a beautiful day.

Maria: Oh, good. Just think. By this time tomorrow, we (relax)

_____ 15 on the beach for three hours.

Charlene: That's right. At this time tomorrow, I (swim) _____ 16 in

the sea. I can't wait! But right now, we need to go shopping. The store (close)

_____ 17 at 7:00.

Maria: I can't go right now. I (meet) _____ 18 you at your house

as soon as I (finish) _____ 19 writing this paper.

Charlene: (you, be) _____ 20 finished by 5:00?

Maria: Sure. See you later!

4 | Review (3a, 3c–3d, 3f)

Write wh- questions about the dialogue in Review 3.

1. *What is Maria doing on Sunday?* _____

2. _____

3. _____

4. _____

5. _____

6. _____

7. _____

8. _____

WRITING: Write an Essay with Supporting Examples

Write an essay about life in the year 2040. Use examples to support your ideas. See page 470 for general writing guidelines. See page 471 for information on writing an essay.

Step 1. Work with a partner. Brainstorm the following topics. Make notes about each one.

clothes   food   shopping
computers   home   transportation

Step 2. Choose two or three of the topics and write sentences about each one.

Step 3. Write a paragraph on each topic. Write a topic sentence, a supporting sentence, and at least one example for each topic.

Topic Sentence	In the year, 2040 our homes will be completely computerized.
Supporting Sentence	Our television, telephone, and computer will be a single machine.
Example 1	For example, while talking on the phone we will see the person
Example 2	we are talking to. We will also exchange pictures and other
	information as we talk.

Step 4. Write an introduction with a thesis statement that refers to your examples. Write a conclusion that restates the thesis statement.

Step 5. Write a title for your essay. Center it at the top of the page.

Step 6. Evaluate your essay.

Checklist

_____ Did you write a title and put it in the right place?

_____ Did your introduction include a thesis statement?

_____ Do your supporting paragraphs have a topic sentence, a supporting sentence, and at least one example?

_____ Does your conclusion restate the thesis statement?

Step 7. Work with a partner or a teacher to edit your essay. Check spelling, vocabulary, and grammar.

Step 8. Write your final copy.

SELF-TEST

A Choose the best answer, A, B, C, or D, to complete the sentence. Mark your answer by darkening the oval with the same letter.

1. By next year, I will _____ here for three years.

   A. be living   Ⓐ Ⓑ Ⓒ Ⓓ
   B. have been living
   C. live
   D. to be lived

2. She'll have graduated _____ June.

   A. for   Ⓐ Ⓑ Ⓒ Ⓓ
   B. until
   C. by
   D. already

3. I'll _____ my essay by 6:00.

   A. have finished   Ⓐ Ⓑ Ⓒ Ⓓ
   B. finishing
   C. have been finishing
   D. be finished

4. We _____ our test results tomorrow.

   A. will know   Ⓐ Ⓑ Ⓒ Ⓓ
   B. will be knowing
   C. are knowing
   D. know

5. We don't have much time. The plane _____ in 30 minutes.

   A. taking off   Ⓐ Ⓑ Ⓒ Ⓓ
   B. take off
   C. takes off
   D. will have been taking off

6. Look at those clouds! It _____ soon.

   A. is going to rain   Ⓐ Ⓑ Ⓒ Ⓓ
   B. is raining
   C. rains
   D. going to rain

7. As soon as I have enough money, I _____ a DVD player.

   A. buy   Ⓐ Ⓑ Ⓒ Ⓓ
   B. will buy
   C. buying
   D. will have bought

8. I'll give her the message when I _____ her.

   A. am seeing   Ⓐ Ⓑ Ⓒ Ⓓ
   B. will see
   C. saw
   D. see

9. Alex: I need some help with this report.
   Julio: Sure. _____ on it tomorrow morning? I can help you then.

   A. You will be working   Ⓐ Ⓑ Ⓒ Ⓓ
   B. Will you working
   C. Will you be working
   D. You are going to be working

10. They _____ to buy a house next year.

    A. will plan   Ⓐ Ⓑ Ⓒ Ⓓ
    B. are going to plan
    C. are planning
    D. will be planning

B **Find the underlined word or phrase, A, B, C, or D, that is incorrect. Mark your answer by darkening the oval with the same letter.**

1. When <u>you will</u> <u>have</u> <u>completed</u>
        A   B   C
   <u>all your courses</u> at the university?
        D

   Ⓐ Ⓑ Ⓒ Ⓓ

2. By the end of the year, I <u>have</u> <u>been</u>
                       A   B
   <u>studying</u> at this college <u>for</u> three years.
     C   D

   Ⓐ Ⓑ Ⓒ Ⓓ

3. We <u>are</u> <u>about to</u> have dinner <u>when</u> the
      A   B   C
   doorbell <u>rang</u>. It was Mr. Jones.
        D

   Ⓐ Ⓑ Ⓒ Ⓓ

4. Janet <u>is</u> <u>studying</u> hard right now <u>because</u>
        A   B   C
   she <u>will intend</u> to go to college next year.
         D

   Ⓐ Ⓑ Ⓒ Ⓓ

5. Our son <u>will</u> not <u>has</u> <u>graduated</u> from
          A   B   C
   college <u>by</u> next summer.
        D

   Ⓐ Ⓑ Ⓒ Ⓓ

6. George <u>is</u> <u>going to</u> study economics,
         A   B
   <u>but</u> he <u>changed</u> his mind and studied
    C   D
   medicine instead.

   Ⓐ Ⓑ Ⓒ Ⓓ

7. The traffic <u>is</u> very bad at <u>the moment</u>,
           A   B
   <u>so</u> they <u>are</u> probably get here late.
    C   D

   Ⓐ Ⓑ Ⓒ Ⓓ

8. Where <u>she will</u> <u>be</u> <u>staying</u> when she <u>goes</u>
         A   B   C   D
   to Canada?

   Ⓐ Ⓑ Ⓒ Ⓓ

9. Next week <u>at this time</u>, <u>I'll be lying</u> on
            A   B
   the beach <u>while</u> you <u>will studying</u>.
          C   D

   Ⓐ Ⓑ Ⓒ Ⓓ

10. <u>Will</u> you <u>be</u> <u>go</u> to the meeting tomorrow
      A   B C
    <u>morning</u>?
      D

    Ⓐ Ⓑ Ⓒ Ⓓ

UNIT 4

NOUNS AND EXPRESSIONS OF QUANTITY

Form

One sheep, two sheep, three sheep ... Don't fall asleep!

REGULAR PLURALS

	Singular	Plural
1. We form the plural of most nouns by adding -s to the singular noun.	book	book**s**
	girl	girl**s**
2. Some regular plurals require changes in the spelling of the noun before we add -s. See page 439 for more information on spelling changes.	dish	dish**es**
	factory	facto**ries**
	knife	kni**ves**

IRREGULAR PLURALS

	Singular	Plural
3. Some nouns form their plural by changing their vowels.	f**oo**t	f**ee**t
	g**oo**se	g**ee**se
	m**a**n	m**e**n
	m**ou**se	m**i**ce
	t**oo**th	t**ee**th
	wom**a**n	wom**e**n
4. Some nouns form their plural by adding a syllable.	child	child**ren**
	ox	ox**en**

	Singular	Plural
5. Some nouns have the same singular and plural form.	aircraft	aircraft
	deer	deer
	fish	fish*
	offspring	offspring
	series	series
	sheep	sheep
	spacecraft	spacecraft
	species	species
6. Some nouns that come from Latin or Greek have plural endings that come from those languages.	bacterium	bacter**ia**
	cactus	cact**i**
	curriculum	curricul**a**
	focus	foc**i**
	fungus	fung**i**
	medium	medi**a**
	memorandum	memorand**a**
	thesis	thes**es**

7. Some nouns have only a plural form. We can also use *a pair of* before these nouns.
 	
    Those **jeans** look great on you.
    That **pair of jeans** looks great on you.
		jeans

		pajamas
		pants
		shorts
		trousers
8. Some nouns end in *-s* but are not plural. **Economics** is interesting to me.	news	
	politics	
	mathematics	
	economics	
	athletics	
	physics	
	rabies	

9. The plural of *person* is usually *people* (not persons), but we can use *persons* in legal contexts.

   I know a **person** who works for your father.
   I know some **people** who work for your father.

   The **person** who had broken into a store was arrested.
   Three **persons** who had broken into a store were arrested.

See pages 292-300 for information on using verb forms with singular and plural nouns.

* *Fishes* is also possible, but it is less common and refers to more than one *species* of fish.

1 | Practice

Complete the sentences with the plural form of the nouns in parentheses.

Joseph Tanner is eighty-nine years old. He is very tall and has large

(foot) _____*feet*_____ , a big nose, and no (tooth) _____ at all.
       1   **2**

His (hobby) _____ are taking (photo) _____ and fixing
              3   **4**

old (watch) _____ . He has several (pet) _____ :
              5   **6**

three (mouse) _____ , five (fish) _____ , and two
              7   **8**

(canary) _____ . He had two (wife) _____ during his life,
              9   **10**

but they both died. His three (child) _____ are all grown up and now have
                                        11

(life) _____ of their own.
      12

2 | Practice

Complete the sentences with *is* or *are*.

1. The news on the Internet _____*is*_____ more up-to-date than in the newspaper.

2. Physics _____ more difficult than mathematics.

3. Sheep _____ more intelligent than deer.

4. Aircraft _____ safer today than twenty years ago.

5. Bacteria _____ spread only through physical contact.

6. In some jobs, jeans _____ more common at work these days than more formal pants.

7. Fish _____ easier to take care of than birds.

8. Nowadays the media _____ the biggest influence on our opinions.

9. Too many species of animal _____ now extinct.

10. The curriculum in this school _____ excellent.

Your Turn

With a partner, discuss each of the sentences in Practice 2. Do you agree with them or not? Explain why. Use the correct singular or plural verb form in your answers.

Example:
I agree that the news on the Internet is more up-to-date because it can be changed every minute of the day.

4b Possessive Nouns; Possessive Phrases with *Of*

Form

Camels are called **"the ships of the desert."** they carry **people's** goods from place to place.

1. We use possessive nouns before singular or plural nouns.

   That **woman's** dress is very beautiful.
   The **teachers'** room is on the second floor.

2. If a noun is singular, we form its possessive by adding an apostrophe + -s (*'s*).

   Suzy is wearing her mother**'s** hat.

3. If a plural noun ends in -s, we form its possessive by adding only an apostrophe (*'*).

   Today is my parents' wedding anniversary.

4. If a plural noun does not end in -s, we form its possessive by adding an apostrophe + -s (*'s*).

   The children**'s** toys are here.
   There is a lot of good men**'s** clothing in this store.

5. If a singular noun ends in *s,* we can write the possessive form with an apostrophe + -*s* or just an apostrophe.

> That was Chris**'s** plan. OR That was Chris**'** plan.
> Sherlock Holmes**'s** hat is funny. OR Sherlock Holmes**'** hat is funny.

We usually pronounce these *s'* endings as though they were written as *s's*. For example, *Chris'* is pronounced like *Chris's,* with two syllables *(chris-es)*.

6. If there are two or more nouns in a possessive phrase, we add the apostrophe to the last noun only.

> That is **Kate** and **Ben's** house.

7. We can also use a possessive noun with no noun following it. In this case it must be clear what we are talking about.

> That's not my cell phone. It's **Pete's**. (*Cell phone* is understood in the second sentence.)

8. In some cases, we use a phrase with *of* instead of an apostrophe to show possession. We usually use the possessive phrase with *of* when we refer to things.

> The title **of this book** is *A Tale of Two Cities*.

Function

1. We often add the possessive *'s* to personal nouns (names like *Maria* and *John*) to show that the person owns or possesses something.

> **Kate's** glasses look good on her.
> My **brother's** school is near here.

2. We use the possessive form of nouns in some expressions of time.

> Next **year's** class schedule is difficult for me.
> **Yesterday's** news was interesting.

We can also use the possessive form of nouns to show a period of time.

> He took a **week's** vacation last year.

3. With places, we can use either the possessive form of nouns or a phrase with *of*.

> The **state's capital** is in Austin.
> OR The **capital of the state** is in Austin.

> The **world's problems** are serious.
> OR The **problems of the world** are serious.

4. We usually use the possessive form when the first noun is a person or an animal.

First Noun	Second Noun	
My brother's	school	is very small.
The cat's	bowl	is in the kitchen.
John's	address	is 85 Valley St.

But when the first of two nouns is a thing, we usually use *of*.

First Noun	Second Noun	
The name	of the school	is Hayes High School.
The name	of the song	is "Take My Heart."
The length	of skirts	is getting shorter this year.

4 | Practice

Eight apostrophes are missing in this paragraph. Add apostrophes in the correct places.

This is a photo of my grandparents' wedding. My grandmothers wedding dress is made of real lace. It used to be her mothers. The color of the bridesmaids dresses matches the flowers. My grandfathers expression is very serious. He

borrowed his brothers best suit for the wedding and it is a little too tight. Mens suits are less formal nowadays. Womens hairstyles are also more casual. I like this photo because it reminds me of the old days.

5 | Your Turn

Write three sentences about the photo in Practice 4 using the possessive forms *'s, s',* or *of*.

Example:
The sleeves of her dress are very wide.

6 | Practice

**Complete the sentences. Use the words in parentheses with the possessive 's or ...of...
as in the examples. Sometimes you will have to add the word *the*.**

Helen: (sister/Jack) _____ *Jack's sister* _____ and I went out
                                     1

     to dinner last night. The food was wonderful, but I can't remember

     (name/restaurant) _*the name of the restaurant*_ . It was something
                                        2

     like (Tony/Place) _____.
                                  3

Pete: Where was it?

Helen: I can't remember (name/street) _____, but it
                                        4

     was on the opposite (side/street) _____ from
                                        5

     (Pizza/Mike) _____.
                                6

     (food/freshness) _____ was incredible, and
                                    7

     you would like (size/portions) _____.
                                    8

Pete: Was it expensive?

Helen: (price/main courses) _____ was a little high,
                                    9

     but if you have (day/specials) _____, you
                                    10

     won't spend much.

Pete: Sounds good. Maybe I'll try it.

7 | Your Turn

**Using the prompts, write five sentences with *of*. With a partner, discuss which
things are important to you when you buy clothing.**

Example:
The style of the pants is important to me, but the name of the designer isn't.

1. the price _____

   _____

2. the fit _____

   _____

3. the quality _____

_____

4. the name of the designer _____

_____

5. the style _____

_____

4c Compound Nouns

Question: What do a **soccer ball,** a pair of **tennis shoes,** an a **paint brush** have in common?

Answer: They're all compound nouns!

1. A compound noun is a noun that is made of two or more simple nouns.

Simple Nouns	Compound Nouns
hair	hairbrush
brush	can opener
can	
opener	

2. We write some compound nouns as one word, for example, *bookstore*. We write others with a hyphen *(-)(T-shirt)*, and others as two words *(hot dog)*. There are no clear rules to tell you how to write a compound noun, and sometimes there is more than one possible way. If you are not sure how to spell a compound noun, look it up in your dictionary.

3. We can form many compound nouns by putting one noun, which acts as an adjective, in front of another noun.

a toothbrush   a candy store

4. We usually form the plural of a compound noun by adding *-s* to the second noun.

> CORRECT: two toothbrushes   two candy stores
> INCORRECT: two ~~tooths~~brushes   two ~~candies~~ stores

Exception: Compound nouns ending in *-in-law* form plurals with the first word.

> I have one **brother-in-law**.
> My wife has three **brothers-in-law**.

5. When we use a number in a compound expression, the noun is singular and we use hyphens between the words.

> CORRECT: We had a two-hour essay exam.
> INCORRECT: We had a two ~~hours~~ essay exam.

> CORRECT: He has a three-year-old son.
> INCORRECT: He has a three-~~years~~-old son.

---

8 | Practice

Complete the sentences with a compound noun that means the same thing as the words in parentheses.

Bob's (son who is sixteen years old) _____ *sixteen-year-old son* _____,
                                                              1

Mark, is taking a (computer course that lasts for three weeks)

_____. Bob is very happy about this and wants to
            2

buy him a (bicycle with ten speeds) _____. Mark tells
                                                3

his father that he now has a (license to drive*) _____.
                                                                    4

Mark has found a car for sale. It's a (car with two doors)

_____. It's a (car that is five years old)
            5

_____, but it looks great. The (person who sell cars)
            6

_____ tells Mark that he can take it for a (test drive
            7

for five minutes) _____. The man says it's a good
                            8

deal. He says that it's a (car worth two thousand dollars) _____,
                                                                            9

but Mark can have it for five hundred dollars! And he doesn't have to pay for it now. He

can get a (loan for five years) _____ to pay for it.
                                            10

*Hint: This compound noun starts with the word *driver's*.

Practice

Jack's class is having a sale to raise money for a trip. He is putting some things in a box to take to the sale. Write a compound noun for each thing in Jack's box. Use a word from list A and a word from list B to create each compound noun.
Use *a* or *an* before each compound noun.

A	B
alarm	brush
camera	case
coat	clock
coffee	driver
computer	hangers
hair	keyboard
lamp	mugs
neck	pot
pencil	shade
screw	sharpener
tea	shoes
tennis	tie

1. _____*an alarm clock*_____

2. _____

3. _____

4. _____

5. _____

6. _____

7. _____

8. _____

9. _____

10. _____

11. _____

12. _____

Your Turn

Work with a partner. Write as many compound nouns as you can with the following words plus words of your own. The pair with the most compound nouns is the winner.

Examples:
lunch time
telephone call

baby	computer	office	shoe	telephone
bicycle	head	paper	station	time

1. _____   7. _____

2. _____   8. _____

3. _____   9. _____

4. _____   10. _____

5 _____   11. _____

6. _____   12. _____

4d Count Nouns and Noncount Nouns

Form / Function

Sue: What's that?
Kumiko: It's sushi. It's made of **rice, fish, seaweed,** and other **things.** We eat it with **chopsticks.**

There are two kinds of nouns: count nouns and noncount nouns.

1. Count nouns name things that we can count: *one chair, two chairs.* Noncount nouns name things we cannot separate and count because we see them as a mass or an abstraction: *rice, love.*

Count Nouns	Noncount Nouns

a. Have singular and plural forms.
 	
   one **book**, two **books**
   a **man**, some **men**
	a. Have only the singular form. They have no plural form.
	
	   milk, weather, gold

b. Take singular or plural verbs.
 	
   This book **is** good.
   Those books **are** good.
   That man **works** here.
   Those men **work** here.
	b. Always take singular verbs.
	
	   Milk **is** good for you.
	   The weather **was** cold yesterday.

c. Can take *some/any/many/few* with the plural form.
 	
   I bought **some** oranges.
   There are **few** oranges.
	c. Can take *some/any/much/little* with the plural form.
	
	   There is **some** milk in the refrigerator.
	   There is **little** milk left.

d. Take *a/an* and numbers.
 	
   I have **an** orange.
	d. Do not take *a/an* and numbers.
	
	   Milk is good for you.*

*We use *a/an, one/two* etc. with noncount nouns such as coffee, tea, water, etc. when we refer to servings.

   We'd like **two coffees**, please.

2. Some nouns can be count or noncount, but with a difference in meaning. Here are some examples.

Noun	Count Meaning	Noncount Meaning
experience	I had a bad **experience** on a boat.	Do you have any **experience** in computer programming?
glass	Would you like a **glass** of water?	The vase is made of **glass**.
hair	He has two gray **hairs** on his head.	His **hair** is gray.
iron	I bought a new **iron**.	The pot is made of **iron**.
time	How many **times** did the phone ring?	I don't have much **time** right now.
wood	The table was made of five different **woods**.	The table is made of **wood**.

3. The following are categories of some noncount nouns:

Categories of Noncount Nouns	Examples
Abstract Words	time, love, happiness, education, information
Activities	sailing, swimming, farming
Fields of Study	history, geography, medicine
Some Kinds of Food	chocolate, meat, bread, milk
Gases	air, oxygen, pollution
Languages	Spanish, Arabic, French
Liquids	water, gasoline, blood
Materials	plastic, cotton, wood
Natural Forces	weather, wind, fire, sunshine
Particles	sand, dust, rice, hair, dirt
Recreation	football, baseball, chess, tennis

11 Practice

Complete the sentences with nouns from the list. Add articles and make them plural if necessary.

experience   glass   hair   time

1. Are the _____*glasses*_____ on this shelf for water?

2. Climbing the Eiffel Tower was _____ I will never forget.

3. My _____ had turned gray when I was only 25.

4. Do you have _____ to help me with my homework?

5. The company wanted someone with _____ in marketing or sales.

6. Russian tea is usually served in _____.

7. I found two white _____ in my beard today.

8. They had met several _____ before.

9. The outside of my office building is made of _____.

12 Practice

Complete the sentences with *much, many, little,* or *few.*

Cars use too _____*much*_____ fuel, make too _____ noise, emit
                        1   2
too _____ toxic chemicals, and take up too _____ space
              3   4
in our cities. This is the opinion of Car-Free Day supporters all around the world.

They point out that too _____ pollution from cars also causes too
                                        5
_____ harmful health effects, and that commuters waste too
              6
_____ time in their daily commute. Most cities, they claim, have
              7
too _____ public transportation and offer too _____
              8   9
opportunities for bicyclists and pedestrians to travel comfortably and safely. Too

_____ people drive when they could easily walk. Just one car-free day a
              10
year can make people aware of how giving up their car could improve their quality of life.

13 | Your Turn

Work with a partner. Which of these things are there too much or too many of in your town or city? Which of them are there too little or too few of? Tell your partner what you think. Does your partner agree or disagree?

Example:
tall buildings

You: I think there are too many tall buildings in our city.
Your partner: I agree, and I think that there are too few parks and trees.

buses	noise	stores	taxis
cycling paths	open space	tall buildings	traffic

4e *Some* and *Any*

Form / Function

I have **some** cash.

1. We use *some* and *any* before plural nouns and noncount nouns to talk about an indefinite quantity.

   I have **some** paper.
   I don't have **any** paper.
   I have **some** plants.
   I don't have **any** plants.

2. We usually use *some* in affirmative sentences and *any* in negative sentences.

   There are **some** messages for you.
   There aren't **any** messages for you.

3. We use *any* after negative-meaning words such as *never, seldom, rarely, hardly,* and *without.*

> He **never** has **any** time.
> I found the store **without any** problems.

4. We usually use *any* in a question for which we don't expect any special answer.

> A: Is there **any** milk in the refrigerator?
> B: Yes, there is. But there isn't much.

> A: Do you have **any** change on you?
> B: Sorry, I don't.

But we usually use *some* in questions when we expect the answer "yes" or when we want to encourage people to say "yes" to an offer or request.

> A: Do you have **some** money for me?   (I think you have money, and I expect the answer "yes.")
> B: Sure. Here it is.

> A: Can I have **some** more cake please?   (I want you to say "yes.")
> B: Of course. Help yourself.

> A: Would you like **some** more coffee?   (I am encouraging you to have more coffee.)
> B: No, thanks.

5. We can use *any* to mean "it does not matter which one."

> You can buy the card from **any** supermarket.
> She can call me at **any** time after 8:00 in the morning.

14 Practice

Underline the correct answer in each sentence.

Tom and Linda are in the ticket line outside a theater. They want to see a play.

Tom: This show is very popular, so there are hardly (some / <u>any</u>) seats left.
1

Linda: You're next, Tom.

Tom: I'd like to buy (some / any) tickets for tonight's show, please. I don't care
2
where they are. (Some / Any) seats will be fine.
3

Ticket Seller: I'm sorry, sir, I don't have anything right now. But if you wait over there,
there may be (some / any) tickets available in ten minutes.
4

Tom: OK. Thanks.

Tom: We should have come last week. My friend Carol came last week, and she got tickets without (some / any) difficulty.

5

Ten minutes later.

Ticket Seller: I do have two seats available now. Cash or credit card?

Tom: Cash. Oh, sorry. I don't have (some / any) cash. I'll pay by credit card.

6

15 Practice

Complete the sentences with *some* or *any*.

Maria: Could you go to the store for me? I want to make spaghetti tonight, and I need tomato sauce and ___some___ olive oil.

1

Carla: Sure! Are there _____ other things that you need?

2

Maria: Well, I don't have _____ cheese. Could you get _____

3   4

parmesan cheese?

Carla: Of course, about half a pound? Oh, what kind of olive oil do you want?

Maria: Oh, _____ kind of olive oil will do . . . as long as it's virgin olive oil

5

from Italy.

Carla: Could you make _____ garlic bread to go with the spaghetti?

6

Maria: Good idea! Get _____ garlic, and get _____ more bread just in

7   8

case we have _____ extra guests.

9

16 Your Turn

Repeat the conversation in Practice 15 with a partner. Change the food words to those that you need for any of the following dishes or one that is your own idea. You can make other changes if you want.

stir fry   cheeseburgers   tacos   pancakes

Example:

You: Can you go to the store for me? I want to make pancakes for breakfast, and I need some eggs and some flour.

Your partner: Sure. Are there any other things that you need?

4f   Much, Many, A Lot Of, A Few, Few, A Little, and Little

Today, there are few white rhinos left. Hunters have killed **many** for their horns.

1. Some quantity expressions such as *many* and *a few* go with plural count nouns. Others such as *much* and *a little* go with noncount nouns.

	Plural Count Nouns	Noncount Nouns
many/much *a lot of*	There aren't **many apples** in this pie. There are **a lot of apples** in this pie.	There isn't **much butter** left. There's **a lot of butter** left.
a few/a little *few/little*	There are **a few eggs** in the refrigerator. There are **few bananas** left.	I have **a little milk**. These cookies require **little sugar**.

2. The choice of *many, much,* and *a lot of* often depends on whether the sentence is an affirmative statement, a negative statement, or a question.

	Affirmative Statement	Negative Statement	Question
many	There are **many** eggs in this cake. (Uncommon)	We **don't** have **many** apples.	**How many** apples are there?
much	I bought ~~much~~ rice. (Incorrect)	I **didn't** buy **much** rice.	**How much** rice is there?
a lot of	I have **a lot of** apples. I bought **a lot of** tea.	I didn't buy **a lot of** rice.	Did you buy **a lot of** apples?

3. We often use *much* and *many* after *too, as, so,* and *very* in affirmative sentences.

> I have **too much** work to do today.
> We enjoyed the dinner **very much**.
> He has **so many** books that he can't get them all in his backpack.

4. We use *a little* and *a few* for positive ideas.

> I still have **a little** work to do. (I have a small amount of work, but some work.)
> The new program has **a few** changes this year. (It has a small number of changes, but some changes.)

5. We use *little* and *few* for negative ideas. *Little* means "not much" or "almost no." *Few* means "not many" or "almost no." We usually use *little* and *few* in formal English.

> FORMAL: I have **little** work to do today. (I have almost no work.)
> INFORMAL: I **don't** have **much** work to do today.

> FORMAL: This year's program has **few** changes. (There are almost no changes.)
> INFORMAL: This year's program **doesn't** have **many** changes.

17 Practice

Complete the sentences with *much, many,* or *a lot of*. There is sometimes more than one possible correct answer.

Julia: What do you think of my new dress? I didn't spend _____*much*_____ money.
1

I got it at a new store on Bleecker Street. You can get _____ real
2

bargains there. This dress had buttons missing, but it didn't need

_____ new buttons. Luckily, I know how to sew, and it didn't take
3

_____ time.
4

Susan: But where are you going to wear it?

Julia: I got a free ticket to the symphony, so I decided to dress up. I have so

_____ casual clothes, but not _____ formal dresses.
5   6

Susan: What make-up are you going to wear with it?

Julia: Oh, I don't usually wear _____ makeup. Do you think I have too
7

_____ lipstick on?
8

18 Practice

Complete the sentences with *a few, a little, few,* or *little*.

January 25, 20XX

Dear Amy,

Can you give me _____*a little*_____ advice? The problem is that I have
1

_____ friends, and I often feel lonely. I work late every night and
2

on weekends. I take care of my mother, so I have _____ opportunities to
3

go out. Can you give me _____ tips on how to meet more people?
4

Yours,
Busy but Lonely

January 30, 20XX

Dear Busy but Lonely,

It's great that you are taking care of your mother, but you have given yourself too

_____ time for your personal life. The first thing you have to do is to set
5

aside _____ hours every week for your social life. Then make a list of
6

_____ friends that you would like to spend more time with. Let them
7

know that you would like to spend _____ more time with them. In
8

_____ weeks, and with just _____ effort on your part,
9   10

your social group will start to grow.

Yours,
Amy

19 │ Your Turn

A. Work with a partner. Imagine that you have one of the problems in the list, or use an idea of your own. Tell your partner about the problem, and ask him or her for advice. Use *many, much, a few, a little, few,* **or** *little* **in your conversation.**

Example:

You: I need some advice. I can't seem to manage my money very well.

Your partner: Hmm. Do you have a budget?

You: No. I just charge things on my credit card. But then I can't pay the whole bill at the end of the month.

Your partner: That can be very dangerous, you know.

You: Really? How?

Your partner: Well, . . .

1. You don't have time for a social life because you have to take care of someone who is sick.

2. You spend too much money and have to pay too much interest on your credit card.

3. You have too many employees, and you don't have enough money to pay them.

4. You have too much furniture and too many things, and you have too little storage space in your apartment or house.

B. Write your conversation.

_____

_____

_____

_____

_____

_____

_____

_____

_____

_____

_____

_____

_____

4g Each, Each (One) Of, Every, Every One Of, Both, Both Of, All, and All Of

Both of the girls are in traditional costumes.
Both are young, and **both** are cute.

1. We use *each* and *every* with singular count nouns. We usually use each when we talk about two people or things. We usually use *every* when we talk about three or more people or things.

   CORRECT: She is carrying a bag in each hand.
   INCORRECT: She is carrying a bag in ~~every~~ hand.

   CORRECT: Every student in the class was happy that day.
   INCORRECT: ~~Each~~ student in the class was happy that day.

2. We use *every* when we are thinking of people or things together in a group as "all."

   Every student must be on time.

3. We use *each* when we are thinking of people or things separately.

   The teacher called **each** student's name.

4. We use *each (one) of* and *every one of* before plural count nouns. We use a word like *the, those, these,* or *your* before the plural count noun.

   Each one of the sisters wore the same clothes.
   I've been to **every one of these** stores.
   Every one of your answers was correct.

5. We use *both (of the)* + a plural count noun to refer to two people, groups, or things. We use *all, all the,* or *all of the* + a plural count noun or a noncount noun to refer to more than two people, groups, or things.

With *both,* we can use *both* + plural count noun OR *both of the* + plural count noun.

CORRECT: **Both movies** were good.
CORRECT: **Both of the movies** were good.
INCORRECT: ~~Both of movies~~ were good.

With *all,* we use *all* + noun if the noun is general. If the noun is specific, we can use *all of the* + noun OR *all* + noun.

A: **All Americans** like hamburgers. (*Americans* is general.)
B: That's not true. My teacher is an American, and he doesn't like hamburgers.
A: Well, **all of the Americans** that I know like hamburgers. (Here, *Americans* is specific.)
OR **All the Americans** that I know like hamburgers. (Here, *Americans* is also specific.)

20 Practice

Match the sentence halves to create sentences that accurately describe the photos.

A   B

_d_ **1.** Both girls   **a.** is smiling.

___ **2.** Both boys   **b.** the children have dark ties.

___ **3.** All   **c.** child is wearing a school uniform.

___ **4.** Every child   **d.** are wearing sweaters.

___ **5.** Each   **e.** are standing in front of a map.

21 Your Turn

Say or write three sentences about students in your class.

Example:
Both Maria and Marta are wearing red sweaters today.

REVIEW

1 Review (4a–4b, 4d–4f)

Underline the correct answer in each sentence.

1. All of the food (<u>was</u> / were) good.

2. The menu had (much / a few) changes.

3. I can't meet you today. I have too (much / many) work.

4. I'd like two cups of (coffee / coffees), please.

5. There (is / are) a lot of (pollutions / pollution) in the world today.

6. Jenny met Tanya and Joseph at the airport and gave a flower to (each / all) of them.

7. I have a (little / few) milk left in my glass.

8. There isn't (many / much) butter on your bread.

9. I watched several (childs / children) play with their toys.

10. You have (any / some) beautiful (cactus / cacti) in your garden.

11. Measles (makes / make) children very sick.

12. There isn't (any / some) steak in the freezer.

13. That pair of pants (looks / look) nice on you.

14. How did I know there are two (trains stations / train stations)?

15. We need a few good (idea / ideas) right now.

16. (Nancy's house / the house of Nancy) is beautiful.

17. (Little / Few) people like the new boss.

18. You can buy tickets from (any / some) student.

19. Don't play those drums! You make too (many / much) noise.

20. The (accident's cause / cause of the accident) was unknown.

21. The (wifes / wives) played tennis while their husbands played golf.

22. I think I ate too (much / many) cheese!

23. Our boss sends us about 20 (memorandum / memoranda) every day.

24. I need to do (any / some) laundry. I don't have (any / some) clean socks to wear.

25. Each one of my friends (is / are) on vacation. I need (a little / few) time off too!

2 Review (4a–4b, 4f)

Complete the sentences with the correct form of the nouns and verbs in parentheses. With some nouns, you will have to use an *of* phrase.

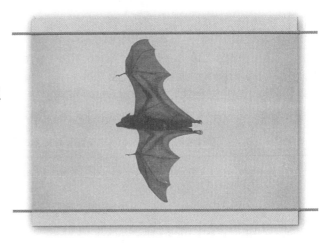

I saw some (bat) _____ *bats* _____
                            1
last night. One was only two (foot)

_____ away from me.
        2
They are very strange looking (creature)

_____. But I also think they're very interesting. I know two (person)
        3

_____ who wrote their (thesis) _____ on bats. I don't
        4   5
remember the (title, paper) _____. However, I do remember that each of
                                    6
them (be) _____ very interesting. I've read lots of (book)
              7

_____ on (bat) _____. I wouldn't say I have a lot of
        8   9
(knowledge) _____ about them, and I don't have much (experience)
                    10

_____ with them. But I do know a few (fact) _____.
        11   12
There aren't many (person) _____ who (like) _____ bats.
                                    13   14
Most (idea, person) _____ about bats (be) _____ wrong.
                            15   16
Bats (not, be) _____ dirty or scary (animal) _____. Rabies
                        17   18
(be) _____ not common in bats. As a matter of fact, bats (clean)
          19

_____ themselves all the (time) _____, just like
        20   21
(cat) _____. Only three (species) _____ of bats (drink)
            22   23

_____ blood. These (type) _____ of bats fly quietly up to an
        24   25
(animal) _____, make a small bite, and drink a little (blood) _____.
                26   27
However, most species of bats (eat) _____ (fruit) _____,
                                            28   29
(pollen) _____, (insect) _____, (spider) _____,
                30   31   32
or other tiny (animal) _____. These (bat) _____ eat a huge
                            33   34
number of (insect) _____ every day. They also pollinate many kinds of
                        35
(plant) _____, and they help (forest) _____ when they drop
            36   37
(seed) _____. They are truly (friend, nature) _____.
          38   39

Review (4a, 4c, 4e–4f)

Complete the sentences with the correct form of the words in parentheses.

Claude: A few (person) ____*people*____ didn't
<u>1</u>

get their invitations for the party tonight.

Michelle: I know. Every one of them (have)

_____ recently moved.
<u>2</u>

Claude: It's lucky that most of them (have) _____ e-mail. By the way, did
<u>3</u>

you call your two (brother-in-law) _____?
<u>4</u>

Michelle: Yes. By the way, do we have any (ice) _____ in the freezer?
<u>5</u>

Claude: I don't think so.

Michelle: How many (time) _____ have I asked you to fill up the ice trays?
<u>6</u>

Well, never mind. We'll buy a few (bag) _____ here at the store.
<u>7</u>

Do we have any (vegetable) _____ at home?
<u>8</u>

Claude: We have some (celery) _____ and (tomato) _____.
<u>9</u>   <u>10</u>

Michelle: Should we cook both (rice) _____ and (potato) _____?
<u>11</u>   <u>12</u>

Claude: Oh, no. That's too much (starch) _____.
<u>13</u>

Michelle: Right. I think we're forgetting a few (thing) _____.
<u>14</u>

Claude: Well, each of us (have) _____ a list in our hands. Let's look at them!
<u>15</u>

Michelle: We need some (fruit) _____. I know we have a lot of
<u>16</u>

(peach) _____. But we don't have many (nuts) _____.
<u>17</u>   <u>18</u>

Oh, look, a can opener.

Claude: What? We already have two (can opener) _____. (two can
<u>19</u>

openers, not, be) _____ enough for you?
<u>20</u>

Michelle: Oh, right. But let's get a couple of (pot holder) _____. We need
<u>21</u>

those. Oh, we need some (toothpaste) _____, too.
<u>22</u>

Claude: Every one of those items in your hands (have) _____ nothing to
<u>23</u>

do with the party.

Michelle: Well, you want my (tooth) _____ to be clean, don't you?

24

Claude: Yes. But we have lots of (thing) _____ to buy. Let's think about

25

them, OK? (time) _____ isn't on our side, you know!

26

4 | Review (4a, 4c, 4f–4g)

Find the errors and correct them.

Tina: Guess what? I'm going to explore the Amazon! It doesn't cost ~~many~~ *much* money.

Marie: Really? I know there are a lot of travels bargain right now, but the Amazon?

Tina: Oh, yes. I've always wanted to go there. How much time have I told you that? All of people I know are surprised. I don't know why.

Marie: Only a few person is that adventurous. Don't forget to pack lots of mosquitos spray.

Tina: Don't worry. The travel agent gave me a few book to read. Each book have a list of thing to bring.

Marie: Well, I don't have a little to do today. Can I help you buy some equipments?

Tina: Sure. I need to buy so much things. I understand there will be a lot of rains. I'll need two cameras bag for my two cameras.

Marie: You know, every one of your vacations have been an adventure. I think I've been to every one of your after-vacation party and listened to all your story. You should start your own tour company and call it "The Adventure of Tina."

Tina: That's a great idea. All of people I know would come. They'd give me a lot of businesses.

Marie: I have a few idea of my own. We can be partners. Both us know a lot about travel.

Tina: Yes! Every one of your ideas are great. How about Brian? Maybe he can give us some offices product. You know, papers, pen, and maybe a few computers keyboard.

Marie: I don't know. Brian never has any times. He's so busy with all his own works.

Tina: Well, there's too many work for just the two of us, don't you think?

Marie: I don't think so. I have almost a month vacation coming to me. I can start doing a few thing while you're gone. Maybe I can get some advices about starting a business. I know a little people who can help us. With a few effort, we'll have our own business!

WRITING: Write a Descriptive Essay

Write an essay that describes a famous thing or place. See page 470 for general writing guidelines. See page 471 for information on writing an essay.

Step 1. With a partner, think of some important things or places your country (or the country you are living in) is famous for. For example:

Mexico: splendid Aztec buildings, great food, beautiful beaches

Step 2. Write as many sentences as you can to describe each of the things or places from step 1. What do these things look like, sound like, smell like, etc. Choose two of the things or places from steps 1 and 2 to write about.

Step 3. Write your essay.

1. Write a paragraph with a topic sentence about each of the things or places that you chose. For example:

    > Many Americans think that Mexican food is nothing but tortillas, ground beef, tomato sauce, cheese, and hot peppers. In fact, there is a lot of variety in Mexican food. For example, Mexicans eat a lot of fish. It makes you feel like you are right on the beach. Everyone knows tomato *salsa*, but there are many other sauces in Mexico. They can be very subtle, and others can be fiery hot. Some Mexican sauces include chocolate.

2. Write an introduction and a conclusion to your paragraph or essay. Your introduction should state the two topics that you have chosen to write about. Your conclusion should summarize the points that you made.

3. Write a title for your essay.

Step 4. Evaluate your essay/paragraph.

Checklist

_____ Did you write a title and put it in the right place?

_____ Did you indent your paragraphs?

_____ Did you write an introduction, two paragraphs, and a conclusion?

_____ Did you write a title and put it in the right place?

Step 5. Work with a partner or a teacher to edit your work. Check spelling, vocabulary, and grammar.

Step 6. Write your final copy.

A **Choose the best answer, A, B, C, or D, to complete the sentence. Mark your answer by darkening the oval with the same letter.**

1. That _____ clothing store has a lot of nice things.

   A. woman's   Ⓐ Ⓑ Ⓒ Ⓓ
   B. women's
   C. woman
   D. women

2. That's _____ new house.

   A. Jackie and Mike   Ⓐ Ⓑ Ⓒ Ⓓ
   B. Jackie and Mikes'
   C. Jackie's and Mike's
   D. Jackie and Mike's

3. She has a _____.

   A. nine years old son   Ⓐ Ⓑ Ⓒ Ⓓ
   B. nine year-old son
   C. son nine year old
   D. nine-year-old son

4. He doesn't eat _____.

   A. any meat   Ⓐ Ⓑ Ⓒ Ⓓ
   B. some meat
   C. of meat
   D. few meat

5. _____ student must take the test.

   A. All   Ⓐ Ⓑ Ⓒ Ⓓ
   B. All of
   C. Every
   D. Every one of

6. At first, she was lonely because she had _____ friends in class.

   A. a few   Ⓐ Ⓑ Ⓒ Ⓓ
   B. few
   C. little
   D. a little

7. How _____ eggs do you need?

   A. much   Ⓐ Ⓑ Ⓒ Ⓓ
   B. more
   C. little
   D. many

8. He wears _____ all the time.

   A. a jeans   Ⓐ Ⓑ Ⓒ Ⓓ
   B. a jean
   C. a pair of jean
   D. jeans

9. There are _____ in that field.

   A. some sheep   Ⓐ Ⓑ Ⓒ Ⓓ
   B. some sheeps
   C. sheeps
   D. many sheeps

10. This _____ classes are difficult.

   A. year's   Ⓐ Ⓑ Ⓒ Ⓓ
   B. years'
   C. years
   D. a year's

B Find the underlined word or phrase, A, B, C, or D, that is incorrect. Mark your answer by darkening the oval with the same letter.

1. I need <u>a few</u> milk and <u>some</u> <u>flour</u> for this
      A   B   C
   recipe, but I don't have <u>any</u>.
                             D

   Ⓐ Ⓑ Ⓒ Ⓓ

2. The <u>women</u> and <u>children</u> of this culture
       A   B
   cover their <u>hairs</u> and paint designs on
               C
   their hands and <u>feet</u> on special occasions.
                    D

   Ⓐ Ⓑ Ⓒ Ⓓ

3. <u>Physic</u> <u>is</u> <u>Chris's</u> favorite subject, so he's
   A   B   C
   going to work on a <u>two-year</u> research
                       D
   project.

   Ⓐ Ⓑ Ⓒ Ⓓ

4. We have <u>few</u> <u>time</u> to make any <u>corrections</u>
            A   B   C
   in a <u>thirty-minute</u> essay exam.
        D

   Ⓐ Ⓑ Ⓒ Ⓓ

5. <u>Babies</u> grow their first <u>teeth</u> when they
   A   B
   are <u>six months old</u> and keep them until
       C
   they are seven or <u>eight-years-olds</u>.
                      D

   Ⓐ Ⓑ Ⓒ Ⓓ

6. <u>Today's</u> <u>news</u> is interesting because
   A   B
   two <u>persons</u> have discovered a new
       C
   <u>bacterium</u> that helps humans.
   D

   Ⓐ Ⓑ Ⓒ Ⓓ

7. There are <u>so much</u> <u>dictionaries</u> at
            A   B
   <u>King's bookstore</u> that you will find one
   C
   without <u>any</u> problems.
           D

   Ⓐ Ⓑ Ⓒ Ⓓ

8. In next <u>semester class</u> schedule, the
          A
   <u>economics</u> class I want <u>is</u> at the same
   B   C
   time as the <u>mathematics</u> class.
               D

   Ⓐ Ⓑ Ⓒ Ⓓ

9. There is <u>a lot of</u> <u>dirt</u> and <u>dusts</u> here
            A   B   C
   because of all the <u>traffic</u> and construction
                       D
   outside.

   Ⓐ Ⓑ Ⓒ Ⓓ

10. The <u>chief</u> cause of this <u>city's</u> <u>pollution</u> is
        A   B   C
    <u>unleaded gasolines</u>.
    D

    Ⓐ Ⓑ Ⓒ Ⓓ

UNIT 5

PRONOUNS AND ARTICLES

5a Subject and Object Pronouns; Possessive Adjectives; and Possessive Pronouns

My wife and **I** are in this photo.
We never argue.

SUBJECT AND OBJECT PRONOUNS

1. We use personal pronouns to replace nouns when it is clear who or what we are talking about. There are three kinds of personal pronouns: subject pronouns, object pronouns, and possessive pronouns. See #3 below for information on possessive pronouns.

    Subject Pronoun: John was not in class yesterday. **He** was sick.
    Object Pronoun: The students are dressed up. Look at **them**.

2. Most of the subject and object forms are different from each other.

SUBJECT PRONOUNS		OBJECT PRONOUNS	
Singular	Plural	Singular	Plural
I	we	me	us
you	you	you	you
he/she/it	they	him/her/it	them

POSSESSIVE ADJECTIVES AND POSSESSIVE PRONOUNS

3. We use possessive adjectives in front of nouns. We use possessive pronouns without nouns.

> Possessive Adjective: I wrote a letter to **my** parents.
> Possessive Pronoun: That's not my backpack. It's **yours**.

POSSESSIVE ADJECTIVES		POSSESSIVE PRONOUNS	
Singular	Plural	Singular	Plural
my	our	mine	ours
your	your	yours	yours
his		his	
her	their	hers	theirs
its		its	

Function

1. We use subject pronouns as the subjects of verbs.

> Dick was at home last night. **He** was studying.
> Where's Linda? **She's** at school.

In formal situations, such as academic writing and formal speaking presentations in business, we use a subject pronoun after the verb *be*.

> Who is it? It is **I**.
> If I were **he**, I would have complained.

However, we normally use the object pronoun after the verb *be* in everyday speech.

> Who is it? It's **me**.
> If I were **him**, I'd have complained.

2. We use object pronouns as the objects of verbs and prepositions.

> That's Linda. I like **her**. (*Her* is the object of the verb *like*.)
> Those children are funny. Look at **them**. (*Them* is the object of the preposition *at*.)

3. We can use *you* to mean "people in general," including yourself and the person you are talking to.

> **You** can get a driver's license when you are sixteen in this state.

We can also use *one* with the same meaning. *One* is more formal and is not used much in everyday speech.

> **One** can get a driver's license when **one** is sixteen in this state.

4. We also use *they* to mean "people in general," but not including yourself and the person you are talking to.

> **They** say the test is difficult, but I haven't taken it myself.

They can also refer to the government or to people in authority.

> **They** are going to build a new hospital in this neighborhood.

5. When a pronoun refers to a person whose gender (male or female) is known, we use the pronoun that matches that person's gender.

> **Jane** came in late for the test. **She** was not allowed to take it.

However, some nouns, such as *worker* or *student,* may refer to either gender or have a general meaning that includes people of both genders. In the past, many people used a singular masculine pronoun or possessive adjective to refer to a noun such as *worker* or *student.* This is no longer acceptable. Now we use both masculine and feminine forms to refer to such nouns.

> ACCEPTABLE: A good **student** always does **his or her** homework.
> NOT ACCEPTABLE: A good **student** always does **his** homework.

However, the use of *his* or *her* can be awkward. To avoid this problem we can often make the noun plural and use a plural pronoun or possessive adjective after it.

> ACCEPTABLE: Good **students** always do **their** homework.

This area of English grammar is changing. It is a good idea to ask your instructors about the pronoun uses that they will accept.

6. With group nouns such as *family, class, crowd, team, group,* and *company,* we can use a singular or plural pronoun to refer to it. We use a singular pronoun when we think of the group as one impersonal unit.

> A family is important to me. **It** has the greatest value for me.

We use a plural pronoun when we think of the group as a number of people.

> I have the greatest **family. They** always support me in whatever I do.
> The **class** thinks that **they** are ready to take the test.

7. We use both possessive adjectives and pronouns to talk about ownership or relationships between people. We put a noun after a possessive adjective, but not after a possessive pronoun.

> That's **her** book.
> It's **hers**.

8. We usually use possessive adjectives with parts of the body and clothes.

> He broke **his** leg.
> She took off **her** coat.

9. The following are indefinite pronouns. Unlike other pronouns, they do not refer to a specific noun.

everyone	someone	anyone	no one
everybody	somebody	anybody	nobody
everything	something	anything	nothing

> **Everyone** knows the answer to this question.
> I saw **someone** standing outside.
> Can you do **anything** about this problem?
> **Nobody** can do the job except Sam.

In formal speech or writing, we use a singular possessive adjective *(her, his)* to refer to an indefinite pronoun. However, in everyday speech we often use a plural possessive adjective *(their)*. Many, but not all, instructors will also accept this in written English.

> FORMAL: **Somebody** left **his or her** keys on the table.
> INFORMAL: **Somebody** left **their** keys on the table.

> FORMAL: **Everyone** must lead **his or her** own life.
> INFORMAL: **Everyone** must lead **their** own life.

10. We can use *it* to refer to a person when we are asking or saying who that person is.

> A: Who is **it**?
> B: **It**'s Ken.

We use *it* to talk about the weather, distance, temperature, and time.

> **It's** warm today.
> **It's** two miles from here.
> **It's** seven o'clock.

We use *it* to refer to animals, especially when we do not know the sex of the animal.

> There's a dog outside. I wonder who **it** belongs to.
> That's my dog. **She**'s 10 years old.

11. Notice the difference between *its* and *it's*.

	Meaning	Example
its	Possessive adjective	I put my laptop back in **its** case.
it's	*It is* or *it has*	**It's** a nice day today. **It's** been nice all week.

1 Practice

Replace the underlined nouns with the correct subject or object pronouns.

Ben is on a business trip. He is leaving a phone message for his wife, Rosie.

Hi Rosie, it's Ben. I left home in a big hurry this morning. Could you do a few things for me?

The electricity bill is on the bookshelf. <u>The electricity bill</u> ₁ *It* is due tomorrow. Please pay <u>the electricity bill</u> ₂ for me.

I left my glasses on the table. I'm afraid <u>my glasses</u> ₃ might get broken. Can you put <u>my glasses</u> ₄ on my desk for me?

Oh, and I forgot it was Jenny's birthday. <u>Jenny</u> ₅ will be upset. Would you mind getting <u>Jenny</u> ₆ a card for me?

Also, remember to take Peter to his soccer game this afternoon. <u>Peter</u> ₇ will be waiting for you at school. Tell <u>Peter</u> ₈ that I hope his team wins.

Let me see . . . I fed the cat this morning, but <u>the cat</u> ₉ didn't eat. Please give <u>the cat</u> ₁₀ some food tonight.

Rosie, I'll be back by 7:00 in the evening. <u>You and I</u> ₁₁ both like Gino's restaurant. I'll call and make a reservation for <u>you and me</u> ₁₂. Is that OK?

2 Practice

Underline the correct word in parentheses.

I work for a small media company in New York, but (<u>my</u> / mine) ₁ friend works for a large advertising company in Los Angeles. (Her / Hers) ₂ office is much bigger than (my / mine) ₃, but (my / mine) ₄ has a better view than (her / hers) ₅. (Our / Ours) ₆ working hours are 40 hours a week, but (their / theirs) ₇ are only 35 hours a week. (Their / Theirs) ₈ vacation is three weeks, while (our / ours) ₉ is only two weeks. (My / Mine) ₁₀ salary isn't bad, but (her / hers) ₁₁ is higher. It makes me think about looking for a new job. What would make you want to change (your / yours) ₁₂?

Practice

Complete the sentences with the correct pronoun (subject, object, or possessive) or possessive adjective.

A. Complete the sentences with I, me, my, mine, you, your, or yours.

John,

I took a book from _____your_____ desk today. I shouldn't have done it,
                        1

but I really needed it to review for _____ exam today because I left
                                            2

_____ on the bus yesterday. So _____ just took
        3   4

_____. Please forgive _____. _____ promise
        5   6   7

to give it back to _____ tomorrow.
                          8

B. Complete the sentences with we, us, our, ours, they, them, their, or theirs.

Our neighbors went on vacation to Florida last year and had a terrible time. But my

family went this year and really enjoyed it. _____ flight was late, but
                                                    1

_____ was on time. _____ hotel was near the beach, but
        2   3

_____ was far away. _____ tour guide told
        4   5

_____ that _____ couldn't go to some of the theme parks,
        6   7

but _____ told _____ that _____ could go
            8   9   10

anywhere we wanted. Our neighbors told _____ that the next time
                                                11

_____ will use _____ travel agency!
        12   13

C. Complete the sentences with she, her, hers, he, him, his, it, or them. Then finish the story by adding sentences of your own.

George met Anna on the first day of math class. _____ fell in love with
                                                        1

_____ immediately. _____ eyes were big and brown, and
        2   3

_____ had a lively personality. He talked to _____, but she
        4   5

wasn't very interested. He gave her _____ telephone number, but she
                                            6

wouldn't give _____ to him. He asked _____ to go to the
                    7   8

movies with _____. _____ refused. _____
                    9   10   11

heart was broken.

One day, he discovered that he knew Anna's roommate. She told him that

_____ should send a letter to Anna, and he did. _____
         12   13
sent _____ back. He sent _____ some flowers.
              14   15

_____ sent _____ back. Finally, George asked Anna's
         16   17
roommate for more advice. _____ roommate said that Anna's favorite food
                                      18
was _____

_____

_____

_____

4 Practice

Some of the sentences in these paragraphs have unacceptable gender-specific pronouns and possessive adjectives. Rewrite those sentences so that they are acceptable.

1.

All students are required to hand in their assignments.
~~Every student is required to hand in his assignment on time~~. If any student does not

understand the assignment, he must ask the instructor for further help. If any student

borrows or copies another person's work and submits this as his work, the instructor may

require him to withdraw from the course.

2.

If my son calls this afternoon, please tell him to call me on my cell phone. I'll be

unable to speak to any other caller unless his business is extremely urgent.

3.

To play this game, each player will need to move his marker around the board and

answer the question in the square he lands on. If a player does not know the answer to a

question, he has to go back to the previous square.

Practice

Complete the sentences with an appropriate pronoun (subject, object, or possessive) or possessive adjective. Some sentences are identified as formal, and some are identified as informal.

1. Would the person who has parked _____*their*_____ car by the main gate, please come to the front desk immediately? (informal)

2. Anyone who wishes to obtain further information should consult _____ doctor. (formal)

3. No one called for me today, did _____? (informal)

4. If anyone wants me to help _____, please ask me. (informal)

5. If anyone requires assistance, would _____ please call for attention? (formal)

6. Everyone has the right to know whether any complaints have been made against _____ conduct. (formal)

7. Did you see someone here just now? I think _____ were asking for me. (informal)

8. A financial advisor should give reliable and accurate advice to every client and advise _____ of all possible risks before making an investment. (formal)

5b Reflexive Pronouns

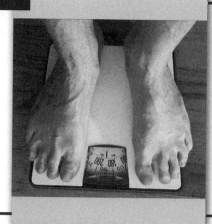

He's weighing himself.

Subject Pronouns	Reflexive Pronouns
I	myself
you (singular)	yourself (singular)
he	himself
she	herself
it	itself
we	ourselves
you (plural)	yourselves (plural)
they	themselves

1. We use reflexive pronouns as objects when the subject and object are the same person (for example, *I* and *myself*).

   We saw **ourselves** in the mirror.
   I told **myself** to hurry.

   Reflexive pronouns are common as the objects of verbs such as *burn, hurt, cut, enjoy, teach, introduce,* and *look at.* There are also common phrases with reflexive pronouns, such as *enjoy yourself* (have a good time), *help yourself* (take something if you want), and *behave yourself* (be good).

   He was cooking dinner when he burned **himself.**
   Are you still hungry? **Help yourself** to some more food.

2. We use reflexive pronouns to emphasize that we are speaking of a specific person and nobody else.

> I repaired the car **myself**.
> I'm sure he knows about the problem. He **himself** spoke to me about it.

3. We use *by* + reflexive pronoun to mean "alone."

> My great-grandmother is ninety years old and lives **by herself**.

6 | Practice

Paul and Mary have invited Tony and Linda to their house for dinner. Match the sentences on the left with the correct responses to the right. Then complete the sentences with the correct reflexive pronouns. You may need to use *by*.

_e_ 1. Hello! Thanks for inviting us!

_____ 2. Mary, this cake is delicious!

_____ 3. Could I have some more cake?

_____ 4. Is this a photo of your twins when they were little?

_____ 5. Does Matthew still live at home?

_____ 6. Is that an automatic light?

_____ 7. What beautiful bookshelves!

a. Of course, Linda, please help _____*yourself*_____

b. Yes, when you go into the room, it goes on _____

c. Yes, they taught _____ to ride bikes when they were only four years old.

d. No, he left home last year, and now he lives _____

e. You're welcome. Please come in and make _____ at home!

f. Thank you, we couldn't make them _____, so a friend made them for us.

g. Thanks, I made it _____.

7 | Your Turn

Which of these things do you prefer to do yourself or ask someone to do for you?

Example:
Student A: Do you cut your hair yourself?
Student B: No, I usually go to the hairdresser.

change a lightbulb	fix your car	mend your clothes
cut your hair	iron your clothes	paint your room

5c *Another, Other, Others, The Other, and The Others*

One woman is wearing a coat;
the others are not.
One is talking on the phone,
another is listening, and **the
other** is going to hang up.

1. We use the different forms of *other* as adjectives or as pronouns.

		Adjective	Pronoun
Indefinite	**Singular**	*another* + singular noun	another
	Plural	*other* + plural noun	others*
Definite	**Singular**	*the other* + singular noun	the other
	Plural	*the other* + plural noun	the others*

*Only plural pronouns take -*s*.

2. Do not use *others* before a plural noun.

   CORRECT: There are other bicycles in the garage.
   INCORRECT: There are ~~others~~ bicycles in the garage.

Function

1. *Another* means one more. We use *another* with singular count nouns.

   Can I have **another** cup of coffee?

2. We use *another* + *two, three, few,* etc. + noun with expressions of time, money, and distance.

   We are going to stay here for **another few days.**
   The place is **another five miles** from here.
   I need **another ten dollars.**

3. *Other* and *others* (without *the*) refer to part of a group beyond those already mentioned.

    > One guest was from Brazil. Another guest came from China. **Other** guests were from Europe. **Others** were from Africa.

4. We can also use *others* to mean other people.

    > Some people enjoy playing football; **others** like watching it.

5. *The other* and *the others* means the rest of a group we are talking about.

    > The movie star has two homes. One is in Malibu, California, and **the other** is in New York City.
    > The movie star also has three expensive cars. One is a Rolls Royce, and **the others** are Ferraris.

6. Here are some common expressions with *other*.

    Each other or *one another* indicate that people do the same thing, feel the same way, or have the same relationship.

    > We understand **each other**.
    > OR We understand **one another**. (I understand you, and you understand me.)

    Every other means every second one.

    > We have a test **every other** week.

    The other day means a few days ago.

    > I saw Jim **the other day**.

---

8 Practice

Complete the sentences with a word or phrase from the list.

another	every other	others	the other
each other	other	the other	the others

I saw Sammy in the park ___*the other*___ day. We had

seen _____ before, but we had never spoken to

_____. Some people go to the park to walk by the lake,

while _____ like to sit on a bench or feed the ducks. I like to

go there at least _____ day. One day, I noticed Sammy on a

bench near the lake. He was looking down, and he seemed to be talking to himself.

Several little boys were near Sammy. One boy was sitting on the bench beside him.

_____ boy was looking
                    6
at Sammy curiously. Three or four

_____ children were
                    7
feeding the ducks in the pond, and

_____ were playing
                    8
in a group. I went over to talk with Sammy.

Then I saw that he was holding a small baby

duck in one hand and feeding it some bread with

_____. He wasn't talking to
                    9
himself. He was talking to the duck.

9 | Your Turn

Write four sentences about the photo in Practice 8. Use *other, another,* etc. in your sentences.

Example:
[Example to come when photo is chosen.]

1. _____

2. _____

3. _____

4. _____

5d The Indefinite Articles *A* and *An; One* and *Ones*

A zebra has stripes. Each **one** has different **ones.**

1. We use the article *a* before words beginning with a consonant sound.*

   a book   **a** girl

2. We use the article *an* before words beginning with a vowel sound.*

   an apple   **an** umbrella

3. We can sometimes use *one* before a noun instead of *a* or *an.*

   I need **one ticket**, not two.

4. We can use *one* and *ones* as pronouns.

   If there aren't any large cakes, get a small **one.**
   If there aren't any large cakes, get two small **ones.**

   *It is the sound, not the letter, that determines whether you use *a* or *an.*
   If an *h* is silent, we use **an: an** hour; **an** honest man. But if it is not silent, we use *a*: **a** hotel; **a** horse.

   If a *u* or *eu* sounds like "yoo," we use *a:* **a** university, **a** European.

   Some letters of the alphabet start with a vowel sound, so we use *an:* **an** x-ray, **an** M.A., but for letters that start with a consonent sound, we use *a:* **a** B.A., **a** YMCA.

Function

A AND *AN*

1. We use *a* and *an* with singular count nouns when we talk about them in general.

   I saw **a** man outside. (The listener does not know which man.)

2. We do not use a singular count noun alone. We always use *a* or *an, the, my,* etc. before it.

> CORRECT: It's a computer.
> INCORRECT: It's computer.

3. We do not use *a* or *an* with noncount nouns or plural count nouns.

> CORRECT: I like music.
> INCORRECT: I like ~~a~~ music.

> CORRECT: Students from all over the world are here.
> INCORRECT: ~~A~~ students from all over the world are here.

4. We use *a* or *an* + a noun when we say what someone or something is.

> She's **an** architect.
> It looks like **an** address book, but it's really **a** computer.

But we don't use *a* or *an* if the noun is noncount.

> A: What's in that bowl?
> B: It's flour and sugar.

5. We use *a* and *an* to show certain measures.

Measure	Example
price in relation to weight	It costs $2.00 **a** pound
frequency	He goes to the doctor once **a** year.
distance in relation to speed	He was driving 70 miles **an** hour.

A OR *AN* AND *ONE*

6. We use *a* or *an* when we talk about something that is not specific. We use *one* when we want to emphasize the number and to be more specific.

> I have **an** umbrella. (not a specific umbrella)
> I have **one** umbrella. (I do not have two.)
> I was disappointed to get just **one card** for my birthday.

7. We can use *one day* to refer to the future.

> **One day**, all cars will run on electricity.

8. We use *a, an,* or *one* with no difference in meaning when we count or measure.

> I have **a/one** bottle of water.
> It costs **a/one** hundred dollars.

ONE AND ONES

9. We usually use *one* or *ones* to avoid repeating a noun. We use *one* for the singular and *ones* for the plural.

> This apartment is bigger than my old **one**. (my old apartment)
> These pants are nicer than the other **ones**. (the other pants)

10. We use *a* or *an* with *one* if there is an adjective before *one*.

> I want to a buy a shirt. I'm looking for **one** right now.
> I'm looking for **a blue one**.

11. We can use *one* or *ones* after *the* if we are referring to a specific noun or nouns.

> This movie is better than **the one** we saw last week.
> I don't like these oranges. I prefer **the ones** we bought yesterday.

12. We can use *one* or *ones* after *this* or *that*.

> Which computer do you prefer, **this one** or **that one**?

13. We use *which one(s)* in questions.

> I like these shoes best. **Which ones** do you like?

---

10 Practice

Complete the questions with *a* or *an*. Then discuss each question with a partner and explain the reason for your choices.

Which do you prefer:

1. _____*a*_____ telephone call or _____*an*_____ email message?

2. _____ one-story house or _____ two-story house?

3. _____ oral exam or _____ written exam?

4. _____ honest man who is unfriendly or _____ friendly man who

   is dishonest?

5. _____ one-dollar coin or _____ one-dollar bill?

6. _____ island in the Caribbean or _____ mountain in the Andes?

7. _____ European car or _____ American car?

8. _____ MRI or _____ X-ray?

11 Practice

A. Complete the sentences with *a*, *one*, or *ones*.

George Crum invented the potato chip in 1853. Crum was _____*a*_____ chef in
                                                        1
Saratoga Springs, New York. French fries were very popular in his restaurant. _____
                                                                              2
day, _____ customer complained that the French fries were too thick. Crum made
        3
some thinner _____, but the customer still didn't like them. So Crum made French
                4
fries that were too thin to eat with _____ fork and hoped to annoy the picky
                                        5
customer. But the customer was happy—and that's the story of potato chips! Now potato
chips are _____ big industry in the United States. The average person there eats
             6
seven pounds of potato chips _____ year. It takes about four pounds of potatoes
                                7
to make _____ pound of potato chips.
            8

B. Answer these questions with complete sentences.

1. What was George Crum's job?

   _He was a chef._____

2. What kind of French fries did he make?

   _____

3. Why did he make them?

   _____

4. How many pounds of potato chips does the average American eat each year?

   _____

12 What Do You Think?

It takes four pounds of potatoes to make one pound of potato chips. Why do you think this is?

13 Practice

Complete the sentences with a word or phrase from the list + *one* or *ones*. In some cases, you do not need a word or phrase from the list. In other cases, you must add *the*.

other	that	which
small	this	white

Customer: A loaf of bread, please.

Salesperson: What kind?

Customer: I'm not sure. What's _____*this one*_____ in front called?
                                  1

Salesperson: It's called country farmhouse white.

Customer: And what's _____ over there called?
                                  2

Salesperson: _____ on the top shelf? It's called German rye.
                  3

Customer: I'll take two of _____ please.
                                  4

Salesperson: Would you like them sliced?

Customer: I'd like _____ sliced, and _____
                            5   6

               unsliced, please.

Salesperson: Anything else?

Customer: Yes, I'd like four muffins.

Salesperson: I have muffins with orange or chocolate frosting. _____
                                                              7

               do you want?

Customer: _____ with orange frosting.
                  8

Salesperson: Small or large?

Customer: _____ please. I don't like
                  9

               large _____.
                              10

14 Your Turn

Working with a partner, create a conversation like the one in Practice 13. Choose a different kind of food shop for your conversation.

Example:
You: I'd like a cake, please.
Your partner: What kind?

5e The Definite Article *The*

The Leaning Tower of Pisa
is in Italy.

We Use *The*	We Do Not Use *The*
1. With count and noncount nouns when it is clear from the situation which people or things we mean or when the noun is mentioned for the second time or is already known. Can you pass me **the** milk please? (the milk that is on the table) I met a man and a woman in the hallway. I didn't like **the** man much, but **the** woman was nice.	1. With plural count nouns and noncount nouns when we talk about something in general. Roses smell sweet. Milk is good for you. (milk in general)
2. When there is only one of something, for example, *the* sun, *the* moon, *the* earth, *the* sky. Would you like to travel around **the** world?	2. With names of days, months, celebrations, drinks, meals, languages (without the word *language*), sports, and games. I'm working on Monday, and I'm playing tennis after lunch on Friday.
3. With countries when they include a count noun, for example *union, republic, states,* and *kingdom.* **the** United Kingdom **the** Federal Republic of Germany With names of plural countries. **the** Netherlands **the** United Arab Emirates	3. With most countries. India China Brazil Canada

We Use *The*	We Do Not Use *The*

We Use *The*

4. With other place names.

Oceans and seas	**the** Pacific **the** Mediterranean
Rivers, canals	**the** Mississippi
Deserts	**the** Sahara
Island groups	**the** Azores
Mountain ranges	**the** Andes
Hotels, theaters, museums, galleries	**the** Ritz, **the** Wang Theater, **the** Guggenheim

5. Before names that end with a prepositional phrase with *of*.

> **the** Statue of Liberty
> **the** Leaning Tower of Pisa
> **the** University of London

6. With the names of musical instruments and scientific inventions.

> He can play **the** guitar.
> Marconi invented **the** radio.

7. Before nationality words ending in *sh, ch, ans,* or *ese,* such as *English, Italian,* and *Japanese,* to mean people of that country. With other nationality endings, we can use or not use *the.*

> **The** Americans love hamburgers.
> OR Americans love hamburgers.

8. With adjectives and adverbs in the superlative form.

> He bought **the most expensive** car.

Also before some adjectives such as *young, old, rich,* and *poor* with a general meaning.

> **The rich** should help **the poor.**

We Do Not Use *The*

4. With other place names.

Continents	Africa, Antarctica
Most countries	India, China, Brazil, Canada
Cities, towns, states	Tokyo, Pleasantville, California
Individual islands	Long Island, Puerto Rico
Lakes	Lake Ontario, Lake Chad
Individual mountains	Mount Everest, Mount Fuji
Streets, parks, squares	Main Street, Central Park, Trafalgar Square

5. With names of hotels or restaurants named after the people who started them.

> McDonald's
> Macy's
> Harrods

6. With some nouns such as *school, college, prison, church,* and *bed,* when we are thinking about the main purpose of the place.

> He is at school right now.
> BUT I didn't like **the** school that I went to last year.

7. With means of transportation such as *by car/bus/plane/train,* etc., to talk about how we travel.

> I go to school by bus.
> BUT I left on **the** 7:15 bus this morning.

8. With names of illnesses.

> He has pneumonia.

But we can say **(the)** flu, **(the)** mumps, **(the)** measles.

We Use *The*	We Do Not Use *The*

9. With a singular count noun to mean something in general.
 	
    The horse is a beautiful animal.
 	
We can also use *a* or *an* to express a general meaning.
 	
    A horse is a beautiful animal.
 	
Or we can use a plural count noun alone.
 	
    Horses are beautiful animals.
	9. With seasons, we may or may not use *the*.
	    I love **(the)** spring in this part of the country.

10. Some expressions with *the* have a general meaning, for example, *the countryside, the mountains, the rain, the wind,* and *the snow.* I love to hear the sound of **the rain.** We usually go to **the mountains** in the summer.	

15   Practice

**Complete the sentences with *a, an,* or *the.*
If no article is needed, write *X.***

<u>   *The*   </u> woman in <u>   </u>
     1   2

photo is tall and slim. Maybe she's

<u>   </u> model or <u>   </u> actress.
     3   4

She is wearing <u>   </u> short black dress.
                5

The dress has no <u>   </u> sleeves and is
                6

made of <u>   </u> silk. Her earrings and
        7

necklace are probably made of <u>   </u>
                       8

diamonds. <u>   </u> woman is standing on <u>   </u> cruise ship that is sailing
         9   10

on <u>   </u> Mediterranean Sea. <u>   </u> sun is shining and <u>   </u>
     11   12   13

woman is looking out at <u>   </u> sea. There is <u>   </u> man standing next to
                     14   15

her. He is wearing <u>   </u> black jacket and <u>   </u> white pants.
                 16   17

<u>   </u> man is not wearing <u>   </u> tie. He is not looking at <u>   </u>
   18   19   20

woman. He is looking at <u>   </u> sea, too. <u>   </u> man is holding
                 21   22

<u>   </u> glass in his hand. <u>   </u> woman is holding <u>   </u> glass in
   23   24   25

her hand, too.

16 Practice

Complete the sentences with *a, an, the,* or *X* (no article).

Madagascar is __an__ island in _____
       1   2
Indian Ocean, off _____ east coast of Africa.
                    3
It is _____ fourth largest island in _____ world.
       4   5
It is sometimes known as _____ Great Red
                          6
Island. The people of Madagascar speak _____
                                         7
many different languages, but _____ official
                               8
language is French. _____ capital is Antananarivo.
                      9
It is _____ picturesque city with _____
       10   11
narrow streets. Archaeologists believe that _____
                                             12
first humans arrived here from _____ Indonesia
                                13
and _____ Malaysia around 2,000 years ago. Madagascar has mountains in _____ central
     14   15
region. It also has _____ tropical rainforests, grasslands, and deserts in _____ west.
                     16   17
After _____ island split from _____ mainland of _____ Africa 88 million years ago,
       18   19   20
many unique species of _____ plants and _____ wildlife developed there. Over half of
                        21   22
its _____ plants and _____ animals are special to Madagascar. We cannot find them
     23   24
anywhere else in the _____ world.
                       25

17 What Do You Think?

1. What makes Madagascar so unique?
2. What parts of Madagascar would you like to visit and why?
3. Why is French the official language of Madagascar?

18 Your Turn

Write a short description of your country.

_____

_____

_____

_____

1 **Review (5a, 5e)**

Complete the sentences with pronouns, possessive adjectives, forms of _other_, or articles. Write X for no article. There may be more than one correct answer.

One-seventh of all the land on Earth is

_____X_____ desert.
     1

_____ deserts are very dry
       2

areas. _____ get less than
            3

10 inches (25 cm.) of rain _____ each year. Most deserts are hot, like
                                   4

_____ Sahara in _____ Africa. _____ deserts
        5   6   7

are cold, such as _____ Gobi in _____ Asia. The coldest
                        8   9

desert of all is _____ Antarctica. _____ Sahara is about
                      10   11

one-third _____ size of _____ Africa. _____
                12   13   14

is almost as big as _____ United States, which is _____ fourth
                          15   16

largest country in _____ world. _____ Sahara was not
                        17   18

always _____ desert. Over millions of years, it has been covered with
             19

_____ ice, _____ water, _____ forests, and
        20   21   22

_____ grass.
        23

Some animals and _____ plants have adapted to life in _____
                        24   25

desert regions. Many desert animals are _____ nocturnal. This means that
                                               26

_____ hide from _____ sun during _____
        27   28   29

day and come out at night when _____ is cooler.
                                     30

Camels are ideally suited for _____ desert life. _____
                                   31   32

wide feet do not sink into _____ sand. Before _____ camels
                                33   34

go on _____ journey, _____ eat and drink for
            35   36

_____ days. They eat so much that _____ humps rise on
        37   38

their backs. Each hump can weigh as much as 100 pounds. Camels use the humps for storage

of _____ fat, which _____ will use up during
         39   **40**

_____ journey.
         41

Camels have _____ survival technique. They have bags in
                         42

_____ walls of _____ stomachs where _____
         43   **44**   **45**

store water. In this way, camels can travel several days with no _____ food
                                                                                              46

except what they draw from _____ fat of their humps.
                                          47

2 Review (5d, 5e)

Complete the sentences with pronouns, possessive adjectives, or articles. Write X for no article. There may be more than one correct answer.

The Olympic Games are _____ *an* _____ international sports competition. Every four
                                1

years athletes from around _____ world compete in either
                                       2

_____ summer or winter Olympic Games. Each takes place in
         3

_____ different city. More than 10,000 athletes from _____
         4   **5**

200 nations take part in _____ Games.
                                  6

_____ first Olympic Games took place in _____
         7   **8**

Olympia, _____ Greece more than two thousand years ago. They were part
                 9

of _____ festival for their chief god, Zeus. _____ ancient
         10   **11**

games took place every four years for 1,000 years until _____ Roman
                                                                           12

emperor cancelled _____ in about the year 400. That was the end of
                              13

_____ Olympics until _____ Frenchman named Baron Pierre
         14   **15**

de Coubertin (1863-1937) persuaded _____ group of countries to bring
                                                  16

_____ Olympics back. De Coubertin was himself _____
         17   **18**

sportsman and educator. In 1896, _____ first modern Olympics took place
                                              19

in _____ Athens, _____ Greece. In the beginning,
         20   **21**

_____ games were not successful, but later they became _____
         22   **23**

successful world event. _____ Winter Olympics first started in 1924 in
                                   24

_____ Chamonix, _____ France.
         25   **26**

3 Review (5a–5b, 5d)

Complete the sentences with pronouns, possessive adjectives, articles, or *one*. Write X for no article. There may be more than one correct answer.

Dear Lisa,

How are ___you___? Thanks for your email message. I enjoyed reading _____.
1 2

I have some news, too. I'm going on vacation next week to _____
3

New York City. Unfortunately, _____ is only for three days. Imagine!
4

I haven't seen _____ Statue of Liberty or been to _____
5 6

show on Broadway! I don't want to go by _____, so I'm going with Melissa.
7

We can share a room so it will be cheaper for _____. Melissa is a
8

shopaholic*, and I'm not, so I'll let her go shopping by _____ and I'll go to
9

_____ museum. There are so many of _____. I want to go
10 11

to a different _____ every day. I want to take _____ photos
12 13

so I can remember everything. The only problem is that my camera doesn't work, but

Melissa said I can use _____. She has _____ digital
14 15

_____.
16

I'll write to you when I come back, and tell you what _____ was like.
17

Take care,

Annie

shopaholic: informal and sometimes humorous term for someone who shops a lot

4 Review (5a, 5c)

Complete the sentences with pronouns, possessive adjectives, forms of *other*, or articles. Write X for no article. There may be more than one correct answer.

Louisa: Hi Ken, how are you? We always seem to run into each ___other___.
1

Ken: Hi Louisa. You're right we see each _____ almost every
2

_____ day.
3

Louisa: I saw your brother Tony the _____ day. He was driving
4

_____ red car, but I don't think he saw _____.
5 6

Ken: He didn't tell _____ he saw _____. By the way,
                                    7   8
         that's his new car. His old _____ broke down and he sold
                                                    9
         _____. _____ old car was red, too.
                    10   11
Louisa: _____ red car! What's the matter with _____?
                    12   13
Ken: He just likes _____ color red.
                                14

5 ## Review (5d–5e)

Find and correct the errors in pronouns and articles. Add pronouns and articles where necessary.

                                                       X   *the*

1. The word "Olympic" comes from name of the town Olympia in ~~the~~ Greece where ^

   first games started.

2. The athletes in the first modern Olympic Games in 1896 were only the men, as in

   ancient the Greece. In 1900, the women became eligible to participate in Games.

3. In 1932, the women could not participate in more than the three events.

4. The five rings on Olympic flag represent five geographic areas of the world: the Europe,

   Asia, Africa, the Australia, and the Americas.

5. Muhammad Ali won a Olympic gold medal in boxing in 1960. At the time, he called

   him Cassius Clay. In 1996, he returned to Olympics and lit Olympic flame at the

   opening ceremony.

6. Before Olympic Games start, runners carry torch all the way from Greece to the site of

   the games. On first day, the last runner lights a huge torch. This flame burns until last

   day.

7. Olympic Games have taken place every four years since 1896, except for 1916, 1940,

   and 1944, during two World Wars.

8. Summer Games were seen on the television for the first time in 1936.

9. In ancient Greece, the prize for the winner was not gold medal. It was branch from a olive

   tree; however, the winners became very famous and were like celebrities in hometowns.

Pronouns and Articles

WRITING: Write a Review of a Movie

Think of a movie that you enjoyed or one that you thought was terrible. Write a five-paragraph review about it. See page 470 for general writing guidelines.

Step 1. Use the following guidelines to organize and write your review. The sentence starters may help you as you write.

Paragraph 1: Give facts about the movie (title, director, screen play writer, actors).

> The movie was directed by ... and written by ...
> Its star is (name of actor) in the title role and (name of actor) in the supporting role ...

Paragraph 2: Introduce the setting (the place and time of the action) and the characters.

> The story is set in (Tokyo, Los Angeles, outer space) ...
> The story takes place (in the early 1800s, during the war in ..., in the present) ...
> The main character is ...

Paragraph 3: Describe the story. Use two paragraphs if necessary.

> It tells the story of (a character) OR it is based on the real life story of (a person) ...
> As the story develops, we learn that ...
> Finally ... OR In the end ...

Paragraph 4: State your reactions and the reasons why you did or didn't like it.

> The story was convincing/not convincing because...
> (Actor's) performance in the movie was exciting/disappointing because...

Paragraph 5: Write a conclusion.

> This movie is/isn't successful because ...
> The movie's story was very engaging, but unfortunately...

Step 2. Evaluate your review.

Checklist

_____ Did you write an introduction that presented basic facts about the movie?

_____ Did you describe the time and place of the movie in the second paragraph?

_____ Did you summarize the story in the third paragraph?

_____ Did you state your reactions to the movie in the fourth paragraph?

_____ Did you summarize your reactions in the fifth paragraph?

Step 3. Work with a partner or a teacher to edit your review. Check spelling, vocabulary, and grammar.

Step 4. Write your final copy.

A   Choose the best answer, A, B, C, or D, to complete the sentence. Mark your answer by darkening the oval with the same letter. A dash (—) in an answer means that no word is needed.

1. He is ninety-two and lives _____.

   A. himself   Ⓐ Ⓑ Ⓒ Ⓓ
   B. by himself
   C. by himselves
   D. by hisself

2. It costs $2.50 _____.

   A. the pound   Ⓐ Ⓑ Ⓒ Ⓓ
   B. pound
   C. one pound
   D. a pound

3. I see better with these glasses than with _____.

   A. the other ones   Ⓐ Ⓑ Ⓒ Ⓓ
   B. the other one
   C. other one
   D. one other

4. Richard went to _____ United Kingdom on business.

   A. an   Ⓐ Ⓑ Ⓒ Ⓓ
   B. a
   C. the
   D. —

5. The satellite will be above _____ earth.

   A. an   Ⓐ Ⓑ Ⓒ Ⓓ
   B. a
   C. other
   D. the

6. Brenda is _____ architect now. She has just finished her degree.

   A. an   Ⓐ Ⓑ Ⓒ Ⓓ
   B. a
   C. the
   D. —

7. That's not my book. It's _____.

   A. your   Ⓐ Ⓑ Ⓒ Ⓓ
   B. yours
   C. yourself
   D. yours book

8. The town is _____ ten miles from here.

   A. more   Ⓐ Ⓑ Ⓒ Ⓓ
   B. other
   C. another
   D. a

9. Bill: I flew to Chicago _____ day, and
           your sister had the seat next to me.
   Linda: No kidding! That's amazing!

   A. the other   Ⓐ Ⓑ Ⓒ Ⓓ
   B. another
   C. other
   D. each other

10. We tried not to look at _____ during the meeting.

   A. every other   Ⓐ Ⓑ Ⓒ Ⓓ
   B. the other
   C. each other
   D. each one

B **Find the underlined word or phrase, A, B, C, or D, that is incorrect. Mark your answer by darkening the oval with the same letter.**

1. There are <u>the salads</u>, sandwiches, and
A
<u>desserts</u> on <u>the tables</u>, so please help
B   C
<u>yourselves</u>.
D

Ⓐ Ⓑ Ⓒ Ⓓ

2. We had spoken to <u>each</u> <u>another</u> before
A   B
Ken introduced <u>us</u> <u>a</u> week ago.
C D

Ⓐ Ⓑ Ⓒ Ⓓ

3. My friend gave <u>me</u> the name of a <u>dentist</u>,
A   B
so I made <u>an appointment</u> to see
C
<u>a dentist</u> next week.
D

Ⓐ Ⓑ Ⓒ Ⓓ

4. <u>They</u> say it's very cold in <u>winter</u> on
A   B
<u>an east coast</u> of <u>the United States</u>.
C   D

Ⓐ Ⓑ Ⓒ Ⓓ

5. He was born in <u>Canada</u>, went to school in
A
<u>Australia</u> and <u>the United States</u>, and
B   C
worked in <u>United Arab Emirates</u>.
D

Ⓐ Ⓑ Ⓒ Ⓓ

6. <u>The Chinese</u> eat a lot of <u>the rice</u>,
A   B
but they don't drink a lot of <u>milk</u> like
C
<u>the Americans</u>.
D

Ⓐ Ⓑ Ⓒ Ⓓ

7. In <u>the United States</u>, <u>people</u> say that
A   B
<u>the time</u> is <u>money</u>, but I don't agree
C   D
with this.

Ⓐ Ⓑ Ⓒ Ⓓ

8. There are two solutions. <u>One</u> would be
A
<u>a miracle</u>, and <u>other</u> is <u>a possibility</u>.
B   C   D

Ⓐ Ⓑ Ⓒ Ⓓ

9. Zebras all seem to be <u>the same</u>, but in
A
fact <u>each ones</u> <u>has</u> its <u>own</u> particular
B   C   D
stripes.

Ⓐ Ⓑ Ⓒ Ⓓ

10. The principal of <u>the school</u> I go to has
A
<u>a flu</u> and won't be <u>at school</u> for <u>a week</u>.
B   C   D

Ⓐ Ⓑ Ⓒ Ⓓ

UNIT 6

MODALS I

6a Introduction to Modal Verbs

1. We use modal verbs with a main verb. Modal verbs add meaning to a main verb.

   Modal   Main Verb

   Betsy is only four, but she **can**   **ride** a bicycle.

   The modal *can* expresses the idea that Betsy has the ability to ride a bicycle. Modals often have several meanings, and two or three modals can share the same meaning.

You **may** take another piece of candy.	*May* expresses permission.
I **may** be late for your party.	*May* expresses possibility.

I **might** be late. I **may** be late. I **could** be late.	*Might, may,* and *could* all express possibility.

2. Here is a list of modals.

can	may	shall	will	must
could	might	should	would	ought to

3. We form statements and questions the same way with all modals. Here are summaries and examples of how modals work. See pages 453-462 for forms not presented in Units 6 and 7.

   Affirmative Statements: Subject + Modal + Verb

   You **should see** a doctor about that cough.

   Negative Statements: Subject + Modal + *Not* + Verb

   They **can't speak** Chinese very well.

   Yes/No Questions: Modal + Subject + Verb
   Short Answers: *Yes/No* + Pronoun + Modal (+ *Not*)

   A: **Could** you **swim** when you were five?
   B: Yes, I **could.**/No, I **couldn't.**

   Wh- Questions: Wh- Word + Modal + Subject + Verb

   When should the children **eat** their dinner?

4. Modal phrases such as *be able to* also add meaning to a main verb. In their function, they are like modals, but they are different in form. We will address both modals and modal phrases in Units 6 and 7.

Modals	Examples of Modal Phrases
can/could	be able to
must	have to
will	be going to *
should	be supposed to *
would	used to
may/might	be allowed to

*See page 44 for *used to* and page 58 for *going to*.

6b *Can, Could,* and *Be Able To* to Express Ability

I **can't hear** you.

1. We use *can* to talk about ability in the present and future.

   Can you drive?
   I **can** play the piano.
   When Tom comes home, he **can** help you with your homework.

2. We use *could* to talk about ability in the past.

   I **could** swim when I was three years old.

3. We can also use the modal phrase *be able to* with the same meaning as *can* and *could*. *Be able to* is not used as often as *can* and *could*.

   Are you able to drive? (present)
   I **was able to** swim when I was three years old. (past)

4. When we want to say that someone had the ability or opportunity to do something in a particular situation which resulted in an action, we use *was/were able to* and not *could*.

> Although the president of the company was at a meeting, we **were able to** speak to him for a few minutes.
> The office was closed today, so I **was able to** do things that needed to be done at home.

5. When we talk about a future ability that we do not have in the present, we use *will be able to,* not *can*.

> CORRECT: He'll be able to walk after his leg heals.
> INCORRECT: He ~~can~~ walk after his leg heals.

6. We must use *be able to,* not *can,* with some grammatical structures, such as with another modal and in the perfect tenses.

> CORRECT: We **might be able to** finish before the library closes.
> INCORRECT: We ~~might can~~ finish before the library closes.

> CORRECT: We**'ve been able to** pass more difficult tests.
> INCORRECT: We ~~can have passed~~ more difficult tests.

7. In particular situations, we usually use *can* or *could* and not *be able to* with stative verbs such as *see, hear, smell, taste, feel, understand,* and *remember.*

> COMMON: When I opened the door, I could smell gas.
> UNCOMMON: When I opened the door, I ~~was able to~~ smell gas.

---

1 Practice

Complete the sentences using the correct form of *be able to* and the verbs in parentheses. Use contractions when possible.

1. Stan (not, swim) *wasn't able to swim* when he was 12 years old.

2. I have to think about it. I (not, make) _____ a decision right now.

3. I regret that I (not, attend) _____ the meeting next Tuesday.

4. Anne broke her right arm last year, but she (use) _____ it very well now.

5. The meeting lasted six hours, but they (not, reach) _____ a decision.

6. Peter has a big disadvantage in Los Angeles because he

(not, drive) _____

7. (you, drive) _____ me home now?

8. We (not, get) _____ our email this afternoon because the

tech people are going to work on the server.

2 | Practice

Complete the sentences with the correct form of *be able to, can,* or *could* plus the verbs in parentheses. Use contractions when possible.

What health hazards do you have if you (not/smell) _____*can't smell*_____?

1

If you don't have the sense of smell, you (not/detect) _____

2

the smell of smoke or bad food. These are just two examples of how the sense of smell

(help) _____ us avoid danger.

3

Scents (affect) _____ our feelings, too. In one study, researchers

4

discovered that when a pleasant scent is introduced into an examination room, students

(get) _____ higher grades! In the future, it is possible

5

that our computers (deliver) _____ scents to our home.

6

We (smell) _____ vanilla, strawberries, or any other scents

7

we choose. Some experts say that working while smelling roses or vanilla

(have) _____ a positive effect on our health.

8

3 | Your Turn

Work with a partner. Make a note of one unusual skill that you have. Your partner will ask you questions to try and guess what the skill is. You will answer yes or no to each question. You can give hints if necessary. When your partner has guessed the skill, tell your partner as many details as you can about how you learned it.

Example:
Your partner: Can you ski?
You: No, but my skill is a sport that you can do in the winter.

6c *Must, Have To,* and *Have Got To* to Express Obligation and Necessity

You **must stop** at the stop sign.

1. We use *must* or *have to* to express obligation or necessity.

    You **have to take** an English exam when you enroll at the university.
    You **must take** an English exam when you enroll at the university.

2. In everyday English, *have to* is more common than *must.*

3. We use *must* when we write forms, signs, and notices.

    The last person to leave the office **must lock** the door.

4. We usually use *must* when the necessity to do something comes from the speaker.
   We usually use *have to* when the necessity comes from outside the speaker.

    Teacher: You **must** give me all your essays by tomorrow.
    Student to a friend: I **have to** write my essay by tomorrow. (The teacher says so.)

5. *Must* usually shows urgent necessity.

    We **must** get her to a doctor right away.

6. *Have got to* has the same meaning as *have to,* but we use it mostly in informal
   spoken English. We use it in affirmative statements. We do not often use it in
   negative statements or questions. We do not use *have got to* in the past tense.

    CORRECT: I have got to go now.
    CORRECT: I haven't got to go now.
    CORRECT: Where have you got to go now?
    INCORRECT: I ~~had~~ got to go early last night.
    CORRECT: I had to go early last night.

In rapid speech, *got to* sounds like *gotta*.

We can contract *have got to* with the subject, but we can't contract *have to*.

CORRECT: I have to buy a new computer.
INCORRECT: I~~'ve~~ to buy a new computer.
CORRECT: I have got to buy a new computer.
CORRECT: I've got to buy a new computer.

7. We can use *have to* for all tenses and forms. There is no past form of *must* or *have got to*. We rarely use *must* for questions.

	Statement	Question
Present or Future	I **must study** for the test now/tomorrow. I **have to study** for the test now/tomorrow.	**Do** I **have to study** for the test now/tomorrow?
Past	They **had to study** for the test yesterday.	**Did** they **have to study** for the test yesterday?

4 Practice

Write rules for each of the following situations. Use the prompts and *must* or *have to*.

1. sit in your assigned seat

   You must sit in your assigned seat.

   OR

   You have to sit in your assigned seat.

2. fasten your seatbelt when the seatbelt sign is on

   _____

3. stay seated when the seatbelt sign is on

   _____

4. turn off your cell phone

   _____

5. talk quietly—if at all

   _____

6. buy your food or drinks at the theater

   _____

7. buy a ticket

_____

8. respect the animals

_____

9. put your litter into a proper container

_____

<u>5</u> Practice

Do you think the following rules should be set by the school or by the class teacher? If you think it should be a school rule, complete the sentence with *must*. If you think the teacher should set the rule, complete the sentence with *have to*.

<u>School Rules</u>

1. You _____*must*_____ pay your fees before you start the class.

2. You _____ attend all the classes.

3. You _____ come to class on time.

4. You _____ turn off your MP3 player in class.

5. You _____ bring a dictionary to class every day.

6. You _____ be quiet when the teacher is talking.

7. You _____ complete all the assignments on time.

8. You _____ take all exams.

9. You _____ type your assignments on a computer.

10. You _____ consult with your advisor if you want to change classes.

<u>6</u> Your Turn

Work with a partner. You and your partner will take the roles of teacher and student. Ask and answer questions about the rules in your school. Think of some rules to add to the ones in Practice 5.

Example:
You: Do I have to pay the fees before I start the class?
Your partner: Yes, you have to pay them when you register for the class.

6d *Not Have To* and *Must Not* to Express Prohibition and Lack of Necessity

Anna is calling her friend. She **doesn't have to do** any homework today.

1. *Have to* and *must* have similar meanings in the affirmative, but in the negative, they have very different meanings.

    We use *not have to* show that something is not necessary. There is another possibility or a choice.

    > You **don't have to help** me today. (It's not necessary. I don't need your help today; you can help me another day.)

    We use *must not* to express prohibition. It means that something is not allowed or is against the law. There is no choice.

    > You **must not** drive over 60 miles an hour. (It's against the law. You are not allowed to drive over 60 miles an hour.)

2. We usually use *must not* to show prohibition in official written forms, notices, and signs. We usually do not use *must not* when we talk to an adult, but we sometimes use *must not* when we tell a child something is not allowed.

    > Billy, you **must not** go near the fire.

3. We can use *not have to* in all tenses. We can use *must not* only to talk about the present and future.

    > You **must not park** in front of the doorway now/later. (present or future)
    > I **didn't have to take** a driver's test when I moved to this state. (past)
    > I **won't have to renew** my driver's license for another five years. (future)

7 | Practice

Complete the schedule with *must* or *don't have to*. Then decide which place each sentence describes. Sometimes more than one place is possible.

airplane   airport   art gallery   hotel   museum   restaurant   theater   zoo

Place

1. Visitors _____*must*_____ buy a ticket before entering.   _____*museum*_____

2. Children under six _____ pay.   _____

3. Guests _____ tip the waiter—service is included.   _____

4. You _____ be quiet during the performance.   _____

5. Guests _____ sign in at the reception desk.   _____

6. Passengers _____ have their hand luggage screened.   _____

7. You _____ switch off your cell phones.   _____

8. Visitors _____ hand in their audio players after the tour.   _____

8 | Practice

Complete the sentences with *must, have to, mustn't,* or *don't have to* and the verbs in parentheses.

When I started my new job, I saw that most of the employees were wearing sweaters

and casual shirts. I'm happy that men (wear) __*don't have to wear*__ a jacket
                                                          1

and tie. In my previous job, we (keep) _____ our jackets on
                                                          2

all day. Here, only the manager (wear) _____ a tie, but he
                                                          3

(keep) _____ his jacket on.
                4

On the other hand, some rules are quite strict. For example, you

(clear) _____ your work space at the end of every day,
                5

and you (put) _____ any personal pictures up. You
                          6

(be) _____ late because there is a staff meeting every day at
              7

8:00 A.M. You (be) _____ absent unless it is absolutely necessary.
                              8

My friend was sick for three days, and she (get) _____ a doctor's
                                                              9
note. That reminds me, I (tell) _____ my manager that I (go)
                                              10
_____ to the dentist tomorrow.
              11

9 Your Turn

**Work with a partner. Compare your previous job and your present job, or your
previous school and your present school. Talk with your partner about the work or
school rules using *must, have to, mustn't,* or *don't have to.***

Example:
At my old job, we didn't have to come in at any specific time. We chose our own hours.
But in my new job, we mustn't ever be late or we'll get in trouble.

6e *Should, Ought To,* and *Had Better* to Give Advice

Function

We **shouldn't pollute** the air.

1. We use *should* and *ought to* to ask for and give advice, to say what is right or
   good in general, or to talk about obligation or duty.

   You **should learn** to drive.
   You **ought to learn** to drive.
   You **shouldn't tell** lies.
   You **ought not to tell** lies. (uncommon)

   In general, we use *should* more than *ought to*.

2. We use *had better* to express a strong recommendation in a specific situation.
   Had better suggests a warning or a threat of bad consequences. It is stronger than
   should or *ought to*. In statements, we usually contract *had* to *'d*.

   You**'d better leave** now, or you'll miss the flight.

3. Even though *had better* contains the word *had,* it refers to the present or the future, not to the past.

4. We use *should* for questions. We do not usually use *had better* for questions. Questions with *ought to* are very rare.

10 Practice

A. Read Lara's description of her problems at work.

I'm having a lot of problems at work. They always give me too much work, and I can never get it finished on time. Also, my cubicle is much too small. I have so many papers and files that there's no room for them, and they end up all over the floor. And you wouldn't believe how hot it is in there. The heat is always on full blast, and it gives me a constant headache. But the worst thing is, I don't think any of my coworkers like me because they never ask me to eat lunch with them.

B. What should Lara do? Write six sentences using *should, shouldn't,* or *ought to.*

1. *She should talk to her supervisor about her workload.*

2. _____

3. _____

4. _____

5. _____

6. _____

C. Work with a partner. Write a conversation between Lara and a friend. The friend gives advice. Lara responds using expressions like these:

That's a good idea! I hadn't thought of that!
I've tried that!
No, that wouldn't work because...

Friend: *I think you should talk to your supervisor about your workload.*

Lara: *I've tried that. She said that she couldn't change it.*

Friend: _____

Lara: _____

Friend: _____

Lara: _____

Friend: _____

11 Your Turn

Work with a partner. Write three problems that you have. Ask your partner for advice.

Example:
You: I don't have anyone to speak English with. What should I do?
Your partner: You should find an English-speaking key pal on the Internet.

6f *Should Have* and *Ought To Have* to Express Regret or a Mistake

Form

He **shouldn't have done** that.

1. We call this form of modals—modal + *have* + past participle—a perfect modal. Perfect modals refer to the past.

AFFIRMATIVE AND NEGATIVE STATEMENTS

Subject	Modal *(Not)*	*Have*	Past Participle
I/You He/She/It We/They	**should** **should not** **shouldn't** **ought to** **ought not to**	**have**	**gone** there.

We rarely use *ought to* in the negative.

YES/NO QUESTIONS				SHORT ANSWERS			
Modal	Subject	*Have*	Past Participle	Yes,		No,	
Should	I/we he/she you they	**have**	**gone** there?	you he/she I/we they	**should have.**	you he/she I/we they	**shouldn't have.**

Yes/no questions with *ought to* are extremely rare.

WH- QUESTIONS*					
	Subject (Wh- Word)	*Should Have*			Past Participle
Wh- Word Is the Subject	**Who**	**should have**			**left** early?
	Which (boy)				**won** the race?
	Wh- Word	*Should*	Subject	*Have*	Past Participle
Wh- Word Is not the Subject	**What**		I		**done** to help you?
	Where		she		**gone**?
	When		they		**taken** the test?
	How	**should**	he	**have**	**completed** the form?
	Which (car)		you		**repaired**?
	Why		he		**left** early?
	Who*		they		**talked to**?

*In formal written English, the wh- word would be *whom*.

Wh- questions with *ought to* are rare.

2. In speech, we contract *should have* to *should've* when *should have* comes before a past participle, or when it is used in a short answer. It is very common to say this, but we do not often write it. Do not make the mistake of writing the contracted form of *should have* as *should of*.

CORRECT: I should have brought more money. (*Should have* sounds like "should've" or "should'a.")

INCORRECT: I should ~~of~~ brought more money.

Function

We use the perfect modal form of *should* or *ought to* to say that something was the best thing to do, but we didn't do it.

I **should have taken** a map with me. (I didn't, and I got lost.)
You **ought to have taken** the job. (You didn't take it. That was a mistake.)
He **shouldn't have missed** the test. (He did miss it. Now he regrets it.)

12 Practice

A. Read the following description of Gary and Julia's holiday.

The Vacation That Went Wrong

Gary and Julia decided to go to Spain for a vacation. They found a cheap hotel and flight package from a new discount travel agency. When they got to the airport, they found that the flight was overbooked. They hadn't phoned to confirm their flight ahead of time, so they had to wait six hours for the next flight. When they got to the hotel, they found that it was not near the beach as the advertisement had said. It was at least two miles away! They went to a nearby restaurant for dinner, but they couldn't speak any Spanish, and Julia had left her phrasebook at home. They couldn't understand the menu, and they ordered meat even though they are both vegetarians. When they got back to their hotel, Gary found that his camera and cell phone had both disappeared. They thought about complaining to the travel agency, but when they got back from their vacation, they were just too tired.

B. What should Gary and Julia have done? Write eight sentences using *should have* and *shouldn't have*.

1. <u>They should have booked the trip with a travel company that they knew about.</u>

2. _____

3. _____

4. _____

5. _____

6. _____

7. _____

8. _____

Your Turn

Write notes about three mistakes that you made in the past that caused a problem. Work with a partner. Think of what you should have or shouldn't have done in each case.

Example:

You: I failed my math exam. What should I have done?

Your partner: You should have studied harder. You shouldn't have spent so much time watching TV.

6g *Be Supposed To* to Express Expectation

Function

You**'re supposed to study** in the library.
You**'re not supposed to sleep.**

1. We use *be supposed to* to talk about what we expect to happen because it is the normal way of doing things or because of an arrangement, duty, or custom.

   You **are supposed to take** something to the host when you go for dinner.

2. There is often a difference between what is supposed to happen and what really happens.

   I **am supposed to go** to the conference tomorrow, but instead I'm going to stay in the office and catch up on my work.
   She **was supposed to call** me yesterday, but she didn't.

3. We can use *be supposed to* in the past tense by using *was* or *were* instead of *am, is,* or *are.*

   The plane **was supposed to arrive** at 9:30, but it arrived an hour late.
   The soccer players **were supposed to practice** on Saturday, but it rained.

14 Practice

Complete the sentences with the correct form of *be supposed to*. Then match the sentences with the phrase that describes what the sentence is about.

The sentence is about . . .

____d____ **1.** I (go) *was supposed to go* to the dentist last Tuesday, but I had too much work.

_____ **2.** (you/not be) _____ in a meeting right now?

_____ **3.** My cousins (visit) _____ us last April, but they cancelled their trip.

_____ **4.** I (not/tell) _____ you this, but I think they are going to give you a surprise party.

_____ **5.** In Japan, you (take off) _____ your shoes before you enter someone's house.

_____ **6.** (not/drive) _____ without a license. It's against the law.

_____ **7.** If you fail the test, the examiner (tell) _____ you why.

_____ **8.** (I/put) _____ my luggage on the bus myself?

a. a generally agreed upon custom

b. a rule or regulation

c. a scheduled event

d. a scheduled event that did not take place

e. an action carried out against the rule

15 Your Turn

Say or write things that you are supposed to or not supposed to do to help the following problems.

Example:
Putting cold water on a burn is supposed to help it. You're not supposed to put butter on it.

a burn   a cold   a headache   a sunburn

REVIEW

1 Review (6b–6c, 6e, 6g)

Underline the correct answers.

What (<u>can</u> / ought to) happen if you
¹
don't prepare for an interview? Will you

(be able to / better not) get the job you
²

really want? If you don't prepare, you'll leave

thinking about what you (should / mustn't) have
³

done and said. You say you want a better job?

Then you (are supposed to / had better) learn
⁴

how to interview for one. You (aren't supposed to / don't have to) attend a class to do it.
⁵

You only have to read this article.

First, you (may / must) remember PPPQ. That's *Preparation, Practice, Personal*
⁶

Presentation, and *Questions*. To prepare for your interview, you (should / couldn't) read as
⁷

much as you can find about the company. You (don't have to / must not) know everything.
⁸

You (ought not / aren't supposed) to be an expert, but (you aren't able / you've got) to
⁹   ¹⁰

show the interviewer that you're interested in the company.

Practice is very important. You (must / may) practice answering questions with some-
¹¹

one. You (may not / cannot) think this is important, but you really (could / ought to)
¹²   ¹³

understand how it feels to answer questions and communicate well.

What clothes (ought / should) you wear? Personal presentation is very important. You
¹⁴

(might / must) get away with wearing a bathing suit if you want to be a lifeguard, but in
¹⁵

most cases you (could / had better) wear more formal clothes to an office interview. You're
¹⁶

(supposed to / able to) look like a professional. You (aren't able to / shouldn't) walk
¹⁷   ¹⁸

into an interview wearing a wrinkled shirt or a pair of jeans. You (may / must) wear
¹⁹

something that you feel good in. During the interview, you don't want to feel that you

(mustn't have / shouldn't have) worn those uncomfortable pants or that bright
²⁰

red dress. You (can / ought to) look and feel confident.
²¹

Always ask questions. You (shouldn't have / are supposed) to be an intelligent person
                                              22
who's interested in this company. You (must / might) never say you have no questions.
                                         23

2 Review (6b–6c, 6e)

Complete the sentences with the correct forms of *be able to, can, could, could have,*
must, have to, have got to, should, ought to, had better, should have, ought to have,
be supposed to, may, **or** *might.* **Some items have more than one correct answer.**

Gina and Sally meet on their university campus.

Gina: Sally! What are you doing here? I thought you (go) <u>*had to go*</u> to the
                                                          1

         media fair today.

Sally: Well, I (go) _____, but my car broke down and I (take)
                                   2

         _____ it to my mechanic earlier this morning.
                    3

Gina: You (call) _____ me. I (take)
                                4

         _____ you, but now it's too late. You know,
                    5

         you (learn) _____ how to ask for help when you need it.
                                 6

Sally: I know. I (not, help) _____ it. I hate to bother people.
                                           7

Gina: You (not, feel) _____ that way with me. I'm you're best
                                       8

         friend. You know you (count on) _____ me to help you
                                                        9

         any time.

Sally: Well, in that case, (you, do) _____ me a favor?
                                                10

Gina: Of course.

Sally: It's only 3:00. If we hurry, we (get) _____ there in time
                                                        11

         for me to see some of the show before it closes.

Gina: Well, let's go then. But we (hurry) _____ because it takes
                                                     12

         almost 30 minutes to get there. By the way, (you, drive)

         _____? I broke my glasses this morning. I (never, throw)
                    13

         _____ away my old pair. I (use) _____
                    14   **15**

         use them right now.

Sally: Yes, (you, always, keep) _____ a spare pair of glasses, in
                                              16

         case of an emergency. Anyway, of course I (drive) _____.
                                                                            17

Gina: Thanks, but you (not, go) _____ over the speed limit. It
       18
makes me too nervous. Besides, it's against the law.

Sally: Okay. No problem. You know, we really (call) _____
                                                          19
Maggie. I know she'd love to come, too. She lives on High Street, so we (stop)

_____ by her house on the way.
       20

Gina: That's a good idea. I (meet) _____ her at the gym this
                                              21
morning but I overslept. Anyway, we (hurry) _____ now.
                                                          22
It's getting late.

3 Review (6b–6c, 6e–6f)

**Complete the sentences with the correct forms of *be able to, can, could, must, have to,
have got to, should, ought to, had better, should have, ought to have, be supposed to,
may,* and *might*.**

Amy: (you find) _Can you find_ someone else to help you study your lines for
                      1
your play today? I (go) _____ to my aunt's house. She's not well.
                                 2

John: Of course. You (not, help) _____ me today. I can get someone at
                                          3
the theater to read my lines with me. I (know) _____ my part by
                                                          4
tomorrow night. Anyway, don't worry about me. You (leave)

_____ now before you miss your bus.
       5

Amy: Oh, I have plenty of time. You know, I (stay) _____ with my
                                                              6
aunt for two days, but instead I'm coming home tomorrow afternoon. That way I

(go) _____ to your dress rehearsal.
          7

John: Oh, don't remind me! I'm not ready. I (take) _____ some time
                                                                8
off from work yesterday to study my script, but I was too busy. Now I don't

know half my lines. What (I, do) _____? Stay up all night? Oh, I
                                          9
(never, take) _____ this part.
                    10

Amy: We (never, go) _____ to the theater that night. Then you
                            11
(never, see) _____ the notice.
                    12

John: You know how much I love to be on stage, but I (never, try out)

_____ for this role. I (know) _____ that I wouldn't
       13   14

have the time. I (do) _____ this sort of thing when I was in
                               15
school. But I'm working full time now.

Amy: I know it's hard, but I really think that you (do) _____ what
                                                                    16
          makes you happy. You've always wanted to play this role. And I know you'll
          be great. Anyway, I (come) _____ home by noon tomorrow.
                                            17
          If that happens, I'll come by right away to help you. Oh, I (never, agree)
          _____ to go there tonight.
                   18

John: No, no. Your aunt needs you right now. You (stay) _____ with
                                                                  19
          her until she's better. You (not, cancel) _____ your plans
                                                            20
          because of me.

Amy: Well, my mother will be there in the morning so it will be all right. Well, I (go)
          _____ now, but I'll see you tomorrow around noon. Good luck!
                   21

4   Review (6b)

Find the errors and correct them.

                                Should
Do you love to paint? ~~Ought~~ you have gone to art school?
Maybe you didn't have the opportunity. You should think it's too
late for you to start now, but that's not true. You have to never
think it's too late to do something that you love. You don't must
spend a lot of money, either. And after you finish our six-week
course, you'll can say that you're an artist. You cannot produce masterpieces for a while,
but you'll be proud of your work.

    Our lessons teach the techniques of watercolor painting. Do you think you can't not do
it? Well, may you draw a picture? Might you brush paper with water? Then you must paint
with watercolors. Call us for a free brochure.

WRITING: Write an Expository Essay

An expository essay explains something. In this essay, you will explain how a visitor should and should not act when going for a meal in a home in your country. See page 470 for general writing guidelines. See page 471 for information on writing an essay.

Step 1. Work with a partner and make notes about what a visitor from another country should remember when going to a home for a meal in your country. Make notes for each part of the visit. Use the following ideas or your own.

1. Arrival

   Being punctual: When to go?
   Greeting: How to?
   Bringing a gift: Necessary or not? What to bring? Whom to give the gift to?
   Ask for a tour of the house?

2. At the table

   What to talk about?
   How to eat: Utensils (use of chopsticks, spoons, fingers, etc.)? Where to put your hands?
   OK to make noise while eating?
   How to refuse food or ask for more?
   What to say about the food?

3. After the meal

   How long to stay?
   How to thank your host?
   Offer to help after the meal?
   What to say before you leave?

Step 2. Write your notes or sentences in an essay. Make sure the body of the essay has the three parts listed above. Write an introduction and a conclusion. Write a title.

Step 3. Evaluate your essay.

Checklist

_____ Did you write an introduction that stated the purpose of the essay?

_____ Did you write three paragraphs in the body? Did they explain what a visitor should do in the three parts of the visit?

_____ Did you write a conclusion that summarized your points in the body?

Step 4. Work with a partner or a teacher to edit your essay. Check spelling, vocabulary, and grammar.

Step 5. Write your final copy.

A Choose the best answer, A, B, C, or D, to complete the sentence. Mark your answer by darkening the oval with the same letter.

1. You _____ be late for your interview tomorrow. It will not look good.

   A. had better not   Ⓐ Ⓑ Ⓒ Ⓓ
   B. better not
   C. had no better
   D. 'd better

2. He _____ to call yesterday, but didn't.

   A. is supposed   Ⓐ Ⓑ Ⓒ Ⓓ
   B. was supposed
   C. supposed
   D. supposing

3. You _____ drive without a seat belt. It's the law.

   A. have to   Ⓐ Ⓑ Ⓒ Ⓓ
   B. are supposed to
   C. must not
   D. don't have to

4. When _____ to help us?

   A. will you be able   Ⓐ Ⓑ Ⓒ Ⓓ
   B. you will be able
   C. you be able
   D. are you be able

5. I have a bad sunburn. I _____ sat in the sun too long.

   A. should have   Ⓐ Ⓑ Ⓒ Ⓓ
   B. shouldn't have
   C. mustn't have
   D. mustn't

6. A few months ago, I _____ to use a computer, but now I even use it to chat with my family.

   A. am not able   Ⓐ Ⓑ Ⓒ Ⓓ
   B. couldn't
   C. wasn't able
   D. couldn't able

7. Tim _____ to wash the dishes. There are no more clean ones.

   A. must   Ⓐ Ⓑ Ⓒ Ⓓ
   B. have got
   C. got
   D. has

8. You _____ to clean your room today. You can do it tomorrow.

   A. have   Ⓐ Ⓑ Ⓒ Ⓓ
   B. don't have
   C. mustn't
   D. can't

9. Rick: _____ go now?
   Anne: Yes, that's a good idea.

   A. Had I better   Ⓐ Ⓑ Ⓒ Ⓓ
   B. Had better I
   C. Had I
   D. Better had I

10. You _____ tell lies.

    A. shouldn't   Ⓐ Ⓑ Ⓒ Ⓓ
    B. ought to
    C. ought better not
    D. had not better

B Find the underlined word or phrase, A, B, C, or D, that is incorrect. Mark your answer by darkening the oval with the same letter.

1. We <u>are supposed</u> <u>to go</u> camping last
       A   **B**
   Saturday, but we <u>had to</u> <u>cancel</u> it because
                      C   **D**
   of the weather.

   Ⓐ Ⓑ Ⓒ Ⓓ

2. You s<u>hould ask</u> <u>your counselor</u> <u>for advice</u>,
        A   **B**   **C**
   or you <u>call</u> the department at
          D
   the university.

   Ⓐ Ⓑ Ⓒ Ⓓ

3. I work from home, so I <u>haven't</u> <u>have to</u>
                          A   **B**
   drive much, but my husband <u>has to</u> <u>do</u> a
                               C   **D**
   lot of driving.

   Ⓐ Ⓑ Ⓒ Ⓓ

4. When he <u>was</u> <u>a child</u>, he <u>couldn't read</u>,
          A   **B**   **C**
   but he <u>was able use</u> a computer.
          D

   Ⓐ Ⓑ Ⓒ Ⓓ

5. We <u>have</u> a test tomorrow, so we
       A
   <u>had better</u> <u>not</u> <u>to go</u> out tonight.
   B   **C**   **D**

   Ⓐ Ⓑ Ⓒ Ⓓ

6. She <u>have</u> <u>got to</u> take the test this year or
        A   **B**
   else she <u>won't</u> <u>be able to</u> apply to college.
            C   **D**

   Ⓐ Ⓑ Ⓒ Ⓓ

7. In most high schools, students <u>must not</u>
                                  A
   <u>to call</u> their teacher by their first names,
   B
   but in college, students <u>are able</u> <u>to call</u>
                            C   **D**
   their professors by their first names if the
   professor allows them to do so.

   Ⓐ Ⓑ Ⓒ Ⓓ

8. You <u>not</u> <u>have to</u> finish high school
       A   **B**
   <u>in order</u> <u>to get</u> a driver's license.
   C   **D**

   Ⓐ Ⓑ Ⓒ Ⓓ

9. We <u>should</u> <u>not have</u> <u>wash</u> the car
       A   **B**   **C**
   yesterday because <u>it's going to rain</u>.
                     D

   Ⓐ Ⓑ Ⓒ Ⓓ

10. You <u>don't have</u> <u>got to</u> show your passport
        A   **B**
    when you <u>fly</u> within the United States,
             C
    but you <u>must show</u> your drivers license or
            D
    another form of photo identification.

    Ⓐ Ⓑ Ⓒ Ⓓ

UNIT 7

MODALS II

7a Shall, Let's, How About, What About, Why Don't, Could, and Can to Make Suggestions

Form / Function

Anne: Let's get a cup of coffee after class.
Lyn: Good idea.

1. We can make suggestions with *shall, let's, why don't, how about,* and *what about.* Notice that all of these, except *let's,* are questions and must end with a question mark.

SHALL		
Shall	Subject	Base Verb
Shall	we	**leave** now?

HOW ABOUT and WHAT ABOUT	
How/What About	Gerund*/Noun
How about	**going** to dinner?
What about	**dinner**?

*A gerund is a base verb + *-ing* that we use as a noun.

LET'S	
Let's (Not)	Base Verb
Let's	**leave** now.
Let's not	

2. A question starting with *why don't* can be a suggestion or a normal question. We expect an agreement or a disagreement in response to a suggestion. We expect an explanation in response to a normal question.

   A: **Why don't you eat** now?
   B: That's a good idea. (The response to the suggestion is an agreement.)

   OR

   B: Because I'm not hungry. (The response to the normal question is an explanation.)

3. Statements with *could* and *can* are sometimes suggestions. Words and phrases such as *maybe* and *if you like* can show that a statement is a suggestion. *Could* is usually more polite than *can* in these suggestions.

COULD and CAN			
(Maybe)	Subject	Modal + Base Verb	*(If You Like)*
Maybe	we	**could** leave now.	**if you like.**
	I	**can** leave now	

Let's and *let us* can also mean that the speaker expects the listener to agree to what the speaker says. The uncontracted form, *let us* is usually formal.

Doctor to a child: Let's listen to your heart.
In a speech: Let us never forget this senator's contribution to our country.
In a religious service: Let us pray.

---

1 | Practice

Complete the sentences with *how about, why don't, shall, could,* or *can*.

Rick and Olivia are having a cup of coffee between classes.

Rick: _____*Shall*_____ we go to the movies tonight?
                        1

Olivia: Great idea! _____ going to that new film at the Avon Cinema?
                        2

Rick: OK. _____ I pick you up at 5:30?
                        3

Olivia: Sure. Maybe we _____ go out to eat afterwards?
                        4

Rick: Great! Or we _____ eat at my place, if you like.
                        5

Olivia: _____ we pick up some take-out Chinese food on the way to
                        6
your house?

Rick: Perfect!

2 | Your Turn

Work with a partner. You and your partner are having a difficult time agreeing on what to do this weekend. Use *shall, let's, how about, what about, why don't, could,* and *can* to make suggestions until you agree on the same activity. Use activities from the list or your own ideas.

Example:

You: Let's go bowling on Saturday.

Your partner: Hmm. The bowling alley is always so crowded on Saturdays. How about going dancing?

You: We went dancing last week. Maybe we could do something at the Culture Center.

Your partner: That's a good idea. Shall we try to get tickets for the ballet?

You: Ugh. I hate the ballet. How about . . .

| a baseball game | a party | dancing | skating |
| a concert | bowling | shopping | swimming |

7b *Prefer, Would Prefer,* and *Would Rather* to Express Preference

Form

They **'d prefer eating** pizza **to** salad.

PREFER and *WOULD PREFER*

STATEMENTS			
Subject	*(Would) Prefer(s)*	Object	*(To* + Object)
I/You/ He/She/It/ We/They	prefer(s) would prefer	coffee	to tea.
		drinking coffee	to tea. to drinking tea.
		to drink coffee.	*

*We do not use *to* + object if the first object is an infinitive.

YES/NO QUESTIONS					SHORT ANSWERS	
Auxiliary	Subject	Base Verb	Object	(To + Object)	Yes,	No,
Do	I/we		coffee?		you **do.**	you **don't.**
	you				I/we **do.**	I/we **don't.**
	they				they **do.**	they **don't.**
Does	he/she	**prefer**			he/she **does.**	he/she **doesn't.**
Would	I/we		coffee	to tea?	you **would.**	you **wouldn't.**
	you				I/we **would.**	I/we **wouldn't.**
	he/she				he/she **would.**	he/she **wouldn't.**
	they				they **would.**	they **wouldn't.**

1. The objects that follow *prefer* and *would prefer* can be nouns, gerunds, or infinitives.

   I prefer **television** to **movies**. (noun objects)
   He prefers **watching** television to **watching** movies. (gerund objects)
   We prefer **to watch** television. (infinitive object)

2. *To* + object is optional if both speakers understand what the second object is.

   I prefer **coffee**. (The listener knows that they are talking about coffee and tea.)

3. After *(would) prefer,* we do not use *to* + object if the first object is an infinitive.

   CORRECT: We prefer to watch movies.
   INCORRECT: We prefer to watch movies ~~to watch television~~.

4. When the object after *prefer* is an infinitive, we can add *than* + another infinitive. We can omit the *to* in the second infinitive.

   I prefer to see movies **than (to) rent videos**.

WOULD RATHER

AFFIRMATIVE AND NEGATIVE STATEMENTS				
Subject	*Would Rather (Not)*	Base Verb	Object	(*Than* + Object) (*Than* + Base Verb + Object)
I/You/ He/She/ We/They	**would rather** **'d rather**	**have**	**tea.**	
			tea	than coffee.
				than have coffee.
I/You/ He/She/ We/They	**would rather not**	**have**	**tea.**	

5. Some verbs (intransitive verbs) do not have objects. In these cases, objects are not necessary with *would rather*.

> I'**d rather** leave now than leave later.
> I'**d rather** not arrive too early.

6. The phrases with *than* are optional if both speakers understand what the object is.

YES/NO QUESTIONS					
Would	Subject	*Rather*	Verb	Object	(*Or* + Object) (*Or* + Base Verb + Object)
Would	I/you he/she/it we/they	**rather**	**have**	tea?	
				tea	**or coffee?** **or have coffee?**

ANSWERS	
Question	Possible Answers
Would he rather have tea?	Yes, he would./No, he wouldn't.
Would they rather have coffee or tea?	They'd rather have tea.

Function

1. We use *prefer, would prefer,* and *would rather* to say that we like one thing more than other things. We usually use *prefer* to state our general preferences, but we use *would prefer* or *would rather* when we are talking about a specific choice, as in a restaurant.

> Which do you **prefer**, beef or chicken?
> **Would** you **prefer** a steak or a hamburger?
> I **prefer** Chinese food to Indian.
> I'**d prefer** to have Chinese food to Indian.

2. When we want to refuse an offer, we usually answer by saying "I'd rather not."

> A: Would you like some coffee?
> B: I'**d rather not**. It makes me nervous.

> CORRECT: I'd rather not.
> INCORRECT: ~~I wouldn't rather~~.

3. When we want to compare two things, we can use *to* after *prefer* + object.

> Helen prefers books **to movies**. (noun object)
> Helen prefers reading books **to watching** movies. (gerund object)

3 | Practice

Bob completed this questionnaire about his preferences. Use the questionnaire to write ten sentences about Bob using *prefer, would prefer,* and *would rather.*

Preferences Quiz

Write your preferences on a scale of 1–5.

| 1 = love, 2 = like a lot, 3 = like, 4 = OK, 5 = dislike |

Fish	1	②	3	4	5
Meat	①	2	3	4	5
Tofu	1	2	3	4	⑤
Jogging	1	②	3	4	5
Tennis	①	2	3	4	5
Classical music	1	2	③	4	5
Rock music	①	2	3	4	5
Chess	①	2	3	4	5
Scrabble	1	2	③	4	5
Eating out	①	2	3	4	5
Eating at home	1	2	3	④	5
Sending email messages	①	2	3	4	5
Writing letters	1	2	3	4	⑤

1. *Bob prefers fish to tofu.*

2. _____

3. _____

4. _____

5. _____

6. _____

7. _____

8. _____

9. _____

10. _____

4 Your Turn

A. Work with a partner. Use the questionnaire in Practice 3 to ask questions about your partner's preferences. Your partner will answer the questions and give reasons for his or her choices.

Examples:
You: Do you prefer jogging to tennis?
Your partner: Yes, I do. / No, I don't. I like tennis because it is more competitive.

You: Do you like eating out?
Your partner: Yes. I would rather eat out than eat at home. It's less work.

B. Tell the class about your partner.

Example:
He prefers jogging to tennis. He's not very competitive.

7c *May, Could,* and *Can* to Ask Permission

Form

Can I **check** this book out of the library?

YES/NO QUESTIONS			SHORT ANSWERS			
Modal	Subject	Base Verb	Yes,		No,	
May	I/we		you	**may.**	you	**may not.**
Could	he/she	**use** your phone?	he/she	**could.**	he/she	**couldn't.**
Can	they		they	**can.**	they	**can't.**

1. We use *may, could,* and *can* to ask permission. We use *may* or *could* with people we do not know or who are in authority. We can use *could* in any situation. We use *can* with friends and family members.

   > Ms. Brown isn't in the office. **May** I take a message?
   > **Could** Sally have another piece of cake, please?
   > Pete, **can** I borrow your dictionary?

   Remember that *can* and *could* sometimes express ability.

   > I **can** make cakes, but I **can't** make pies.
   > She **couldn't** swim until last year.

2. It is polite to use *please* when we ask permission. *Please* usually goes after the subject or at the end of the sentence. We put a comma before it if it is at the end of the sentence.

   > Could I **please** borrow the car?
   > Could I borrow the car, **please**?

3. When we use *could* to ask permission, it refers to the present or future. Remember that *could* also has the meaning of past ability.

   > **Could** she **take** some more potatoes, please? (permission)
   > **Could** she **swim** when she was five? (*could* = past ability)

4. When we ask permission with *could,* the short answer uses *may* or *can.*

   > A: Could I borrow your dictionary?
   > CORRECT: B: Yes, of course you can/may.
   > INCORRECT: B: Yes, of course you ~~could~~.

5. We can use expressions other than short answers to answer requests for permission.

   > A: Could I use your phone?
   > B: **Yes, of course.**
   >   OR **Sure.**
   >   OR **No problem.**
   >   OR **Go ahead.**

6. When we refuse to give permission, we usually also offer an apology and/or an explanation.

   > A: **May** I sit here?
   > B: I'm sorry, but I'm saving this seat for my friend.

Practice

Complete the sentences about a zoo with *can* or *can't*. Then identify the meaning of *can* or *can't* by writing *permission* or *ability* on the line.

1. You ____can____ buy popcorn there. ____ability____

2. You _____ feed the animals. It isn't good for them. _____

3. You _____ take photos. It doesn't hurt the animals. _____

4. You _____ see the snakes when they hide in the rocks. _____

5. We _____ see the elephants if their area is open now. _____

6. You _____ stay after dark. The zoo is closed then. _____

7. You _____ see everything today because the zoo is too large. _____

8. Children under five _____ get in free. _____

6 Practice

A. Read each dialogue. Complete each request with *may, could, can,* or *would.* Then write the correct response from the list.

1. Employee: *Could/May* I leave work a little early today?

   Boss: _____

2. Passenger A: _____ I borrow your newspaper for a moment?

   Passenger B: _____

3. Customer: _____ I have another cup of coffee?

   Server: _____

4. Teacher: _____ Susan come to school early tomorrow? I want to help her with her math.

   Parent: _____

5. Student: _____ I hand in my paper a day late?

   Teacher: _____

6. Child: _____ you give me five dollars, please?

   Parent: _____

7. Husband: _____ you mind if I close the window?

   Wife: _____

Responses
Sure! Right away.
Of course. What time should she be there?
Of course.
No. It's getting cold in here.
Certainly not! I've already given you your allowance this week!
I'm sorry, but the date can't be changed.
Certainly. That's fine.

B. Write *formal* or *informal* for each of the situations in Practice A.

1. _____formal_____   **5.** _____

2. _____   **6.** _____

3. _____   **7.** _____

4. _____

---

7 | Your Turn

Work in groups of three. Choose two of the situations from Practice 6, or use two of your own ideas. Tell each of your situations to your two partners. Your partners will act out a request and a response.

Example:
You: One passenger on a train to another.
Partner 1: May I close the window? It's cold in here.
Partner 2: Sure. That's fine. OR I'd rather you didn't.

7d Will, Can, Could, Would, and Would You Mind to Make Requests

Kate: **Could** you **make** a copy of this for me?

Tom: Sure

WILL, CAN, COULD, AND WOULD

REQUEST			POSSIBLE ANSWERS	
Modal	Subject	Base Verb	Accept	Decline
Will	you	**pick up** my mother at the airport?	Yes, of course.	Sorry, I can't.
Can			I'd be happy to.	
Would			Certainly.	I'm not sure. When?
			Sure.*	No way!*
Could			No problem.	

Sure, No problem, and *No way!* are informal. *No way!* is sometimes also humorous.

WOULD YOU MIND

REQUEST		POSSIBLE ANSWERS	
Would You Mind	Gerund	Accept	Decline
Would you mind	**mailing** this for me?	Of course.	Sorry, I can't.
		(No,) I'd be happy to.	I won't have time. Sorry.
		(No,) I'd be glad to.	No way!
		Sure.	

1. We use *would* and *could* to make polite requests.

   > Boss to employee:
   > **Could** you **make** a copy of this, please?
   > **Would** you **answer** these letters for me, please?

2. We use *will* and *can* for more direct and informal requests.

   > Mother to daughter:
   > **Will** you **turn** down the TV, please?
   > **Can** you **pass** me the salt?

3. We use *please* to make a request more polite. We can put *please* at the end of the sentence or between the subject and the verb. If we put *please* at the end of the sentence, we put a comma before it.

   > Could you make a copy of this, **please**?
   > Could you **please** make a copy of this?

4. We may agree to do a polite request. However, when we cannot do it, we usually apologize and give a reason.

   > Boss: Could you finish that report for me this morning?
   > Employee: **I'm sorry, I can't.** I'll be in a meeting.

5. We can also use *would you mind* + a gerund to make a polite request.

   > A: **Would you mind waiting** a few minutes longer?
   > B: No, that's OK. OR Yes, I would. I've already been waiting for an hour.

   A negative answer to *would you mind* means that you will do what the person wants. A positive answer—*Yes, I would*—means that you are not willing to do it.

6. Compare these answers to polite requests.

   Request with *would/could* + base verb (Do not answer with *would* or *could*.)

   > Boss: Would/Could you come to my office?
   > Employee: Yes, of course. INCORRECT: Yes, I ~~would/could~~.

   Request with *would you mind* + gerund (You can answer with *would*.)

   > Receptionist: Would you mind waiting a few minutes longer?
   > Visitor: No, that's OK. OR Yes, I would. I've already been waiting for an hour.

Practice

For each of the following situations, write three different requests and responses that would be appropriate to the situation.

1. It's very hot and stuffy in your office. The windows are all closed. The heat is on high. The door is closed. There are two coworkers in the office with you. What requests could you make?

   Request A: _Would you mind opening the window?_

   Reply: _I'd be happy to._

   Request B: _____

   Reply: _____

   Request C: _____

   Reply: _____

2. You are on the train that you take every day to work. You realize that you left your train pass at home. It costs a lot to buy a ticket on the train, and you don't want to do that. What requests could you make to the train conductor?

   Request A: _____

   Reply: _____

   Request B: _____

   Reply: _____

   Request C: _____

   Reply: _____

3. Your daughter's room is very messy, she hasn't finished eating her dinner, and she hasn't done her homework. But now she wants to go out to her friend's house. What requests could you make to your daughter?

   Request A: _____

   Reply: _____

   Request B: _____

   Reply: _____

   Request C: _____

   Reply: _____

7e *May, Might,* and *Could* to Express Possibility

Form

I **could be** in this traffic jam for a long time.

PRESENT

Subject	Modal *(Not)*	Base Verb
I/We He/She/It You We/They	**may** **may not** **might** **might not** **could***	**be** there.

*No negative for *could* in this meaning.

YES/NO QUESTIONS			SHORT ANSWERS			
Modal	Subject	Base Verb	Yes,		No,	
Could	I/we you he/she/it they	**get** there early?	you I/we he/she/it they	**could.**	you I/we he/she/it they	**couldn't.**

1. We do not contract *may not* or *might not* when they express possibility.

   CORRECT: He may not be there yet./He might not be there yet.
   INCORRECT: He ~~mayn't~~ be there yet./He ~~might't~~ be there yet.

2. When *could* refers to the present, we do not use it in the negative.

   CORRECT: They may/might not be on time.
   INCORRECT: They ~~could not~~ be on time.

3. We can form yes/no questions about possibility with *could,* but not with *may* or *might*. However, we often respond to yes/no and wh- questions in the present progressive or the future tenses with *may* or *might*.

   A: Are you leaving soon?   A: Is John still in his office?
   B: I don't know. I **might/may**.   B: He **might/may be**.

4. *Maybe* and *may be* both express possibility, but they have different forms. *Maybe* is an adverb. It is one word and always comes at the beginning of a sentence.

   Maybe that's Ted at the door.

   May be is a modal + a verb *(be)*. It is always two words.

   Ted **may be** in the library.

   Pronunciation Note: *Maybe* is pronounced with stress on the first syllable. *May be* is pronounced with stress on both syllables.

   MAYbe that's Ted at the door.
   Ted MAY BE in the library.

PAST

5. We use the perfect modal form (modal + *have* + a past participle) to express possibilities with these modals in the past.

AFFIRMATIVE AND NEGATIVE STATEMENTS			
Subject	Modal *(Not)*	*Have*	Past Participle
I/You He/She/It We/They	**may/may not*** **might/might not*** **could** (no negative**)	**have**	**been** there yesterday.

   *The contraction of *may not* and *might not* is very rare.
   **Could not* expresses past impossibility.

YES/NO QUESTIONS				SHORT ANSWERS			
Modal	Subject	*Have*	Past Participle	Yes,		No,	
Could	I/we	have	taken the wrong road?	you	could have.	you	couldn't have.
	you			I/we		I/we	
	he/she			he/she		he/she	
	they			they		they	

6. In statements and short answers, we can contract a modal + *have* to "may've," "might've," and "could've." We do not usually write this contraction. Although they sound like "may of," "might of," and "could of," be sure that you do not spell these speech contractions with *of*.

       CORRECT: We might have (might've) taken the wrong road.
       INCORRECT: We might ~~of~~ taken the wrong road.

7. We use *could,* not *might* or *may,* in yes/no questions.

Function

PRESENT AND FUTURE

1. We use *may, might,* and *could* to talk about present and future possibility.

    I **may be** there tomorrow.
    I **might be** there tomorrow.
    I **could be** there tomorrow.

    A: Who is at the door?
    B: I don't know. It **may** be Ken.

    I'm not sure what I'm going to do tomorrow. I **might** go to the library.
    Where is Ted? I'm not sure, but he **could** be in his room.

2. We use *may not* and *might not,* but not *could not,* to express that something will possibly not happen.

    She **might not** come tomorrow. (Possibly she will not come.)
    The rain has stopped. I **may not** need an umbrella. (Possibly I won't need an umbrella.)

PAST

3. We use the perfect modal form (modal + *have* + past participle) of *may, might,* or *could* to express that something was possible in the past.

> He **may have** already **gone**.
> Maria is late. She **might have missed** her train.
> I can't find my glasses. I **could have left** them at work.

4. We use the negative with *may have* and *might have* (but not *could have*) to say that something possibly did not happen in the past.

> I **may not have put** my glasses in my bag as usual.
> They **might not have heard** about it yet.

5. We use *could have* and *might have* (but not *may have*) when something was possible in the past, but it did not happen.

> We were lucky. There **could have been** a bad accident.
> It was dangerous to climb that wall. You **might have fallen**.

6. We use *couldn't have* to say that something was impossible in the past.

> You **couldn't have seen** Mary on the street. I know she's in Beijing!

---

10 | Practice

A. Read about Agatha Christie.

Agatha Christie was a famous British author of mystery novels. But there was an incident in her own life that was mysterious—just like those in her novels. She married at the age of 24. Twelve years later, her husband Archie asked for a divorce because he had fallen in love with a younger woman. At this time, Agatha was upset by the death of her mother, and she suddenly disappeared. She was missing for three weeks. The police, the press, and her husband searched for her everywhere. Finally, they found her. She was staying in a small hotel in Harrowgate, England, using the name Mrs. Neele. She told the police that she had lost her memory. No one knows why she went there or what she did during those three weeks. Soon after, she divorced her husband, and six months later she married again. She never talked about her mysterious disappearance incident again.

B. Write sentences in response to the following questions that express possibilities of what may, might, or could have happened to Agatha Christie. Try to think of two or three possible answers for each question.

1. Why did Agatha Christie suddenly disappear?

   She might have been so sad that she needed to be alone for awhile.

   _____

   _____

2. Why did she go to a small hotel?

   _____

   _____

   _____

3. Why did she use a different name?

   _____

   _____

   _____

4. Why didn't she tell anyone where she was going?

   _____

   _____

   _____

5. How do you think the police were able to find her?

   _____

   _____

   _____

6. Why do you think she never talked about the incident again?

   _____

   _____

   _____

Your friend was absent from class yesterday. What happened? Write five possibilities with *may have, might have,* or *could have* + a past participle.

Example:
He could have had a dental appointment.

1. _____

2. _____

3. _____

4. _____

5. _____

7f *Should* and *Ought To* to Express Probability

They **should be** here by now.

1. We use different modals for different degrees of certainty.

    I **will be** there tomorrow.   100% sure
    I **should be** there tomorrow.   90% sure
    I **ought to be** there tomorrow.   90% sure

2. We use *should* or *ought to* to say that something is probable at the time of speaking or in the future.

    Maria **should be** at work now. She's usually there at this time.
    I **ought to pass** the English test easily. I have studied hard and know everything.

3. We use the perfect modal form of *should* or *ought to* when we think something has probably happened, but we don't know for sure.

> Their plane **should have landed** by now.
> Their plane **ought to have landed** by now.

We also use this form when we expect something to happen that has not happened.

> I was surprised to hear that he didn't pass the test. He **should/ought to have passed** it.

12 Practice

Read about Jim. Write sentences using *should* or *ought to* and one of the phrases from the list. Some sentences require a modal + base verb; others require a perfect modal. Some sentences must be negative.

Jim is a very reliable, punctual, and hardworking person. He is a sales manager in a computer software company and has worked there for four years. He thinks his job is a little boring. He goes to night school, and he has recently applied for the position of senior sales manager in his company.

be at the office by now	get an interview soon
be in good physical shape	get the new job
earn a higher salary	have to borrow money
feel tired by noon	need repairs yet
finish it before going home	reply to it by now
get a high grade	

1. It is after 9:00 A.M.

   Jim *should be at the office by now.*

2. You left him a phone message this morning.

   He _____

3. He started writing a report yesterday morning.

   He _____

4. He's just had a week's vacation.

   He _____

5. He earns a good salary.

   He _____

6. He's studied hard for his Spanish exam next week.

   He _____

7. He's just bought a new car.

It _____

8. He swims at the gym every day.

He _____

9. Jim applied for a better job in the company two weeks ago.

He _____

10. His job performance reviews are excellent.

He _____

11. When he is senior sales manager, he _____

 Your Turn

Write two sentences about your life and your future career. What will probably happen? Give a reason for your statement.

Example:
I should get into a good university because I studied hard for the exams.
I'm a really good soccer player, so I should be able to get on the school team.

7g *Must, Must Not,* and *Can't* to Make Deductions

Form

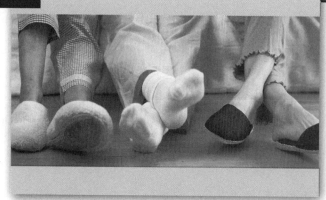

They **must be** at home.

PRESENT

Subject	Modal	Base Verb
I/You He/She/It We/They	**must (not)** **can't**	**be** hungry.

PAST

Subject	Modal	*Have*	Past Participle
I/You He/She/It We/They	**must (not)** **can't**	**have**	**been** hungry.

1. In this meaning, we use *must* in the affirmative and the negative (*must* or *must not*), but we use *can* only in the negative (*can't*).

2. In this meaning, we do not contract *must not*.

3. Questions in these forms are very rare.

Function

PRESENT

1. We use *must (not)* to express deductions (or a good guess) based on information we have about a present situation, and when we are almost 100 percent sure that something is true.

> Dana **must know** New York City very well. She has lived in the city all her life.
> Eddie comes to class every day, but today he isn't in class. He **must not feel** well.

2. We use *can't* to make a deduction that is, in our opinion, 100 percent true.

> I saw Rob a minute ago, so he **can't be** at home.
> We had lunch half an hour ago. You **can't be** hungry.

PAST

3. We use the perfect modal form of *must* or *can't* for deductions about the past.

> You did a lot of walking yesterday. You **must have been** tired.
> She **can't have seen** us on campus yesterday. We weren't there.

We can also use *couldn't have* instead of *can't have* in this meaning.

> She **couldn't have seen** us on campus yesterday.
> What **can** she **have seen**? What **could** she **have done**?

14 Practice

You are talking about your neighbors. Complete the sentences using *must* or *can't*.

1. There are no lights on.

   They _____*must*_____ be out.

2. They bought a new car.

   They _____ make a lot of money.

3. The husband comes home late and looks tired.

   He _____ work a lot.

4. We never see any children.

   They _____ have any children.

5. The woman leaves in the morning and comes home in the evening.

   She _____ work.

6. She dresses in expensive suits and carries a briefcase.

   She _____ be a factory worker.

7. People do not come to their house.

   They _____ have many friends.

8. They always buy a lot of fresh food.

   They _____ like to eat well.

15 Practice

Complete the sentences about life 500 years ago with *can't have* and *must have* and the past participle of the verbs in parentheses.

1. People (die) _*must have died*_ when they had infectious diseases because there

   were no antibiotics.

2. Travel to far away places (be) _____ long and dangerous without trains

   or planes.

3. Europeans (go) _____ to Australia because they didn't know it existed.

4. Many children (have) _____ a good education because there were no

   schools for them.

5. Many people (work) _____ at home or a farm because the economy

was not industrialized as it is today.

6. Many children (work) _____ to help their parents because it was

difficult to make a living then.

7. Big castles (be) _____ cold places in winter.

8. Life (be) _____ easy for many people then.

16 Practice

A. Read about Rapa Nui.

Rapa Nui, also called Easter Island, is a small island in the middle of the South Pacific Ocean. It is over 2,000 miles from Tahiti and Chile, and it is one of the most isolated places on earth. It is best known for the mystery of the moai—giant statues that stand on high cliffs around the island. Each statue has a human form, and a few of them have a separate stone of red volcanic rock on their heads.

We do not know where the original people of Rapa Nui came from, or what these giant statues represent. We also do not know how they transported the statues from the quarries* to the ceremonial sites around the island. Each statue weighs about 14 tons! The people had no metal tools or machinery of any kind. They transported 288 statues to their final locations, but there were 397 statues, all fully carved, still in the quarry. There were also 92 statues abandoned on the road from the quarry to their final location. Some statues were later knocked down and damaged. The stone for these statues did not come from the ceremonial sites but from the quarries. Archaeologists have discovered that the island was once covered with thick palm forests, but today there are no trees and not enough vegetation to support a population. At one time, the population of Rapa Nui reached 10,000, but today there are no descendants of this culture. There are no written records to explain the mystery of the island.

*Quarries: holes in the ground from which people get building stones.

B. Write your conclusions about what must have happened, must not have happened, or can't have happened on the island.

1. How did the ancient people transport these giant statues?

They can't have used machines.

2. Why were some statues abandoned on the road?

_____

3. What did the statues represent?

_____

4. Did the ancient people of the island carve the statues before or after they transported them to their final locations?

_____

5. Why did the ancient people of the island go to so much trouble to carve and transport these statues?

_____

6. How and why did the ancient population disappear?

_____

7. Why did they leave no written records?

_____

8. How did archaeologists discover facts about Rapa Nui's population?

_____

17 **Your Turn**

Imagine that your instructor hasn't come to class for two days. She/He hasn't phoned the school, and no one has seen her/him. Say or write five things that must, might, could, or can't have happened.

Example:
She might have had an accident.
He must not be able to call.

7h The Progressive and Perfect Progressive Forms of Modals

Form

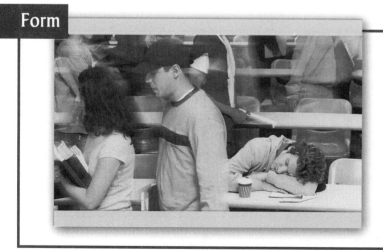

He **must have been sleeping** all through the class.

THE PROGRESSIVE FORM

AFFIRMATIVE AND NEGATIVE STATEMENTS

Subject	Modal (Not)	Be	Verb + -ing
I/You He/She/It We/They	**may** **may not** **might** **might not** **could** **could not** **couldn't** **should** **should not** **shouldn't** **must** **must not**	**be**	**working.**

YES/NO QUESTIONS				SHORT ANSWERS			
Modal	Subject	*Be*	Verb + *-ing*	Yes,		No,	
Could	I/we you he/she they	**be**	**working?**	you I/we he/she/it they	**could (be).**	you I/we he/she/it they	**couldn't (be).**
Should				you I/we he/she they	**should (be).**	you I/we he/she they	**shouldn't (be).**

THE PERFECT PROGRESSIVE FORM

Subject	Modal (Not)	Have Been	Verb + -ing
I/You He/She/It We/They	**may** **may not** **might** **might not** **could** **could not** **couldn't** **should** **should not** **shouldn't** **must** **must not**	**have been**	**working.**

YES/NO QUESTIONS				SHORT ANSWERS	
Modal	Subject	*Have Been*	Base Verb + *-ing*	Yes,	No,
Could	I/we you he/she/it they	**have been**	**working?**	you I/we he/she/it they **could have been.**	you I/we he/she/it they **couldn't have been.**
Should				you I/we he/she/it they **should have been.**	you I/we he/she/it they **shouldn't have been.**

1. In speech, we often contract the modal + *have:* "May've," "might've," "could've," "should've," and "must've." They sound like "might of," "could of", etc., but be sure not to spell the *'ve* part of the contraction as *of*.

   CORRECT: She should have been here by now.
   INCORRECT: She should ~~of~~ been here by now.

2. We can form yes/no and wh- questions with *could* and *should* in the progressive and progressive perfect forms.

   It's midnight, and John's light is still on. **Could** he **be studying**?
   The test is tomorrow. What **should** I **be studying**?

   I saw John's light on at midnight last night. **Could** he **have been studying**?
   Why **should** he **have been studying** at that time?

Function

1. We use the progressive form of modals to say that something is in progress at the time of speaking.

   He **may be staying** at his uncle's house. (He's not home right now.)

2. We use the perfect progressive form of modals to say that something was in progress at a time in the past.

   They **must have been eating** dinner when we called.

18 Practice

Complete the sentences with the progressive or perfect progressive form of a modal and the verbs in parentheses.

1. A man is sitting on a bench in a train station early one morning. He has no luggage.

   He (wait) _could be waiting_ for someone.

2. His raincoat and hair are wet. The floor is wet. It (rain) _____.

3. He looks very tired. He (work) _____ late last night.

4. There is a used and folded newspaper next to him. He (read) _____ it.

5. There is an empty paper coffee cup next to the newspaper. He (drink)

   _____ coffee.

6. There is also a bouquet of red roses next to him. The person he is meeting must be his

   wife or girlfriend. The man is looking at his watch and combing his hair. The person

   (come) _____ on the next train.

7. The train comes from Medham, but there are other towns where the train stops on the

   way. She (come) _____ from Medham.

8. There is a big university in Medham. She (study) _____ there.

9. The train is coming and has now stopped. The woman (get off) _____

   the train any minute.

10. The two meet. They are looking at each other and smiling. They (feel)

    _____ very happy.

19 Practice

Read the situations and write sentences about it with *may*, *might*, *could*, **or** *must* **in the progressive or perfect progressive form. Use one of the following prompts for each situation.**

they/celebrate a birthday	they/have an argument
they/cook on the grill	new neighbor/move in
they/expect a lot of guests	they/plan this party for some time
the neighbors/have a party	they/play music too loud to hear anything

1. What's happening at our neighbors' house? I heard a man and a woman shouting at each other this morning.

   They must have been having an argument.

2. I live in a five-story building. I heard a lot of noise on the stairs yesterday.

3. The front door of the neighbor's house is open, and all the hall lights are on.

4. I can hear a lot of loud music next door and people laughing and talking.

5. There is smoke and the smell of delicious food coming from the back yard.

6. They sent out invitations several weeks ago.

7. A delivery man from Christine's Bakery took a huge cake box into the Smith's house.

8. I phoned them to complain about the noise, but no one answered.

20 Your Turn

Imagine that there is a lot of noise coming from the classroom next door. People are laughing, and you can hear music. Write or say three things that must, might, may, or can't be happening.

Example:
They must be having a party.

REVIEW

1 Review (7b, 7d–7f)

Complete the sentences using the words and phrases from the list. Sometimes there is more than one correct answer.

can	may	shall
could	may not	should
could not	might	would prefer
couldn't	ought	would you mind

This ___may/might/could___ be a story that you do not believe. Nevertheless,
1

it _____ give you something to think about.
2

_____ taking the time to read my story?
3

Winchester House is a 160-room mansion in San Jose, California. You

_____ have heard about it, but every year, thousands of people go
4

to see this mansion. _____ they all be interested in the building's
5

unusual architecture? Some _____ be, but not all. Some
6

_____ to skip the secret passages and staircases that go nowhere
7

and go straight to some of the more interesting areas. There, they

_____ see the rooms where Sarah Winchester's ghost has appeared.
8

In the years since Sarah's death in 1922, visitors to the mansion have reported hearing

mysterious footsteps and slamming doors. These reports _____ not
9

surprise the tour guide, who heard his name whispered in a room when no one else

was there.

_____ I tell you more? _____ I add to
10   11

this strange story? With your permission, I'll say that a caretaker heard breathing behind

him when he was alone. He _____ have been mistaken, but that's
12

not what most people think. Some visitors have felt cold spots in warm rooms. Others

have smelled soup cooking in a kitchen with no pots on the stove. Certainly, soup

_____ have been cooking in a kitchen with no pots and no fire on
13

the stove!

Allen Weitzel, a director at Winchester House, _____ have been
                                                        14
working in his office one morning. However, he wasn't working because everything on his
desk was completely wet. Nothing else in the room had a drop of water on it.
"_____ explaining this?" he _____ have
          15   16
asked when he unlocked the door and entered the room that morning. It just
_____ be that Sarah was behind him laughing.
          17
    Some people claim to have seen Sarah's image in certain parts of the house. I
_____ to know. I'm one of them.
          18

2 Review (7e, 7g)

Underline the correct words.

There's a mystery in the African country of Zimbabwe that archaeologists (can / <u>may</u>) solve
                                                                              1
someday. Right now, however, they can only keep trying. The ruins of Great Zimbabwe lie in
a beautiful valley. If you have been there, you (can / might) have seen the great wall going
                                                      2
around the top of a rocky hill. Ruins cover the hill and the valley to the south. These ruins
are the walls of buildings made of small pieces of cut stone piled one on top of the other.
Archaeologists believe the builders (might / ought to) have used almost a million stones.
                                            3
No one knows who the builders were. Some people think they (should / could) have been
                                                                    4
visitors from other countries. However, most of the evidence indicates that the builders
(should / must) have been the Africans who first lived in Zimbabwe. The Zimbabweans
      5
certainly (would rather / prefer) that explanation.
              6
    There are no ruins like these anywhere else in the world. Dating of the stones shows that
the first buildings (should / could) have been built as long ago as 1100 C.E. The rest of
                          7
Great Zimbabwe was built during the 14th century. As many as 30,000 people (will / may)
                                                                                  8
have lived there. No one knows why the people eventually left the area. (Would / Could)
                                                                              9
there have been a drought? It's certainly possible. That many people (must / could) have
                                                                        10
needed a lot of water. Other theories are that the people (should / might) have left to find
                                                              11
new land for their cattle, or that they (could / must) have been attacked by outsiders.
                                          12

There (could / must) have been a good reason why they abandoned this great kingdom. No
      13
one knows. You (can't / can) make your own guess.
              14

For centuries, Great Zimbabwe lay silent as trees and bushes grew over it. It

(should / might) have been unknown for many more years, but a hunter named Adam
      15
Renders found the site in 1868. We know a lot about it now, and, thanks to the work of the

archaeologists, we (ought to / must) know more in the future. But Great Zimbabwe will
                           16
remain a place of awe and mystery.

3 Review (7a–7e)

**Complete the sentences using the words and phrases from the list. Sometimes there is
more than one correct answer.**

can't	let's not	must	why don't
could	may	prefer	will
could have	may not	rather not	would you mind
couldn't have	maybe	should have	

1. Margaret isn't here right now. ___*Could/May*___ I ask who's calling?

2. The sun seems to be coming out. I _____ need an umbrella after all.

3. You _____ gone to the soccer game today. It was cancelled!

4. It's four o'clock. They _____ been here by now.

5. He _____ know a lot about plants. He's been working at the garden
   center for years.

6. She _____ be in the office today. She's on vacation.

7. _____ you call Mr. Winters, please? I need to confirm our schedule.

8. _____ we go out for dinner? There's a great new restaurant in the mall.

9. _____ stay home today. It's a great day for the beach!

10. I _____ going to the movies tonight to going shopping.

11. It was a terrible day, but it _____ been worse.

12. I'm very busy right now. I'd _____ go to that meeting.

13. It's a good thing that you didn't drive into the city. You _____ been
    caught in that traffic jam.

14. I know you're in a hurry. _____ we could finish this another time.

15. _____ changing my appointment? I won't be in town tomorrow.

16. _____ you please turn down that radio? It's too loud!

Review (7e–7h)

Find the errors and correct them.

Brenda: Good morning, Neil. How ~~is~~ about getting a cup of coffee?

Neil: Sorry, I can. I'm late for a meeting with Foster.

Brenda: Then you'll be happy to hear that Foster isn't in the office today. He can't be out sick.

Neil: But that can't not be true! I thought I saw him coming into the building an hour ago. I musn't be mistaken. What a relief!

Brenda: Well, that's lucky for you. Now, I'm going to get some coffee. Would you like some?

Neil: Actually, I would rather tea.

Brenda: Fine. By the way, has David left for Djakarta yet?

Neil: Yes, he's on the way. He would be there in three hours. No, wait. I forgot about the time difference. Actually, his plane ought to land an hour ago.

Brenda: He can know Djakarta very well by now. He's been there at least a dozen times.

Neil: Yes, he has. Oh, that reminds me. I should be going to Mexico City next week. It isn't certain yet, but may you check on flight times for me this morning?

Brenda: No.

Neil: Oh, no problem. I can have some time to do it myself this afternoon. By the way, does everyone know that we're having a group meeting at 3:00 today?

Brenda: I think most people know, although a few could not have heard about it yet.

Neil: Then how don't we make an announcement? I'll write it down and give it to Betty.

Brenda: Good idea, but I think Betty should have already gone to lunch.

Neil: Lunch! It's 10:00 in the morning! She may be at lunch!

Brenda: Oh, you're right. It's been such a busy morning that it feels like I've been here four hours!

WRITING: Write a Business Letter

Write a business letter in which you complain about a product or a service.

Step 1. With a partner, brainstorm ideas for your letter. Think of (or imagine) something you have bought and were unhappy with. Write down your ideas, and make notes about what you would like to tell the company about the problem.

Step 2. Pay attention to the format and organization of this letter. Notice that a business letter is short and direct, but also polite.

---

126 Longwood Avenue
Boston, MA 02116
March 20, 20XX

Mr. James Smithson
President, Real Mobility, Inc.
2003 N. Mountain Avenue
Los Angeles, CA 90027

Dear Mr. Smithson:

I am writing to express my disappointment with my cellular phone service with your company.

I signed a contract with Real Mobility on February 15, 20XX. The service was supposed to start on February 16, but it didn't start until February 20. When I called your customer service department, the representative ...

I think you will agree that it is unfair for me to have to pay for phone service that I can't use all the time. Would you please arrange for me to receive a full refund of the money that I have paid? My account number is 100-265-983.

Sincerely,

Sarah MacKay

Sarah MacKay

Introduction: State the problem simply and briefly.

Body: Give specific information about the problem.

Conclusion: Summarize your position and tell what you want.

Signature: Sign your name and type it below your signature.

Step 3. Write a letter of complaint in the format above, on a computer if possible.

Step 4. Evaluate your letter.

Checklist

_____ Did you use the format of the example letter?

_____ Is your letter short, direct, and polite?

_____ Did you follow the organizational model of the example letter?

_____ Did you sign your name in writing and also type it?

Step 5. Work with a partner or a teacher to edit your letter. Check spelling, vocabulary, and grammar.

A **Choose the best answer, A, B, C, or D, to complete the sentence. Mark your answer by darkening the oval with the same letter.**

1. Would you mind _____ me tomorrow?

   A. meet   Ⓐ Ⓑ Ⓒ Ⓓ
   B. to meet
   C. meeting
   D. if you meet

2. I'd rather _____ home. I'm too tired to go out.

   A. stay   Ⓐ Ⓑ Ⓒ Ⓓ
   B. staying
   C. not stay
   D. to stay

3. _____ go home. It's getting late.

   A. Why don't   Ⓐ Ⓑ Ⓒ Ⓓ
   B. Let's
   C. Can
   D. How about

4. May I _____ my dictionary during the test?

   A. use   Ⓐ Ⓑ Ⓒ Ⓓ
   B. using
   C. to use
   D. rather use

5. There's someone at the door. Who _____ it be?

   A. must   Ⓐ Ⓑ Ⓒ Ⓓ
   B. may
   C. will
   D. could

6. He _____ arrived home by now. It only takes 20 minutes to get here from the airport.

   A. might   Ⓐ Ⓑ Ⓒ Ⓓ
   B. should have
   C. should
   D. ought to

7. People wait six months for an appointment with him. He _____ a very good doctor.

   A. must be   Ⓐ Ⓑ Ⓒ Ⓓ
   B. may be
   C. should have been
   D. would rather be

8. It's midnight and John's light is still on. _____ studying?

   A. Could he   Ⓐ Ⓑ Ⓒ Ⓓ
   B. Should be
   C. Could he be
   D. Must he be

9. Jenny: Was that Franco in that car?
   Valerie: It _____ him. He left town for his vacation yesterday.

   A. could have been   Ⓐ Ⓑ Ⓒ Ⓓ
   B. couldn't
   C. couldn't have been
   D. shouldn't have

10. Ed: Will the flight be delayed this evening?
    Rosa: It _____. The snowstorm is still very bad.

    A. can't be   Ⓐ Ⓑ Ⓒ Ⓓ
    B. won't
    C. may be
    D. maybe

B Find the underlined word or phrase, A, B, C, or D, that is incorrect. Mark your answer by darkening the oval with the same letter.

1. The extreme weather conditions could

   <u>causing</u> droughts, <u>and</u> <u>food</u> may <u>get</u>
     A   B   C   D

   expensive.

   Ⓐ Ⓑ Ⓒ Ⓓ

2. <u>Would</u> you prefer <u>eat</u> here or <u>in</u> a
     A   B   C

   <u>restaurant</u>?
     D

   Ⓐ Ⓑ Ⓒ Ⓓ

3. <u>It's</u> summer south of the Equator now, so
     A

   it <u>should</u> <u>been</u> warm in Argentina.
   <u> </u>B   C   D

   Ⓐ Ⓑ Ⓒ Ⓓ

4. <u>Would</u> you <u>mind</u> <u>work</u> <u>an extra hour</u> on
     A   B   C   D

   Friday?

   Ⓐ Ⓑ Ⓒ Ⓓ

5. Jack <u>prefer</u> <u>a video game</u> <u>to</u> <u>a walk</u> in
         A   B   C   D

   the park.

   Ⓐ Ⓑ Ⓒ Ⓓ

6. <u>I'm</u> hungry, so <u>let's</u> <u>us</u> <u>start</u> dinner soon.
     A   B   C   D

   Ⓐ Ⓑ Ⓒ Ⓓ

7. <u>May</u> Matt <u>uses</u> your computer tonight, <u>or</u>
     A   B   C

   <u>do</u> you need it?
     D

   Ⓐ Ⓑ Ⓒ Ⓓ

8. Why <u>we don't</u> <u>leave</u> early so we <u>can get</u>
         A   B   C

   there <u>on time</u>?
          D

   Ⓐ Ⓑ Ⓒ Ⓓ

9. He <u>must</u> <u>have sleeping</u> <u>when</u> I <u>called him</u>
       A   B   C   D

   last night.

   Ⓐ Ⓑ Ⓒ Ⓓ

10. I <u>can't</u> help you, <u>but</u> <u>may be</u> Tony <u>can</u>.
        A   B   C   D

    Ⓐ Ⓑ Ⓒ Ⓓ

UNIT 8

THE PASSIVE VOICE, CAUSATIVES, AND PHRASAL VERBS

8a The Passive Voice: Overview

The Colosseum in Rome **was built** by the Romans. Competitions **were held** there. Today, some sports arenas **are named** after this building.

1. To form the passive voice, we change the object of an active voice sentence into the subject of a passive one. The subject of the active sentence can become the agent in a passive sentence. The agent tells who or what did the action in a passive sentence. It is introduced with the preposition *by*.

	Subject	Verb	Object
Active Voice	The pilot	**flew**	the airplane.
Passive Voice	The airplane	**was flown**	by the pilot.

2. We form the passive voice with a form of the verb *be* + a past participle. Questions use an auxiliary verb before the subject.

Subject	*Be*	(Other Auxiliary Verb)	Past Participle	
The Great Wall	**was**		**built**	by the Chinese.
The tourists	**are**	**being**	**shown**	around by the guides.

YES/NO QUESTIONS				
Auxiliary Verb	Subject	(Other Auxiliary Verb)	Past Participle	
Was	the Great Wall		**built**	by the Chinese?
Has	it	**been**	**visited**	by many people?

WH- QUESTIONS				
Wh- Word	Auxiliary Verb	Subject	(Other Auxiliary Verb)	Past Participle
When	**was**	the Great Wall		**built**?
How many people	**has**	it	**been**	**visited** by?

3. We form passive voice sentences with transitive verbs, which take objects. We cannot form passive voice sentences with intransitive verbs.

TRANSITIVE VERB	**fly**
Active Sentence:	The pilot **flew** the plane.
Passive Sentene:	The plane **was flown** by the pilot.

INTRANSITIVE VERB	**arrive**
CORRECT:	The plane arrived on time.
INCORRECT:	The plane ~~was arrived~~ on time.

Some common intransitive verbs are *appear, arrive, become, come, go, happen, occur, rain,* and *stay.* Motion verbs such as *go, come, walk, run,* and *arrive* are often intransitive.

Some transitive verbs do not have passive forms. These include stative verbs such as *cost, fit, have, resemble, suit,* and *weigh.*

CORRECT:	You resemble your father.
INCORRECT:	You ~~are resembled by your father~~.

Some verbs can be either transitive or intransitive. A good dictionary will tell you which verbs are transitive, intransitive, or both. Here are some examples.

Verb	Transitive Use	Intransitive Use
leave	She **left** her keys at home.	She **left** early.
move	I can't **move** that box.	Don't **move.** There's a snake next to your foot.
drive	I can **drive** a truck.	I'm tired. Would you **drive?**
play	We **play** soccer on weekends.	The children **play** nicely together.
work	Can you **work** this machine?	This computer won't **work.**

The Passive Voice, Causatives, and Phrasal Verbs

4. We use the passive voice in the following tenses. Note that the form of *be* is in the same tense as the tense of the active verb.

Tense	Active Voice	Passive Voice
Simple Present	He **washes** the car.	The car **is washed** by him.
Present Progressive	He **is washing** the car.	The car **is being washed** by him.
Present Perfect	He **has washed** the car.	The car **has been washed** by him.
Simple Past	He **washed** the car.	The car **was washed** by him.
Past Progressive	He **was washing** the car.	The car **was being washed** by him.
Past Perfect	He **had washed** the car.	The car **had been washed** by him.
Future with *Will*	He **will wash** the car.	The car **will be washed** by him.
Future with *Be Going To*	He **is going to wash** the car.	The car **is going to be washed** by him.
Future Perfect	He **will have washed** the car.	The car **will have been washed** by him.

We do not use the passive voice with some tenses because they sound awkward. These tenses are the present perfect progressive, the future progressive, the past perfect progressive, and the future perfect progressive.

5. Object pronouns (*me, him, her,* etc.) in the active voice become subject pronouns (*I, he, she,* etc.) in the passive voice.

ACTIVE SENTENCE			PASSIVE SENTENCE		
Subject	Verb	Object	Subject	Verb	
Thousands of people	elected	**her.**	**She**	was elected	(by thousands of people.)
The Chinese	built	**it.**	**It**	was built	(by the Chinese.)

Function

1. We use the passive voice when the agent (who or what does something) is not known or unimportant.

   The Great Wall **was built** hundreds of years ago. (The people who built the wall are not important to the meaning of the sentence.)

2. When we use *by* + an agent, it is usually because the subject of the sentence is more important than the agent, but we want to express them both.

   The economy was hurt **by last year's bad weather.**

We do not use *by* + an agent when the agent is a pronoun such as *you* or *they* used with a general meaning.

> Active Sentence: In this school, you obey the rules. (*you* = people in general)
> Passive Sentence: In this school, the rules are obeyed ~~by you~~.

Sometimes we do not use *by* + an agent because we do not want to mention the agent.

> Teacher: Some very basic grammar errors **were made** in last week's test.
>   (The teacher doesn't want to say who made the errors.)

3. We often use the passive voice to make a sentence more impersonal, in situations involving rules, instructions, announcements, advertisements, or processes.

> Passengers **are requested** to show their passports along with their boarding passes.
> The time of the press conference **will be announced** later today.

4. We often use the passive when the agent is obvious from the meaning of the sentence.

> Olive oil **is used** a lot ~~by Italians~~ in Italy. (It is obvious that Italian people use it.)

☐1☐ Practice

Some of the following statements are true; some are false. If the statement is false, make it negative. Then follow it with a true statement using a word from the list. Use the present or past passive in your statement. If the statement is true, write "true" in the blank. Discuss your answers with a partner.

Alexander Graham Bell   Edmund Hillary and Tenzing Norgay
Brazil   earthquakes
calcium   Greece
discs

1. Coffee is grown in Italy.

   Coffee is not grown in Italy.

   It is grown in Brazil.

2. The telephone was invented by Picasso.

   _____

   _____

3. Bill Gates started Microsoft.

_____

_____

4. The Taj Mahal in India was built by an emperor in memory of his wife.

_____

_____

5. The summit of Mount Everest was reached by Marco Polo.

_____

_____

6. The world's first Olympic Games were held in France.

_____

_____

7. Blood pressure is measured on the Richter scale.

_____

_____

8. *Hamlet* was written by Shakespeare.

_____

_____

9. Sugar is needed for strong bones.

_____

_____

10. Data on a computer is stored on plates.

_____

_____

2 Practice

Rewrite the headlines as complete sentences. Use the present perfect or simple past passive. Make any other changes that are necessary. (Remember that headlines often omit articles and words like *people*.)

1. Movie Star Questioned in Murder Case

   A movie star has been questioned in a murder case. OR

   A movie star was questioned in a murder case.

2. Higher Wages Demanded by Teachers

   _____

3. Twelve Injured in Friday's Earthquake

   _____

4. Plane Captured by Hijackers

   _____

5. Airport Closed; All Flights Canceled (Write two sentences.)

   _____

   _____

6. Ten Hospitalized After Gas Explosion

   _____

3 Practice

Rewrite the following newspaper paragraphs in the passive voice where appropriate. State the agent if it is important to the story.

1.
   Snowstorms have cut off many towns in the north. Snow has blocked the main highway to the north. People are unable to clear the road because the snow is still coming down heavily.

   Many towns in the north have been cut off by snowstorms

   The main highway...

   _____

   _____

2.

Somebody has stolen a total of two million dollars from the National Bank in New York City. Medical emergency workers took two guards to the hospital. The police have arrested three men in connection with the robbery. They are questioning another man.

_____

_____

_____

_____

3.

The Coast Guard found two teenage boys in a small boat far offshore yesterday. The boys and the boat had been missing since last Friday. The two boys were alive but weak. They took the boys to the hospital. Doctors expect them to recover soon.

_____

_____

_____

_____

4.

The police are seeking* two men in connection with a robbery at a gas station. They held up the cashier, but they did not injure him. While they were stealing the money, one of the men tied up the cashier. The men escaped in a black truck which the police think they used in other robberies in the same area.

_____

_____

_____

_____

* _Seek_ means "look for." The past participle of _seek_ is _sought_.

| 4 | Your Turn |

Find or create yourself three newspaper headlines from the news this week. Ask the class to make full passive sentences from each of them. Discuss whether it is possible to write all headlines in the passive voice.

Example:

Local Student Chosen for Big Scholarship—A local student has been chosen for a big scholarship.

8b The Passive Voice of Modals and Modal Phrases

Certain animals should be protected.

1. To form the passive voice of a modal expressing the present or the future, we use a modal + *be* + a past participle.

Subject	Modal	*Be*	Past Participle	
The sign	can		seen	by everyone.
The report	may		finished	on Tuesday.
The car	could*		repaired	in two days.
The work	might		given	to us.
The garbage	should		thrown out.	
His decision	ought to	be	respected.	
The rules	must		obeyed.	
Claudia	has to		told	the truth.
The workers	had better		paid	this week.
We	are supposed to		informed	about the delay.
We	will		invited	to the reception.
The date	is going to		changed.	

*Could can refer to the past, present, or future, depending on the context.

2. To form the passive voice of a perfect modal (modal + *have* + past participle), we use a modal + *have been* + a past participle.

Subject	Modal	*Have Been*	Past Participle	
The project	should		finished	this week.
The Great Wall	must	have been	built	a long time ago.
We	ought to		informed	of the change.
The house	had better		cleaned.	

3. To form the past passive of expressions with *be* or *have,* we use the past forms of those verbs.

Subject	*Be/Have* Expression	Past Participle	
The students	**had to be**	**told**	that the trip had been canceled.
The house	**was supposed to be**	**painted**	the next day.
The computers	**were going to be**	**repaired,**	but weren't.

Function

1. We use the passive of *will* or *going to* to talk about the future.

    A new drug **will be produced** soon.
    More tests **are going to be performed** soon.

2. We use *can* to talk about ability in the present and future. We use *could* to talk about ability in the past.

    Our lives **can be extended** by this drug.
    The computer **could be repaired**, but the monitor **couldn't**.

3. We use *may, might,* and *could* to talk about present or future possibility.

    The new drug **may be tested** on patients this year.
    The drug **could be sold** in pharmacies in a year or two.

4. We use *should, ought to, had better,* and *must* to express advice or necessity.

    It **should be sold** to anyone who wants it.
    It **must be regulated** by law.

5. We use perfect modals with *can, could, should, ought to, may, might, must,* and *had better* to refer to the past.

    They **should have been told** about the change in the schedule.
    This report **must have been written** by one of the best students.
    They **can't have been held up in traffic**. The roads are clear at this hour.

5 Practice

Read about elephants in Sri Lanka. Use the words in parentheses and the passive modal to complete the sentences. Some sentences refer to the past; others refer to the present.

Elephants are very important in Sri Lanka. They are important culturally, as they often lead religious processions. They are also important economically, as they (can/use) _____*can be used*_____ to haul timber. There used to be tens of

1

thousands of wild elephants in Sri Lanka, but now there are only around 3,000.

Why did so many elephants disappear? Some of the working elephants

(may/mistreat) _____ when they got old or sick.

2

Some of the wild elephants (may/shoot) _____ by

3

villagers who were trying to protect their crops. Other elephants

(may/force) _____ to leave the forests as the

4

human population increased over the years.

What (can/do) _____ to help save them?

5

How (can/more elephants/save) _____?

6

Sri Lankan authorities have decided that in the future many elephants

(will/move) _____ to protected

7

areas so people and crops won't be hurt, and the elephants

(can/preserve) _____ in safety. Better conservation

8

programs (will/establish) _____. Wildlife experts say

9

that more (should/do) _____ in the past to protect

10

the elephant population. This gracious and majestic animal

(must/not/allow) _____ to die out.

11

6 **Your Turn**

Write a paragraph about an environmental problem in your community. State the problem and write three or four sentences about what can be done to help solve it. Use passive modals in your sentences.

Example:
There are too many cars in the city where I live. Cars should be banned from downtown. Downtown should be reserved as a pedestrian area. Parking lots could be built near downtown, and people could be taken to the stores and businesses by train or bus.

8c The Passive Voice with *Get; Get* + Adjective

Form

They have to get washed soon.

1. We sometimes use *get* in place of *be* in passive voice sentences.

Subject	*Get*	Past Participle	
I	**got**	**hurt**	by the falling tree branch.
You	**get**	**frightened**	by thunderstorms.
She	**gets**	**bored**	by long movies.
We	**will get**	**paid**	early this month.
They	**might get**	**delayed**	by the snowstorm.

2. We can also use *get* + an adjective. We can use *get* in any tense.

Subject	Get	Adjective
I	**will get**	**angry** if I'm late.
You	**got**	**cold.**
He/She/It	**gets**	**full** after a big meal.
We	**are getting**	**hungry.**
They	**get**	**thirsty** after a run.

3. The past participles of many verbs can be adjectives. We can use them after *get*.

Subject	Get	Past Participle as Adjective	
I	**will get**	**tired**	before the day ends.
He	**gets**	**bored**	quickly.
You	**got**	**scared,**	didn't you?

Function

1. We often use *get* + a past participle or *get* + an adjective in conversation instead of *be* + a past participle or *be* + an adjective. We rarely use the passive voice or *get* + adjective in formal writing.

2. We use *get* to emphasize action or change. We often use *get* in this way to suggest that something happens accidentally, unexpectedly, or unfairly.

   The vase **got broken** when I bumped into the table. (accidentally)
   She got awarded a big prize. (unexpectedly)
   I got blamed for losing the money. (unfairly)

3. When we use *get* + a past participle or an adjective, *get* usually means *become*.

   I **got hungry** by 11:00 in the morning. (= I became hungry by 11:00 in the morning.)

4. In some expressions, *get* does not mean *become*.

   get washed (wash oneself)
   get dressed (dress oneself)
   get started (begin doing something; or begin a trip)

5. We usually use *get,* not *become,* before the words *engaged, married,* and *divorced,* in speech and in writing.

   They **got engaged** last month. (It is possible to say *became engaged,* but this is rather formal.)
   They **got married** at the end of the year. (We do not use *become* with *married.*)
   We **got divorced** in January. (We do not use *become* with *divorced.*)

7 Practice

A. Read about Princess Diana's life. Use *get* + one of the words from the list to complete the missing information. Use the correct tense. (Use *involved* twice.)

blamed	divorced	jealous
criticized	engaged	killed
depressed	involved	married

Princess Diana was born on July 1, 1961. Who could have known then how tragically her life would end? It was in 1980, on a trip to visit the royal family at Balmoral Castle, that she _____*got involved*_____ romantically with Prince Charles. Diana and
1

Charles _____ on July 29, 1981, and from that moment on,
2

Diana was followed everywhere by photographers and journalists. Diana and Charles

_____ in St. Paul's Cathedral in London. But after her marriage,
3

Diana _____ about her life with Charles and the royal family. People
4

said that Charles _____ because of Diana's popularity. She was
5

beautiful and glamorous, but she understood the lives of ordinary people. They had two

sons, but their marriage was not happy. They _____ on August 28th,
6

1996. Afterwards, Diana _____ in humanitarian causes,
7

helping people with AIDS, and campaigning against landmines. On September 6th, 1997,

Diana and her friend Dodi Al Fayed _____ in a car crash in Paris.
8

The Queen wanted a private funeral. But the British public wanted a public funeral to

express their grief. The Queen _____ for not showing enough
9

emotion about Diana's death. In the investigation, the driver of the car, Henri Paul,

_____ for causing the crash by driving when drunk.
10

B. Work with a partner. Ask your partner questions about the facts in the story.

Example:
You: What happened in 1980?
Your partner: Diana got romantically involved with Prince Charles.

8 | Practice

A. Read the sentences about Janice. What kind of person is she? Write *B* for the sentences in which *get* means *become*. Write *O* for sentences with other meanings of *get*.

    _O_   **1.** Janice gets up at 8:00 A.M.

    _B_   **2.** If she doesn't sleep enough, she gets tired by the end of the day.

                3. She gets dressed before having her breakfast.

                4. She gets her briefcase ready the night before.

                5. She gets irritated when the bus is late.

                6. She always gets her work done by the end of the day.

                7. She doesn't like it when her boss gets angry.

                8. She gets bored if she is not busy.

                9. She would like to get another job next year.

                10. She likes to go home before it gets dark.

                11. She usually gets sleepy by 9:00 P.M.

B. Discuss Janice with a partner. Give a reason why each of these characteristics applies (or doesn't apply) to her.

1. Janice is (a) punctual (b) lazy (c) confident.

2. Janice is (a) efficient (b) hardworking (c) impatient.

3. Janice is (a) energetic (b) ambitious (c) nervous.

The Passive Voice, Causatives, and Phrasal Verbs

9 Your Turn

Ask a partner these questions. Do you have the same or different reactions?

Example:

You:	When do you get irritated?
Your partner:	When I get held up in traffic.
You:	I don't get irritated in traffic, but I do get irritated when I have to wait in line for a long time.

1. When do you get angry?
2. When do you get bored?
3. When do you get depressed?
4. When do you get irritated?
5. When do you get worried?

8d *It* + a Passive Voice Verb + a *That* Clause

Form / Function

It **is said that** chocolate is actually good for you.

1. We can use *it* + a passive voice verb + a *that* clause to avoid mentioning an agent. We use this structure with past participles such as *believed, confirmed, considered, estimated, feared, hoped, known, mentioned, reported, said,* and *thought.*

ACTIVE SENTENCE	PASSIVE SENTENCE		
	It	Passive Verb	*That* Clause
People say that he is a billionaire.	**It**	**is said**	**that** he is a billionaire.

2. We can also use the subject of the active *that* clause as the subject of the passive sentence.

ACTIVE SENTENCE	PASSIVE SENTENCE		
	Subject	Passive Verb	*To Be*
People say that he is a billionaire.	He	**is said**	**to be** a billionaire.

10 Practice

Rewrite the sentences using *It is . . . that . . .*

1. We believe that calcium builds strong bones and teeth.

   It is believed that calcium builds strong bones and teeth.

2. We know that fruits and vegetables are important for our health.

   _____

3. Many doctors think that some fruits and grains can help to prevent cancer.

   _____

4. People say that fruit improves your immune system.

   _____

5. We believe that nuts help to lower cholesterol.

   _____

6. Dentists know that eating too much sugar can be bad for our teeth.

   _____

11 Practice

Work with a partner or the class. Complete the following statements with a noun + a passive voice verb. Use the past participles of verbs like *think, say, expect, report, or consider* + the infinitive in parentheses.

1. (to be) *Nora Jones is thought to be* _____ the best singer of

   the decade.

2. (to taste) _____ delicious, but I

   have never eaten it/one/them.

3. (to win) _____ the World Cup

   this year.

4. (to have) _____ a financial

recovery this year.

5. (to be) _____ good for your health.

| 12 | **Your Turn** |

Say or write five sentences with *is said, is known, has been known, is reported,* **etc. Use the following topics or think of your own.**

Example:
The Japanese are known to have a healthy diet.

1. the Japanese
2. hamburgers
3. computers
4. the United States
5. my country

8e   Present and Past Participles Used as Adjectives

Form

Ted felt **frustrated**.

1. We can use present participles* and past participles as adjectives.

Base Verb	Present Participle as Adjective	Past Participle as Adjective
tire	My job is **tiring**.	I'm **tired**.
relax	We had a **relaxing** vacation.	We felt **relaxed**.
excite	The game was **exciting**.	Everyone was **excited**.
shock	The **shocking** news spread quickly.	Shocked citizens demonstrated in the streets.

228

Present and past participles used as adjectives generally describe feelings. The two forms have different meanings.

1. Present participial adjectives describe someone or something that causes a feeling.

>   The game was **exciting** (to me).
>   Ted is **boring** (to Sandra).

2. Past participial adjectives describe someone who experiences a feeling.

>   I am **bored**. (by the movie).
>   He is really **confused** (by the question).

3. Here are some common participles used as adjectives.

Present Participle	Past Participle
amazing	amazed
amusing	amused
boring	bored
confusing	confused
depressing	depressed
embarrassing	embarrassed
exhausting	exhausted
frightening	frightened
impressive	impressed
interesting	interested
relaxing	relaxed
shocking	shocked
surprising	surprised

Present participle is another term for verb + -ing.

13 Practice

Read the story about a terrifying experience. Underline the correct adjectives in each underlined pair.

I had a (terrified / <u>terrifying</u>) experience when I went to Michigan a few years ago.
                          1
I had been driving all day, and I was completely (exhausted / exhausting). I stopped at
                                                                    2
the first hotel I could find. It was an old hotel near the center of a small town. The hotel

looked a little rundown, and its dark windows were quite (depressed / depressing), but I
                                                                        3
was so (tired / tiring) that I couldn't drive any farther to look for a better place. The desk
          4
clerk looked very (surprised / surprising) that I had stopped there. The hotel wasn't cheap,
                    5
and when I saw the room, it was a little (disappointed / disappointing). I didn't notice any
                                                        6
other guests around. I went to my room and tried to watch TV, but all the programs were

(bored / boring). So I decided to read for a while until I felt (relax / relaxing) enough to
    7   **8**
fall asleep. Suddenly I heard a strange creaking noise outside my door. It was very dark.

I couldn't see anything through the window. I was really (frightened / frightening). I went
                                                                        9
back to bed. Then I heard the sound again, so I leapt out of bed and opened the door.

There was nothing there at all, but I noticed the front of the door was covered in scratch

marks. I packed all my things and ran for my car. I have never been so (terrified / terrifying)
                                                                                    10
in all my life.

14 Your Turn

Work with a partner. Tell your partner about an experience you have had. It can be a terrifying experience, an amusing experience, or an interesting experience. Use some present or past participles in your description.

8f Causative Sentences with *Have*, *Get*, and *Make*: Active Voice

Form

I **have** the optician **check** my eyes every year.

1. We can form causative sentences with *have, get,* and *make* as the main verb.

THE CAUSATIVE WITH *HAVE* AND *MAKE*

Subject	Have/Make	Object	Base Verb
We	**have**	**our son**	**do** the dishes.
She	**had**	**her assistant**	**copy** the report.
The boss	**is going to make**	**everyone**	**work** late.
Tom's mother	**can make**	**him**	**stay** home tonight.

THE CAUSATIVE WITH *GET*

Subject	Get	Object	To + Base Verb
Tom	**gets**	**his sister**	**to do** the dishes for him.
I	**got**	**my friend**	**to drive** me here.
We	**are going to get**	**the store**	**to give** us a refund.
The boss	**should get**	**the staff**	**to work** late tonight.

2. We use a base verb after *have* and *make,* but we use *to* + a base verb after *get.*

3. We can use any tense or modal that makes sense in causative sentences.

4. We use the normal rules to form negative statements, questions, and short answers with the causative.

Negative Statements	We **don't make** our son do the dishes. She **didn't have** her assistant copy the report. The boss **isn't going to make** everyone work late. Tom's mother **might not make** him stay home tonight. Tom **didn't get** his sister to do the dishes for him.	
Yes/No Questions and Answers	**Do** you **have** your son do the dishes? **Did** she **have** her assistant copy the report? **Is** the boss **going to make** everyone work late? **Can** Tom's mother **make** him stay home tonight? **Did** you **get** your friend to drive you here?	No, I **don't.** Yes, she **did.** No, he**'s not.** Yes, she **can.** Yes, I **did.**
Wh-Questions and Answers	Who **gets** his sister to do the dishes for him? Who **does** Tom **get** to do the dishes for him? What **does** Tom **get** his sister to do? Who **made** Tom do the dishes? What **did** she **have** her assistant copy? Where **did** they **have** the taxi take them? When **will** you **have** the students take the test? Why **did** you **make** the children go to bed?	Tom **does.** His sister. The dishes. His mother **did.** The report. To the train station. Tomorrow. Because they were tired.

Function

1. We use the causative to talk about something that we require or arrange for someone else to do.

> I **had** the stylist **cut** my hair really short. (It's the stylist's job to cut my hair. I told him to cut it really short.)

2. We use *have* in a causative sentence when we normally expect someone, like a salesperson in a store, to do something for us.

> He **had** the salesperson **show** him 12 pairs of shoes.
> My boss **has** us **prepare** a progress report every week.

3. We use *get* when there is some difficulty involved, or when we have to persuade someone to do what we want.

> It took a long time, but I finally **got** my boss to **let** me take a week off.
> The teenager **got** his parents to **let** him take the car, but they told him to be very careful.

4. We use *make* when one person has power and/or authority over another. The person who does the action does not want to do it.

> The children's mother **made** them go to bed. (The mother has authority and power.)
> The robber **made** the clerk give him the money. (The robber does not have authority but does have power.)

15 Practice

A famous film director, Robert Ebbits, is traveling to New York City. His personal assistant is giving the hotel instructions. Rewrite the sentences as causatives.

Assistant: Mr. Ebbits will be arriving at your hotel tomorrow, and I want to make sure that everything is arranged for him.

Hotel Receptionist: Yes, of course. What can I do for you?

1. He likes to wake up punctually at 6:00 A.M. (have/the front desk/call him)

   Please have the front desk call him at 6:00 A.M.

2. He likes to read three daily newspapers first thing in the morning. (have/bellhop/deliver)

   _____

3. He likes to have fresh fruit and coffee for breakfast at 7:00 A.M. (have/room service/bring)

   _____

4. He doesn't like fresh flowers in his room. (have/the florist/put)

   Don't _____

5. He needs three shirts to be washed every day. (have/the laundry/wash)

   _____

6. He needs a computer, an Internet connection, a fax machine, and a flat-screen TV installed in his room as soon as he checks in. (get/the technical staff/install)

   _____

7. He wants his shoes polished and left outside his door every morning. (have/the bellhop/polish)

   _____

8. He needs a limousine waiting for him in front of the hotel each day at 9:00 A.M. (get/a chauffeur/bring)

   _____

8g Causative Sentences with *Have* and *Get*: Passive Voice

Mary is **getting** the house **cleaned** because her in-laws are coming tomorrow.

1. We can form passive causative sentences with *have* and *get,* but not with *make.*

Subject	*Have/Get*	Object	Past Participle	
I	**have**	**my hair**	**styled**	by Lorenzo.
We	**have had**	**our car**	**serviced**	twice this year.
She	**had**	**her winter coat**	**cleaned**	last week.
He	**is getting**	**his car**	**washed**	this afternoon.
You	**should get**	**your eyes**	**tested**	soon.

2. When we use *have* or *get* in a passive causative sentence, we do not use *to* with the past participle.

   CORRECT: He got his hair cut.
   INCORRECT: He got his hair ~~to~~ cut.

3. We can use the causative with modals and in all tenses.

4. We use the normal rules to form negative statements, questions, and short answers.

Negative Statements	I **don't have** my hair styled by Lorenzo. He **isn't getting** his car washed this afternoon.	
Yes/No Questions	**Did** she **have** her winter coat cleaned last week? **Should** I **get** my eyes tested?	Yes, she **did.** No, you **shouldn't.**
Wh- Questions	Who **had** the car serviced? What **did** John **have** serviced?	John **did.** The car.

1. We use the passive form of the causative when we want to stress what was done and not who did it. We do not use *by* + an agent when we don't know who did it, or when it is not important who did it.

   > She **has** her hair **styled** every week.
   > I **got** the refrigerator **fixed**.

2. We use a *by* + an agent when it is important to mention the person doing the service.

   > She **has** her hair **styled** by Lorenzo. (The speaker wants to mention the agent, Lorenzo.)
   > I must **get** my suit **cleaned** this week. (The speaker is not interested in mentioning the agent.)

3. We can use the causative with *have* when something unpleasant or unexpected happens to someone.

   > We **had** our passports **stolen** when we went on vacation.

16 Practice

Write one sentence about what you can have done (or get done) at each of these places.

1. copy shop	3. garage	5. laundromat	7. optician's
2. dentist's office	4. hair salon	6. dry cleaner's	8. tailor's

1. *You can get copies made at a copy shop. You can also get them bound.*

2. _____

3. _____

4. _____

5. _____

6. _____

7. _____

8. _____

Your Turn

What things would you have someone do for you, or have done for you, if you were in these situations? Talk with a partner.

Example:
If I were in the hospital, I would have my husband bring me something to read, and I would have flowers delivered.

1. if you were staying in an expensive hotel
2. if you were the president of a huge company
3. if you were in the hospital with a broken leg

8h Phrasal Verbs

Form / Function

They're **putting on** makeup.

1. Phrasal verbs are very common in English. A phrasal verb consists of a verb + a particle. A particle is an adverb such as *up, down, away, out*. A verb followed by a particle has a different meaning from the verb alone. Sometimes we can guess the meaning of a phrasal verb.

   We **stood up**. (We got on our feet from a seated position.)

2. Sometimes we cannot guess the meaning of a phrasal verb. In these cases, we have to learn the special meaning of the phrasal verb.

   I'll **look up** the word. (I'll find information about the word in a dictionary, thesaurus, etc.)

INTRANSITIVE PHRASAL VERBS

3. Some phrasal verbs are intransitive. They do not take objects.

Subject	Verb + Particle
My car	**broke down** last night.
They	**eat out** every Saturday night.

Here are some common intransitive phrasal verbs.

Phrasal Verb	Meaning	Phrasal Verb	Meaning
break out	happen suddenly and unexpectedly	go out	leave the house; not stay home
break down	stop working (as a machine)	grow up	become an adult
break up	separate	hang up	end a phone conversation
dress up	put on nice clothes	show up	appear; be present
eat out	eat in a restaurant	speak up	speak loud/louder
fall down	fall to the ground	stand up	arise from a sitting position
get up	arise from a bed or a chair	start over	begin again
give up	stop trying to do something	stay up	remain awake
go down/up	increase/decrease	take off	go up (as an airplane); suddenly succeed (as a business); leave (informal)
go on	continue	work out	exercise

Some of these phrasal verbs can take objects, but the meaning is different.
Phrasal verbs, like other verbs, can have different meanings.

> The plane **took off** on time. (intransitive.)
> We **took off our coats** because it was too warm.
> (transitive; *take off = remove a piece of clothing*.)

4. Some intransitive phrasal verbs can be followed by a prepositional phrase, but the meaning of the phrasal verb does not change.

> Bob and June **broke up**.
> June **broke up with** Bob.
>
> I **get up** every time I hear a noise.
> She **got up from** her chair when the visitor arrived.

TRANSITIVE PHRASAL VERBS

5. Most phrasal verbs are transitive. Transitive verbs take objects.

Phrasal Verb	Object
Take off	your shoes.

There are two kinds of transitive phrasal verbs: separable and inseparable. Separable phrasal verbs are very common. Inseparable phrasal verbs are less common.

6. With separable phrasal verbs, the particle can go before or after a noun object. But when the object is a pronoun, the particle always follows the object.

	Subject	Verb	Particle	Object	Particle	
SEPARABLE PHRASAL VERBS						
Noun Object	I	**take**	**out**	the garbage		every morning.
	I	**take**		the garbage	**out**	every morning.
Pronoun Object	I	**take**		it	**out**	every morning.

INCORRECT: I take ~~out it~~.

7. With inseparable phrasal verbs, the particle always goes before the object.

	Subject	Verb	Particle	Object	
INSEPARABLE PHRASAL VERBS					
Noun Object	She	**got**	**over**	**her cold**	quickly.
Pronoun Object	She	**got**	**over**	**it**	quickly.

INCORRECT: We ~~came an interesting museum across~~.
INCORRECT: She ~~got her cold over quickly~~.

Here are some common separable and inseparable phrasal verbs and their meanings. Some of these phrasal verbs have additional meanings. Check a dictionary for other meanings.

Separable Phrasal Verbs	Meaning	Separable Phrasal Verbs	Meaning
bring up	raise a child; state something/someone as a topic	put on	place a piece of clothing on your body
call off	cancel something	set up	arrange for something
call up	telephone someone	start over	start something again
do over	do something again	tear down	destroy something completely
drop off	leave someone/ something somewhere	think over	reflect on someone/something
give up	quit something	think up	invent something
go over	review something	turn down	lower the volume on something
leave out	omit someone/ something	turn up	increase the volume on something
pick up	meet someone and take him/her somewhere	use up	use something until there is no more
put back	place something in its original location	wake up	cause someone to stop sleeping
put off	postpone someone/ something	work out	solve something

Inseparable Phrasal Verbs	Meaning
call for	come get someone
check into	register at a hotel; inquire into something
come across	find or discover someone/something by chance
get over	recover from something
go over	review something
look after	take care of someone/something
look into	investigate something
put up with	tolerate someone/something
run into	meet someone by chance

Practice

Read Mr. Jackson's schedule. Then answer the questions. Use pronouns in your answers. Remember that the position of pronouns is different for separable and inseparable phrasal verbs.

From: Company Management Tour Services

To: Interglobal Corporation, Inc.

Re: Mr. Jackson's Schedule, April 16–18, 20XX

16 April

Pick up Mr. Jackson from the airport at 6:45 P.M.

Drop off Mr. Jackson at his hotel at 7:30 P.M.

Mr. Jackson will check into the hotel at 7:35 P.M.

Meet tour guide who will look after Mr. Jackson during his stay.

17 April

Tour guide will call for Mr. Jackson at 7:00 A.M.

Set up a meeting to discuss the contract with the president at 9:00 A.M.

If the president decides to call off the meeting, we will call up Mr. Jackson immediately.

Afternoon and evening free; guided tour of city.

18 April

Pick up Mr. Jackson from the hotel at 10:30 A.M.

Meeting with president to go over the contract from 11:00 to 12:30 P.M.

Drop off Mr. Jackson at the airport at 1:15 P.M.

1. What time will they pick up Mr. Jackson from the airport?

   They will pick him up at 6:45 P.M.

2. What time will they drop off Mr. Jackson at his hotel?

   _____

3. What time will Mr. Jackson check into his hotel?

   _____

4. Who will look after Mr. Jackson during his stay?

   _____

5. What time will the tour guide call for Mr. Jackson the next morning?

   _____

6. For what time will they set up a meeting with the president?

   _____

7. What will they do if the president decides to call off the meeting?

   _____

8. What time will they pick up Mr. Jackson from the hotel on the final day?

   _____

9. When will Mr. Jackson go over the contract with the president?

   _____

10. What time will they drop off Mr. Jackson at the airport?

    _____

19 Practice

A. Complete the sentences with particles from the list. Use *down* two times. Use *up* four times.

across	out
after	over
down	up

I was born and brought _____*up*_____ in Madrid. I was left alone a lot as a child and

1

learned to look _____ myself. I did a lot of reading. One winter, while I was

2

getting _____ the flu, I came _____ a book about Sherlock Holmes, the

3   4

famous fictional detective. I loved it! And that's when I started thinking _____

5

mystery stories of my own and writing them _____. I designed elaborate covers for

6

the books and used _____ all the paper in the house. I gave them as presents to

7

my family and challenged them to work _____ the solution to the crimes in my

8

stories. My mother tried to get me to give _____ mystery stories and try some

9

other form of fiction, but it was no good. Even now that I am older, I still read mysteries

in my spare time. There's nothing like a good mystery to calm you _____ after a

10

hectic day.

B. Here is a list of synonyms for the phrasal verbs in part A. Write each phrasal verb next to the correct synonym.

1. find by accident   *come across* _____

2. invent   _____

3. make a note of   _____

4. quit   _____

5. raise   _____

6. recover from   _____

7. relax   _____

8. solve   _____

9. take care of   _____

10. use all of   _____

20 Your Turn

Take turns asking a partner these questions. Each one has a synonym for a phrasal verb in italics. In your answer, use a phrasal verb with a similar meaning as the italicized verb.

Example:
You: Where were you *raised*?
Your partner: I was *brought up* in Monterrey.

1. Where were you *raised*?

   _____

2. Who *cared for* you when you were a child?

   _____

3. Describe a day when you *found something by accident*.

   _____

   _____

   _____

4. Do you find it easy to *invent* excuses? Describe one time when you needed to invent and excuse.

   _____

   _____

   _____

5. When do you usually *exercise*? What kind of exercise do you do?

   _____

   _____

6. How do you go about *solving* a problem?

   _____

   _____

   _____

7. What kind of food or drink would you like to *quit*?

   _____

8. What makes you *feel relaxed* after a hectic day?

   _____

   _____

The Passive Voice, Causatives, and Phrasal Verbs

8i ◆ Prepositions Following Verbs, Adjectives, and Nouns; Other Combinations with Prepositions

Alberto is **thinking about** something.

We use prepositions not only to show time, place, manner, and agent, but also in combination with verbs, adjectives, and nouns, and in many common expressions.

1. We use many verbs together with specific prepositions.

> You must **concentrate on** your work!
> I love to **listen to** the birds in the early morning.

Here are some common examples of verb and preposition combinations.*

Preposition	Examples			
about	think about	dream about		
at	laugh at	shout at	smile at	
for	account for	fight for	search for	wait for
from	come from	derive from	recover from	
in	believe in	delight in	result in	
of	think of	dream of		
on	concentrate on	depend on	plan on	rely on
	insist on			
to	belong to	contribute to	listen to	lead to
	speak to			

*Some verbs can take more than one preposition. For example, if you think **about** something, you consider it. If you think **of** something, it comes to your mind.

I **thought about** the problem all night.
I **thought of** a great place to go on Saturday night.

2. We use many adjectives with specific prepositions.

Are you **worried about** the test?
We are very **proud of** her.

Preposition	Examples			
about	angry about	excited about	worried about	
at	bad at	expert at	good at	surprised at (also *by*)
for	responsible for			
from	free from			
in	interested in	successful in (also *at*)		
of	afraid of	aware of	envious of	fond of
	proud of	tired of	typical of	
to	compared to	essential to	married to	opposed to
	related to	similar to		
with	bored with (also *by*)	disappointed with	pleased with	

3. We use many nouns with specific prepositions.

The **cost of food** has risen.
The senator didn't like the **results of the government's policies**.
I didn't know the **answer to her question**.

Preposition	Examples			
for	demand for	need for	reason for	
in	change in	decrease in	increase in	rise in
of	cause of	cost of	danger of	evidence of	example of
	possibility of	result of	supply of	trace of	use of
on	impact on			
to	answer to	invitation to	reaction to	reply to	solution to
	threat to			

4. Here are some other common expressions that end in prepositions.

Preposition	Examples			
of	as a result of	because of	in spite of	in view of
	on account of	on behalf of	with the exception of	
to	according to	prior to		

5. There are also many common expressions that begin with prepositions.

Preposition	Examples			
at	at first	at last	at present	at the moment
	at times			
by	by accident	by chance	by land	by sea
	by air	by day	by night	
in	in common	in existence	in general	in the future
	in the past			
on	on fire	on land	on purpose	on the other hand
	on the whole			

21 Practice

Complete the sentences in each section with phrases from the list from that section.

A.
Nouns + Prepositions

an increase in   a threat to   one example of
an impact on   changes in

What is global warming? Global warming is _____*an increase in*_____ the earth's
                                                                    1
temperature, which in turn causes many _____ climate. These
                                                          2
changes may have _____ plants, wildlife, and humans.
                                3
_____ a change caused by global warming is the rise in sea level,
                4
which may be _____ coastal communities and the people and
                              5
animals that live there.

B.
Adjectives + Prepositions

essential to   free of   opposed to   responsible for

What causes global warming? Most of the energy that is _____

1

the creation of the light and heat in our homes is produced by burning coal and gas, which

produces carbon dioxide. The carbon dioxide traps heat in the earth's atmosphere. Carbon

dioxide is _____ about half of our global warming. Many

2

environmentalists are _____ fossil fuels like coal and gas. They say

3

we should try to develop energy that is _____ pollution, such as

4

wave or wind energy. Then it will be possible to protect the climate as well as the animals

and people who live on the earth.

C.
Verbs + Prepositions

account for   contribute to   result in
come from   recover from

Another cause of global warming is a reduction in ozone in the outer layer of the

earth's atmosphere. Ozone is a gas that absorbs ultraviolet (UV) rays that

_____ the sun. Chlorofluorocarbons (CFCs) are chemicals that are

1

used in aerosols, air conditioners, refrigerators, and throwaway food containers. Scientists

believe that CFCs _____ the destruction of the ozone layer and

2

_____ a thinner layer of ozone in the outer atmosphere. As more of

3

the sun's ultraviolet rays enter our atmosphere, this _____ an

4

increase in cases of skin cancer. What can we do? Using CFC-free products is one way to

help our planet to _____ the damaging effects of ozone depletion.

5

---

[22] **Your Turn**

Talk with a partner about the causes and effects of global warming. Can you think of any solutions? Use some of the noun, verb, and adjective + preposition combinations from Practice 21.

REVIEW

1 Review (8a, 8e, 8i)

Underline the correct words.

Wouldn't you like to be able to (have / <u>get</u>) the weather to do what you want? Do you ever (get angry / have anger) because the weather is (depressing / depressed) and you want to have a (relaxing / relaxed) day at the beach? Well, you're not alone. Everyone would like their wishes to (be obeyed / obey). However, the weather (is obeying / obeys) no one. Everyone should delight (in / about) that fact because the weather has a big impact (on / for) our planet and is essential (on / to) our survival.

The sun (got worshipped / was worshipped) by ancient people. They believed (in / on) its importance to life on earth even though they didn't understand how it makes plants grow and how it affects the weather. The sun is (amazed / amazing). Our air, oceans, and land (are heated / heat) by the sun's energy. As the seasons change, the Earth (is / has) bathed in different amounts of energy from the sun. The result (for / of) this is a planet that has areas of hot and cold. The weather (gets / is getting) powered by these differences. Huge areas of hot and cold air (have / are) created by the heat and cold coming off water and land. These air masses must (have moved / move), or the cold areas (would get / are getting) colder, and the hot areas (would get / are getting) hotter. Fortunately, the earth keeps everything (on / in) balance by moving cold water and air from the poles toward the tropics, while warm water and air flow from the tropics toward the poles. As these areas of heat and cold move (around / over) and meet, wind, rain, and storms (are / have) produced. Crops grow, rivers run, and life on our planet goes (about / on).

Are you (having / going) to make the weather change? No, of course not. But (in / on) reality, you don't really want to.

2 Review (8a, 8b, 8d)

Read about Zanskar. Use the words in parentheses and the passive voice to complete the sentences. Some sentences require present tense verbs; others require past tense verbs.

High in India's western Himalayas, there is a kingdom called Zanskar. It (say)

___is said/has been said___ that Zanskar is invisible because it (know)
           1

_____ by so few people in the outside world.
        2

For nine months every year, the Sensi-la Pass into Zanskar (block)

_____ by snow. In the winter, there is only one route that
        3

(can, take) _____ by travelers. It is a 112-mile journey through a
           4

deep canyon on a frozen river. Traffic (can, carry) _____ on the river
                  5

for only a few short weeks each year before the ice starts to melt. It is a very dangerous

journey. Along the way, shelter (provide) _____ to travelers by caves
                  6

200 to 300 feet high on the canyon walls. Shelter (provide) _____
                  7

by these caves for at least a thousand years. Because Zanskar is so remote, it has remained

independent for over 900 years. During this time, kingdoms around it (conquer)

_____ by outside armies many times.
        8

The little-known kingdom of Zanskar (rule) _____ by unknown
                9

kings from 930 to 1836 C.E. Then it (take over) _____ by the Hindu
              10

Dogras. In 1846, Zanskar (seized) _____ by the British, who never
           11

set foot on the land. Neither the Dogras nor the British ever took any interest in Zanskar.

In fact, Zanskar (ignore) _____ by most explorers until the
           12

1820s, when the country (visit) _____ for the first time by a
           13

European. He was a Hungarian student named Alexander Csoma de Koros. Csoma de Koros

was no ordinary student. It (can, say) _____ that he performed one
           14

The Passive Voice, Causatives, and Phrasal Verbs

of the greatest achievements in travel for his day when he crossed Asia alone on foot.

In his travels, de Koros had met an English explorer named William Moorcroft who advised him to study the Tibetan language. After that, Csoma de Koros (introduce) _____ by Moorcroft to the King of Zanskar's secretary.

15

Csoma de Koros (invite) _____ to spend time at a Zanskar monastery.

16

He stayed there a year and returned one of Europe's first Tibetan scholars.

3 Review (8f–8g)

Complete the sentences using *have, get,* or *make* and the verbs in parentheses in the active or passive voice. Use the correct tense.

1. Even though we're busy, I _____*got*_____ my boss (give) _____
   me the day off tomorrow.

2. When I was a child, I didn't like to do house work, but my mother _____
   me (clean) _____ my room before I could go out to play.

3. I _____ my computer (upgrade) _____ twice since I've
   owned it.

4. I _____ the painter (paint) _____ the room again after
   he painted it with the wrong color.

5. How does that teacher _____ her students (stay) _____
   so quiet?

6. My knee has been hurting for a week. I really have to _____ it
   (examine) _____ by a doctor.

7. My son's grades are too low. From now on, I _____ him
   (finish) _____ his homework before he goes out to play with his friends.

8. When will you _____ the students (take) _____ their
   examinations?

9. Who will John _____ (help) _____ him paint his apartment?

10. How can I _____ her (wear) _____ this dress if she
    doesn't want to?

4 Review (8h–8i)

Complete the sentences with phrases from the list.

demand for	pick up	tear up
dream of	solution to	trace of
impact on	take off	use up

At times, hikers _____*dream of*_____ getting extra help along the trail.* A day of
          1

hiking with a backpack full of equipment can _____ a lot of energy.
                                                    2

Well, now there's a new _____ the problem. You can
                              3

_____ that heavy backpack and _____ your
         4   5

pace, because llamas are here to help. In South America, llamas have worked as pack

animals that carry heavy loads for 6,000 years. But now there's a new

_____ them among hikers throughout the U.S. and Canada. One of
         6

the big advantages of using llamas is their low _____ the
                                                       7

environment. They don't _____ the trail like horses and mules.**
                               8

They leave barely a _____ their visit.
                            9

*trail: A path used for hiking, horseback riding, etc.
**mule: An animal that is a cross between a donkey and a horse

5 Review (8c, 8h)

Find the errors and correct them.

Melinda: Did you hear that Joe and Marian are ~~being~~ married? [*getting* written above *being*]

Patrick: No way! They broke last month.

Melinda: They did, but I guess they decided to start out. Anyway, I don't know how she

puts with him.

Patrick: Him! You're not trying to have me believe that he's the problem, are you?

Melinda: No, you're right. Their problems must cause by both of them. I still can't believe

they're engaged. Do you think we can get them change their minds?

Patrick: I doubt it. Remember what write by Shakespeare: "Love is blind." Anyway,

don't be so worry. They'll work up their problems. They'll probably end over

being very happy.

WRITING: Write a Cover Letter

When you send an application form or a résumé to a company or a school, you send a cover letter with it. The purpose of a cover letter is to make the reader interested in reading your résumé or application. A cover letter has the format of a business letter (see page 207).

Step 1. Pay attention to the format and organization of this letter.

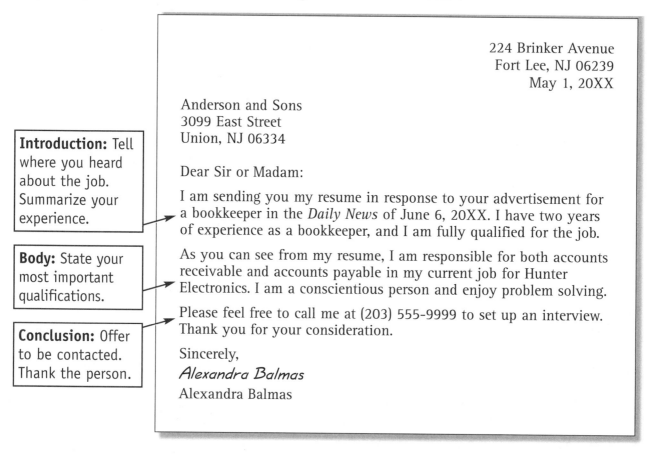

Introduction: Tell where you heard about the job. Summarize your experience.

Body: State your most important qualifications.

Conclusion: Offer to be contacted. Thank the person.

224 Brinker Avenue
Fort Lee, NJ 06239
May 1, 20XX

Anderson and Sons
3099 East Street
Union, NJ 06334

Dear Sir or Madam:

I am sending you my resume in response to your advertisement for a bookkeeper in the *Daily News* of June 6, 20XX. I have two years of experience as a bookkeeper, and I am fully qualified for the job.

As you can see from my resume, I am responsible for both accounts receivable and accounts payable in my current job for Hunter Electronics. I am a conscientious person and enjoy problem solving.

Please feel free to call me at (203) 555-9999 to set up an interview. Thank you for your consideration.

Sincerely,
Alexandra Balmas
Alexandra Balmas

Step 2. Write a cover letter for a job that you would like to have. Type it on plain white paper (use a computer if possible). Send an original, not a photocopy.

Step 3. Evaluate your letter.

Checklist

_____ Did you use the format of the example letter?

_____ Did you follow the organizational model of the example letter?

_____ Do you think your letter would interest the reader? Would you get an interview?

Step 4. Work with a partner or a teacher to edit your letter. Check spelling, vocabulary, and grammar.

Step 5. Write your final copy.

A **Choose the best answer, A, B, C, or D, to complete the sentence. Mark your answer by darkening the oval with the same letter.**

1. You have to get a photo _____ for your passport.

   A. taking (A) (B) (C) (D)
   B. took
   C. taken
   D. to take

2. This is an example _____ a multiple-choice question.

   A. of (A) (B) (C) (D)
   B. in
   C. at
   D. to

3. I am going to the dentist next week to have _____.

   A. my teeth clean (A) (B) (C) (D)
   B. clean my teeth
   C. my teeth cleaned
   D. cleaning my teeth

4. The test results _____ next Monday.

   A. will have posted (A) (B) (C) (D)
   B. will posted
   C. will post
   D. will be posted

5. Hurry up and _____!

   A. get dress (A) (B) (C) (D)
   B. get dressed
   C. to get dressed
   D. getting dressed

6. _____ there was once water on the planet Mars.

   A. It is said that (A) (B) (C) (D)
   B. It is said to
   C. They say it was
   D. Says it

7. Ted is _____ about what to do.

   A. confuse (A) (B) (C) (D)
   B. confusing
   C. confused
   D. get confused

8. _____ the facts, we need more time.

   A. In view to (A) (B) (C) (D)
   B. In view of
   C. On view of
   D. By view of

9. I was late, so I _____.

   A. woke up him (A) (B) (C) (D)
   B. woke him up
   C. wake him
   D. him wake up

10. She's very _____ her job.

   A. a success in (A) (B) (C) (D)
   B. successful in
   C. successful for
   D. successful with

B   **Find the underlined word or phrase, A, B, C, or D, that is incorrect. Mark your answer by darkening the oval with the same letter.**

1. Today's meeting <u>was postponed</u> <u>because of</u>
                    A   **B**
   a schedule conflict and a new time for the
   meeting <u>will been</u> <u>announced</u> later today.
            C   **D**

   Ⓐ Ⓑ Ⓒ Ⓓ

2. There has been an <u>increase in</u> demand for
                   A
   the buildings that <u>were built</u> in this area
                 B
   at the turn of the century; that is why
   they <u>are be</u> <u>renovated by</u> investors.
       C   **D**

   Ⓐ Ⓑ Ⓒ Ⓓ

3. Diamonds <u>are found</u> <u>in</u> different colors
           A   **B**
   and, <u>on general</u>, only shine when they
        C
   <u>are cut and polished</u>.
         D

   Ⓐ Ⓑ Ⓒ Ⓓ

4. A strange <u>coincidence</u> <u>was happened</u> when
            A   **B**
   the news <u>was</u> <u>announced</u> this
        C   **D**
   morning.

   Ⓐ Ⓑ Ⓒ Ⓓ

5. Some kinds of <u>fish cannot</u> <u>be ate</u>
              A   **B**
   <u>because of</u> contamination <u>from</u> industrial
     C   **D**
   waste.

   Ⓐ Ⓑ Ⓒ Ⓓ

6. In the past, <u>it was said</u> <u>that computers</u>
             A   **B**
   were too <u>complicating</u> for people to use
           C
   and <u>would be used</u> only for scientific
        D
   purposes.

   Ⓐ Ⓑ Ⓒ Ⓓ

7. <u>It is best</u> not <u>to leave out</u> multiple choice
     A   **B**
   questions on a test and <u>go them over</u>
                    C
   <u>at the end</u>.
     D

   Ⓐ Ⓑ Ⓒ Ⓓ

8. Everyone <u>was amazing</u> that
           A
   the painting <u>was stolen</u> with
            B
   <u>all the security precautions</u>
           C
   <u>were taken</u>.
     D

   Ⓐ Ⓑ Ⓒ Ⓓ

9. After the ancient artifacts <u>discovered</u>,
                    A
   construction on the site <u>was stopped</u>
                 B
   <u>by</u> the <u>city</u>.
     C   **D**

   Ⓐ Ⓑ Ⓒ Ⓓ

10. We <u>will have</u> <u>our computers service</u> next
         A   **B**
    week <u>by a company</u> that
         C
    <u>was recommended</u> by the bank.
        D

    Ⓐ Ⓑ Ⓒ Ⓓ

UNIT 9

GERUNDS AND INFINITIVES

9a ◆ Gerunds as Subjects and Objects; Verbs Followed by Gerunds

Daydreaming is useful.
Wanda **enjoys daydreaming.**

1. A gerund is a base verb + *-ing* that works like a noun. For example, a gerund can be a subject or an object in a sentence.

GERUND AS SUBJECT

Gerund Subject	Verb	
Painting	is	my favorite hobby.
Cycling	is	good exercise.
Scuba diving	takes	a lot of money.

GERUND AS OBJECT

Subject	Verb	Gerund Object
I	enjoy	**painting.**
He	stopped	**cycling.**

2. A gerund is always singular. When one gerund is the subject of a sentence, it takes a singular verb.

    Painting makes me happy.

    But if two gerunds form a subject, the verb is plural.

    Cycling and **diving are** my favorite sports.

3. Do not confuse a gerund with the present progressive.

    Cycling is a good sport. (*Cycling* is a gerund.)
    He **is cycling** in the park right now. (*Cycling* is part of the present progressive verb.)

1. We use a gerund as a noun.

   Painting is relaxing for me.

2. We can use a gerund after the following verbs and verb phrases.

admit	finish	quit
appreciate	give up	recall
avoid	imagine	resent
can't help	involve	resist
consider	keep/keep on	risk
continue	(not) mind	stand
delay	postpone	suggest
deny	practice	tolerate
discuss	prevent	understand
enjoy	put off	

   Have you **finished doing** your homework?
   I **enjoy walking** in the rain.

3. We usually use *go* + a gerund to describe recreational activities.

   We **went sightseeing** yesterday.
   Let's **go surfing**.

   Here are some expressions with *go* + a gerund.

go biking	go hiking	go shopping
go bowling	go hunting	go skating
go camping	go jogging	go skiing
go canoeing	go running	go swimming
go dancing	go sailing	go sightseeing
go fishing	go scuba diving	go surfing

1 Practice

Complete the sentences with the gerund form of verbs from the list.

camp	cycle	exercise	sail	sleep
climb	dive	jog	ski	swim

We are a very active family. In the winter, when there is snow, we pack up our skis and

go _____*skiing*_____ every weekend. In the summer, we take our tents and go

_____2_____ in the mountains. Our son Mark prefers mountain

_____3_____. We often go to the coast and do a lot of _____4_____,

_____5_____, and _____6_____. During the week, I take my running

shoes to work so I can go _____7_____ on my lunch break if the weather is good.

And when my husband gets home from work, he takes his bike and goes

_____8_____ for an hour or so. _____9_____ regularly is very good for

our health, and we're usually so tired at the end of the day that we don't have any

problems _____10_____ at night.

2 Practice

Rewrite the sentences using gerunds.

1. The doctor said I could get heart disease.

The doctor said I risk _getting heart disease_

2. "It might be a good idea to go on a diet," she said.

She suggested _____

3. I decided not to drink coffee.

I decide to give up _____

4. It's difficult not to drink coffee when I'm tired.

It's difficult to avoid _____

5. I think that I shouldn't eat ice cream.

I want to stop _____

6. I sometimes buy a small bag of potato chips. They are so good!

Sometimes I can't resist _____

7. It's OK to count calories at every meal.

I don't mind _____

8. I used to cook a lot of rich food.

I used to enjoy _____

9. I have to learn to make new dishes with fewer calories.

I have to practice _____

10. I want to take care of my health.

I don't want to put off _____

---

3 | Your Turn

Put the following list of activities in order from the most dangerous to the least dangerous, in your opinion. Then write a reason for each one of your choices. Discuss your opinions and reasons with a partner.

cycling   mountain climbing   skateboarding
hiking   scuba diving   swimming
jogging   skydiving

Activity	Reason
(Most dangerous) **1.**	
2.	
3.	
4.	
5.	
6.	
7.	
8.	
(Least dangerous)	

Example:

You: I think that scuba diving is dangerous because there may be sharks in the water.

Your partner: I disagree. I don't think that sharks attack people very often.

9b Gerunds as Objects of Prepositions; Gerunds after Certain Expressions

Is he really interested **in studying** plant life in Antarctica?

1. Prepositions are words like *about, against, at, by, for, in, of, on, to, with,* and *without*. The noun or pronoun that comes after a preposition is the object of the preposition. A gerund works like a noun and therefore can also be the object of a preposition.

   She is interested **in him**.   (pronoun)
   She is interested **in seeing** him. (gerund)

   Here are more examples of prepositions + gerunds.

	Preposition	Gerund	
What do you like	**about**	**living**	in a big city?
I am good	**at**	**learning**	languages.
He has plans	**for**	**decorating**	the house.
She stops him	**from**	**coming**	here.
He is interested	**in**	**working**	for us.
She is tired	**of**	**doing**	this job.
He insists	**on**	**checking**	my work.
They look forward	**to**	**seeing**	us tomorrow.
There's no point	**in**	**having**	a car in the city.

2. We use a gerund after many common expressions.

Expression	Example
Be busy	I'll **be busy doing** housework tomorrow.
Can't stand	He **can't stand waiting** in long lines.
Have difficulty/trouble	She **has difficulty learning** languages.
It's a waste of time/money	**It's a waste of time washing** the car because it's going to rain later.
*It's no use	**It's no use worrying** about it. There's nothing you can do.
It's not worth	**It's not worth waiting** in line for hours to see the game. We can see it on television.

*We can also say *there's no use (in) worrying about it.*

4 Practice

Jane has recently gone to an interview for a new job. Match the two halves of the interviewer's statements and questions.

_h_	**1.** Thank you	**a.** of taking on responsibility?
	2. We are excited	**b.** in solving a problem.
	3. We are thinking	**c.** in working with databases?
	4. Are you interested	**d.** about talking to you regarding this opportunity.
	5. Tell us about a time when you succeeded	**e.** to seeing you again.
		f. of hiring someone to manage our computer databases.
	6. Are you capable	
	7. Are you good	**g.** at dealing with stressful work situations?
	8. What are your plans	**h.** for coming to this interview.
	9. What would stop you	**i.** for developing your career?
	10. We look forward	**j.** from coming to work for us?

5 Practice

Read the numbered sentence in each of the following groups. Then circle the letter, a, b, c, or d, of the sentence with the same meaning.

1. I can't type your report because I'm too busy typing my own report.
   a. I can type my report but not yours.
   (b.) I can't type your report and mine, too.
   c. I'll type your report after I type mine.

2. It's not worth watching movies in the theater because they come out on DVD very quickly.
   a. The films are not good enough to watch in the theater.
   b. You might as well wait for the DVD to come out.
   c. Going to the cinema is too expensive.

3. There's no point in living in the city if you don't go out.
   a. If you don't go out, you don't benefit from living in the city.
   b. You don't have to go out if you live in the city.
   c. If you like to go out, you shouldn't live in the city.

4. It's a waste of time complaining about your cell phone service.
   a. If you don't complain, the service will be bad.
   b. If you complain, they will waste your time.
   c. The service will be bad whether you complain or not.

5. The exam is over. It's no use worrying about it now.
   a. Worrying about the exam will not help you now.
   b. You can't worry about the exam because it is over.
   c. You don't have to worry about the exam now that it's over.

6. I can't stand spending all of my money before the end of the month.
   a. I don't ever spend all of my money before the end of the month.
   b. Spending all of my money before the end of the month is OK with me.
   c. I really don't like spending all of my money before the end of the month.

6 Your Turn

Tell a partner two things that you are good at, interested in, and tired of.

Example:
I am good at drawing and playing basketball. I'm interested in movies and music.
I'm tired of eating the food here, and I'm tired of living in my apartment.

9c Verbs Followed by Infinitives

They **want to see** if they have passed the test.

1. We form an infinitive with *to* + a base verb. With some verbs, we use the verb + an infinitive.

Subject	Verb	Infinitive
We	agreed	**to look** after the children.
My parents	promised	**to visit** me this summer.
Everybody	wants	**to succeed.**

Here are some verbs that take infinitives.

afford	expect	need	refuse
agree	hope	plan	seem
appear	learn	pretend	threaten
decide	manage	promise	want

He can't **afford to buy** a computer.
She **threatened to resign** from the committee.

2. After some verbs, we can use the verb + an object + an infinitive.

Subject	Verb	Object	Infinitive
They	**encouraged** **asked** **persuaded**	**her**	**to stay.**

Here are some verbs that follow the pattern of verb + object + infinitive.

advise	invite	prefer	tell
allow	order	remind	warn
ask	permit	require	
encourage	persuade	teach	

3. With some verbs, we can use either of the structures in points 1 and 2 on page 263.

ask	help	want
expect	need	would like

The teacher **wants to leave** early. (The teacher will leave early if he can.)
The teacher **wants us to leave** early. (We will leave early because the teacher wants this.)

---

7 Practice

Our neighbor, Rose, phoned us last night and this is what she said. Rewrite the sentences using the verbs in parentheses. Remember that some verbs need an object.

1. She said, "Please come to my house for a barbecue* with us on Saturday." (invite)

   She invited us to come to her house for a barbecue
   on Saturday.

2. She said, "Don't forget to bring the children." (remind)

   _____

3. She said, "Don't knock on the door loudly, or you'll wake up the baby." (warn)

   _____

4. She said, "Could you please bring a salad?" (would like)

   _____

5. She said, "I'm going to make a big chocolate cake. You'll love it." (promise)

   _____

6. She said, "Please come at 6:00 P.M." (want)

   _____

7. She said, "Try to be on time." (encourage)

   _____

8. She said, "You will be able to cook your own meat if you want." (allow)

   _____

9. She said, "You'll stay for a game of softball** too, won't you?" (expect)

_____

10. She said, "You don't know how to play softball? Don't worry. Just watch me play." (teach)

_____

Barbecue: An informal meal which is cooked and usually eaten outdoors
**Softball:* A game similar to baseball

9d Verbs Followed by a Gerund or an Infinitive

Form / Function

She **loves to draw.**
She **loves drawing.**

Some verbs can take either an infinitive or a gerund. With some verbs, there is no difference in meaning, but with other verbs there is a difference in meaning.

1. These verbs can take either an infinitive or a gerund with no difference in meaning.

begin	hate	love
continue	like	start

It **started to snow**.
OR It **started snowing**.

2. With these verbs, there is a difference in meaning between the infinitive and gerund forms.

Verb	We Use Verb + Gerund:	We Use Verb + Infinitive:
forget	To say that we forget something after we have done it. I **forgot going** to their house. (I went there, but I forgot about it.)	To say that we forget something and don't do it. I **forgot to go to** the post office. (I was supposed to go there, but I didn't because I forgot.)
regret	To say that we regret something we have already done in the past. I **regret telling** him that I bought a car. (I told him I bought a car.)	To say that we regret something we have to do now. I **regret to tell** you that you have failed the test.*
remember	To say that we remember something after we have done it. I **remember going** to their house. (I went there, and I remember it.)	To say that we remember something before we do it. I **remembered to go** to the post office. (First I remembered, then I went there.)
stop	To say what we are doing before we stop. The class **stopped talking** when the teacher entered the room.	To say why we stop. The teacher **stopped to talk** to the principal when he entered the classroom.
try	To say that we intend to do an experiment to see what happens. I'll **try switching** the computer on and off to see if it will work.	To say that we intend to make an effort to see if we can do something. I **tried to fix** the computer, but I couldn't.

*Regret + infinitive is usually formal English.

9 | Practice

Sherry is on the phone with her sister Susan. Read their conversation and underline the correct form in each underlined pair. Circle both forms if both are correct.

Susan: I've been thinking about our trip to Vermont last fall.

Sherry: Yeah. It was really great. Do you remember (to climb / <u>climbing</u>) up that steep
1
mountain?

Susan: Yes. I'll never forget (to walk / walking) under all those red and gold leaves. I love
2
(to hike / hiking) in the mountains.
3

Sherry: You know, I don't have copies of your photos. Please don't forget
(to send / sending) them to me. Mine are terrible. I always try (to take / taking)
4   5
them at special angles, but they never come out well.

Susan: Sure. I'm sorry that I forgot (to mail / mailing) them. Sherry, how about another trip
6
next year? I was thinking that we could try (to go / going) on one of those organized
7
tours. I know you hate (to travel / traveling) by bus, but it's really inexpensive.
8

Sherry: I know, but you don't have any freedom.

Susan: It's not that bad. They let you stop (to take / taking) photos along the way, and
9
you get time on your own. I started (to look / looking) for some information on
10
the Internet, but I got busy and couldn't finish.

Sherry: Well, we can check into them. You know, I can't stop (to think / thinking) about our
11
Vermont trip. I agree that we should start (to plan / planning) another one soon.
12

10 | Your Turn

Write a short paragraph that could be part of an e-mail message to a family member or a friend. Write three or four sentences and use at least three verbs from the list.

begin	enjoy	hate	remember	stop
continue	forget	love	start	try

Example:
    You know how much I love skiing. Did you know that I began to ski when I was only four years old? ...

9e Infinitives after Certain Adjectives, Nouns, and Indefinite Pronouns

Form

She has a lot of homework **to do.**

1. We use infinitives after certain adjectives.

	Adjective	Infinitive	
It is	**important**	**to know**	a foreign language.
He was	**pleased**	**to see**	me.
We were	**disappointed**	**to hear**	the news.

Here are some adjectives that take infinitives.

afraid	determined	hesitant	proud
ashamed	eager	likely	ready
careful	happy	pleased	willing

2. We can use infinitives after nouns or after indefinite pronouns like *something* or *anything*.

	Noun/Pronoun	Infinitive
Do you have	**anything**	**to read?**
I have	**something**	**to eat.**
It's	**time**	**to leave.**
I have some	**letters**	**to write.**

1. The adjective in many adjective + infinitive combinations describes a feeling or attitude.

   > She was **happy to hear** the news.
   > We were **eager to try** the new restaurant.

2. When infinitives follow nouns, they often mean that there is an obligation or a necessity.

   > I have some **letters to write**. (I must write some letters.)
   > It's **time to leave**. (It's necessary for us to leave now.)

3. We use *for* + a noun or an indefinite pronoun when we need to say who does an action in the infinitive.

   > It's convenient **for everyone** to have a computer in the classroom.
   > I have some work **for James** to do.
   > Do you have something **for me** to read?

II Practice

Complete the sentences with the infinitive form of the verbs from the list.

| aim for | do | finish | hear | think |
| be | find out | have | plan | travel |

Dear Henry,

    I was very happy to _____*hear*_____ that you have decided to apply for
<u>   1   </u>

graduate school next year. As you know, your mother and I were very concerned

_____ that you were thinking of taking a year off. Of course, we'll
<u>   2   </u>

support you, whatever you decide. But I'm sure you realize that it's very important for you

_____ your education. After you graduate from college, you'll have time
<u>   3   </u>

_____ and do other things. But now it's good to have something
<u>   4   </u>

_____. It's good for everyone _____ a goal in life. That
<u>   5   </u>   <u>   6   </u>

has always been my philosophy. When you are young, it's easy _____
                                                                       <u>   7   </u>

that the future is not important. But believe me, and I know from experience, the

time _____ for the future is when you are young, not when it's too late
<u>   8   </u>

_____ anything about it. Take my advice. Finish your education. It'll make
9

your mother and me so proud _____ there on your graduation day.
10

Love,
Dad

12 **Your Turn**

Complete the sentences. Explain your answers to a partner.

Example:
It's never too late to learn new things. For example, my grandmother has learned how to use a computer.

It's very important to . . .
It's never too late to . . .
There is never enough time to . . .
It's good to have something to . . .

9f *Too* and *Enough* Followed by Infinitives

Form

She's **too** young to use a computer.
She isn't old **enough** to use a computer.

1. *Too* comes before an adjective or adverb. We use *for* + an object when we need to say who does the action in the infinitive.

Subject	Verb	*Too* + Adjective/Adverb	(*For* + Object)	Infinitive
It	is	**too cold**	**(for the girls)**	**to go** to the beach.
He	spoke	**too quickly**	**(for me)**	**to understand.**
It	isn't	**too late**	**(for us)**	**to go.**

2. *Enough* comes after an adjective or an adverb.

Subject	Verb	Adjective/Adverb + *Enough*	(*For* + Object)	Infinitive
It	isn't	**warm enough**	**(for the girls)**	**to go** to the beach.
He	spoke	**loudly enough**	**(for us)**	**to understand.**
She	is	**old enough**		**to go.**

3. *Enough* comes before a noun.

Subject	Verb	*Enough* + Noun	(*For* + Object)	Infinitive
There	isn't	**enough time**	**(for them)**	**to finish.**
We	have	**enough money**		**to buy** the CDs.

Function

1. When we use *too,* it has a negative meaning. It means that something is more than necessary or more than is wanted.

> She is **too** young to drive. (It is impossible for her to drive.)
> I'm **too** tired to go. (I cannot go.)

Do not confuse *too* with *very. Very* means to a great degree; to a great extent. It does not suggest more than necessary.

> I am **very** busy, but I can help you.   (I am busy, but it is possible for me to help you.)
> I am **too** busy to help you.   (I can't help you because I am busy.)

2. When we use *enough* in an affirmative sentence, it has a positive meaning. It implies that there is as much of something as is needed.

> She is **old enough** to drive.

But when we use *enough* in a negative sentence, it means that something is less than necessary or less than is wanted.

> This coffee is **not warm enough** to drink.

3. *Enough* usually comes before a noun. However, in formal English it occasionally follows a noun.

> INFORMAL: I have **enough** time.
> FORMAL: There is time **enough**.

13 Practice

Rewrite the sentences using *too* and *not . . . enough* and the words in parentheses.

Last week I went to a new restaurant with a friend. It was terrible!

1. The tea was so hot that we couldn't drink it.

(hot/for us) *The tea was too hot for us to drink.*

(cool/for us) *The tea wasn't cool enough for us to drink.*

2. The server spoke so fast that I couldn't understand her.

(fast/for us) _____

(slowly/for us) _____

3. The words on the menu were so difficult that I couldn't pronounce them.

(difficult/for me) _____

(easy/for me) _____

4. The room was so dark that I couldn't see the food.

(dark/for me) _____

(bright/for me) _____

5. The music was so loud that we couldn't have a conversation.

(loud/for us) _____

(quiet/for us) _____

6. I was so shy that I couldn't complain.

(shy) _____

(brave) _____

7. We were so disappointed that we didn't leave a tip.

(disappointed) _____

(satisfied) _____

8. We were so tired that we couldn't walk home.

(tired) _____

(energetic) _____

Your Turn

Tell a partner about yourself using *so* + adjective/adverb + *that*. Then ask your partner to tell the class about you using *too* or *not . . . enough*. Use the words in the list or your own ideas.

Example:

You: In the morning, I am usually so sleepy that I can't make breakfast.
So I usually eat at school.
When I was younger, I was so shy that I couldn't make many friends.
Now I'm more outgoing.

Your partner: My partner is usually too sleepy in the morning to make breakfast.
She eats at school instead.
Also, when she was younger, she wasn't outgoing enough to make many friends. She says she's more outgoing now.

ambitious	friendly	optimistic	sleepy
athletic	hungry	outgoing	thirsty
busy	lazy	pessimistic	
energetic	lucky	shy	

9g   The Infinitive of Purpose

Form / Function

We went to the jewelry store **to look** at rings.

1. We can use an infinitive to talk about the purpose of an action. This often explains why someone does something.

     I am saving **to buy** a new car.   (My purpose in saving is to buy a new car.)
     I went to Miami **to see** Susan.   (My purpose in going to Miami was to see Susan.)

2. We can also use *in order to* + a base verb instead of an infinitive to explain a purpose. This is usually more formal.

> I drank a lot of coffee **in order to stay** awake.
> We left early **in order to get** there on time.

3. In formal English, we use *in order not to* to express a negative purpose. In informal English, we usually use a clause with *so*.

> FORMAL: All employees should attend the meeting **in order not to** miss important news.
> INFORMAL: All employees should attend the meeting **so** they won't miss important news.

4. We can also use *for* + an object to show purpose.

> I went to the pharmacy **for** some medication.
> I went to the pharmacy **to buy** some medication.

15 Practice

Jan is planning a trip to Colorado. Write sentences using the infinitive of purpose to tell what she will need these items for. Use the phrases from the list.

boil water	find her way	keep mosquitoes away	sleep in
carry things	keep food cold	see in the dark	start a fire

1. matches *She needs matches to start a fire.* _____

2. a tent _____

3. insect repellent _____

4. an ice chest _____

5. a kettle _____

6. a flashlight _____

7. a backpack _____

8. a compass _____

Your Turn

What things do you need to buy or do before going on vacation? Where do you go to get them? Say or write sentences using *to* or *for*.

Example:
I usually go to the drugstore to get some air sickness pills and some sunscreen.
I sometimes go to the bookstore to look for guide books about the place I'm going.

9h Perfect Infinitives and Perfect Gerunds; Passive Voice of Infinitives and Gerunds

Form

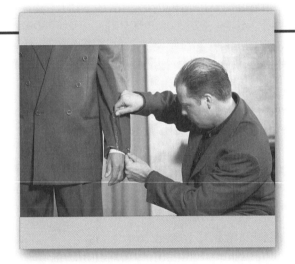

The sleeves **need to be shortened.**

ACTIVE FORMS OF INFINITIVES AND GERUNDS	
Form	Example
Simple Infinitive	Bob wanted **to do** the work by 5:00.
Simple Gerund	I enjoy **going** to parties.
Perfect Infinitive	Bob wanted **to have done** the work by 5:00, but he wasn't able to.
Perfect Gerund	I enjoyed **having gone** to Amy's party.

PASSIVE FORMS OF INFINITIVES AND GERUNDS*	
Form	Example
Simple Infinitive	She was lucky **to be awarded** the prize (by the judges).
Simple Gerund	I enjoy **being invited** to parties (by my friends).
Perfect Infinitive	She was lucky **to have been awarded** the prize (by the judges).
Perfect Gerund	I enjoyed **having been invited** (by Amy) to Amy's party.

*The agent may or may not be stated.

1. We use the perfect infinitive or perfect gerund to talk about something that happened at a time earlier than the main verb.

   > My English seems **to have gotten** better. (My English got better before the time of speaking.)

   > I remember **having met** her a year ago. (I met her before the time of speaking.)

2. We can also use the simple and perfect forms of infinitives and gerunds in the passive voice. The agent may or may not be mentioned. As in the active voice, we use the perfect form to talk about something that happened at a time earlier than the main verb.

   > Thomas didn't expect **to be called** into the meeting (by his boss). (simple infinitive)
   >
   > He was glad **to have been called** into the meeting (by his boss). (perfect infinitive)

   > Chloe dislikes **being given** extra work (by her boss). (simple gerund)
   >
   > She disliked **having been given** extra work last week (by her boss). (perfect gerund)

3. We can use simple and perfect gerunds as introductory phrases. See page 394 for more information on this kind of phrase.

   > Before **deciding** on my destination, I talked to friends.
   > **Having decided** to go on vacation, I called my travel agent.

4. We usually use an infinitive after the verb *need*.

   > I **need to go** to the bank.

   But sometimes we use a gerund after *need*. In these cases, the gerund has a passive meaning. It usually shows that it is necessary to improve or fix something.

   > My suit **needs cleaning**.
   > His car **needs servicing**.

   We can also use a passive infinitive with the same meaning.

   > My suit **needs to be cleaned**.
   > His car **needs to be serviced**.

17 Practice

Complete the sentences with the simple or perfect form of infinitives or gerunds of the verbs in parentheses. Some answers must be in the active voice; others must be in the passive. Write one word on each line.

1. Kate was relieved (hear) __to__ __have__ __heard__ the news.

2. She was not really surprised (choose) _____ _____ _____ _____ as the best

   student by the class.

3. (receive) _____ _____ the highest score in every test, she was very happy.

4. She was pleased (be) _____ _____ so successful.

5. It had been hard for her (spend) _____ _____ _____ so much of her

   time studying.

6. She missed (not/see) _____ _____ _____ the latest movies.

7. (tell) _____ _____ _____ by her parents she would not get any more money,

   she had had no choice.

8. She also wanted (recognize) _____ _____ _____ as the intelligent child in her

   family instead of her brother!

18 Practice

Complete the sentences using the perfect gerund form of the verbs in parentheses. Some sentences require the active voice. The others require the passive.

Joe is writing an e-mail message to a new key pal. He is writing about his first job.

My first job was as a journalist for a local newspaper.

(spend) _____ *Having spent* _____ four years in college earning a
                                1

degree in English, I thought I would be able to do the job easily. I was

pleased at (find) _____ the perfect job. After
                        2

(make) _____ many corrections on my first article,
                   3

my boss advised me to work harder. I tried hard, but I couldn't do better. After

(warn) _____ that I could lose my job, I started to worry.
                   4

I think most people would get worried after (tell) _____
5
that they would lose their job. I felt like a complete failure. I felt angry at

(treat) _____ unfairly. I told my uncle that after
6

(lose) _____ this job, I thought I would never find a job
7

again. (hear) _____ that, my uncle offered me a job
8

as his personal assistant working for his magazine!

19 Practice

**Rewrite the sentences using *need* + a gerund and *need* + a passive infinitive.
Use verbs from the list.**

clean	do	repair	sweep
cut	paint	replace	wash

We've just rented a house, but there are a lot of problems!

1. The windows are dirty.

   They need cleaning.

   They need to be cleaned.

2. The front gate is broken.

   _____

   _____

3. The grass is too long.

   _____

   _____

4. The floors are dusty.

   _____

   _____

5. The paint is coming off the walls.

   _____

   _____

6. The curtains are dirty.

_____

_____

7. The gas stove in the kitchen is old. We need a new one.

_____

_____

8. We have a lot of things to do!

_____

_____

20 Your Turn

What things need to be done in your house or apartment? Make a list and tell your partner about it.

Example:
My windows need to be cleaned.

9i Gerunds and Base Verbs with Verbs of Perception

Form

I **saw** a man **playing** music to a snake.

After some verbs of perception such as _see, hear, feel, smell, listen to, look at, notice, watch,_ and _observe,_ we can use an object + a verb + _-ing_ (present participle) or a base verb.

Subject	Verb	Object	Base Verb + -ing OR Base Verb
I	heard	Susan	**playing** the piano.
I	heard	Susan	**play** the piano.
We	saw	them	**leaving.**
We	saw	them	**leave.**

Function

There is usually little difference in meaning between the base verb + -ing and the base verb. However, in general, we use the base verb + -ing when we perceive (*hear, see, notice*) part of the action in progress.

I saw him **sleeping** in front of the television.

We use the base form when we perceive the whole action from beginning to end.

I saw him **sleep** through the whole movie from beginning to end.

21 Practice

Read the following questions. Is the question about a single complete action or an action in progress? Underline the correct form.

What would you do if . . . ?

1. . . . you saw someone (<u>steal</u> / stealing) your car?

2. . . . you saw someone (leave / leaving) their car lights on?

3. . . . you heard someone (break / breaking) into your house at night?

4. . . . you noticed some parents (shout / shouting) at their child?

5. . . . you heard someone (scream / screaming) and (fall / falling) down the stairs?

6. . . . you noticed a mouse (crawl / crawling) towards your chair?

7. . . . you saw a spider (sit / sitting) on your computer?

22 Your Turn

Say or write answers to the questions in Practice 21.

9j ◆ Person + Gerund

He insisted on **my leaving** the game.

1. In informal English, when we use a gerund to talk about what a person is doing, we usually use an object pronoun (*me, you, her, etc.*) + a gerund, or, if it is a person's name, the name (David) + a gerund.

   They insisted on **us going** with them.
   We were surprised at **David forgetting** to attend.

   In formal English, we usually use a possessive pronoun or noun.

   They insisted on **our going** with them.
   We were surprised at **David's forgetting** to attend.

2. In both informal and formal English, we use the object form after perception verbs such as *see, hear,* and *feel.*

   CORRECT: I saw him arriving.
   INCORRECT: I saw ~~his~~ arriving.

---

23 Practice

Rewrite the sentences with a person + a gerund. Give answers in both informal and formal English.

1. David forgot to call me on my birthday. I was surprised.

   I was surprised at David forgetting to call me on my birthday.

   I was surprised at David's forgetting to call me on my birthday.

2. He often phones me at work when I am busy. I don't like it.

_____

_____

3. He phones in the evening before 9:00. I don't mind.

_____

_____

4. He takes me dancing every Saturday night. My parents don't approve of it.

_____

_____

5. His friends talk on their cell phones all the time. I can't stand it.

_____

_____

6. I sometimes go out with other friends. He doesn't like me for it.

_____

_____

7. My parents tell me that David is not good enough for me. I don't listen to them.

_____

_____

8. My parents are always telling me what to do. I am tired of it.

_____

_____

24 | Your Turn

Complete the sentences with true facts about yourself.

Example:
I can't stand people telling me what to do.

1. I can't stand people telling me _____.

2. I don't mind people telling me _____.

3. My friends criticize me for _____.

REVIEW

1   Review (9a–9d, 9f–9g, 9i)

Complete the sentences with a gerund or an infinitive.

Jack: I heard you went (camp)_____*camping*_____ over the weekend. I thought you
        1
        hated (do) _____ any outdoor activity.
        2

Betty: I like (shop) _____ in flea markets, don't I?
        3

Jack: Yes, (shop) _____ is your favorite pastime. But who persuaded
        4
        you (sleep) _____ under the stars?
        5

Betty: You know I have trouble (say) _____ no. Anyway, I couldn't
        6
        avoid (go) _____. It was Stephanie's birthday. Besides, none of
        7
        us had enough money (stay) _____ in a hotel.
        8

Jack: I see. Well, tell me all about it. I can't wait (hear) _____.
        9

Betty: Do you really want to hear me (talk) _____ about it? It's a
        10
        very sad story. It all started at 5:00 Saturday morning. I was trying (get)
        _____ some sleep when the phone rang. "It's time (get)
        11
        _____ up!" Stephanie said. Three hours later, we arrived at the
        12
        campground. We put up our tent, but I was still too sleepy (do)
        _____ anything! I was also very upset because I'd forgotten
        13
        (bring) _____ my feather pillow. After the tent was up, we went
        14
        (hike) _____. At first, I refused (go) _____. But
        15   16
        I was too afraid (stay) _____ alone. We hiked and hiked. It was
        17
        awful. Terry warned me (stay) _____ on the path. But I saw
        18
        some wild flowers (grow) _____ in a field. I can't resist
        19
        (pick) _____ flowers. How did I know there was poison ivy*
        20
        there! Now I'm going crazy with all the (itch) _____. Not to
        21
        mention the insect bites. I had forgotten (bring) _____ my
        22
        insect spray. Finally, we got back to camp. All I thought about was

poison ivy: a plant that irritates the skin and makes it itch

(eat) _____ dinner. But they said it was too early (eat)
                 23

_____. They had (swim) _____ on their mind. By
         24   25

that time I was too tired (argue) _____. After they left, I
                                         26

thought I'd try (do) _____ some (cook) _____,
                            27   28

but there wasn't a stove. I tried (start) _____ a fire in the
                                                 29

firepit. After an hour, I got a small stick of wood (light) _____.
                                                                    30

Then it started (rain) _____. There was no use even (think)
                              31

_____ about dinner. I decided I needed (go)
         32

_____ to bed. I had big plans for (sleep) _____.
         33   34

Then I discovered the leak in my tent.

2 Review (9b-9c, 9e, 9g–9h)

Complete the sentences with the correct gerund or infinitive form of verbs from the list.

be	do	rest	sleep	work
compete	meet	run	swim	worry
cycle	prepare	see	win	

I have always dreamed about _____competing_____ in a triathlon. Tomorrow I'll see
                                              1

that dream come true. I'm nervous but, there's no use _____ about it. It's
                                                               2

more important for me _____ be part of this competition than
                              3

_____ it. I'm sure I'll have difficulty _____ tonight. But I'll
         4   5

have plenty of time _____ my sore muscles tomorrow night. I'm looking
                           6

forward to _____ all the other athletes at 5:00 in the morning. At 7:00,
                  7

we'll start the triathlon by _____ in a lake for 2.4 miles. The next event
                                    8

requires us _____ over mountains and through deserts for 112 miles. Those
                   9

who are left can look forward to _____ 26.2 miles through the city streets.
                                          10

I insist on _____ this even though it's very difficult. _____
                   11   12

very hard _____ for this event, I want _____ my dream
                 13   14

come true.

3 Review (9c–9e, 9g, 9j)

Complete the sentences with the gerund or infinitive form of verbs from the list.

do	join	pay	snow
go	learn	read	think
hear	pack	remind	write

I'm so happy _____ that you're finally _____ on that

             1   **2**

trip to Tibet. I've always wanted _____ something like that. I was thinking

                                         3

about _____ you, but I'm saving my money _____ for my

          4   **5**

tuition next semester. Right now, it's more important for me _____ about

                                                      6

my future. I hope you don't mind my _____ you _____

                                      7   **8**

some warm clothes. In those mountains, it can start _____ at any

                                                  9

time of year. There are many great books about Tibet, so I hope you have done a lot

of _____. It's important _____ about a place before

          10   **11**

you visit. Well, have a wonderful time. Remember _____ me a letter!

                                                              12

4 Review (9a–9e, 9g)

Complete the sentences with the correct gerund or infinitive verb form.

The appeal of (travel) ___*traveling*___ by bicycle is easy (understand)

                                      1

_____. It's healthy, good for (meet) _____ people, and

          2   **3**

anyone can do it. But (ride) _____ around a city park and (cycle)

                                    4

_____ around a country are two very different things. Before you take off

          5

on a bicycle tour, you need (be) _____ fit. Touring companies say that

                                        6

before anyone starts (think) _____ about a cycling tour, they need (get)

                                      7

_____ in shape. They can do this by (start) _____ long

          8   **9**

before the trip starts. They urge people (get) _____ out and bike every

                                        10

weekend in order (prepare) _____ themselves for 50-mile daily rides.

                                      11

Without some (train) _____, riders can count on plenty of sore muscles.

                          12

If you can't get outside (ride) _____ on the roads, then you must do some

                                    13

indoor exercise. You also need (do) _____ some (cross-train)

                                    14

_____ In addition to (cycle) _____, you can do some

          15   **16**

(run) _____ 17 , (hike) _____ 18 or even (swim)

_____ 19 . (Get) _____ 20 ready for a bike trip, you should start

(build) _____ 21 your muscles four to six weeks ahead of time.

　　It's a good idea (know) _____ 22 what you can do before (commit)

_____ 23 yourself. "People need (have) _____ 24 some knowledge

of their abilities," says Dr. Ross of the Sports Institute. "Obviously, if someone can't go

up the stairs without (lose) _____ 25 their breath, they're not ready

(cycle) _____ 26 a couple of hundred miles."

　　If you are physically ready and like (cycle) _____ 27 , you're going

(love) _____ 28 a cycle tour. There are tours all over the world, for all

levels, even beginners. So you don't have (be) _____ 29 a professional

(participate) _____ 30 . There's nothing like (be) _____ 31

outdoors and (see) _____ 32 a country on a bicycle. It's like (have)

_____ 33 a great adventure. And there is something about (ride)

_____ 34 with other people that makes a trip more fun.

WRITING: Write an Essay of Analysis

An essay of analysis gives reasons or causes of something. See page 470 for general writing guidelines. See page 471 for information on writing an essay.

Step 1. Work with a partner or a group and analyze the topics. Make notes of the causes or reasons for each topic.

1. the causes of heart disease
2. the major causes of pollution in the world
3. how weather affects our lives
4. why marriage is good

Step 2. Choose one of the topics in Step 1, or think of your own.

Step 3. Write your essay.

1. Write a paragraph on each of the causes or reasons you have listed in your thesis statement. Make sure you have supporting examples and details for each.

2. Write an introduction to the topic. In your introduction, write a thesis statement: state your method of analysis (for example causes or reasons) and state your organizational method (for example, number of causes or reasons). Also summarize your key points. Here is an example of an introductory paragraph. The thesis statement is in bold.

> Preventing heart disease is a major public health effort in the United States. Some researchers say that heart disease appears to be on the decline, but we must persuade more people to pay attention to the risk that they face. One way to do this is by educating them about the causes of heart disease. **There are many causes of this deadly disease; however the three major causes are high blood pressure, genetic predisposition, and an unhealthy lifestyle.**

3. Write a conclusion. Restate your thesis statement and also state that there may be causes other than the ones you have listed.

4. Write a title for your essay.

Step 4. Evaluate your essay.

Checklist

_____ Did you write an introduction with a thesis statement?

_____ Did you write a paragraph about each of the points in the thesis statement?

_____ Are your reasons or causes clear? Do they support the thesis statement?

Step 5. Work with a partner or a teacher to edit your essay. Check spelling, vocabulary, and grammar.

Step 6. Write your final copy.

A **Choose the best answer, A, B, C, or D, to complete the sentence. Mark your answer by darkening the oval with the same letter.**

1. _____ a foreign language can sometimes be difficult.

   A. To learning   Ⓐ Ⓑ Ⓒ Ⓓ
   B. Learning
   C. Learn
   D. Be learning

2. I enjoyed _____ him write his essay.

   A. helping   Ⓐ Ⓑ Ⓒ Ⓓ
   B. to help
   C. help
   D. for to help

3. He _____ correcting my pronunciation.

   A. insist on   Ⓐ Ⓑ Ⓒ Ⓓ
   B. insist
   C. insists on
   D. insists to

4. We advised _____.

   A. to him not to go   Ⓐ Ⓑ Ⓒ Ⓓ
   B. him not go
   C. him not to go
   D. not him to go

5. On the way home, we stopped _____ some gas.

   A. getting   Ⓐ Ⓑ Ⓒ Ⓓ
   B. get
   C. to get
   D. for getting

6. We were eager _____ the new game.

   A. to try   Ⓐ Ⓑ Ⓒ Ⓓ
   B. trying
   C. try
   D. for to trying

7. We _____ to finish the test.

      Ⓐ Ⓑ Ⓒ Ⓓ
   A. didn't enough have time
   B. didn't have enough time
   C. had not time enough
   D. did not enough time have

8. The teacher saw _____ during the test.

   A. the student to cheat   Ⓐ Ⓑ Ⓒ Ⓓ
   B. cheat the student
   C. the student cheating
   D. cheating the student

9. He left a note for himself in order _____ forget.

   A. not   Ⓐ Ⓑ Ⓒ Ⓓ
   B. not for
   C. not to
   D. for not

10. We have an important issue _____.

    A. for discuss   Ⓐ Ⓑ Ⓒ Ⓓ
    B. for discussing
    C. to discussing
    D. to discuss

B Find the underlined word or phrase, A, B, C, or D, that is incorrect. Mark your answer by darkening the oval with the same letter.

1. Drinking enough water is important
   A   B   C
   in order not get dehydrated.
              D

   Ⓐ Ⓑ Ⓒ Ⓓ

2. After I finished doing my homework,
               A   B
   I decided go for a walk.
       C   D

   Ⓐ Ⓑ Ⓒ Ⓓ

3. The teacher was pleased see her students
                      A
   do well on their final exam before
   B   C
   graduating.
   D

   Ⓐ Ⓑ Ⓒ Ⓓ

4. We had been told by our teacher not
       A   B
   using the internet for our research.
   C   D

   Ⓐ Ⓑ Ⓒ Ⓓ

5. After having a wonderful time
          A
   hiking and seeing friends at the camp,
   B
   I look forward to go there again
     C   D
   next year.

   Ⓐ Ⓑ Ⓒ Ⓓ

6. Meg: Could you help me with these
           math problems?

   Matt: Sorry. I don't have time enough
                                    A
           now, but I can help you later.
           B   C   D

   Ⓐ Ⓑ Ⓒ Ⓓ

7. We decided to go on a trip to the
      A
   mountains but forgot taking the map, so
                        B   C
   we stopped to buy one at a gas station.
                D

   Ⓐ Ⓑ Ⓒ Ⓓ

8. Watching bears in the wild are exciting
   A   B   C
   and fun, but we must remember to keep
                                   D
   our distance.

   Ⓐ Ⓑ Ⓒ Ⓓ

9. In order to be not late for the flight and
   A   B
   have enough time for breakfast, I suggest
        C
   getting up at five in the morning.
   D

   Ⓐ Ⓑ Ⓒ Ⓓ

10. I always enjoy to go to the airport
                   A
    because it's nice to sit and watch the
                      B
    planes taking off and landing.
           C   D

    Ⓐ Ⓑ Ⓒ Ⓓ

UNIT 10

AGREEMENT AND PARALLEL STRUCTURE

10a Subject-Verb Agreement: General Rules Part 1

Form / Function

All the students in the photo **have** graduated.
Everyone is happy.

In an English sentence, the subject and the verb must agree in number. This means that a singular subject must have a singular verb, and a plural subject must have a plural verb.

Singular: John **is** a lawyer.
(*John* is a singular subject, and *is* is a singular form of the verb *be*.)
Plural: John and Alice **are** lawyers.
(*John and Alice* is a plural subject, and *are* is a plural form of the verb *be*.)

We form singular and plural forms of *be* differently from other verbs.

	Singular		Plural	
The verb *be* (present and past)	I	am/was	we	are/were
	you	are/were	you	
	he/she/it	is/was	they	
Other verbs in the present tense*	I	run	we	run
	you		you	
	he/she/it	runs	they	

*Note: *I* is a singular subject, and *you* can also be a singular subject, but they both take the base form of the verb. Only third person singular subjects (*he, she, it, Tom,* etc.) take the *-s* form.

Most of the time, subject-verb agreement is clear, but in some cases, even native speakers have to be careful. Here are some rules for special situations.

1. A sentence with two subjects joined by *and* takes a plural verb.

    The physics laboratory **and** the library **are** located on the first floor.

2. Some words like *mathematics* and *news* end in *-s,* but they are singular and take a singular verb.

> Mathematics **is** not my favorite subject.
> The news **is** good.

Other examples are *politics, physics, economics, aeronautics, electronics,* and *measles.*

3. When we use a gerund as the subject, it is always singular.

> Swimming **is** my favorite sport.

But if a subject has two gerunds, it is plural.

> Swimming and biking **are** my favorite sports.

4. When we use *each, every,* or *any* as an adjective in front of a subject, it takes a singular verb. This also includes indefinite pronouns like *everyone* and *everything.*

> Each of the subjects in a sentence **has** to agree with its verb.
> Everyone **wants** something from us.

5. When we use *all, almost all, most,* or *some* in front of a subject or as a subject, the subject takes a plural verb.

> **All** the students **eat** lunch at 12:00.   (*all* + a subject)
> **Most eat** in the cafeteria.   (*most* is the subject)
> **Some** of the students **eat** at home.   (*some* is the subject)

6. Two singular subjects joined by *or* take a singular verb. See page 307 for information on *either . . . or* and *neither . . . nor.*

> Thursday or Friday **is** the best day to go.

Two plural subjects joined by *or* take a plural verb.

> **Are** the boys or the girls going to leave first?

If one subject is singular and the other is plural, the verb agrees with the subject that is closest to it.

> I think that the potatoes or the chicken **is** burning.

> I think that the chicken or the potatoes **are** burning.

1 Practice

Complete the sentences using the singular or plural form of the verbs in parentheses.

Every student whose first language is not English and who wants to go to college

in the United States (have) _____*has*_____ to take an exam called TOEFL® (Test of
1

English as a Foreign Language). This exam tests your knowledge and skills in grammar,

vocabulary, reading, writing, and listening. Mathematics (be) _____
2

not included in the test. Reading (be) _____ the subject most students
3

have difficulty with. But listening and writing (be) _____ also difficult for
4

many students. Each student (apply) _____ to take the test individually.
5

The test can be taken on a computer or with pen and paper. Neither the handwritten test

nor the computerized test (be) _____ marked by a person. Everything,
6

except the essays, (be) _____ scored by computer. Each student
7

(receive) _____ a score by mail a few weeks later. Most colleges in the
8

country (require) _____ a certain score on this exam. Taking tests (be)
9

_____ a skill that requires a lot of practice.
10

2 Your Turn

What is the process of applying for college in your country? Write sentences explaining what every student has to do, what most students have to do, etc.

Example:
Every student has to write an essay.
Most students have to go to an interview.

10b Subject-Verb Agreement: General Rules Part 2

Form / Function

Here is your paper.
There are only two mistakes.
You got an A.

1. Prepositional phrases do not affect the verb. The verb always agrees with the subject.

   The value of his investments **is** dropping every day.

Subject	Prepositional Phrase	Verb	Complement
The value	of his investments	**is** dropping	every day.
One	of the students	**is**	here.
The directions	for operating this machine	**are**	confusing.

Phrases like *along with*, *together with*, *accompanied by*, *as well as*, and *in addition to* also do not affect the verb.

The surgeon, together with his team of doctors, **is** visiting the patient.

My parents, along with my brother, **are** going to visit me tomorrow.

2. When we begin a sentence with *here* or *there*, the verb may be singular or plural depending on the noun that follows.

There **are** many students in class today.

Here **is** the result of all your efforts.

3 | Practice

Complete the sentences with a singular or plural form of the verb *be*.

There ____*are*____ twenty students in my daughter's class. Elena, along with
         1

all the other students, _____ taking a test right now. The subject of the
                               2

test _____ mathematics. All of the children _____
          3   4

allowed to use a calculator, which makes it easier. The instructions for the exam

_____ on the board. There _____ a separate answer sheet
         5   6

for each section of the exam. The answers _____ written in pencil. My
                                                7

daughter, along with all the other students in the class, _____ trying hard
                                                                 8

to pass the exam. All of the children, except Elena, _____ having trouble
                                                          9

with the questions. Elena is one of the few students who _____ able to
                                                              10

finish all the questions on time.

4 | Your Turn

**Describe the photo. What are all the
people doing? What are some of the
people doing? What is one person doing?**

_____

_____

_____

_____

_____

_____

_____

_____

_____

_____

_____

_____

_____

10c Subject-Verb Agreement with Quantity Words

Three hundred dollars is enough.

1. We usually use a singular verb with expressions of time, money, distance, weight, and measurement. We do this because we think of the subject as a single unit.

   > Ten dollars **is** all the money I have.
   > Three miles **is** not far to run.
   > Three weeks **is** a long time to wait for the results of the test.
   > Twenty minutes **is** not enough time for an essay.
   > Two cups of milk **is** what we need for this recipe.
   > Two thirds of this box of cereal **has** been eaten.

2. We use the subject *the number of* + plural noun with a singular verb.

   > The number of students in our class **is** twenty.

   We use the subject *a number of* + plural noun with a plural verb.

   > A number of important people **are** here today.

3. When we use expressions of quantity such as *some of, a lot of,* and *three-quarters of* as the subject, the verb agrees with the pronoun or noun that follows *of*.

   > Some of the orange **is** still good. (*some of the orange* = a part of the orange)
   > Some of it **is** still good.
   > Some of the oranges **are** still good.
   > Some of them **are** still good.

However, we use a singular verb with these subjects: *one of the* + plural noun, *each of the* + plural noun, *every one of the* + plural noun, and *none of the* + plural noun.

> **One of the** students is sick.
> **Each of the** students is ready for the test.
> **Every one of the** students is on time for the test.
> **None of the** students **is** late.

In informal speech, we often use a plural verb with *none of the*.

> None of the students **are** late.

5 Practice

Look at the photo of the women having a friendly game of cards. Complete the sentences with the following quantity words.

a number of   each of the   none of the   one of the   the number of (use twice)

1. _____ *The number of* _____ women

   playing cards is four.

2. _____ women

   are sitting down at a table and playing cards.

3. _____ women

   is not holding a card.

4. _____ women

   is playing cards.

5. _____ are wearing jeans.

6. _____ cards on the table is unclear.

Make two sentences about the photo on your own.

7. _____

8. _____

Read the sentences about the chart. Fill in the correct form of the verb in parentheses.

STUDENT SURVEY				
	Eat Dinner	Do Homework	Watch TV	Talk on the Phone
Student 1	20 minutes	60 minutes	90 minutes	45 minutes
Student 2	20 minutes	120 minutes	30 minutes	90 minutes
Student 3	20 minutes	60 minutes	90 minutes	15 minutes
Student 4	20 minutes	30 minutes	45 minutes	0 minutes
Student 5	60 minutes	90 minutes	120 minutes	30 minutes
Student 6	20 minutes	120 minutes	0 minutes	45 minutes
Student 7	60 minutes	60 minutes	30 minutes	20 minutes
Student 8	20 minutes	90 minutes	45 minutes	50 minutes
Student 9	20 minutes	60 minutes	60 minutes	120 minutes
Student 10	60 minutes	90 minutes	15 minutes	30 minutes
Student 11	60 minutes	30 minutes	45 minutes	45 minutes
Student 12	20 minutes	60 minutes	90 minutes	75 minutes
Student 13	20 minutes	120 minutes	120 minutes	15 minutes
Student 14	20 minutes	90 minutes	30 minutes	20 minutes
Student 15	20 minutes	30 minutes	90 minutes	0 minutes
Student 16	60 minutes	30 minutes	60 minutes	20 minutes
Student 17	20 minutes	90 minutes	120 minutes	0 minutes
Student 18	60 minutes	60 minutes	30 minutes	20 minutes

1. There (be) _____are_____ 18 students in this survey.

2. Two thirds of the students (spend) _____ twenty minutes eating dinner.

3. One third of the students (spend) _____ one hour on eating dinner.

4. None of the students (do) _____ homework for more than two hours.

5. All of the students (spend) _____ some time on homework.

6. One of the students never (watch) _____ TV.

7. Half of the class (watch) _____ TV for an hour or more.

8. Two thirds of the class (talk) _____ on the phone for less than an hour.

9. One sixth of the class (talk) _____ on the phone for more than an hour.

10. A number of students (not talk) _____ on the phone.

7 | What Do You Think?

1. Is forty minutes a long time to talk on the phone?
2. Is twenty minutes enough time to finish your homework?
3. Is more than one hour too much time to spend on eating dinner?
4. Is two hours enough time to spend watching TV?

8 | Your Turn

A. Interview six students in your class. Ask them how much of their time they spend on each of these activities every day.

Example:

You: How much time to you spend exercising every day?
Your classmate: I exercise for about an hour each day.

exercising   eating   sleeping   watching TV

B. Tell the class about the results of your survey.

Example:

None of the students exercises for more than one hour a day.

C. Write a paragraph about the results of your survey.

_____

_____

_____

_____

_____

_____

_____

_____

_____

_____

_____

_____

_____

10d Parallel Structure

A good baseball player needs **stamina, concentration,** and **skill.**

1. We can use the conjunctions *and, but, or,* and *nor* to connect words or phrases. The words before and after these conjunctions must have the same grammatical form. When this is the case, there is parallel structure.

Grammatical Form	Example
Nouns	The essay had mistakes in **grammar** and **organization.**
Adjectives	His speech was neither **short** nor **good.**
Verbs	She **arrives** at seven and **leaves** at nine.
Adverbs	Does she work **slowly** or **quickly?**
Gerunds	**Dancing** and **watching** movies are my favorite weekend activities.
Infinitives	I like **to swim** but not **to fish.**

2. When a parallel structure has more than two parts, we use a comma to separate each part.

   The book contained **stories, poems,** and **plays.**
   His chores are **washing the dishes, cleaning the bathroom,** and **watering the flowers.**
   The instructor expects students **to attend** every class, **to do** all the assignments, and **to hand in** homework on time.

3. If a parallel structure has only two parts, we do not use a comma between them.

   I can speak Chinese and English.

9 Practice

Underline the parallel structure in the following sentences. Then write what grammatical form (nouns, adjectives, verbs, adverbs, gerunds, or infinitives) the parallel structure contains.

1. The colors you choose for your <u>clothes</u> and for your <u>home</u>, <u>office</u>, and <u>car</u> can have an effect on you. _____nouns_____

2. Colors have been known to ease stress, to fill you with energy, and even to reduce pain and other physical problems. _____

3. When you decide to paint your apartment, you shouldn't choose colors quickly or carelessly. _____

4. For example, the colors blue and green have a calming, relaxing, and peaceful effect.

   _____

5. On the other hand, the color red excites, stimulates, and warms the body.

   _____

6. The color yellow also energizes and stimulates the body, but not as much as the color red. _____

7. The color yellow is good for remembering things and relieving depression.

   _____

8. If you are sleeping and eating poorly, then orange is the color for you.

   _____

10 Practice

Underline and correct the errors in parallel structure in the sentences. Then write what grammatical form (nouns, adjectives, verbs, adverbs, gerunds, or infinitives) the parallel structure contains. Some sentences have no errors.

1. Blue makes people feel cooler in hot and <u>humidity</u> environments. _____adjectives_____
   humid

2. Try wearing black to feel strong and self-confidence. _____

3. Orange is the color for reducing fatigue and stimulate the appetite. _____

4. When you surround yourself with the color blue, you can help back problems, painful, and insomnia. _____

5. The color green helps people with emotional problems, heart problems, and cancer. _____

6. Yellow stimulates the mind, energizes the body, and creates a positive attitude. _____

7. The effect of color on our moods, healthy, and way of thinking has been studied for years. _____

11 Practice

Underline and correct the errors in parallel structure. Some sentences have no errors.

health
1. In order to maintain youth and good <u>healthy</u>, we need to have a combination of
nutrition
exercise and proper <u>nutritional</u>.

2. Exercise is good for our physical health and psychologically.

3. Regular exercise improves digestion, increases energy, burns fat, and lowering blood cholesterol.

4. It also reduces stress and anxious, which are the main reasons for many illness and conditions.

5. Also, regular exercise elevating mood, increases feelings of well-being, and reduces anxious and depression.

6. When you start an exercise program, remember to start out slowly, listen to your body, and gradually increase the strength and long of the exercise.

7. There are many different forms of moderate exercise including daily walking, bicycling, or even gardening.

12 Your Turn

Complete each sentence with your own words using parallel structure.

1. The night before a test, it is important to _____,

_____, and _____.

2. On the day of the test, you must be _____,

_____, and _____.

3. During the test, you must _____,

_____, and _____.

4. After the test, you can _____,

_____, and _____.

10e Coordinating Conjunctions

The ostrich is a bird, **yet** it doesn't fly.

1. We use a conjunction like *and, but, or, so, yet,* and *for* to connect two main clauses. We usually put a comma before the conjunction in a main clause.

    Susan has many problems, **but** she always looks happy.

    We can begin a sentence with *and* or *but*. Some instructors do not accept this usage. Check with your instructor.

    Susan has many problems. **But** she always looks happy.

2. We also use *so, for,* and *yet* to join two independent clauses. We usually use a comma before these conjunctions.

    I was very hungry, **so** I ate the whole cake.
    The actor doesn't appear in public, **for** he doesn't like publicity.
    He told me he would give back my money, **yet** he didn't.

    So, for, and *yet* also have other meanings.

    She is **so** smart. (adverb—*so = very*)
    I haven't finished **yet**. (adverb)
    I bought it **for** you. (preposition)

13 Practice

Punctuate the sentences with commas and periods. Use capital letters where necessary. Do not add other words.

Terry Fox was born in 1958 in Canada. ~~he~~ *He*
played soccer and basketball in high school for he loved sports
when he was eighteen he had problems with his knee so he went
to the doctor the doctor told him he had bone cancer and would
lose his leg this was a terrible shock yet Terry had an idea he
decided he could help people even with one leg his idea was to
run across Canada to collect money to fight cancer after the
operation he got an artificial leg and started to prepare for the
run his progress was very slow but he did not give up in 1980 he
started his run and called it the "Marathon of Hope" he ran 26
miles a day, seven days a week this was amazing but it was more
amazing because he had only one leg later that year Terry got sick again and had to stop
running he received letters from all over the world and Canadian television showed a
program about him the program collected $10 million for the Canadian Cancer Society
Terry Fox collected almost $24 million for cancer he died in 1981 but his story did not end
with his death Terry Fox events started all over the world and collected millions of dollars
to help fight cancer.

14 Practice

Punctuate the sentences with commas and periods. Use capital letters where necessary. Do not add other words.

A.
Dolphins live in the sea, yet they are
mammals. ~~they~~ *They* breathe air and give live birth
to their young young dolphins are intelligent
and sensitive animals their brains are almost
as large as ours and they have a language of

Agreement and Parallel Structure

more than 30 sounds for communicating with each other they live in groups of several hundred and always help any dolphins that may be in danger

dolphins are friendly to humans and there are many reports of dolphins helping people in danger in one case in 1983, a helicopter crashed into the Java Sea and it was a dolphin that saved the pilot's life the dolphin pushed the rubber raft for nine days until it reached the coast.

B.

Family names usually go from parents to children but some family names have the phrase "son of" to make the connection clear this happens in Scottish and Irish names, such as MacDonald or O'Connor *Mac* and *O'* mean "son of" so *MacDonald* means "son of Donald" and *O'Connor* means "son of Connor."

15 Your Turn

Write a paragraph describing your classroom. Use coordinating conjunctions and the correct punctuation.

Example:

Our classroom has a blackboard, desks, and chairs, but it doesn't have computers.

10f Correlative Conjunctions: *Both ... And; Not Only ... But Also; Either ... Or; Neither ... Nor*

Form / Function

Malaika Mills is appearing **not only** in a movie **but also** in a play this year.

1. Correlative conjunctions come in two parts, for example, *both ... and*. We use these conjunctions to compare two ideas. We use the same grammatical form after each part of a correlative conjunction. Here are some examples of parallel structure with correlative conjunctions.

Parallel Structure	Example
both + verb + *and* + verb	Ben **both** studies **and** works.
not only + adjective + *but also* + adjective	Mary is **not only** generous **but also** intelligent.
either + noun + *or* + noun	I have to do **either** my homework **or** my chores.
neither + gerund + *nor* + gerund	He enjoys **neither** skiing **nor** hiking.

2. When we connect two subjects with *both ... and,* we use a plural verb.

   Both his brother **and** sister **are** in town.

3. When we connect two subjects with *not only ... but also, either ... or,* or *neither ... nor,* we use a singular or plural verb depending on the subject that is closest to the verb.

   Neither the doctor **nor** the nurse **is** with the patient.

   Neither the doctor **nor** the nurses **are** with the patient.

16 Practice

Circle the correct form of the verbs in parentheses.

1. Both vitamin C and calcium (is /(are)) important for good health.

2. Both your teeth and bones (need / needs) calcium.

3. Either milk or products from milk (contain / contains) a lot of calcium.

4. Both children and the elderly (require / requires) calcium.

5. Neither chicken nor pork (have / has) much calcium.

6. Not only milk products but also dark green vegetables (contain / contains) calcium.

7. Neither the liver nor the blood (make / makes) calcium.

8. Either food or drink (give / gives) the body the calcium it needs.

17 Practice

Combine the sentences into one with *both ... and, not only ... but also, either ... or* or *neither ... nor.*

1. Fruits have vitamin C. Vegetables have vitamin C.

   Both fruits and vegetables have vitamin C.

2. Heat destroys vitamin C. Exposure to air destroys vitamin C.

   _____

3. You can take vitamin C naturally in food. You can take vitamin C in tablet supplements.

   _____

4. Rice does not have vitamin C. Pasta does not have vitamin C.

   _____

5. Oranges have a lot of vitamin C. Lemons have a lot of vitamin C.

   _____

6. They say vitamin C prevents heart disease. They say vitamin C prevents colds.

   _____

7. Vitamin C does not prevent cancer. Vitamin C does not prevent infection.

   _____

8. Natural vitamins are good for the body. Synthetic vitamins are good for the body.

   _____

18 Your Turn

A. Complete the sentences about you and a partner in your own words.

Example:
Neither my partner nor I like baseball.

1. Neither my partner nor I _____

2. Not only I but also my partner _____

3. Both my partner and I _____

B. Report the information from part A to the class.

Example:
Both my partner and I like most sports, but neither of us likes tennis. My partner likes not only team sports but also individual sports such as running marathons.

C. Write a paragraph about what one of your classmates reported.

_____

_____

_____

_____

_____

_____

_____

_____

1 Review (10a–10c)

Underline the correct words.

Animals with a backbone (is / <u>are</u>)₁ vertebrates. Scientists have recently discovered the earth's smallest vertebrate. It is the "stout infantfish."

When scientists first looked under the microscope, they instantly recognized it as something special. It is not only the world's smallest fish, but also (light / the lightest)₂. This new species (are / is)₃ no longer than the (wide / width)₄ of a pencil. Both the male and the female (is / are)₅ quite small. The female stout infantfish (measure / measures)₆ a third of an inch. The male (is / are)₇ just over one quarter of an inch. Each of these fish (weigh / weighs)₈ very, very little. A load of 500,000 stout infantfish (weigh / weighs)₉ barely one pound. Of course, no one (have / has)₁₀ that many. As a matter of fact, there (is / are)₁₁ only six specimens of this fish in laboratories today. The stout infantfish (are / is)₁₂ very rare.

Neither the males (or / nor)₁₃ the females (have / has)₁₄ color, except for the eyes. Every one of these fish (lacks / lack)₁₅ teeth, scales, and certain characteristics typical of other fish. Two months (is / are)₁₆ not very long, but that (is / are)₁₇ how long the stout infantfish live.

Everyone (want / wants)₁₈ to know more about this tiny fish, but it is very hard to find them. Fishing (is / are)₁₉ not the way to catch them, of course. The only ways (is / are)₂₀ diving and (to explore / exploring)₂₁ the deep ocean.

Scientists are very excited about the discovery of the world's smallest and lightest fish. Many (say / says)₂₂ that discovering the stout infantfish (demonstrate / demonstrates)₂₃ that scientists do not yet possess a complete list of marine (animal / animals)₂₄. In fact, many important species (remain / remains)₂₅ undiscovered.

2 Review (10a–10b, 10d, 10f)

Underline the correct words.

The Maldives (<u>is</u> / are) an island republic located in the northern Indian Ocean. A
<u>1</u>
chain of 1,190 islands (makes / make) up the Maldives. (All / Each) of the islands is a coral
<u>2</u> <u>3</u>
island. The 1,190 islands (is / are) organized into 26 groups called "atolls." The capital of
<u>4</u>
the Maldives (is / are) Male. The climate (is / are) tropical. It (is / are) hot and
<u>5</u> <u>6</u> <u>7</u>
(humidity / humid). The weather throughout the islands (is / are) dry from November to
<u>8</u> <u>9</u>
March, but it is (rains / rainy) from June to August. November or January (is / are) the
<u>10</u> <u>11</u>
best month to visit the islands. The islands (is / are) small but (beautiful / beauty). There
<u>12</u> <u>13</u>
(is / are) many lovely beaches. Tourism (is / are) the largest industry. Fishing for the many
<u>14</u> <u>15</u>
species of fish in the warm waters (is / are) the second largest. The Maldivian people also
<u>16</u>
(sells / sell) many of their beautiful crafts. Coconuts, sweet potatoes, and corn (is / are)
<u>17</u> <u>18</u>
their main agricultural products.

The Maldives (is / are) near the major sea routes in the Indian Ocean. Many ships on
<u>19</u>
their way to Africa or Asia (has / have) crashed on Maldivian reefs. In 1602, a Frenchman
<u>20</u>
named Francois Pyrard (hits / hit) a reef and (lost / loses) his ship. He swam slowly
<u>21</u> <u>22</u>
and (desperate / desperately) to shore. He could (neither / either) leave the island nor
<u>23</u> <u>24</u>
(rebuilding / rebuild) his ship right away. He decided to make the best of things by studying
<u>25</u>
the culture, (learn / learning) the language, and later (write / writing) a book. The book
<u>26</u> <u>27</u>
(was / were) one of the most detailed books on early life in the Maldives.
<u>28</u>
There (was / were) so many shipwrecks in the 1800s that the British ordered a survey
<u>29</u>
of the islands so that the sailors would have accurate maps and (chart / charts). However,
<u>30</u>
neither charts, maps, (or / nor) good sailing skill (was / were) of much help. The wrecks
<u>31</u> <u>32</u>
continued. To this day, it (is / are) still a dangerous area.
<u>33</u>

Agreement and Parallel Structure

Review (10a-10d)

Find the errors and correct them.

We measure things to find out
how wide, ~~taller~~ *tall*, hot, cold, or ~~heavily~~ *heavy*
they are. We needs accurate
measurements in science and
everyday activities such as cooking

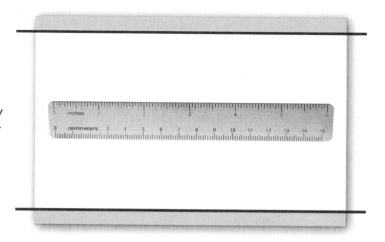

and when we sew. There is different types of instruments for measuring, and different instruments is used to measure long, wide, volume, mass, and temperature.

In the old days, people used objects along with their hands and feet for measuring. Having systems for measuring have always been important. Some cultures still uses ancient methods for measuring. One of these methods are the abacus. The abacus have been used in China since ancient times. With the abacus, you can add, subtraction, multiplying, and do division. Most people uses calculators to do that today. Each method have its own advantages.

There is many measuring tools. Every one of them are useful. We can measure long and width by using a ruler or a tape measure, and we measure weight by using a scale.

The metric system originated in France in 1795. It uses meters to measure length and grams for measuring weight. Most countries and scientists uses this system. The United States use the U.S. customary system. This system utilize feet and inches to measure length and pounds and ounces measures weight.

Two methods of measuring temperature is Fahrenheit and Celsius. Americans measures temperature by using the Fahrenheit scale. Fahrenheit register the freezing point of water as 32° and the boiling point as 212°. Most other countries uses Celsius. Celsius register the freezing point as 0° and the boiling point as 100°.

Which measuring systems do your country use?

4

Review (10a, 10c–10f)

Find the errors and correct them. Some of the errors are in punctuation.

Neil Armstrong and Buzz Aldrin walked on the moon on July 21, 1969. Neither
of them ~~are~~ *is* still there, of course, and one of their experiments are. Armstrong and Aldrin
wasn't only walking and jumped around on the moon. They was busy placing instruments
on the surface and conducted experiments. About an hour before the end of their final
moonwalk, they set up a science experiment, a two-foot wide panel with 100 mirrors. This
panel, along with many other objects, is still on the moon today, for no one have gone
back to get them. Neither the U.S. or any other country have gone back to the moon. The
exact number of objects on the moon are unknown. However, astronauts landing on the moon
today would find only one piece of equipment that are still working—the panel. None of the
other experiments are still running. The panel, called a "lunar laser ranging retroreflector
array," is small and simplicity, or it give scientists lots of important information.

The operation of the panel is simple. The mirrors on the panel points at Earth. A laser
pulse shoots out of a telescope on Earth, crossing the Earth-moon space, so hits the
mirrors. The mirrors sends the pulse straight back. On Earth, scientists measure the travel
time and determining the moon's distance, not only quickly but very accurate. For decades,
scientists, along with an occasional researcher, has traced the moon's orbit and learned
many remarkable things.

Everyone seem to have something to gain. The lunar laser ranging retroreflector array
have provided information to many fields of science. Physics are a good example. Physicists
has used the laser results to check Einstein's theories of gravity and relativity. So far,
Einstein are still considered correct, so who know whether the lunar laser ranging retroreflector array will someday tell us something different!

Agreement and Parallel Structure

WRITING:

An essay of definition gives the writer's opinion of the meaning of a concept. See page 470 for general writing guidelines. See page 471 for information on writing an essay.

Step 1. Choose one of the terms below. With a partner or a group, brainstorm ideas about what these terms mean. Think of specific examples or situations that explain them.

1. friendship
2. happiness
3. a stranger
4. good parents

Step 2. Choose one of the terms above, or think of your own.

Step 3. Write your essay.

1. Write your body paragraphs. Each paragraph of your essay must illustrate a part of the definition stated in your thesis. Support each part with examples.

2. Write an introduction that defines the term you have chosen. You may define the term using a dictionary (name the dictionary and quote from it). In your thesis statement, tell how you are going to define it and give two or three aspects of the definition that you will write.

> Friends play a major role in a person's life. When you find a friend, your life changes. All of us have a different definition of what a friend is. According to the *American Heritage College Dictionary,* a friend is "a person whom one knows, likes, and trusts." For me, too, a friend is someone that I know, like and trust, but a friend is also someone with whom you share the same moral values, whom you support in times of need ...

3. Write a conclusion that summarizes your definition. Give a final comment on the term.

4. Write a title.

Step 4. Evaluate your essay.

Checklist

_____ Did you write a thesis statement in your introduction?

_____ Did you give details, examples, or situations that support your thesis statement?

_____ Did you summarize and comment on your term in the conclusion?

Step 5. Work with a partner or a teacher to edit your essay. Check spelling, vocabulary, and grammar.

Step 6. Write your final copy.

314

A **Choose the best answer, A, B, C, or D, to complete the sentence. Mark your answer by darkening the oval with the same letter.**

1. Kate runs and _____.

   A. lifts weights   Ⓐ Ⓑ Ⓒ Ⓓ
   B. is lifting weights
   C. weight lifting
   D. is doing weight lifting

2. The doctor recommended eating healthier meals and _____.

   A. to do exercise   Ⓐ Ⓑ Ⓒ Ⓓ
   B. doing exercise
   C. exercise
   D. to exercise

3. The store sells not only vitamins _____.

   A. but also food   Ⓐ Ⓑ Ⓒ Ⓓ
   B. also sells food
   C. but sells food
   D. but also is selling food

4. Neither his grammar _____ good.

   Ⓐ Ⓑ Ⓒ Ⓓ
   A. or his reading skills are
   B. nor his reading skills is
   C. nor his reading skills are
   D. or his reading skills are not

5. He told me he would help me, _____ he didn't.

   A. so   Ⓐ Ⓑ Ⓒ Ⓓ
   B. for
   C. and
   D. yet

6. Both the students _____ at the meeting.

   Ⓐ Ⓑ Ⓒ Ⓓ
   A. and also the teachers
   B. and the teachers was
   C. and the teachers were
   D. but also the teachers were

7. He exercises regularly, _____ he is in good health.

   A. so   Ⓐ Ⓑ Ⓒ Ⓓ
   B. but
   C. yet
   D. for

8. I hope to go to college _____.

   A. and study economic   Ⓐ Ⓑ Ⓒ Ⓓ
   B. or to study economics
   C. and also to study economics
   D. and study economics

9. She wants to take either _____ next semester.

   A. physics nor chemistry   Ⓐ Ⓑ Ⓒ Ⓓ
   B. physics and chemistry
   C. physics or chemistry
   D. physic or chemistry

10. Air _____.

   Ⓐ Ⓑ Ⓒ Ⓓ
   A. both contains oxygen and water
   B. contains both oxygen and water
   C. both oxygen and water contains
   D. both contain oxygen and water

B Find the underlined word or phrase, A, B, C, or D, that is incorrect. Mark your answer by darkening the oval with the same letter.

1. Each of the students in the class have
   A   B   C
   a grammar book and a reading book.
   D

   Ⓐ Ⓑ Ⓒ Ⓓ

2. Having a cold can make you feel tired,
   A   B
   miserable, and weakness.
   C   D

   Ⓐ Ⓑ Ⓒ Ⓓ

3. The number of students who passed the
                    A   B
   test were fewer than expected.
        C   D

   Ⓐ Ⓑ Ⓒ Ⓓ

4. Mathematics are my favorite class, but
                A   B
   I also like physics and chemistry.
        C   D

   Ⓐ Ⓑ Ⓒ Ⓓ

5. The principal of the school, along with
   A   B
   the teachers and custodians, were present
                  C   D
   at the meeting.

   Ⓐ Ⓑ Ⓒ Ⓓ

6. The news about the economy are both a
   A   B   C
   surprise and a relief.
            D

   Ⓐ Ⓑ Ⓒ Ⓓ

7. Each of the students agreed that
   A   B
   twenty minutes are not enough for an
                    C   D
   essay exam.

   Ⓐ Ⓑ Ⓒ Ⓓ

8. Many people in the world has neither
                          A   B
   food to eat nor clean water to drink.
              C   D

   Ⓐ Ⓑ Ⓒ Ⓓ

9. Our teacher expects us to be on time,
                A   B
   to do all our homework, and sitting
   C   D
   quietly in class.

   Ⓐ Ⓑ Ⓒ Ⓓ

10. Everybody in our class enjoy doing
    A   B   C
    quizzes.
    D

    Ⓐ Ⓑ Ⓒ Ⓓ

UNIT 11

NOUN CLAUSES AND REPORTED SPEECH

11a Noun Clauses Beginning with *That*

I hope **that I have passed the test.**

Main Clause	Noun Clause (with *That*)
I think	**(that) she's a movie star.**
She hopes	**(that) people won't notice.**

1. Noun clauses act as nouns in a sentence. In this unit, most of the noun clauses act as objects. In the first example in the chart, the noun clause *that she is a movie star* is the object of the verb *think*.

2. We use an object noun clause with a main clause. The main clause always comes first. We do not use a comma between the two clauses.

Function

1. We use *that* clauses after certain verbs that express feelings, thoughts, and opinions. Here are some of them.

agree	expect	hope	presume	remember
assume	fear	imagine	pretend	suppose
believe	feel	know	prove	suspect
decide	figure out	learn	read	show
discover	find	notice	realize	teach
doubt	forget	observe	recognize	think
dream	guess	predict	regret	understand

2. We often omit *that* from a noun clause, especially when we speak. The meaning of the sentence does not change.

> Linda: I think **it's raining**.
>   OR I think **that it's raining**.
> John: I hope **we don't get wet**.
>   OR I hope **that we don't get wet**.

3. When the introductory verb is in the present tense, the verb in the noun clause can be in the present, past, or future, depending on the meaning of the sentence.

> I believe he**'s** here (now).
> I believe he**'ll** be here (in a few minutes).
> I believe he **was** here (a few minutes ago).

4. In conversation, to avoid repeating the *that* clause after verbs such as *think, believe,* and *hope,* we can use *so* or *not* in response to a yes/no question.

> Ken: Is Nancy here today?
> Pat: I **think so**. (I think that Nancy is here today.)
> Ken: Has the rain stopped?
> Pat: I don't **believe so**. (I don't believe that the rain has stopped.)
> Ken: Are we having dinner soon?
> Pat: I'm **afraid not**. (I want us to have dinner soon, but we are not going to.)

	With These Verbs	Question	Answer
Positive Verb + *So*	think		I **think so.**
	believe		I **believe so.**
	be afraid		I'm **afraid so.**
	guess		I **guess so.**
	hope	Has the rain stopped?	I **hope so.**
Negative Verb + *So*	think		I don't **think so.**
	believe		I don't **believe so.**
Positive Verb + *Not*	be afraid		I'm **afraid not.**
	guess		I **guess not.**
	hope		I **hope not.**

5. In formal English, a noun clause can also be the subject of a sentence. In this case we cannot omit the word *that*.

That prices are going up is clear.

It is more common to say the same thing with the word *it* as the subject and with the noun clause at the end.

It is clear **(that) prices are going up.**

Practice

Match the two halves of the sentences to make predictions about the future.

What will happen by the year 2050?

___d___ **1.** Population experts predict

_____ **2.** Food scientists expect

_____ **3.** Energy scientists think

_____ **4.** Astronauts will prove

_____ **5.** Robots will figure out

_____ **6.** People will realize

a. that renewable energy will replace fossil fuels.

b. that they are smarter than humans.

c. that it is possible to survive on Mars.

d. that the world's population will be over 9 billion.

e. that everyone needs to speak one language.

f. that most of our food will be genetically modified.

2 What Do You Think?

With a partner, ask and answer the questions. Answer with *think, believe, be afraid, guess,* or *hope* + *so* or *not*.

1. Will the world's population continue to increase?

2. Will hunger in the world disappear by the year 2050?

3. Will people stop using cars?

4. Will scientists figure out a way for humans to live on Mars?

5. Should everyone speak the same language?

3 Your Turn

Write five predictions about the future. Use verbs from the list.

discover   expect   predict   prove   think

Example:
I predict that everyone will learn English on the Internet by the year 2050.

1. _____

2. _____

3. _____

4. _____

5. _____

11b Noun Clauses Beginning with Wh- Words (Indirect Wh- Questions)

I don't know **why he takes his computer on camping trips.**

Main Clause	Noun Clause (Indirect Question)*
She wanted to know	**who I was.**
	where they came from.
	why he called.
I don't know	**when he arrives.**
	what she said.
	how they did it so fast.

Indirect question is the name of this type of noun clause.

1. Noun clauses may also begin with wh- words. Sentences with noun clauses beginning with wh- words are also called indirect questions.

   Direct Question: Why did he call?
   Indirect Question: I don't know why he called.

2. Although wh- clauses begin with a question word, they do not follow question word order. Instead, they use statement word order.

   CORRECT: I know where **she is**.
   INCORRECT: I know where ~~is she~~.

3. We use a question mark at the end of a sentence if the main clause is a direct question and a period at the end of a sentence if the main clause is a statement.

	Main Clause	Noun Clause (Indirect Question)
Main clause is a question	**Can you tell me**	where the elevators are?
Main clause is a statement	**I wonder**	where the elevators are.

1. We usually use an indirect question to express something we do not know or to express uncertainty.

   I don't know **how much it is.**

2. We often use indirect questions to ask politely for information.

   Direct Question: What time does the train leave?
   Indirect Question: Can you tell me what time the train leaves?

---

4 Practice

Rewrite each question as a main clause + a wh- noun clause. Be sure to use correct punctuation at the end of the sentences.

You are going to a job interview. What questions will you ask?

1. How many people does your company employ?

Can you tell me _how many people the company employs?_

2. When did the company first get started?

I'd like to know _____

3. Where is the head office?

Can you tell me _____

4. What are the job benefits?

Can you tell me _____

5. How many vacation days do people get?

I wonder _____

6. What is the salary?

Can you tell me _____

7. Who will my manager be?

I'd like to know _____

8. When does the job start?

Can you tell me _____

9. How many people are you going to interview for this job?

Can you tell me _____

10. When can you tell me the results of this interview?

If you don't mind, I'd like to know _____

Practice

Rewrite each direct question as an indirect question (a main clause + a wh- noun clause). Be sure to use correct punctuation at the end of the sentences.

You have a job interview tomorrow, and you are asking a friend to help you prepare. Your friend is telling you about the questions that they will probably ask you.

1. They will probably ask _what your current job title is._
   (What is your current job title?)

2. They will want to know _____
   (What are your job duties?)

3. They will ask _____
   (What qualifications do you have?)

4. They will want to know _____
   (Who was your previous employer?)

5. They will ask _____
   (How long did you work in your last job?)

6. They will want to know _____
   (Why did you leave your last job?)

7. They will ask _____
   (What was your salary?)

8. They will want to know _____
   (Why do you want the job?)

9. They will ask _____
   (How did you find out about the job?)

10. They will want to know _____
   (When can you start work?)

6 | Your Turn

Work with a partner. Think of an unusual job. Imagine that you went to a job interview for this job and write five wh- questions the interviewer asked you. Tell the class about the questions using a main clause + a wh- noun clause. Your classmates should guess the job.

Example:
(The unusual job was a lion tamer.)
They asked (me) why I was interested in lions.

◆ 11c Noun Clauses Beginning with *If* or *Whether* (Indirect Yes/No Questions)

I wonder **if he understands me.**

Yes/No Question	Main Clause	Noun Clause (Indirect Yes/No Question)
Did he see you?	Do you know	**if/whether he saw you (or not)?**
Are they angry?	I don't know	**if/whether they're angry (or not).**
Is she at home?	I wonder	**if/whether she's at home (or not).**

1. Noun clauses with *if* or *whether* are indirect yes/no questions.

   Direct Question: Are they angry?
   Indirect Question: I don't know if they are angry or not.

2. *If* and *whether* noun clauses must begin with *if* or *whether*. They do not follow question word order. Instead, they use statement word order.

   CORRECT: Do you know if this is the director's office?
   INCORRECT: Do you know ~~is this~~ the director's office?

3. We can add the phrase *or not* to the end of an *if/whether* clause if the clause is short.

> I don't know if she's here **or not.**
> I don't know whether she is here **or not.**

We can also put *or not* immediately after *whether,* but not after *if.*

> CORRECT: I don't know whether or not she is here.
> INCORRECT: I don't know if ~~or not~~ she's here.

Function

1. *If* and *whether* at the beginning of a noun clause have the same meaning. We usually use *whether* in more formal situations.

2. We usually use *if/whether* clauses following verbs of mental activity.

> I can't remember **if I turned off my computer.**
> I wonder **whether he has sent me a message.**

3. We use *if/whether* clauses in polite questions.

> Do you know **if Mr. Gallo is in the office today**?
> Can you tell me **whether Flight 213 has arrived or not**?

7 Practice

Rewrite each question as a main clause + an *if/whether* noun clause. Be sure to use correct punctuation at the end of the sentences.

You are thinking of having a birthday party at the Paradise Restaurant. Ask your friend about the restaurant.

A: Did we eat lunch there together last year, or didn't we?

B: I can't remember *if we ate lunch there together last year.*
                                                                        1

A: Did we like the food?

B: I can't remember _____
                                                                        2

A: Are they open for lunch on Saturday?

B: I don't know _____
                                                                        3

Noun Clauses and Reported Speech

A: Is there a fixed price lunch menu?

B: We can ask _____
　　　　　　　　　　　　　　　　　　　　4

A: Are there enough tables for fifty guests?

B: I don't know _____
　　　　　　　　　　　　　　　　　　　5

A: Do they have live music?

B: I can't say _____
　　　　　　　　　　　　　　　　　　　6

A: Can they order a special birthday cake?

B: I wonder _____
　　　　　　　　　　　　　　　　　　　7

A: Do they have a vegetarian meal option?

B: I'm not sure _____
　　　　　　　　　　　　　　　　　　　8

A: Do they have high chairs for children?

B: I wonder _____
　　　　　　　　　　　　　　　　　　　9

A: Is it a good idea to go there, or isn't it?

B: We need to decide _____
　　　　　　　　　　　　　　　　　　　10

---

8 | Your Turn

Work with a partner. Imagine that you are planning to stay at an expensive hotel. Your friend knows the hotel quite well. Ask your friend five questions about the hotel.

Example:
You:　　　　　I wonder if they have a sports center.
Your partner:　Of course. They have a huge sports center with an Olympic-sized pool.

11d Quoted Speech

James Dean said, **"Dream as if you'll live forever. Live as if you'll die today."** He died at the age of 24 when his car crashed.

1. See page 468 for punctuation rules for quoted speech.

2. We use quoted speech to show the exact words someone uses. We use quoted speech in novels, stories, and newspaper articles. In these examples, notice where the "said" phrase is. Notice that it can go before or after its subject.

> Story about James Dean: "Dream as if you'll live forever. Live as if you'll die today," **James Dean said.**
> OR **James Dean said,** "Dream as if you'll live forever. Live as if you'll die today."
>
> Newspaper article: "I will not vote for this law," **said Senator Smith.**

9 Practice

Read the following fable from Aesop. Use the correct punctuation and capitalization for quoted speech. Note that when the speaker changes, we start a new paragraph.

The Travelers and the Sea

Two travelers were walking along the seashore. They saw something far out on the waves.

"Look," said one. "There is a big ship coming from far away with gold and riches on it." The object they saw came nearer to the shore.

No said the other that's not a treasure ship. It's a fisherman's boat with the day's catch of good fish

The object came even nearer to the shore. The waves washed it up on the shore.

It's a chest of gold lost from a shipwreck they both said. Both travelers rushed to the beach, but they found nothing but a wet piece of wood.

Moral: Do not let your hopes carry you away from reality.

Read the story. Use the correct punctuation and capitalization for quoted speech.

The Travelers and the Purse

Two men were traveling together along a road when one of them picked up a purse.
"How lucky I am," he said, "I've found a purse. Judging by its weight it must be full of gold."

Don't say *I* have found a purse said his companion. Instead, say *we* have found a purse and how lucky *we* are. Travelers should share the fortunes and misfortunes of the road

No, no replied the other angrily. *I* found it and *I* am going to keep it

Just then they heard a shout of "Stop! Thief!" and when they looked around, they saw a mob of people with clubs coming down the road.

The man who had found the purse began to panic.

We'll be in trouble if they find the purse on us he said

No, no replied the other you wouldn't say *we* before, so now stick to your *I*.
Say *I* am in trouble

Moral: We cannot expect anyone to share our misfortunes unless we are willing to share our good fortunes also.

---

11 Your Turn

Write what your teacher said in class today in quoted speech.

Example:
My teacher said, "I want you to do all the exercises on quoted speech by the next lesson."

◆ 11e Reported Speech: Statements

Benjamin Franklin said **that nothing was certain except death and taxes.**

1. *Say* and *tell* are examples of reporting verbs. If a reporting verb is in the present, there is no change in tense in reported speech. We can omit *that* with no change in meaning.

> Quoted Speech: Mary **says**, "I **am** happy."
> Reported Speech: Mary **says** (that) she **is** happy.

2. If the reporting verb is in the past tense (*said, told*), the verb tense changes when we report it. Here are some common tense changes.

Quoted Speech	Reported Speech
Mary said, "I **do** all the work."	Mary said that she **did** all the work.
Mary said, "I**'m doing** all the work."	Mary said that she **was doing** all the work.
Mary said, "I **did** all the work."	Mary said that she **had done** all the work.
Mary said, "I**'ve done** all the work."	Mary said that she **had done** all the work.
Mary said, "I**'ve been doing** all the work."	Mary said that she **had been doing** all the work.
Mary said, "I**'ll do** all the work."	Mary said that she **would do** all the work.
Mary said, "I **can do** all the work."	Mary said that she **could do** all the work.

3. Pronouns can change in reported speech. The change depends on the meaning. Here are some common examples.

	Quoted	Reported	Quoted Example	Reported Example
Subject Pronouns	I	he, she	Sam said, "**I**'m leaving."	Sam said that **he** was leaving. (Sam was leaving.)
	you (singular)	I	Sam said, "**You**'re leaving."	Sam said that **I** was leaving. (The speaker is leaving.)
		he, she	Sam said, "**You**'re leaving."	Sam said that **he** was leaving. (Sam was talking to a boy or a man.)
	we	they	Sam said, "**We**'re tired."	Sam said that **they** were tired. (*They* includes Sam and other people.)
	you (plural)	we	Sam said, "**You**'re tired."	Sam said that **we** were tired. (*We* includes Sam and other people, but not Sam.)
		they	Sam said, "**You**'re tired."	Sam said that **they** were tired. (*They* includes a group of other people, but not Sam or the speaker.)

	Quoted	Reported	Quoted Example	Reported Example
Object Pronouns	me	him, her	Sam said, "It's for **me**."	Sam said that it was for **him**. (It was for Sam.)
	you (singular)	me	Sam said, "It's for **you**."	Sam said that it was for **me**. (It was for the speaker.)
		him, her	Sam said, "It's for **you**."	Sam said that it was for him/her. (Sam was talking to a man/woman.)
	us	us	Sam said, "It's for **us**."	Sam said that it was for **us**. (*Us* includes the speaker.)
		them	Sam said, "It's for **us**."	Sam said that it was for **them**. (*Us* includes Sam, but not the speaker.)
	you (plural)	us	Sam said, "It's for **you**."	Sam said that it was for **us**. (*Us* includes the speaker and other people, but not Sam.)
		them	Sam said, "It's for **you**."	Sam said that it was for **them**. (*Them* includes other people, but not Sam or the speaker.)
Possessive Forms	my	his, her	Sam said, "**My** son is sleepy."	Sam said that **his** son was sleepy. (The son is the speaker's.)
	your (singular)	my	Sam said, "**Your** son is sleepy."	Sam said that **my** son was sleepy. (The son is the speaker's.)
		his, her	Sam said, "**Your** son is sleepy."	Sam said that **her** son was sleepy. (The son belongs to a woman, not Sam or the speaker.)
	our	their	Sam said, "We have a gift for **our** neighbors."	Sam said that they had a gift for **their** neighbors. (The neighbors are not the speaker's.)
	your (plural)	our	Sam said, "**Your** garden is beautiful."	Sam said that **our** garden was beautiful. (The garden belongs to the speaker and other people.)
		their	Sam said, "**Your** garden is beautiful."	Sam said that **their** garden was beautiful. (The garden belongs to other people, but not Sam or the speaker.)

4. Time expressions can also change in reported speech. Again, it depends on the meaning. Here are come common changes.

Quoted	Reported
now	then
today	that day
tonight	that night
yesterday	the day before
tomorrow	the next day
this week/month/year	that week/month/year
last week/month/year	the week/month/year before
next week/month/year	the week/month/year after
two weeks/months/years ago	two weeks/months/years before

Quoted Speech: She said, "I'm going on vacation **today**."
Reported Speech: She said that she was going on vacation **that day.**

Quoted Speech: Tom explained, "I finished all of the work **yesterday**."
Reported Speech: Tom explained that he had finished all of the work **the day before**.

5. Here are two additional common changes.

Quoted	Reported
here	there
come	go

Quoted Speech: They said, "We'll be **here** when you arrive."
Reported Speech: They said that they would be **there** when we arrived.

Quoted Speech: My mother said, "I hope you can **come** over for dinner."
Reported Speech: My mother said that she hoped I could **go** over for dinner.

12 | Practice

It's a very busy time at the office, so the manager asked the staff to work on Saturday morning. Report the answers the staff gave him.

1. Susan said, "I can't work because I am having my car fixed and won't be able to get here."

   Susan said that she couldn't work on Saturday because she was having her car fixed and she wouldn't be able to get there.

2. Mary Ann said, "I have made other arrangements, and I can't change them now."

_____

_____

3. Ted explained, "I'll be out of town. I'm taking my children to see their grandparents."

_____

_____

4. Stanley complained, "I'm too tired. I need Saturday and Sunday to relax."

_____

_____

5. Steve insisted, "I'll work on Saturday morning, but only if I get paid double."

_____

_____

6. Kate wondered, "Why do I have to come in if the others aren't?"

_____

_____

7. You said, "_____"

_____

_____

13 Practice

Your friend is in the hospital, and she can't call her telephone answering service. She has asked you to listen to her phone messages. Write the messages using reported speech.

Message 1:

This is Cindy from the dentist's office. I'm calling to remind you that you have a dental appointment tomorrow at 10:00.

Cindy called from the dentist's office. She was calling to remind
you that you have a dental appointment tomorrow at 10:00.

Message 2:

Hi, it's Janet. I just want to say hello. I'll call you later.

_____

_____

Message 3:

My name is Ken Stevens. I've been trying to reach you to talk about the new work schedule. My number is 678-9542. Please call me back.

_____

_____

Message 4:

This is Tony from the Travel Shop. Your tickets will be ready tomorrow. If you'd like us to mail them to you, we can send them by regular mail or express mail. Let me know.

_____

_____

Message 5:

It's Jim. My boss gave me two tickets for the Wild Rockers concert next week. Do you want to go with me?

_____

_____

Message 6:

It's your mother, dear. I called you at work and you weren't there. I've been calling you at home, but there is no answer. Where are you? I'm worried. Please call me.

_____

_____

Message 7:

It's Mother again. It has been twenty-four hours, and I still haven't heard from you. Something has to be wrong. Please call me.

_____

_____

14 Your Turn

What interesting things did people say to you yesterday? Use reported speech.

Example:
My friend told me that he saw Ben Affleck in the street yesterday.

11f Reported Speech: Questions

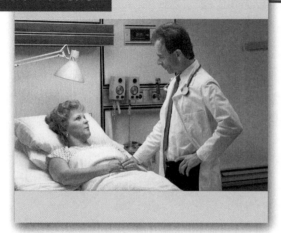

The doctor asked **how I felt.**

1. Like indirect questions, questions in reported speech use statement word order.

   Direct Question: Will it rain this afternoon?
   Indirect Question: I want to know if it will rain this afternoon.
   Reported Question: She asked me if it would rain this afternoon.

   Direct Question: Where is my CD player?
   Indirect Question: She wonders where her CD player is.
   Reported Question: She asked me where her CD player was.

2. Reported questions use a reporting verb such as *ask*. They report someone
   else's words.

3. Reported questions use the same tense, pronoun, and time expression changes as
   reported statements (see page 329).

4. After *ask,* we can use an object (*me, Nancy*) to say who asked the question.

   I **asked Nancy** if she was* busy.
   He **asked me** where I had gone.
   He **asked** to leave early.

5. After the verb *tell* we must use an object.

   CORRECT: He told me what he wanted.
   INCORRECT: He told what he wanted.

*In formal English, *was* would be *were.*

15 Practice

Sue lived in Los Angeles for a few years, and now she is back in her home town. She meets an old friend named Jeff. Rewrite Sue's questions as reported questions.

1. Jeff: How are you?

   He asked her how she was.

2. Jeff: When did you get back?

   _____

3. Jeff: Did you like Los Angeles?

   _____

4. Jeff: Why didn't you stay there longer?

   _____

5. Jeff: Are you living in your old neighborhood?

   _____

6. Jeff: Are you still living alone?

   _____

7. Jeff: What are you doing for a living now?

   _____

8. Jeff: Would you like to play tennis with me again, like old times?

   _____

9. Jeff: Do you have the same cell phone number?

   _____

10. Jeff: Can I call you tonight?

   _____

16 Your Turn

Think of four questions to ask your partner about his/her future. Your partner will answer your questions. Then, you will report to the class what you wanted to know and your partner's answers.

Example:

You: What subject do you want to study in college?
Your partner: I want to study chemistry.
You: Where do you want to study?
Your partner: At the state university.
You: I asked my partner what subject she wanted to study. She told me that she wanted to study chemistry. I also asked her where she wanted to study, and she answered that she wanted to study at the state university.

11g Reported Commands, Requests, Offers, Advice, Invitations, and Warnings

The police officer warned me **not to do** it again.

VERB + OBJECT + (NOT) + INFINITIVE

	Quoted Speech	Reported Speech			
		Subject	Verb	(Object)	(*Not* +) Infinitive
Commands	"Wait."	They	**told**	**me**	**to wait.**
	"Don't get lost."	She	**told**	**us**	**not to get** lost.
Requests	"Talk quietly, please."	We	**asked**	**them**	**to (please) talk** quietly.
	"Could you not drive so fast?"	I	**asked**	**him**	**not to drive** so fast.
Advice	"You should call her."	He	**advised**	**me**	**to call** her.
	"We shouldn't eat so much."	She	**advised**	**us**	**not to eat** so much.
Invitations	"Would you like to have lunch with us?"	They	**asked**	**me**	**to have** lunch with them.
Warnings	"You'd better not be late."	She	**warned**	**them**	**not to be** late.
	"We'd better be careful."	He	**warned**	**us**	**to be** careful.

VERB + (*NOT*) + INFINITIVE

	Quoted Speech	Reported Speech		
		Subject	Verb	(*Not* +) Infinitive
Threats	"I won't give you the money."	She	**threatened**	**not to give** me the money.
Promises	"I'll take you to the movies tomorrow."	I	**promised**	**to take** her to the movies the next day.
Offers	"Can I help you?"	He	**offered**	**to help** me.

Notice that the verbs *tell, ask, advise,* and *warn* are followed by an object + (*not*) + an infinitive.

Tell, advise, and *warn* must be followed by an object.

CORRECT: They told us to come early.
INCORRECT: They told to come early.

We can use *ask* with or without an object.

WITH OBJECT: George asked Alex to play the guitar. (George wants Alex to play the guitar.)
WITHOUT OBJECT: George asked to play the guitar. (George asked permission to play the guitar.)

---

17 **Practice**

Rewrite the following sentences using the reporting verbs in parentheses.

Your teacher is giving some instructions before a test.

1. Listen carefully. (tell)

   He told us to listen carefully.

2. Don't talk. (tell)

   _____

3. Please put all your books and papers away. (ask)

   _____

4. Please do not try to copy your neighbor's work. (ask)

   _____

5. I will tell the boss if you use the company car for personal business again. (threaten)

   _____

6. Cheating will be severely punished. (warn)

   _____

7. Check the answers carefully before handing in your paper. (advise)

   _____

8. You will get a prize if you finish all the questions. (promise)

_____

9. Would someone like to help me give out the papers? (invite)

_____

10. Would you like me to repeat the instructions? (offer)

_____

| 18 | **Your Turn** |

Choose a verb from the list. Say or write a sentence that corresponds to one of the verbs in the list, but do not use the verb in your sentence. Ask a partner to guess which verb you chose. Continue with other verbs from the list.

advise	ask	invite	offer
promise	tell	threaten	warn

Example:
I will help you with your homework, if you do the dishes. (corresponds to a promise)

11h The Subjunctive in Noun Clauses

Our teacher demanded that the class **be** quiet.

1. The subjunctive form is the base form of the verb. It has no present, past, or future form. It has no singular or plural. We put *not* before the base verb to form the negative.

2. We use the subjunctive form in *that* clauses following certain verbs of command, urgency, or request. Here are some verbs that are followed by the subjunctive in noun clauses.

advise	desire	request
ask	insist	require
command	propose	suggest
demand	recommend	urge

Our teacher **insists** that we **be** on time.
The officer **asked** that he **show** his passport.
They **recommended** that he **not try** to fix the computer himself.

3. We can also use *should* after the verbs *suggest* and *recommend*.

I **suggested** that she **should take** the test soon.

4. We also use the subjunctive form in *that* clauses following adjectives of urgency. These statements are similar to commands, but they are impersonal and therefore softer.

It's **vital** that you **make** a decision right now.   (impersonal and softer)
Make a decision right now!   (strong)
I insist that you make a decision right now.   (strong)

Here are some adjectives of urgency.

advisable	critical	essential	important	urgent
best	desirable	imperative	necessary	vital

19 Practice

Rewrite the following sentences using the subjunctive.

A 17-year-old boy was arrested for stealing CDs from a music store. He was sent to a youth correctional facility for two months. What were the opinions of different people involved in the case?

1. The judge: Go to jail for two months.

   The judge recommended *that he go to jail*

   for two months.

2. The parents: He must get another trial.

The parents demanded _____

3. The lawyer: Why doesn't he do community service?

The lawyer suggested _____

4. The police officer: He must repay the money to the store owner.

The police officer insisted _____

5. The store owner: Could he please return the CDs?

The store owner requested _____

6. What is your opinion?

I recommend _____

20 Practice

Write one solution for each of the problems. Use the subjunctive and verbs from the list.

create	improve	reduce	stop
develop	protect	restrict	try

1. Many wildlife species are endangered.

It is urgent _____

2. We are running out of fossil fuel.

It is imperative _____

3. Our cities are overcrowded.

It is desirable _____

4. There are too many cars.

It is essential _____

5. Our climate is heating up too rapidly.

It is critical _____

6. We produce too much plastic waste.

It is advisable _____

7. Too many people are dying from hunger.

It is vital _____

8. There are too many wars.

It is critical _____

21 Your Turn

In groups, choose one of the following cases. Imagine the opinions of different people involved in the case. Say and write sentences about the case using *recommend, insist, suggest,* and *demand*.

Example:
The train conductor insisted that the boy get off at the next station.

1. A 15-year-old boy was traveling on a train alone. He didn't have a ticket. (boy, train conductor, other passengers)

2. A friend of yours spent over three thousand dollars on a credit card to buy luxury clothes and jewelry. (friends, you)

3. A man pretended that his car had been stolen so that he could claim insurance. Actually, the car had broken down and he couldn't afford to repair it. (man, insurance company, representative, man's wife)

_____

_____

_____

_____

_____

_____

_____

_____

_____

_____

REVIEW

1 **Review (11a–11c, 11e–11g)**

Rewrite the quotes as reported speech.

1. Cindy said, "Matthew, get out of bed, or you'll be late for your interview."

   Cindy told <u>Matthew to get out of bed or he'd be late for</u>

   <u>his interview.</u>

2. Matthew said, "Why didn't you get me up earlier?"

   Matthew wanted to know _____

3. Cindy said, "I went to the gym."

   Cindy said that _____

4. Matthew said, "Did I set my alarm clock or not?"

   Mathew couldn't remember _____

5. Cindy suggested, "Matthew, you'd better hurry if you want to get that job."

   Cindy suggested that _____

6. The interviewer had said, "Be here on time."

   The interviewer had insisted _____

7. Cindy said, "Why did you sleep so late?"

   Cindy said she didn't understand _____

8. Matthew explained, "I was preparing for the interview until 2:00 A.M."

   Matthew explained that _____

9. Cindy asked, "How do you expect to get there, Matthew?"

   Cindy asked _____

10. Matthew asked, "Can you drive me there?"

    Matthew wondered if _____

11. Cindy asked, "How far is it to the office?"

    Cindy wanted to know _____

12. Matthew said, "It's about 20 miles."

    Matthew explained that _____

2 Review (11a–11c, 11e–11g)

Rewrite the quotes as reported speech.

1. Michael asked, "Are we going to the museum today, Susan?"

   Michael asked Susan *if they were going to the museum.*

2. Susan asked, "Could you get my umbrella?"

   Susan asked _____

3. Michael asked, "Is it raining now?"

   Michael wanted to know _____

4. Michael asked, "Is the museum open on Mondays?"

   Michael wanted to know _____

5. Susan said, "I'm really excited about seeing the new abstract art exhibit."

   Susan said _____

6. Michael said, "My car isn't running."

   Michael said _____

7. Susan said, "Don't worry because my mother can take us."

   Susan told _____

8. Michael suggested, "Let's go by bus."

   Michael suggested _____

9. Susan asked, "What time does the next bus come?"

   Susan wanted to know _____

10. Michael said, "It'll be here in five minutes."

    Michael told Susan _____

11. Michael said, "Did I give you the discount tickets?"

    Michael couldn't remember _____

12. Susan said, "Don't look for them now."

    Susan recommended _____

13. Susan warned, "We'll miss the bus."

    Susan warned Michael that _____

Review (11a–11e)

Read the following fable from West Africa. Find and correct the errors in noun clauses and quoted and reported speech.

Ananse lived with his family. One year there was no rain, so the crops did not grow.

Ananse ~~that~~ knew ^*that* there would not be enough food to feed everyone. One day his wife

asked Will it rain at all this summer?

I don't believe so he replied. You know, I prefer to die than to see my children starve.

Therefore, I will allow myself to die so that there will be enough food for the family.

Ananse then told to his wife that he wants the family to bury me on the farm and to put

into my coffin all the things I will need for my journey into the next world. He said, "It's

critical that you left my grave open. I want my soul to be free to wander. And I insist that

no one visits the farm for three months after my death.

The next morning, Ananse's family found him dead. But Ananse was only pretending.

At night he would lift the lid of his coffin and take food from the farm. One day his son,

Ntikuma, realized that there wasn't much food in the house and that he must visit the farm

to get some. He said he needed to go today to get what little food the farm had to feed

the family. Where is all the corn and millet? he said to himself when he got to the farm.

His mother told him the food was disappearing at night. It's a thief exclaimed Ntikuma.

I want to know who is he.

Ntikuma carved a statue from wood and covered it with tar*. Then he placed the

figure in the field. That evening, Ananse came out of his coffin and saw the figure. Good

evening he said. I don't know you. Please tell me who are you? The figure did not reply.

Ananse got angry, so he slapped the figure. His hand stuck fast. Ananse shouted If I don't

let go of my right hand, he'll hit you with his left! He hit the figure with his left hand. He

hit the statue with his right leg, then the left. Ananse struggled as the figure fell. He was

stuck was very clear.

tar: a dark, thick, sticky petroleum-based material used, for example, to build roads and roofs

The next day Ntikuma and others went to the field. I wonder Ananse caught the thief someone asked. Then they found Ananse. He was so ashamed he didn't know what to do, so he turned into a spider and climbed up a tree where he could not be seen.

This story is a West African fable meant to teach a lesson about selfishness.

4 Review (IIc–IIe, IIh)

Find and correct the errors in noun clauses and quoted and reported speech.

"I want more excitement," said one traveler.

I want different things to do said another.

When asked, many travelers have insisted that we don't want to do just one thing while we're on vacation. In response, many tour operators now offer combination packages, or "combos." David Rose of High Roads Traveled says We now offer combo packages that mix several activities in one outing. Mr. Rose recommends that a traveler takes a combo if he or she likes fun and adventure. People love these trips is very clear, he adds.

Combo packages mix hiking, cycling, biking, climbing, rafting, horseback riding, or other activities. Ron Clair of Ways Traveled says, "Combos are his most popular trips.

"Sunbathing at the beach all week is a thing of the past, says Margaret Erikson, author of *Your Adventure.* Can I tell you why are combos so popular? she asks. She continues today travelers demand tour operators that will give them a variety of adventures. Will this trend continue? I believe so. Sometimes I wonder the old car trip will eventually fade away.

Some people wonder if or not they must be a superior athlete to take a combo adventure. Top athletes do things on their own says Mary Miller of High Mountain Bike Tours. She adds that my company is oriented toward vacations for the average person. She does say that I talk to a client first and advises he or she prepare. She says, "It's important that you are doing some cycling or hiking before you go on any adventure vacation. But I urge that every client remembers that our tours are designed to be enjoyed at your own pace and in your own style.

Do you know where are you going on your next vacation? If you're into major thrills, a combo adventure just may be what are you looking for.

WRITING: Write a Fable or a Legend

All cultures have stories. A fable is a story that teaches a lesson, which is called a "moral." The moral is usually stated at the end of the fable. In many fables, animals speak and act as humans do. A legend is a story, usually about famous people or events, that is handed down from generation to generation. It may be based in historical reality.

Step 1. Think of a legend or fable that you know. Tell it to your partner. Discuss its meaning to the culture it comes from.

Step 2. Write the events of your story in order.

Step 3. Write the story. Include quoted and reported speech from the characters. Write a title for your story. Here is an example of a fable.

> ### The Fox and the Crow
>
> One day a fox was walking through the forest when he noticed a crow up in a tree. The crow had a piece of cheese in its beak, and the fox was hungry. "That cheese looks delicious," the fox said to himself. He wondered how he could get the cheese. He thought, and then he said, "Good morning, beautiful bird. You are indeed beautiful, and I am sure that you have a beautiful voice. Let me hear you sing." The crow ruffled his feathers and looked proud. Then he opened his beak to sing. Immediately the cheese fell out. The fox snatched it up and ran away.
>
> *Moral: Never trust someone who flatters you.*

Step 4. Evaluate your fable or legend.

Checklist

_____ Did you tell the events in the order in which they occurred?

_____ Did you use quoted and reported speech?

_____ Did you write a title for the story?

_____ If you wrote a fable, did you write a moral at the end?

Step 5. Work with a partner or a teacher to edit your fable or legend. Check spelling, vocabulary, and grammar.

Step 6. Write your final copy.

SELF-TEST

A **Choose the best answer, A, B, C, or D, to complete the sentence. Mark your answer by darkening the oval with the same letter.**

1. I wondered where _____.

   A. he came from   Ⓐ Ⓑ Ⓒ Ⓓ
   B. did he come from
   C. came he from
   D. he did come from

2. My mother said, "Don't come in with your dirty shoes."
   My mother warned me _____ in with my dirty shoes.

   A. to come   Ⓐ Ⓑ Ⓒ Ⓓ
   B. not come
   C. not came
   D. not to come

3. I don't know _____ the right place.

   A. is this   Ⓐ Ⓑ Ⓒ Ⓓ
   B. if is this
   C. if this is
   D. this is

4. Ed: Is Jim in his office?
   Kathy: _____.

   A. I think Jim is   Ⓐ Ⓑ Ⓒ Ⓓ
   B. I think
   C. I think so
   D. Yes, Jim is

5. "I'll see you soon," she said. But we didn't see each other for a long time. She said _____.

   A. she will see me soon   Ⓐ Ⓑ Ⓒ Ⓓ
   B. she would see me soon
   C. I would see her soon
   D. she see me soon

6. "Don't drive too fast."

   He told _____ drive fast.
   A. not to   Ⓐ Ⓑ Ⓒ Ⓓ
   B. to
   C. us not to
   D. to us not to

7. He asked, "Where do you want to go?"
   He asked where _____.

   A. did I want to go   Ⓐ Ⓑ Ⓒ Ⓓ
   B. I want to go
   C. I wanted to go
   D. do I want to go

8. It is urgent that she _____ a decision right now.

   A. makes   Ⓐ Ⓑ Ⓒ Ⓓ
   B. is able to make
   C. make
   D. to make

9. Can you tell me what time _____?

   A. the train arrives   Ⓐ Ⓑ Ⓒ Ⓓ
   B. does the train arrive
   C. the train does it arrive
   D. arrives the train

10. "Have you finished your exams?" he asked. "Yes," I answered.
    He asked _____ my exams.

        Ⓐ Ⓑ Ⓒ Ⓓ
    A. whether I have finished
    B. whether did I finish
    C. if I had finished
    D. if I have finished

B Find the underlined word or phrase, A, B, C, or D, that is incorrect. Mark your answer by darkening the oval with the same letter.

1. The teacher <u>warned</u> <u>us</u> <u>that</u> <u>not to</u> cheat
               A   B   C   D
during the test.

2. The interviewer <u>asked</u> <u>to me</u> when
                   A   B
<u>I wanted</u> to start <u>working</u>.
   C   D

Ⓐ Ⓑ Ⓒ Ⓓ

3. <u>Can you tell me</u> where <u>can I</u> get
     A   B
information about trains and <u>where</u>
                          C
<u>I can</u> buy tickets?
  D

4. Paul asked if <u>did</u> they <u>told</u> <u>me</u> when they
              A   B C
<u>were leaving</u>.
   D

Ⓐ Ⓑ Ⓒ Ⓓ

5. <u>Do you know</u> <u>if or not</u> we <u>need</u> <u>to get</u> a
     A   B   C   D
visa to enter the country?

Ⓐ Ⓑ Ⓒ Ⓓ

6. Ted <u>said that</u> he <u>hadn't</u> <u>fill out</u> the
        A   B   C
application form <u>yet</u>.
            D

Ⓐ Ⓑ Ⓒ Ⓓ

7. <u>It is</u> <u>imperative that</u> <u>I fail not</u> any of
   A   B   C
my courses this year <u>if</u> I want to apply
                    D
to a university.

Ⓐ Ⓑ Ⓒ Ⓓ

8. Tony called from Boston <u>yesterday</u> and
                         A
<u>told me</u> that <u>it was</u> extremely cold <u>here</u>.
  B   C   D

Ⓐ Ⓑ Ⓒ Ⓓ

9. I <u>don't know</u> what <u>did happen</u> to <u>him</u>
     A   B   C
after I <u>left</u> school.
      D

Ⓐ Ⓑ Ⓒ Ⓓ

10. He <u>invited</u> <u>us</u> to <u>going</u> to the theater
      A   B   C
<u>next Sunday</u>.
   D

Ⓐ Ⓑ Ⓒ Ⓓ

UNIT 12

ADJECTIVE CLAUSES

12a Adjective Clauses with Subject Relative Pronouns

A police officer is a person **who doesn't usually smile on the job.**

1. An adjective clause, like an adjective, describes or gives more information about a noun.

   We have **noisy** neighbors.   (The adjective *noisy* describes the noun *neighbors*.)

   I have neighbors **that are very noisy.**   (The adjective clause *that are very noisy* describes the noun *neighbors*.)

2. We introduce an adjective clause with the relative pronouns *who, whom, that,* or *which*. The relative pronoun refers to a noun in the main clause.

   I have a friend **who** lives in Mexico City.

3. When the relative pronoun comes before the verb in the adjective clause, the relative pronoun is the subject of the clause. It is a subject relative pronoun.

MAIN CLAUSE	ADJECTIVE CLAUSE	
	Subject Relative Pronoun	
I have a friend	**who**	lives in Mexico City.
I have neighbors	**that**	are very noisy.
I live in a building	**that/which**	has very thin walls.

4. We use *who* or *that* to refer to people.

5. We use *which* or *that* to refer to things. In careful writing, some people prefer *that*, not *which*, to refer to things.

See pages 361-362 for information on when we must use *who* or *which*, not *that*.

6. A subject relative pronoun always has the same form. It does not change for singular, plural, feminine, or masculine words.

> That's the **man who** works in my office.
> That's the **woman who** works in my office.
> Those are the **people who** work in my office.

7. The verb in an adjective clause is singular if the subject relative pronoun refers to a singular noun. The verb is plural if it refers to a plural noun.

> Ken is a man **who works** in my office. (*Man* is third person singular, so the verb is also third person singular.)

> Tony and Fred are men **who work** in another department. (The noun *men* is plural, so the verb is plural.)

1 Practice

Read the paragraphs about inventors and their inventions. Then answer the questions using adjective clauses with subject relative pronouns.

1. Mary Anderson invented the windshield wiper in 1903. She wanted to make streetcars safer in the rain. Her invention allowed the driver to control the wipers from inside the streetcar.

   a. Who was Mary Anderson?

   She was the person *who invented the windshield wiper.*

   _____

   b. What was the purpose of her invention?

   She wanted to invent something _____

   _____

2. Contact lenses were first made in 1887 by the German doctor Adolf Fick. His first lenses were for animals and were made from heavy brown glass. In 1889, August Muller made lenses to help people see things at a distance.

    a. Who was Adolf Fick?

    He was a German doctor _____

    _____

    b. What kind of lenses did August Muller make for people?

    August Muller made lenses _____

    _____

3. Levi Strauss and Jacob Davis were tailors. Many people went to California to look for gold in the 1890s. Strauss and Davis sold tents to them. Soon they developed the idea of making workpants from the tent material, and blue jeans were invented. The idea is still popular today.

    a. Who were Strauss and Davis?

    Strauss and Davis were tailors _____

    _____

    b. What kind of people bought the tents?

    People _____

    _____ bought the tents.

    c. What kind of pants did they sell?

    They sold pants _____

    _____

---

2   Your Turn

Work with a partner. Think of an interesting object, person, or animal. Describe it in a one-sentence definition using a relative clause. Ask your partner to guess what you are describing. If your partner can't guess, give more information.

Example:
You: I'm thinking of a black and white bird that can swim but can't fly.
Your partner: Is it a penguin?
You: Yes, it is.

12b Adjective Clauses with Object Relative Pronouns

Form / Function

These are the oranges **that I picked myself.**

1. When the relative pronouns *who (whom), that,* or *which* come before a noun or pronoun, the relative pronoun takes the place of the object. It is an object relative pronoun.

2. When the relative pronoun comes before a noun or a pronoun, the relative pronoun is the object of the adjective clause.

MAIN CLAUSE	ADJECTIVE CLAUSE
Claudia is the woman	**that/who/whom** we met yesterday.
Where is the book	**that** Tom put on the table?

3. We use *that, who,* or *whom* to refer to people. We rarely use *whom* except in formal English.

4. We use *that* or *which* for things.

   See pages 361-362 for information on when we must use *who* or *which,* not *that.*

5. The relative pronoun can be the object of a preposition. In conversational English, we usually put the preposition at the end of a clause and omit the relative pronoun. However, in formal English, we put the preposition at the beginning of the clause. When this is the case, we use *whom* and *which.* We do not use *who* or *that.*

	Main Clause	Adjective Clause
Informal	Where's the person	**who/that** I should speak **to?**
	That's the company	**that/which** we signed the agreement **with.**
Formal	Where is the person	**to whom** I should speak?
	That is the company	**with which** we signed the agreement.

6. We often omit object relative pronouns, especially when we speak.

On the street today, I ran into a man (who/whom) I knew a long time ago.
There's the set of keys (that) I lost yesterday!
Where's the person (that) I should speak to?

But we do not omit subject relative pronouns.

CORRECT: I have a friend **who** lives in Mexico City.
INCORRECT: I have a friend lives in Mexico City.

3 Practice

A. Match the words with the correct definitions.

_h_	**1.** We use this machine to keep food cold.	**a.** bank
____	**2.** We eat this sauce with burgers and French fries.	**b.** dictionary
____	**3.** We speak on this machine over long distances.	**c.** doctor
____	**4.** We ask this person for help when we see a fire.	**d.** firefighter
____	**5.** We go to this place when we need to borrow a book.	**e.** ketchup
____	**6.** We use this to see objects far away.	**f.** library
____	**7.** We look in this book when we need to know the meaning of a word.	**g.** lightbulb
____	**8.** We use this to see in the dark.	**h.** refrigerator
____	**9.** We ask this person for help when we are sick.	**i.** telephone
____	**10.** We go to this place when we need to borrow money.	**j.** telescope

B. Write a sentence using an adjective clause with an object relative pronoun for each item in part A.

1. _A refrigerator is a machine that we use to keep food cold._

2. _____

3. _____

4. _____

5. _____

6. _____

7. _____

8. _____

9. _____

10. _____

---

4 **Your Turn**

Work with a partner. Take turns asking and answering questions with *what* or *who* and the following prompts. Use adjective clauses with object relative pronouns.

Example:
a book you always like to look at

You: What is a book that you always like to look at?
Your partner: *A China Journey* is a book that I always like to look at. It has
                   beautiful artwork.

1. something you can't live without
2. a food you always think about
3. a show on TV you always like to watch
4. a person you look up to

---

5 **Your Turn**

Make a list of the three most important inventions of the past 100 years. Then say or write sentences with adjective clauses to describe them. Ask a partner to guess what they are.

Example:
You: It's a machine that you use for storing and working with information.
Your partner: It's a computer.

12c Adjective Clauses with *Whose*

Flamingoes are birds **whose feathers are pink** because of the food they eat.

1. We use the relative pronoun *whose* to show possession. We always use a noun after *whose*. We cannot omit *whose*.

   The English teacher **whose** course I'm taking is walking in front of us.

2. The noun after *whose* is the thing that the person or thing in the main clause possesses.

   That's the student **whose application** we just read.

3. Adjective clauses with *whose* usually show possession for people or animals, but sometimes they refer to things.

   I want to go to the university **whose engineering department** is the best.

4. Do not confuse *whose* with *who's*.

	Meaning	Example
Who's	who is	I know a man **who's** from Egypt.
Whose	shows possession	I know a man **whose** family is in Egypt.

6 Practice

Combine the sentences using *whose* in an adjective clause.

1. Martin Luther King, Jr., was a civil rights leader.
His most famous speech contains the words
"I have a dream."

   Martin Luther King, Jr., was a
   civil rights leader whose most
   famous speech contains the words
   "I have a dream."

2. Abraham Lincoln was a president of the United States. His most famous achievement
was freeing African-Americans from slavery.

   _____

   _____

3. Benjamin Franklin was an American statesman and inventor. His most famous invention
was the lightning rod.

   _____

   _____

4. Wilbur and Orville Wright were brothers. Their aircraft was the first wooden, piloted,
heavier-than-air, self-propelled machine to fly.

   _____

   _____

5. Dorothea Lange was a photographer. Her photos made people realize the poverty of
workers during the Great Depression.

   _____

   _____

6. Alice Walker is an African-American writer. Her novel *The Color Purple* received the
Pulitzer Prize in 1983.

   _____

   _____

7. Elizabeth Cady Stanton was a leader of the American women's rights movement. Her lifetime of work helped women gain the right to vote in the United States.

_____

_____

8. Neil Armstrong was an astronaut. His most famous achievement was walking on the moon.

_____

_____

| 7 | **Your Turn**

Say or write sentences about other famous people that you know about.

12d *When, Where, Why,* and *That* as Relative Pronouns

Form / Function

Holland is a place **where people wear clogs.**

1. We can use *when* and *where* to introduce an adjective clause.

Relative Pronoun	Function	Example
Where	refers to a place	That's the building **where** he works.
When	refers to a time	I remember the day **when** I met you.

Notice that the relative pronouns *where* and *when* can be replaced with *that* or *which* + a preposition.

> That's the building **where** he works. =
> That's the building **(that)** he works **in**. (OR **in which he works**)

> I remember the day **when** I met you. =
> I remember the day **(that)** I met you **on**. (OR **on which I met you**)

2. When we use *where* or *when,* we do not use a preposition in the adjective clause.

> CORRECT: That's the building where he works. (no preposition)
> INCORRECT: That's the building where he works ~~in~~.

3. After the word *reason,* we can use *why* or *that* in an adjective clause.

> Is there a reason **why/that** you want to go to that university?

4. We can omit *when, why,* and *that* without changing the meaning.

> I remember the day I first met you.
> Is there a reason you want to go to that university?

We can also omit *where* if we use a preposition.

> That's the building he works in.

---

8 | Practice

Complete the sentences with the correct relative pronouns: *that, who, where, when,* or *why.*

A.

In 1666, there was a terrible plague in London. Isaac Newton went to stay in the country ___*where*___ his mother had a farm. While he was sitting under an apple tree
                   1
one day, an apple fell on his head. Suddenly, Newton realized the reason _____
                                                                              2
objects on the earth fall downwards. It is because they are pulled towards the earth's center by the force of gravity. Newton proposed that gravity was a universal force
_____ holds planets in their orbits. His universal law led to a principle
   3
_____ we now take for granted; the same physical laws are true anywhere in
   4
the universe. The day _____ an apple fell on Newton's head changed our view
                         5
of the world and the universe.

B.

Louis Braille was the man _____ invented books for the blind. Louis became
                                1
blind at the age of four. It was a time _____ there were very few schools for the
                                          2
blind. Blind people were not sent to school, but learned skills like weaving and woodwork
so they could earn a living. Louis was sent to a school in Paris _____ there were
                                                                  3
very few books. The books were written with raised letters _____ made them heavy
                                                              4
and difficult to read. Louis invented a code of raised dots _____ he arranged to
                                                              5
represent each letter of the alphabet. The first Braille book was published in 1827.

C.

Alexander Graham Bell is best known for the invention of the telephone. He first
developed the "harmonic telegraph," a device _____ could send a number of
                                              1
telegraph messages at the same time over a single telegraph wire. In 1875, Bell and his
assistant Watson developed this into a machine _____ could transmit the sound
                                                2
of the human voice. The day _____ Bell first spoke to his assistant in the next
                             3
room changed history forever. Soon after, Bell and Watson went to Philadelphia
_____ they exhibited their invention at the Centennial Exposition, an exhibition
   4
to celebrate America's 100th birthday. Everyone _____ saw the new invention
                                                 5
was amazed at the idea of instant two-way communication.

---

9 | Your Turn

Use the prompts to describe your feelings. Discuss your answers with a partner.

Example:
A place where I feel peaceful is in my kitchen. It's especially nice at times when I am
cooking dinner for my family.

a place where you feel peaceful
a reason why you feel anxious
a time when you feel happiest

12e Defining and Nondefining Adjective Clauses

My grandmother, **who is seventy**, has just started to drive.

1. There are two kinds of adjective clauses: defining clauses and nondefining clauses.* All of the types of adjective clauses in sections 12a to 12d in this unit have been defining adjective clauses.

2. We use a defining adjective clause to identify nouns. They tell us which person, thing, etc. the speaker means.

   I know the woman **who works at the registration office**.
   (The clause *who works at the registration office* tells us which woman.)

3. We use a nondefining adjective clause to add extra information about the noun it refers to. We can omit this information because it is not necessary to identify the noun. We begin a nondefining clause with the relative pronouns *who(m)*, *which*, or *whose*. The relative clause follows the noun in the main clause that it refers to.

   My grandmother, **who is seventy**, has just passed her driving test.

   The adjective clause *who is seventy* adds extra information about my grandmother. We know which grandmother the speaker means without this information.

4. We use commas before and after a nondefining clause. If a nondefining clause ends a sentence, we do not use a comma after it. We use a period.

   My apartment, **which is in the center of town,** is very small.
   Jane Kendall, **who is one of my best friends,** has decided to live in New York.
   I'm very excited about my vacation, **which begins tomorrow.**

   In speech, we pause before and after a nondefining clause.

   My apartment [pause], **which is in the center of town,** [pause] is very small.

   *These clauses are also called restrictive and nonrestrictive clauses.

5. We use *who, whom, which,* and *whose* as relative pronouns in nondefining clauses. We do not use the relative pronoun *that* in a nondefining clause. We also do not omit relative pronouns in a nondefining clause.

> CORRECT: He gave me the documents, which I put in my briefcase.
> INCORRECT: He gave me the documents, ~~that~~ I put in my briefcase.
> INCORRECT: He gave me the documents, I put in my briefcase.

6. As with defining adjective clauses, we use some forms of nondefining adjective clauses only in formal English.

> ### *Whom* as Object
> Formal: The college president, **whom** I met last night, will attend our meeting.
> Informal: The college president, **who** I met last night, will attend our meeting.
>
> ### Preposition + *Which* or *Whom*
> Formal: My senator, **from whom** I expect support, has agreed to meet with me.
> Informal: My senator, **who** I expect support from, has agreed to meet with me.
>
> Formal: This meeting, **for which** I will travel to Washington, will be next week.
> Informal: This meeting, **which** I will travel to Washington for, will be next week.

7. We sometimes use expressions of quantity with *of* in an adjective clause. Examples are *some of, many of, much of, none of, all of, both of, each of, several of, a number of, a little of,* and *a few of.* These are more common in written English than in speech. Note the structure and the use of commas.

> A number of my friends, **some of whom you know,** will be coming tomorrow.
> She gave me a lot of advice, **most of which was not very useful.**

---

10   Practice

Underline the adjective clauses in this reading about fables. Mark defining adjective clauses as *D* and nondefining as *ND*. Add commas as necessary.

>   *D*
> Fables are stories <u>that have animals in them</u>, but the animals behave as people do.
>
>   *ND*
> The truth is that fables, <u>which seem to be about animals</u>, are really about people.
>
> The animal characters do all the things that people do that can get us into trouble. At the
>
> end of the fable, there is a moral which is the lesson people should learn.

We have all heard of Aesop whose fables are world famous. However, we are not sure if he was the person who wrote them. They say that Aesop who lived a long time ago in Greece was an African slave. Aesop's stories of which he wrote about 350 are short and entertaining. These fables which give us lessons about life have been popular through the ages.

II Practice

A worker is talking about a coworker. Complete the sentences with the words in parentheses and *of which* or *of whom*.

A: Let's go to lunch with Barbara.

B: Not with Barbara. I don't like her.

A: Why not?

B: Well, she always tries to give advice, (most) _____*most of which*_____ is

    1

    completely useless.

A: That's not so bad.

B: And she talks about all the designer clothes she has, (none) _____

    2

    we ever see on her. She tells everyone about how much money she spends on things,

    (all) _____ can't be true because we all know how much she makes.

    3

A: I see.

B: She talks about her two "beautiful" children, (both) _____ look

    4

    like her, and she is definitely not a beauty.

A: Uh-huh.

B: She always talks about choosing a medical school for her son and daughter,

    (neither) _____ are doing very well in high school.

    5

    She also talks about her wonderful husband and how good he is to her,

    (a little) _____ must be true, because he has put up

    6

    with her for so many years!

A: Uh-huh. Oh! Hi, Barbara. Would you like to go to lunch . . . with me?

Write a short paragraph of four or five sentences about the teacher, the students, and the lessons in your class. Use defining and nondefining relative clauses.

Example:

My teacher, whose name is Ms. Adams, is a wonderful person. The students in my class, most of whom are my age, find English difficult. The biggest problem that most of us have in English grammar is articles.

12f Using *Which* to Refer to an Entire Clause

Form / Function

She's finished her classes, **which makes her happy.**

1. We can use a nondefining clause with *which* to refer to a whole clause. Look at these sentences.

> Example A: We had to wait for over an hour. **It** made us feel hungry and irritable.
> Example B: We had to wait for over an hour, **which** made us feel hungry and irritable.
>
> Example C: He gave me the money. **This** was very kind of him.
> Example D: He gave me the money, **which** was very kind of him.

In examples A and C, the pronouns *it* and *this* refer to the entire sentence that comes before. We can use *which* in the same way, and it can refer to the whole main clause, as in examples B and D.

2. We usually use this form in spoken English and not often in formal writing.

13 Practice

Combine each sentence in A with the correct follow-up sentence in B.

A.

__c__   **1.** The teacher encouraged me.

_____   **2.** The teacher corrected my paper in red ink.

_____   **3.** She let us use the Internet to do our research.

_____   **4.** We didn't have tests every week in this class.

_____   **5.** We wrote about the news of the day.

_____   **6.** We worked with other students in class.

_____   **7.** The teacher always paid a lot of attention to us.

_____   **8.** We lost points when we handed in homework late.

a. That was easier than finding books from the library.

b. This made us feel less pressure.

c. This motivated me to work harder.

d. That made us feel like she cared about us.

e. That helped me make new friends.

f. It made me read newspapers and listen to the news.

g. It meant I had to do my homework on time.

h. That helped me find my mistakes.

B.

Now combine the pairs of ideas into one sentence with *which*. Take turns reading the sentences with a partner. Remember to pause before *which*.

1. _The teacher encouraged me, which motivated me to work harder._

2. _____

3. _____

4. _____

5. _____

6. _____

7. _____

8. _____

14 **Your Turn**

Write a sentence that would naturally go with each of the following sentences. Then combine the two using *which*.

1. _I heard the news about the principal of the school._   This was a shock to me.

   I heard the news about the principal of the school, which was a shock to me.

2. _____ This was a nice surprise.

   _____

3. _____ This made it more difficult.

   _____

4. _____ This was very kind of her.

   _____

5. _____ This irritated me.

   _____

6. _____ This disappointed me.

   _____

12g Reduced Adjective Clauses

The man **sitting on his car** has a problem.

1. We can reduce an adjective clause to an adjective phrase. An adjective phrase modifies a noun. An adjective phrase does not have a subject and a verb. Instead, it has a present participle (base verb + *-ing*) for the active voice or a past participle for the passive voice. Remember that regular past participles end in *-ed,* but many past participles are irregular. See page 438 for a list of them.

   Adjective Clause: The girl **who is waiting at the bus stop** is my sister.
   Adjective Phrase: The girl **waiting at the bus stop** is my sister.

   Adjective Clause: The information **that was found on that Website** was incorrect.
   Adjective Phrase: The information **found on that Website** was incorrect.

2. We can only reduce adjective clauses that have a subject relative pronoun.

   Adjective Clause: The man **who is sitting in the corner** is well known.
   Adjective Phrase: The man **sitting in the corner** is well known.

   Adjective Clause: The man **who I sat next to** was well known.
   Adjective Phrase: (Not possible. *Who* is not a subject pronoun in this example.)

3. There are two ways to reduce an adjective clause.

   a. If the adjective clause has a form of *be,* we omit the subject relative pronoun and the form of *be.*

   Clause: Do you know the woman **who is standing by the window**?
   Phrase: Do you know the woman **standing by the window**?

   Clause: The words **that are underlined in red** have errors.
   Phrase: The words **underlined in red** have errors.

b. If there is no form of *be* in the adjective clause, we can omit the subject pronoun and change the verb to the present participle (*-ing* form).

Clause: Anyone **who wants to send a message** can use these computers to do so.
Phrase: Anyone **wanting to send a message** can use these computers to do so.

Clause: The Inuit have about 70 words **that describe different kinds of snow.**
Phrase: The Inuit have about 70 words **describing different kinds of snow.**

4. If the adjective clause is defining, then the adjective phrase is also defining, and we don't put commas around it. But if the adjective clause is nondefining, the adjective phrase is also nondefining, and we must use commas.

Defining Clause: Scientists **who were working before 1898** didn't know about the element radium.
Defining Phrase: Scientists **working before 1898** didn't know about the element radium.

Nondefining Clause: Marie Curie, **who worked at the Sorbonne in Paris,** discovered the element radium in 1898.
Nondefining Phrase: Marie Curie, **working at the Sorbonne in Paris,** discovered the element radium in 1898.

5. If an adjective phrase follows a noun and starts with a noun, we call it an *appositive.* Use commas around an appositive if it is nondefining. Do not use commas if it is defining.

Adjective Clause: Marie Curie, **who was a winner of the Nobel Prize,** discovered radium.
                                               Noun   **Noun**
Appositive: Marie Curie, **a winner of the Nobel Prize,** discovered radium.

15 | Practice

Read about the writer Hans Christian Andersen and underline the adjective clauses. Then rewrite the clauses in reduced form using participles or appositives.

famous for his fairy tales
Hans Christian Andersen was a writer <u>who is famous for his fairy tales</u>. He wrote stories

that are well known all over the world like *The Ugly Duckling, The Princess and the Pea,* and

The Little Mermaid. Andersen, who was born in Denmark in 1805, is still a popular writer today.

As a boy who was growing up in poverty, Hans had a hard life. His father, who was a shoemaker, could not even afford to make leather shoes for him, so he wore wooden shoes. His mother, who was unable to read or write, never encouraged him. His father died when he was eleven, so he went to work in a factory. Hans, who was dreaming of becoming an actor, could not work there for long. At age fourteen, he went to Copenhagen, which was the capital city of Denmark, to become an actor. Hans, who wanted his dream to come true, tried hard for three years, but he was not successful. The theater managers who saw him act said he was not a good actor, and they needed people with an education.

Hans Christian Andersen

Hans, who was feeling very disappointed, decided to go back to school. At age seventeen, he went to school with much younger students. Hans was tall, with big hands and feet, and he had a very big nose. The other students laughed at him. The lessons were difficult, but Hans, who was studying hard, got good grades. However, he was unhappy and wrote down his feelings. He later used these thoughts in his diary for his stories. *The Ugly Duckling*, which is a fairy tale about a baby duck with no friends, was really about himself.

Hans, who was like a child, was shy and sensitive, and he got hurt easily. He wanted to get married, but he was not successful. Andersen, who was getting disappointed, decided he would not marry.

At age thirty, he wrote his first fairy tales. The stories, which were thought to be too adult at first, were soon a great success. Andersen became famous, but he continued to be a shy and lonely man until he died at age seventy.

16 Practice

Complete the sentences with the past participle of verbs from the list.

drink   eat   fry   grow   mash   ripe   sell   serve   take

1. Most of the coffee _____*grown*_____ in Brazil is exported.

2. The most popular hot beverage _____ by Americans is coffee.

3. Strawberries, bananas, tomatoes, and other fruits _____ in supermarkets are often unripe when they are picked.

4. Much of the fast food _____ by young people contains a lot of fat.

5. Hamburgers are eaten _____ on a bun.

6. Food _____ from the freezer must be defrosted before cooking.

7. Some people like potatoes _____ with butter; others like them _____ in oil.

8. Roquefort is a French cheese _____ in caves.

17 Your Turn

Work with a partner, a group, or alone. Write a fairy tale that you know (you can make changes to it) using reduced relative clauses. Read the fairy tale to the class.

Example:
Once upon a time, there was a little girl living in a forest . . .

_____

_____

_____

_____

_____

_____

_____

_____

1 Review (12a–12b, 12e–12f)

Underline the correct word in each sentence. Use formal English.

1. 1. John McDouall Stuart, (<u>who</u> / whom) was a British explorer, was the first man (<u>who</u> / whom) crossed Australia's center from the south coast to the Northern Territory.

2. Australia's vast unknown interior, (that / which) is very hot and dry, was a great challenge to explorers in the 1800s.

3. The natural forces (who / that) stopped him were extremely difficult to overcome.

4. The expeditions, for (that / which) he prepared for months, always ended in failure.

5. Other explorers (who / whom) Stuart met at the time had all failed, too.

6. They gave him advice, some of (whom / which) was useful, but most of (that / which) was not much help.

7. There was a shortage of water (who / that) he had to overcome, as well as hard, sharp grasses on (that / which) the horses and camels could not walk.

8. Natives, from (who / whom) he had to escape, chased him with their weapons.

9. Anyone (who / which) tried to cross Australia in those days had a very difficult time.

10. On his sixth expedition in 1862, Stuart was a man (who / whom) did not turn back.

11. He followed rivers and openings in the mountains, (that / which) made it possible for him to finally reach the sea near Darwin. He had crossed Australia for the first time!

12. No one knows the reason (why / which) Stuart stayed only one day. He returned almost a skeleton and had to be carried away. He died almost penniless at 51, but everyone remembers the important and difficult journey (who / that) he made.

2 | Review (12a, 12e)

Complete the sentences with the correct relative pronouns. Sometimes more than one pronoun is possible.

Some astronauts train in a laboratory _____*that*_____ is under water. Peggy

Whitson is an astronaut _____ has trained there. Where is the laboratory
                                    2

_____ she has trained? The lab, _____ is located three
          3   4

miles off the coast of Florida, is 62 feet below the surface of the ocean. This lab,

_____ is part of a National Aeronautical and Space Administration (NASA)
          5

program, is called Aquarius.

Is there a reason _____ astronauts train under water? Yes. Both space
                              6

and deep water are strange, difficult places for humans to live and work in,

_____ is why the lab is excellent for training astronauts. Whitson,
          7

_____ is only one of the astronauts _____ train in the lab,
          8   9

finds life under water similar to life in space.

The Aquarius crew, most of _____ are scientists and astronauts, stay in
                                        10

the lab for weeks. They live in an area _____ is similar in size to the space
                                                    11

station. The crew members, _____ leave the lab and go into the water,
                                      12

practice building and attaching structures to Aquarius, _____ is good
                                                                      13

practice for space walks. The crew members, _____ mission is also to
                                                          14

conduct experiments, work hard while they are in Aquarius.

Astronauts are not the only people _____ use Aquarius. This lab,
                                              15

_____ is so valuable to NASA, is actually owned by the National Oceanic
          16

and Atmospheric Association (NOAO). The people _____ work benefits the
                                                            17

most from the underwater lab are marine biologists.

3 | Review (12a–12f)

Complete the sentences with the correct relative pronouns. Use informal English.

Rick: So this is the place _____*where*_____ you come to read.
1

Maria: That's right. The public library is the only place _____ it's quiet.
2

Rick: My sister, _____ I introduced to you last week, told me you've
3

been here every night for a week.

Maria: Yes, the author _____ book I'm reading now is going to give a
4

lecture at my school. I want to finish the book before he comes.

Rick: Do you mean the man _____ sailed around the world twice?
5

Maria: Yes. He sailed a boat _____ was only 25 feet long,
6

_____ is small for the open ocean. He actually had two boats.
7

One boat, _____ turned over while he was sailing around Cape Horn, sank.
8

Rick: I read about that. He lost his mast* in a violent storm, _____
9

must have been a terrible experience. The Horn is an area _____
10

waters are full of sunken ships. I know a woman _____ rolled
11

over twice in her sailboat, _____ she was sailing there.
12

Maria: I'm fascinated by people _____ do adventurous things. My
13

grandmother, _____ is 80 now, lived in Kenya for 10 years.
14

Rick: Really? How interesting. Oh, no! Someone took the book _____
15

I put on this table. I need that book! My teacher, _____
16

I expect to get an A from, asked me to get it for her.

Maria: The man _____ was standing here must have taken it.
17

Rick: Oh, no! The library card _____ Ms. Daniels gave me was in that book!
18

Maria: No, no. You gave me the card, _____ I then put in my pocket.
19

You had a pile of books _____ you were about to drop.
20

Rick: You're right. Oh, I see the man _____ took my book. See? He's
21

the one _____ the librarian is speaking to. I'll just go and get it
22

back from him.

mast: A pole that holds up a sail on a sailboat

**Find the errors and correct them.
Some errors are in punctuation.**

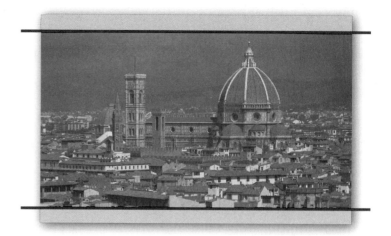

On the morning of November 4,
which
1966, ~~that~~ was a terrible day for art
lovers, it was raining very hard in
Italy. For many days, terrible rains
had fallen on Italy which cities are
filled with the world's greatest works of art. The Arno River, fill quickly, threatened to flood. Just before dawn, the Arno River that flows through Florence overflowed its banks, sending water into the countryside. The citizens of Florence which had been sleeping, awakened to find their city under water. Florence who is a famous art center was under 14 feet of water and mud in some places. Thousands of art works many of whom were priceless masterpieces were also under water. Suddenly Florence was a city who was a graveyard of the world's finest art.

The Florentines that survived by climbing to their rooftops faced a terrible disaster. The city that they loved was flooded. The greatest art works in the world many which had survived for hundreds of years were buried in water and mud. But Florence is a city in whom there are many art lovers.

On the morning after the flood, art students formed a human chain and pulled the art works out of the water. Within 24 hours, people which restored paintings began arriving in the city. It was a time that many people came together for a common cause—to save the art work. This disaster from who the Florentines never expected to recover caught the interest of people around the world. Donations came from everywhere. Experts worked tirelessly and much was saved. To be sure, many books and manuscripts who were very valuable were lost to the flood, but many were rescued. Perhaps most important, the flood of 1966 taught lessons will not be forgotten. Experts developed new methods whom protect artworks from natural disasters. People which worked on the art also developed new techniques will help keep art safe for future generations.

A process is a series of steps that leads to an end. For example, a set of instructions on how to set up a computer is a process. Steps usually occur one after the other, but sometimes they happen at the same time. The order of the steps must be clear. If not, the process cannot be followed accurately. We can use time markers such as *first, then,* and *next* for the main steps. See page 470 for general writing guidelines. See page 471 for information on writing an essay.

Step 1. Discuss these process topics with a partner. Take notes on the important steps in the process.

a. How courtship works in your country
b. How you prepare for a wedding

c. How you prepare for a New Year's celebration
d. How you prepare for a religious holiday

Step 2. Choose one of the topics from Step 1, or use your own.

Step 3. Write your essay.

1. Choose three or four of the main steps for your topic. Write a paragraph for each step. Be sure to give details for each one. Use some adjective clauses in your paragraphs. Here is an example paragraph.

> Next, we prepare special food for this celebration. Dishes that are from an old tradition are prepared in a special way. For example, we always have a fish dish. The fish, which must be fresh, is boiled . . .

2. Write an introduction to the essay. Include a thesis statement stating the number of steps and briefly summarize them.

3. Write a conclusion. Your conclusion can summarize the information in the body and state why this process is important.

4. Write a title for your essay.

Step 4. Evaluate your essay.

Checklist

_____ Did you write an introduction, a paragraph for each step, and a conclusion?

_____ Did you write a title and put it in the right place?

_____ Did you present the order of the steps correctly and clearly?

_____ Would a reader who does not know the process understand it from your essay?

Step 5. Work with a partner or a teacher to edit your essay. Check spelling, vocabulary, and grammar.

Step 6. Write your final copy.

A **Choose the best answer, A, B, C, or D, to complete the sentence. Mark your answer by darkening the oval with the same letter. A—in an answer means that no word is needed to complete the sentence.**

1. That's the doctor _____ husband is an attorney.

   A. she's   Ⓐ Ⓑ Ⓒ Ⓓ
   B. who
   C. which
   D. whose

2. Tom, _____ was in our office yesterday, called me this morning.

   A. whose   Ⓐ Ⓑ Ⓒ Ⓓ
   B. who
   C. that
   D. which

3. Where is the person _____ I should give this?

   A. who   Ⓐ Ⓑ Ⓒ Ⓓ
   B. whom
   C. to whom
   D. to who

4. I remember the office _____ you worked when you first came to this city.

   A. which   Ⓐ Ⓑ Ⓒ Ⓓ
   B. where
   C. whom
   D. that

5. Do you remember Jo Brown, _____ worked with last year?

   A. which I   Ⓐ Ⓑ Ⓒ Ⓓ
   B. I
   C. who I
   D. who

6. Jack found the information _____ was looking for on the Internet.

   A. he   Ⓐ Ⓑ Ⓒ Ⓓ
   B. who
   C. for which
   D. that

7. The person _____ the award was given will appear on television tonight.

   A. whom   Ⓐ Ⓑ Ⓒ Ⓓ
   B. who
   C. to whom
   D. who to

8. I don't like the book _____ our teacher chose for us.

   A. —   Ⓐ Ⓑ Ⓒ Ⓓ
   B. whom
   C. what
   D. who

9. I have applied to two universities, _____ are in this city.

   A. both which   Ⓐ Ⓑ Ⓒ Ⓓ
   B. both of which
   C. of which
   D. both of whom

10. Prague, _____ capital of the Czech Republic, is a beautiful city.

    A. that is the   Ⓐ Ⓑ Ⓒ Ⓓ
    B. the
    C. where
    D. is being

B Find the underlined word or phrase, A, B, C, or D, that is incorrect. Mark your answer by darkening the oval with the same letter.

1. I went <u>to visit</u> a friend <u>his</u> father is the
           A   B

   <u>president</u> of <u>your brother's</u> college.
      C   D

   Ⓐ Ⓑ Ⓒ Ⓓ

2. I remember <u>the hotel</u> <u>for which</u> we <u>stayed</u>
             A   B   C

   at <u>that</u> your friend owned.
      D

   Ⓐ Ⓑ Ⓒ Ⓓ

3. We enjoyed <u>watching</u> the show <u>that</u> you
               A   B

   <u>told us</u> <u>about</u> it.
     C   D

   Ⓐ Ⓑ Ⓒ Ⓓ

4. An <u>author</u> <u>who's</u> books <u>I like</u> a lot <u>is</u>
       A   B   C   D
   Stephen King.

   Ⓐ Ⓑ Ⓒ Ⓓ

5. <u>His collection</u> of paintings, <u>most of them</u>
       A   B

   <u>are</u> from the twentieth century, <u>is</u> famous.
    C   D

   Ⓐ Ⓑ Ⓒ Ⓓ

6. My brother, <u>who his</u> company <u>makes</u> toys,
              A   B

   <u>has moved</u> to <u>another city</u>.
     C   D

   Ⓐ Ⓑ Ⓒ Ⓓ

7. <u>The organization</u>, <u>it</u> <u>having many members</u>,
       A   B   C

   <u>is</u> famous throughout the world.
    D

   Ⓐ Ⓑ Ⓒ Ⓓ

8. <u>Do you</u> know <u>the name</u> of <u>the teacher is</u>
     A   B   C

   <u>standing</u> by the window?
     D

   Ⓐ Ⓑ Ⓒ Ⓓ

9. All of the facts <u>what</u> <u>I have told</u> you <u>are</u>
                A   B   C

   true and <u>can be found</u> in this book.
           D

   Ⓐ Ⓑ Ⓒ Ⓓ

10. <u>This course</u>, <u>which</u> I <u>had</u> to buy this
       A   B   C

    book, <u>will be</u> very useful for me.
        D

    Ⓐ Ⓑ Ⓒ Ⓓ

UNIT 13

ADVERB CLAUSES

13a Adverb Clauses of Time

Ricky listens to music **while he does his homework.**

1. There are many kinds of adverb clauses. We recognize them by their special clause markers* (conjunctions), for example, *when, as soon as, where, although,* and *because.*

2. Adverb clauses of time and place work like adverbs. They tell when and where something happens.

   I do my homework **as soon as I come home from school.**
   While I do my homework, I listen to music.

3. An adverb clause of time is a dependent clause. It must be used with a main clause. When an adverb clause comes at the beginning of a sentence, we put a comma after it. We do not use a comma when it comes at the end.

Clause Marker	Use	Examples
as while when whenever	To say that things happen at the same time. *Whenever* has the additional meaning of "every time."	**As** I was driving down the street, I saw Susan. I watch television **while** I'm having breakfast. They were sleeping **when** they saw the bear. I order the fish **whenever** I go to that restaurant.
when** before after	To say that things happen one after another.	**When** he finished his test, he left the room. The show had begun **before** we arrived. **After** he finished his course, he found a job.

*See Page 463 for more information on adverb clause markers.
**We can use *when* instead of *while, as, before,* and *after* if the order of events is clear from other information in the sentence.

   When/While/As I was writing my essay, I had a brilliant idea.
   The movie had begun when/before we arrived.
   When/after he finished his degree, he quickly found a job.

Clause Marker	Use	Examples
as soon as once	To say that one thing happens quickly after another.	Please feed the dog **as soon as** you get home. **Once** he got home, he fed the dog.
the first time the next time the last time	To say which of several occurrences of something that we are talking about.	**The first time** I ate sushi, I hated it. **The next time** I ate it, I liked it a little bit. **The last time** I ate it, I ate all of it.
until	To say that something continues up to the time when something else happens.	You must stay in class **until** you finish your essay.
as long as*	To say that something continues to the end of something else.	I will dance **as long as** the band plays. (When the band stops playing, I will stop dancing.)
by the time	To say that something happens no later than the time when something else happens.	I will have finished my work **by the time** you come home.
since	To say that something happens between a point in the past and the present.	I've seen a lot of the city **since** I came here.

*We can also say *so long as*.

1 | Practice

A. Read about Helen Thayer's life.

Helen Thayer was the first woman to walk to the North Pole alone and unaided. She walked and skied for 27 days, pulling a 160-pound sled for 364 miles. She had no help from aircraft, dog teams, or snowmobiles. Helen was born in New Zealand. Here are some facts about her life:

B. Match the sentences to learn more about Helen Thayer.

   _b_   **1.** She was attacked by polar bears.

            2. She was resting at night.

            3. She knew she would not give up.

            4. She returned home.

            5. She returned from her trip.

a. She achieved her goal.

b. Her dog Charlie protected her.

c. She has traveled all over the world, giving talks about her amazing experiences.

d. She wrote a book, *Polar Dream,* about her amazing adventure.

e. She talked to Charlie about her thoughts and plans.

C. Using the clause markers in parentheses, combine the pairs of sentences from part B.

1. (when) *When she was attacked by polar bears, her dog Charlie*

        protected her.

2. (while) _____

_____

3. (until) _____

_____

4. (as soon as) _____

_____

5. (since) _____

_____

2 | What Do You Think?

What is your opinion of Helen Thayer's achievement? Which fact do you find most surprising or interesting?

3 | Your Turn

Work with a partrner. Tell your partner about a personal goal that you have achieved. What did you do before? What did you do after? How has your life changed since you achieved that goal?

Example:
I achieved a goal when I got my drivers license. After I got it, I was able to drive myself to school, and I became a lot more independent.

13b Adverb Clauses of Reason and Result

Mona has a headache **because she has too much to do.**

1. There are several kinds of sentences that express a reason or a result. In these examples, notice that both the result and the reason can be in a main clause or an adverb clause.

   Result (main clause)
   I felt tired in the morning

   Reason (adverb clause)
   because I had gone to bed very late.

   Reason (main clause)
   I had gone to bed very late,

   Result (adverb clause)
   so I felt tired in the morning.

2. We use these clause markers to introduce clauses of reason.

   as   because   since   so

   Clauses with *because, as,* and *since* can go at the beginning or end of the sentence. We put a comma after the clause if it comes at the beginning. Result clauses with *so* must go at the end of the sentence. We put a comma in front of them.

   The children shouldn't have any ice cream now **because they're going to have dinner in half an hour.**
   As/Since the weather is bad, we shouldn't go out tonight.
   I got up very early, **so I needed another cup of coffee.**

   Do not confuse *because* with *because of*. Both show reasons, but *because of* is followed by a noun, not a subject and a verb.

   Because it was raining, we stayed home.
   Because of the rain, we stayed home.

Since and *as* mean about the same thing as *because,* but they suggest a meaning like "It is a fact that . . . " or "It is true that . . . "

Remember, *since* is also a time clause marker. See page 381.

3. We can use *so* + adjective/adverb + *that* or *such* + adjective + noun + *that* to show a result. They have the same meaning.

> The sandwich was **so** tasty **that** I had another one.
> It was **such** a tasty sandwich **that** I had another one.

We can also use *such* + a noun with or without an adjective. In informal English, we can omit the *that* clause.

> It was **such** a terrible disaster (that it was on the evening news).
> It was **such** a disaster (that it was on the evening news).

When we speak, we often omit *that.*

> It was **such** tasty soup (that) I had another bowl.
> The movie was **so** good (that) I saw it three times.

4. There are other clause markers that introduce clauses of result. These markers introduce main clauses, not dependent clauses, so their punctuation is different. Clauses with these markers always go at the end of the sentence. Sometimes they can also be a separate sentence.

Main Clause (Reason)	Clause Marker	Main Clause (Result)
Our teacher was sick;	**as a result,**	our class was canceled.
I don't know much about computers;	**therefore,**	I can't help you.
The weather is very severe;	**consequently,**	all flights will be delayed.

We can punctuate the long clause markers *as a result, therefore,* and *consequently* in two ways. We can put a semicolon before the clause marker and a comma after it, or we can write two sentences with a comma after the clause marker.

> One Sentence: I don't know much about computers; **therefore,** I can't help you.
> Two Sentences: I don't know much about computers. **Therefore,** I can't help you.

We can use *and* before these clause markers. In these cases, we use a comma between the two clauses.

> He was very qualified, **and so** he got the job.
> Our teacher was sick, **and as a result** our class was canceled.

4 | Practice

Complete the sentences with *so* or *because*. Add commas where necessary.

1. On Monday, I got up early _____*because*_____ I had an important meeting.

2. I had gone to bed late _____ I felt tired when I got up.

3. I needed more energy _____ I drank some coffee.

4. I took an umbrella _____ it was raining.

5. It was an important interview _____ I wore my best suit.

6. I was feeling rather nervous _____ my boss was going to be there.

7. There was a lot of traffic _____ my bus was late.

8. My papers got mixed up _____ I dropped my briefcase.

9. My suit got mud on it _____ I was standing too near the cars, and it was raining.

10. I finally arrived in a complete mess. I was one hour late. The office was empty. I found a note which said, "Punctuality is very important to this company _____ you are fired."

5 | Practice

Rewrite each of the sentences in two ways, once using *so . . . that* and once using *such a/an . . . that*.

Esmeralda was lost in the forest. She wandered through the trees all day until she came to a small house.

1. The door to the house was very small. She had to stoop down to go in.

   The house was so small that she had to stoop down to go in.

   It was such a small house that she had to stoop down to go in.

2. The chairs and tables were very delicate. She was afraid to touch them.

   _____

   _____

3. A delicious cake was on the kitchen table. She ate three slices.

   _____

   _____

4. The house was very beautiful. She felt like she wanted to stay there forever.

_____

_____

5. The bed was very soft. She couldn't help lying down.

_____

_____

6. She heard some soft music. She fell asleep immediately.

_____

_____

7. She had a very peaceful dream. She didn't want to wake up.

_____

_____

8. She heard a loud noise. She woke up suddenly.

_____

_____

9. The moon was very bright. She could see outside as though it were day.

_____

_____

6 | What Do You Think?

Finish the story in your own words.

7 | Your Turn

Tell a partner about something that was good, horrible, or difficult for you. Use an idea from the list or one of your own.

Example:
I once saw a movie that was so good that I went to see it three times. It was about people in a small mountain village.

a movie
something to eat
a grammar point

13c Adverb Clauses of Purpose

Maria writes everything down
so that she can remember it.

1. We use clauses of purpose to answer the questions *what for?* and *for what purpose?* We use the clause markers *so that* or *in order that** to introduce adverb clauses of purpose. In speech, we can omit *that* when we use *so that*.

    I'm saving money **so (that)** I can buy a car.
    We saved a lot of money **in order that** we could take a long vacation.

2. We can introduce a phrase (not a clause) of purpose with *in order to* + a base verb.

    I'm saving money **in order to** buy a car.

3. We often use *so that* with *can, can't, will,* or *won't* for the present or future, and *could, couldn't, would,* or *wouldn't* for the past. We sometimes, but not often, use *may* or *might* in place of *can* or *could*.

    He writes down everything **so (that)** he **can** remember it.
    She gets up early **so (that)** she **won't** be late.
    He wrote down everything **so (that)** he **could** remember it.
    She got up early **so (that)** she **wouldn't** be late.
    He wrote it down **so that** he **might** remember it.

    *In order that is rare.

8 | Practice

Complete the sentences with *so that* to show purpose or *therefore* to show result. Add commas, semicolons, periods, and capital letters where necessary.

Joanna wanted to go to the United States ___*so that*___ she could improve her

                                                             1

English. She enrolled in an English program at a university _____ she could learn

             2

quickly. She lived with her uncle and aunt, who wanted to speak their language with her

_____ she couldn't practice English at home. At first, her English wasn't very good.

   3

_____ she had to work hard. She learned to keep a notebook with her at all times

   4

_____ she could write down new idioms and expressions that she heard. Also, she

   5

joined some clubs at the university. Many American students became her friends

_____ she was able to practice with them.

   6

After six months, her English was very good. _____ she decided to return

                                                   7

home. She bought a computer _____ she could stay in touch with her American

                           8

friends. Now she is looking for a job in tourism _____ she will be able to use her

                                           9

English at work.

9 | Your Turn

Talk about yourself with a partner. Use *so that* for purpose and *so* or *therefore* for result. Use ideas from the list or your own.

Example:
I watch a lot of American movies so that I can improve my English.
It's important for me to have good English, so I practice as much as possible.
OR It's important for me to have good English; therefore, I practice as much as possible.

speak good English
improve my vocabulary/grammar
make friends
be successful
get married
travel a lot

13d Adverb Clauses of Contrast

Even though Tony apologized, Anne is still angry with him.

1. We use adverb clauses of contrast to show that two ideas differ, often in an unexpected or unusual way. We introduce them with the following clause markers.

   although   even though   though   whereas   while

   > **Although** there was a snowstorm, all the trains were on time.
   > **Even though** there was a snowstorm, all the trains were on time.
   > **Though** there was a snowstorm, all the trains were on time.

2. *Even though* is more emphatic than *although*. *Though* is not as formal as *even though* or *although*.

3. In informal English, we can also use *though* to mean "however." In this case, it often comes at the end of a sentence. There is often a comma before it in writing.

   > It is very cold outside. It's nice and warm in here, **though**.
   > = It's very cold outside; however, it's nice and warm in here.

4. We can also use *while* and *whereas* to introduce contrast between two ideas.

   > Jim has dark hair, **while** his brother has light hair.
   > Jim has dark hair, **whereas** his brother has light hair.

5. We can also show contrast between two ideas by using the transitional main clause markers *however* or *nevertheless*. Note the position and punctuation with *however* and *nevertheless*.

   > I enjoy living in the city; **however,** the cost of living is quite high.
   > I enjoy living in the city. **However,** the cost of living is quite high.

   > I enjoy living in the city; **nevertheless,** I'm going to move to the suburbs soon.
   > I enjoy living in the city. **Nevertheless,** I'm going to move to the suburbs soon.

10 Practice

Match the clauses and then combine them into sentences using *although, even though, while,* or *whereas*. Use correct punctuation.

_f_	**1.** Samuel is rich	**a.** he doesn't know what to spend it on
_____	**2.** Samuel has a lot of "friends"	**b.** he doesn't like his job
_____	**3.** Samuel works very hard	**c.** none of them would help him if he were in trouble
_____	**4.** Samuel has a lot of money	
_____	**5.** A lot of people want to meet him	**d.** none of them feels like home
		e. he doesn't want to meet them
_____	**6.** Samuel has several houses	**f.** he isn't happy

1. _Although Samuel is rich, he isn't happy._

2. _____

3. _____

4. _____

5. _____

6. _____

11 Practice

Rewrite four of the sentences from Practice 11 using *however* or *nevertheless*. Use correct punctuation.

1. _Samuel is rich; however, he is unhappy._

2. _____

3. _____

4. _____

13e Adverb Clauses of Condition

Claudia's parents said they'd buy her
a car **only if she graduated.**

1. Clauses of condition show that one thing depends on another. We use these
   markers to introduce clauses of condition.

even if	in case	unless
if	only if	whether or not

2. *If* clauses are adverb clauses of condition. The *if* clause contains the condition
   and the main clause contains the result. We use the simple present tense in the
   if clause, even if the main clause refers to the future.

   > **If** I feel better tomorrow, I'll go to class.
   > I'll stay in bed **if** I don't go to class.

3. We use *whether or not* to say that a situation will not be affected by one thing or
   another. *Even if* is close in meaning to *whether or not*. It means that no matter
   what the condition, the result will not change.

   > **Whether or not** I feel well tomorrow, I'm going to school.
   > OR **Whether** I feel well **or not** tomorrow, I'm going to school.
   > **Even if** I am sick tomorrow, I'm going to school.
   > (I don't care if I am sick. It doesn't matter. I'm going to school tomorrow.)

4. We use *unless* to mean "if . . . not."

   > **Unless** I feel well, I won't go to school.
   > (If I don't feel well, I won't go to school.)

   > You can't see the doctor **unless** you have an appointment.
   > (You can't see the doctor if you don't have an appointment.)

We often use *unless* in threats and warnings.

> You can't go out **unless** you finish your homework.
> **Unless** you have an emergency, you must attend class.

5. We use *only if* to mean there is only one condition for a certain result.

> My parents will buy me a new computer **only if** I pass this class.
> (If I don't pass this class, they won't buy me a computer.)

When we put *only if* at the beginning of a sentence, we must invert the subject and the verb.

> **Only if** I pass this class will my parents buy me a computer.

6. We use *in case* to talk about things we do because we think something else might happen.

> I'll make some extra food **in case** John wants to stay for dinner.
> (I will make some extra food now. Then if John wants to stay, there will be enough food for him, too. If he doesn't want to stay for dinner, it doesn't matter.)

See Unit 14 for more information on clauses of conditon.

12 Practice

Write sentences that express rules for using computers in the library. Match the halves of the following sentences using adverbial clause markers from the list. Use each marker only once (but more than one may be possible for some answers).

| even if | in case | unless |
| if | only if | whether |

___*a*___ **1.** You may not use the computer

_____ **2.** Children under six may use the computer

_____ **3.** You need to get a new password

_____ **4.** Ask a librarian for assistance

_____ **5.** The maximum time per person is one hour

_____ **6.** You may use the computer for the maximum time

a. you have already registered with the library

b. you can't log on to the Internet

c. they are accompanied by an adult

d. another student is waiting

e. other students are waiting or not

f. you forget your old one

1. <u>You may not use the computer unless you have already registered with the library.</u>

2. _____

_____

3. _____

_____

4. _____

_____

5. _____

_____

6. _____

_____

13 Your Turn

Write rules for one of the following situations, or use your own idea. Use adverb clauses of condition in your rules.

borrowing books from your school or public library
using your local sports center or swimming pool
using the kitchen in an apartment shared by several students

_____

_____

_____

_____

_____

_____

_____

13f Reduced Adverb Clauses

Since starting class, I have
made a lot of friends.

1. We can reduce an adverb clause to a modifying adverb phrase in the same way we reduce adjective clauses to adjective phrases. An adverb phrase does not have a subject or a verb. It consists of a present or past participle and an adverb clause time marker. The present participle replaces verbs in the active voice, and the past participle replaces verbs in the passive voice.

   Adverb Clause: **Before I came** to the United States, I took some English classes.
   Adverb Phrase: **Before coming** to the United States, I took some English classes.

   Adverb Clause: The Internet was for the use of university and government scientists **when it was originally invented.**
   Adverb Phrase: **When originally invented,** the Internet was for the use of university and government scientists.

   We can use modifying adverb phrases with verbs of any tense in the main clause.

   Before going to Korea, I **will take** some Korean classes. (main verb is future)
   When completed, these products **sell** around the world. (main verb is present)

2. The modifying adverb phrase can come before or after the main clause. We use a comma after the adverb phrase when it comes at the beginning of a sentence.

   Since starting this class, she has made a lot of friends.
   She has made a lot of friends **since starting** this class.

3. We can only change an adverb clause to an adverb phrase when the subject of the main clause and the adverb clause are the same.

> Adverb Clause: While **I** was traveling across Europe, **I** noticed the differences in architecture.
> Adverb Phrase: While traveling across Europe, I noticed the differences in architecture.

> Adverb Clause: While **I** was traveling across Europe, the **differences** in architecture became very clear.
> Adverb Phrase: (No reduction possible)

We can sometimes omit *while* and still keep the meaning "at the same time."

> **Traveling** across Europe, I noticed the differences in architecture.

4. We do not use *because* in an adverb phrase. We omit *because* and use only the *-ing* phrase. This gives the same meaning as *because*.

> **Because he wanted** to pass the class, he studied very hard.
> **Wanting to pass** the class, he studied very hard.

5. We sometimes use *upon* or *on* in place of *when* in an adverb phrase. The meaning is the same.

> Adverb Clause: **When we entered** the house, we took off our shoes.
> Adverb Phrase: **Upon entering** the house, we took off our shoes.
> Adverb Phrase: **On entering** the house, we took off our shoes.

|14| Practice

Complete the sentences about Julia's study routine with reduced adverb clauses. Some sentences require an adverb from the list; others do not. Some sentences require present participles; some require past participles.

| after | once | when |
| before | since | while |

Julia is a very organized person, and she has a definite study routine. She gets up at 6:00

every morning and goes running for 30 minutes (begin) ___*before beginning*___
1

work. (run) _____, she thinks about the day ahead and plans
2

her schedule. (come back) _____ from her run, she takes
3

a shower and eats breakfast. Then she sets herself a goal for each part of her day.

(set) _____ her goals, she also estimates
                    4

how long each one will take and which ones are most important.

(complete) _____, her goals are checked
                  5

off on a calendar above her desk. This helps her to track her progress.

(hope) _____ to get high grades in her courses
            6

this semester, she has set herself a strict schedule. She studies for four hours every

morning. She sometimes listens to music (study) _____.
                          7

(eat) _____ lunch, she goes to classes or to the
            8

library to do research. (start) _____ to use this
                  9

study schedule, she has found that her grades have improved, and she is able to

get her work completed on time. (check) _____ by her
                        10

teacher, her assignments are organized in a special folder according to date and topic.

(file) _____ neatly, her work will be easier to find when she
            11

needs to review for her exams.

15 Practice

Read the sentences. Can they be reduced or not? Write Y (for *yes*) or N (for *no*) next to each one. If the sentence can be reduced, rewrite it.

   Y   **1.** After she finishes an assignment, Julia checks her work carefully.

             After finishing an assignment, Julia checks her work carefully.

           2. When her work is completed, Julia's friends can call her up on the phone.

            _____

_____ **3.** Since she started her new schedule, Julia has been much happier.

_____

_____ **4.** When the instructor gives a new assignment, Julia starts work on it immediately.

_____

_____ **5.** While the instructor is handing out the grades, Julia feels very anxious.

_____

_____ **6.** Julia knows that she must stay healthy, so she runs every day and eats lots of fruit.

_____

_____ **7.** Before she returns home, she goes to the coffee shop with her friends.

_____

_____ **8.** When Julia gets a good grade, her parents are very pleased.

_____

16 | Your Turn

Tell a partner about your study or work routine. Ask and answer questions like the following, or use your own ideas.

Example:
I feel very tired in the morning, so after getting up, I take a shower. While showering, I listen to loud music on the radio. That helps me wake up . . .

What do you do before starting work/school?
What do you do while working/studying?
What do you do after finishing work/school?

REVIEW

1 | Review (13a–13b, 13d–13e)

Underline the correct words.

Paul Gaugin was born in Paris, (<u>but</u> / even though) he spent part of his childhood in
Peru before his family returned to France. (Even though / While) a young man, he worked
as a sailor; (whereas / however), he eventually settled down and got married. (While as /
While) he was married, he worked as a stockbroker and had five children. (As / Although)
time went by, Gaugin took up painting as a hobby. (After / Before) a few years, he realized
that he wasn't happy (in case / unless) he was painting. (As / When) he was 35, he quit
his job and started to paint full time; (although / however), he could not make enough
money to support his family. (Even though / Because) his wife loved him, she felt she had
to leave. She took the children to her family in Denmark (as / so) they could have food and
clothes. (Whereas / Although) they had been happy for a time, Gaugin and his wife never
lived together again.

(Because / While) Gaugin had a unique style of painting, he had difficulty selling his
work; (nevertheless / consequently), he refused to give up. He was painting in large shapes
and bright colors, (whereas / because) other artists were painting the old way, with small
detail and dark colors. There were a few other artists, such as Vincent Van Gogh, who were
trying new things, (so that / but) they weren't selling their works either; (nevertheless /
consequently), they were very poor.

Gaugin got tired of it all, (so / when) in 1891 he decided to go to the island of Tahiti in
the South Pacific. (After/ While) landing there, he moved into a grass hut and started to
paint. Gaugin went back to France in 1893. He hoped to sell his paintings; (however /
although), the trip was not a success. Two years later, Gaugin went back to Tahiti—never
to return home. In 1901, he went to the Marquesas Islands where he died penniless and
alone. Like Van Gogh, he was considered a failure as an artist; (as a result / nevertheless),
after their deaths they became famous. Today their paintings sell for millions of dollars.

Read this Greek myth and complete the sentences using the adverbial clause markers from the list. Sometimes there is more than one correct answer. Add commas and semicolons where necessary.

after	because	even though	so
although	but	however	therefore
as	by the time	if only	unless
as soon as	consequently	since	when

Pyramus and Thisbe were in love, _____so_____ they wanted to be together.

1

_____ they were neighbors, they could never meet.

2

_____ their parents disliked each other, they forbade Pyramus and

3

Thisbe to see one another. _____ there was a space in the wall between

4

their houses, _____ the young lovers were able to whisper to each

5

other. _____ their parents forbade it, they wanted very much to be

6

together. _____ they were so much in love, this was too much to endure.

7

_____ a while, Pyramus came up with a plan. They couldn't marry

8

_____ they ran away. They agreed to meet outside the city. Thisbe

9

arrived at the place under a mulberry tree* _____ a lion with bloody

10

jaws frightened her away. _____ she left, the lion found her scarf

11

and ripped it up. _____ Pyramus came along, he found the bloody

12

scarf and the lion's footprints. He thought Thisbe had been killed. _____

13

he had arrived sooner, he could have saved her! _____ he could not

14

accept the thought of living without Thisbe, he took his sword and stabbed it into his

body. _____ the blood spurted** upward, it dyed the white mulberries red.

15

_____ Thisbe returned, her lover was dying.

16

_____ she took the sword and killed herself. The parents saw how

17

much their children had loved each other _____ they buried them in

18

a single urn.*** _____ that time, the mulberry tree has produced

19

red berries.

  * *mulberry:* A tree that bears a red fruit

  ** *spurted:* (of a liquid) to shoot upward with force

*** *urn:* a kind of vase

3 | Review (13b–13e)

A. Match the clauses.

although	even though	so that
because	however	whereas
but	nevertheless	
even if	so	

_____i_____ **1.** Jeff is starting a new job today

_____ **2.** He set his alarm clock

_____ **3.** He changed his clothes three times before leaving home

_____ **4.** Jeff wanted to drive his car today

_____ **5.** He's going to take the bus today

_____ **6.** He will usually take the bus

_____ **7.** He thinks he's well prepared for a job as a computer programmer

_____ **8.** Jeff had several jobs while he was in school

_____ **9.** Jeff has met his new boss

_____ **10.** He is determined to succeed in this job

a. a friend offered to drive him

b. it is difficult at first

c. he would wake up on time

d. he had chosen a suit the night before

e. he has never worked in an office

f. he hasn't met any of his coworkers

g. he wants to save money on gas

h. he's afraid they'll ask him something he doesn't know

i. he's a little nervous

j. it is in the shop for repairs

B. Combine the clauses in Part A using adverbial markers from the list. Sometimes more than one marker is possible.

1. _Jeff is starting a new job today, so he's a little nervous._

2. _____

3. _____

4. _____

5. _____

6. _____

7. _____

8. _____

9. _____

10. _____

Find the errors in clause markers and correct them. Watch for missing punctuation.

As
~~As soon as~~ more and more people try cross-country, or Nordic, skiing, it is becoming more popular than ever. There are several reasons why. In

order ski downhill or snowboard, you must have deep snow where to do cross-country skiing you need only a few inches of snow on the ground. While you do downhill skiing you need to go to a special area and take lifts to the top of the mountain, nevertheless when do cross-country skiing, you can use any field or forest. You don't need to buy lift tickets to ski along a forest trail because cross-country skiing doesn't cost very much to do.

Because of you're not rushing down a hill at a high speed Nordic skiing is safe and easy to learn. It's good for you too. Since you're enjoying your winter surroundings, you're also getting a good physical workout. While you're ready to go cross-country skiing it's easy to find good cross-country routes. Even there's no snow where you live most mountain ski areas have miles and miles of trails.

Since it became a popular sport cross-country skiing was often the only way people could travel in snow country. In cold areas of the north, people couldn't go anywhere though they strapped on their skis. Because some people still cross-country ski out of necessity, most people do it for fun. Before go cross-country skiing, you probably should take a lesson. It may seem hard at first since most instructors say that people are usually gliding along after only a few hours.

WRITING: Write an Essay of Comparison or Contrast

When we compare, we look at the similarities between two things. When we contrast, we look at their differences. See page 470 for general writing guidelines. See page 471 for information on writing an essay.

Step 1. Choose a topic from the list below. Take notes on the similarities or differences between the two things. Decide whether you want to write an essay of comparison or an essay of contrast.

1. life in the country and life in the city
2. transportation now and transportation twenty years ago
3. owning a car or travel by public transportation
4. studying in a foreign country or study in your country

Transportation Now and 20 Years Ago

Similarities	*Differences*
most people drive cars	*some cars are more efficient now*
air travel for long distance	*air travel less comfortable then*
few areas have mass transit	*some cars run on electricity now*

Step 2. Choose two or three points of comparison or contrast.

Step 3. Write your essay. Use some of the words and phrases of comparison and contrast on page 463. Write a title for your essay. Organize your essay like this.

1. Introduction: State your topic and include a thesis statement that explains what you are going to say.

2. Body: Write a paragraph on each of the points you chose in Step 2.

3. Conclusion: Summarize your points and restate your thesis statement.

Step 4. Evaluate your essay.

Checklist

_____ Did you write an introduction with a thesis statement, one paragraph for each point of comparison or contrast, and a conclusion?

_____ Do your paragraphs support your thesis statement?

_____ Did you use some words and phrases of comparison or contrast?

Step 5. Work with a partner or a teacher to edit your essay. Check spelling, vocabulary, and grammar.

Step 6. Write your final copy.

A **Choose the best answer, A, B, C, or D, to complete the sentence. Mark your answer by darkening the oval with the same letter.**

1. _____ she arrives, she will check in to a hotel.

   A. As soon as   Ⓐ Ⓑ Ⓒ Ⓓ
   B. It is when
   C. Since
   D. As

2. _____ she was late, she didn't hurry.

   A. For   Ⓐ Ⓑ Ⓒ Ⓓ
   B. Nevertheless
   C. However
   D. Although

3. The movie was so good _____ saw it three times.

   A. although I   Ⓐ Ⓑ Ⓒ Ⓓ
   B. that I
   C. for I
   D. because I

4. We didn't go on a picnic _____ it was raining.

   A. although   Ⓐ Ⓑ Ⓒ Ⓓ
   B. because of
   C. because
   D. as a result

5. She went to the library _____ return a book.

   A. in order to   Ⓐ Ⓑ Ⓒ Ⓓ
   B. so to
   C. because
   D. so that to

6. It was _____ a difficult poem that nobody in class understood it.

   A. so   Ⓐ Ⓑ Ⓒ Ⓓ
   B. too
   C. such
   D. that

7. Take some food with you _____ you get hungry on the way.

   A. in case   Ⓐ Ⓑ Ⓒ Ⓓ
   B. unless
   C. even if
   D. while

8. You should see a doctor _____ you don't feel well.

   A. unless   Ⓐ Ⓑ Ⓒ Ⓓ
   B. if
   C. in order to
   D. because of

9. _____ the best qualifications, she got the job.

   A. Because having   Ⓐ Ⓑ Ⓒ Ⓓ
   B. Because she having
   C. Having
   D. Because having

10. _____ sitting on a train, he had an idea.

    A. While   Ⓐ Ⓑ Ⓒ Ⓓ
    B. While he
    C. He was
    D. While was

B Find the underlined word or phrase, A, B, C, or D, that is incorrect. Mark your answer by darkening the oval with the same letter.

1. <u>Even</u> he has <u>a number of</u> relatives <u>who</u>
    A   B   C
live close by, he never visits <u>them</u>.
                           D

2. She has <u>so</u> a good memory <u>that</u> she can
        A   B
remember a <u>person's</u> exact words <u>even</u> a
           C   D
week later.

3. He repeated <u>all</u> the new <u>vocabulary</u>
          A   B
<u>in order</u> remember <u>it</u>.
  C   D

4. <u>Why don't we</u> close all the windows <u>case</u>
   A   B
<u>it rains</u> <u>while</u> we are not home?
  C   D

5. <u>She is</u> very <u>organized</u> at work; <u>therefore</u>,
  B   B   C
her apartment is very <u>messy</u>.
                      D

Ⓐ Ⓑ Ⓒ Ⓓ

6. <u>Because working</u> from home, Ken <u>had</u>
      A   B
<u>little</u> <u>contact</u> with people.
  C   D

Ⓐ Ⓑ Ⓒ Ⓓ

7. She called her mother <u>soon as</u> <u>she</u> heard
                    A   B
<u>she</u> <u>had passed</u> the test.
  C   D

Ⓐ Ⓑ Ⓒ Ⓓ

8. Whether <u>or not</u> <u>I pass</u> the test tomorrow,
         A   B
I <u>will call</u> you <u>or not</u>.
     C   D

Ⓐ Ⓑ Ⓒ Ⓓ

9. <u>I'll take</u> my umbrella with me now <u>if</u> it
  A   B
<u>rains</u> <u>later</u>.
  C   D

Ⓐ Ⓑ Ⓒ Ⓓ

10. Only if <u>I</u> <u>found</u> a job here <u>I would</u> <u>move</u>
        A B   C   D
to this city.

UNIT 14

CONDITIONAL SENTENCES

14a Real Conditional Sentences in the Present and Future

If you **water** a plant, it **grows.**

1. We use two clauses in a conditional sentence, a dependent *if* clause and a main clause. The *if* clause states a condition, and the main clause states a result.

2. The *if* clause can come before or after the main clause with no change in meaning. If the *if* clause comes first, we put a comma after it.

3. A sentence that expresses a real condition has a present tense verb in the *if* clause, and a present or future verb in the main clause.

4. *If* clauses can go at the beginning or the end of a sentence. We put a comma after the *if* clause if it comes first.

   If you water a plant, it grows.
   A plant grows **if you water it.**

IF CLAUSE			MAIN CLAUSE		
Subject	Present Tense Verb		Subject	Present or Future Tense Verb	
If you	**water**	a plant,	it	**grows.**	
If it	**rains**	tomorrow,	we	**will go**	to a movie.

1. We use the present real conditional (present tense in the main clause) to say that something always happens in a specific situation.

   If I **eat** too much, I **don't** feel well.

2. We use the present real conditional to talk about a general fact that is always true.

   If you **heat** butter, it **melts.**

3. We use the future real conditional (future tense in the main clause) to talk about something that may possibly happen in the future.

> If it **rains**, we **will go** to a movie. (It may rain, or it may not. But if it does, we will go to a movie.)

> If my parents **come** to visit me this summer, I'**m going to take** them to New York.

4. We can also use *should* after *if* when we are less sure of something.

> If I **see** Tony, I'll tell him. (Perhaps I will see Tony.)
> If I **should see** Tony, I'll tell him. (I am less sure I will see Tony.)

5. We can also use the imperative in the main clause of a future conditional sentence.

> If you see Tony, **tell** him to wait.
> If the phone rings, please **pick** it **up**.

☐ Practice

With a partner, read the proverbs and decide what they mean. Then rewrite the proverbs using *if* sentences in the present tense. (Note: *He who . . .* is a way of starting a proverb. It means "a person who . . .")

1. Don't cry over spilt milk. (*spilt* = spilled)

   If you make a mistake, there is no point in crying about it.

2. Look before you leap. (*leap* = jump)

   _____

3. Many hands make light work. (*light* = easy)

   _____

4. Where there's smoke, there's fire.

   _____

5. An apple a day keeps the doctor away.

   _____

6. It never rains, but it pours. (= Every time it rains, it pours.)

   _____

7. Fish and guests smell after three days.

   _____

8. First things first. (First things come first.)

_____

9. Nothing ventured, nothing gained. (_ventured_ = risked, tried)

_____

10. He who hesitates is lost.

_____

11. He who pays the piper calls the tune. (a piper plays a flute-like instrument; _calls the tune_ = decides which song will be played)

_____

12. He who laughs last laughs best.

_____

2 Practice

Read the recipe. Then match the two halves of the sentences.

Chocolate Brownies

Ingredients	Directions
1/2 cup butter	Heat the butter and chocolate slowly until they melt. Mix the eggs and add the sugar and vanilla gradually. Add the butter and chocolate mixture to the egg mixture and stir with a spoon, not an electric mixer. Stir in the flour and the nuts. Bake for 25 minutes in a 9 x 9-inch pan. Eat the brownies the same day or wrap them in foil.
4 oz. chocolate	
4 eggs, at room temperature	
1/2 teaspoon salt	
2 cups sugar	
1 teaspoon vanilla	
1 cup sifted flour	
1 cup chopped nuts	

____d____ **1.** If you don't heat the butter and chocolate slowly,

_____ **2.** If you use an electric mixer,

_____ **3.** If you don't sift the flour,

_____ **4.** If you bake them for an hour,

_____ **5.** If you wrap the brownies in foil,

a. the mixture will get lumpy.

b. they will burn.

c. they will stay fresh for several days.

d. the butter will burn.

e. the mixture will get too smooth.

3 | Your Turn

What cooking tips do you know? Think of something you know how to cook or use an idea from the list.

Example:
If you put a boiled egg in cold water, it will be easier to peel.

boiling eggs
keeping bread fresh
preventing crying when chopping an onion
making rice
making coffee or tea

14b Unreal Conditional Sentences in the Present or Future

Form

What **would** you **do** if you **saw** someone breaking into your house?

A sentence that expresses an unreal condition in the present or future has a past tense verb in the *if* clause, and *would* or *could* + a base verb in the main clause.

IF CLAUSE			MAIN CLAUSE		
Subject	Past Tense Verb		Subject	*Would/Could* + Base Verb	
If I	**had**	a problem,	I	**would tell**	you.
If we	**were**	on vacation,	we	**would be**	on the beach.
If she	**weren't***	so busy,	she	**could help**	you.
If I	**were***	you,	I	**wouldn't accept**	that offer.

*Careful speakers usually use *were* when the subject is *I, he, she, it,* or a singular noun. However, many people use *was*. In academic and formal business situations, it's better to use *were*.

1. We use *if* + simple past in the *if* clause and *would/could* + base verb in the main clause to talk about an unreal, hypothetical, or contrary-to-fact situation in the present or future.

   > If you **got up** earlier, you **wouldn't be** late for work every morning. (But you do not get up earlier.)
   > If I **had** a lot of money, I'**d travel** around the world. (But I don't have a lot of money.)

2. We often use *were* as a way of giving advice. The *if* clause with *were* makes the sentence sound softer.

   > A: Do you think that I can turn my paper in a few days late?
   > B: If I **were** you, I'**d ask** the instructor.

3. We can use *could* instead of *would* in the main clause. *Could* means *would be able to*.

   > If I **had** more time, I **could help** you.
   > If I **had** a computer, I **could send** you email tomorrow.

4 Practice

Write what you would and wouldn't do in each situation. Give a reason for your advice.

1. If you found a wallet with $500 in it in a taxi, what would you do? Why?

   If I found a wallet with $500 in it, I would give it to the driver.

   Maybe the person who lost it would call the taxi company.

   If I found a wallet with $500 in it, I wouldn't keep it.

   I don't think that's honest.

2. If a burglar broke into your house at night, and you were alone, what would you do? Why?

   _____

   _____

   _____

   _____

   _____

3. If you saw someone stealing some cans of soup in the supermarket, what would you do? Why?

_____

_____

_____

_____

_____

4. If a car hit a cyclist, the driver didn't stop, and the cyclist was left lying injured in the road, what would you do? Why?

_____

_____

_____

_____

_____

5 | **Your Turn**

Think of a situation where you had to make a difficult decision. Describe the situation to a partner. Your partner will try to imagine what he or she would do in that same situation.

Example:
Once the clerk at the supermarket gave me $20 too much in change. I noticed it, but I didn't say anything. I just kept the money. I still feel bad about it.
What would you do in that situation?

14c Unreal Conditional Sentences in the Past; Mixed Conditional Sentences

If we **had left** earlier, we **wouldn't be** in this traffic.

UNREAL CONDITIONAL SENTENCES IN THE PAST

IF CLAUSE			MAIN CLAUSE		
Subject	Past Perfect Verb		Subject	Would/Could + Base Verb	
If I	**had worked**	harder,	I	**would have done**	better.
If Isis	**hadn't been**	so busy,	she	**might have helped**	you.
If we	**hadn't helped**	the man,	he	**could have died**.	

MIXED CONDITIONAL SENTENCES

IF CLAUSE			MAIN CLAUSE		
Subject	Verb		Subject	Verb	
If we	**had left**	earlier,	we	**would be**	home now.
If Dad	**had given**	me the car,	we	**could drive**	to the beach.
If they	**hadn't broken**	the DVD,	they	**could be watching**	a movie now.
If I	**were**	you,	I	**would have**	walked.

UNREAL CONDITIONAL SENTENCES IN THE PAST

1. We use the past unreal conditional to talk about an unreal, hypothetical, or contrary-to-fact situation in the past. Both clauses refer to unreal conditions in the past.

> If she **had had** the opportunity, she **would have gone** to college.
> (But she didn't have the opportunity, and she didn't go to college.)

> If you **had seen** the movie, you **would have enjoyed** it.
> (But you didn't see the movie, so you didn't have the opportunity to enjoy it.)

> If it **hadn't rained** all morning, we **would have gone out**.
> (But it did rain all morning, and we didn't go out.)

2. We can use the modals *would, might,* and *could* in the main clause.

We use *would have* + past participle in the main clause if we think the past action was certain.

> If I **had seen** you yesterday, I **would have given** the money to you then.
> (I would definitely have given it to you.)

We use *might have* + past participle in the main clause if we think the past action was possible.

> If you **had taken** the test, you **might have passed** it. (It's possible that you would have passed it.)

We use *could have* + past participle to say that someone would have been able to do something in the past.

> We **could have eaten** in the park if we **had brought** some food with us.
> (We would have been able to eat in the park.)

In some parts of the United States, people use *would have* + a past participle in the *if* clause, as well as in the main clause.

> If you would've said something, I wouldn't have bought it.

This usage is not generally considered to be grammatically correct.

MIXED CONDITIONAL SENTENCES

3. Conditional sentences can have mixed tense sequences, but the tenses must make sense in the context.

| Past Unreal Conditions. | If he **had played** basketball in high school, he **would be** a great college player now. (He didn't play football in the past, and he isn't a great college player now.) | Present Unreal Conditions. |

| Present Unreal Conditions. | If John **were** my child, I **would have encouraged** him to play basketball, not football. (John is not my child now. I didn't encourage him to play basketball.) | Past Unreal Conditions. |

6 Practice

A. Read the story of Romeo and Juliet.

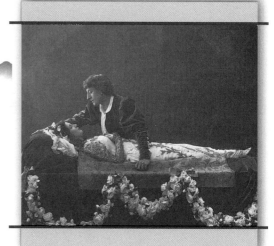

Romeo and Juliet are in love, but their families hate each other. The young couple know that they will never get permission to marry, so they decide to marry secretly. A friendly friar* agrees to perform the marriage ceremony. After the ceremony, Romeo finds his friends in a fight. Romeo kills Juliet's cousin because the cousin had killed his best friend. Romeo is then sent away from the city as a punishment. Juliet's father wants Juliet to marry another man, so Juliet goes to the friar for help. He gives her a sleeping potion** to make her appear dead, and he says that he will send a message to Romeo to come and take her away. However, Romeo never receives the message. When he hears of Juliet's death, he goes to the tomb to see her dead body. In despair, he drinks poison and dies. At that moment, the friar's drink wears off, and Juliet wakes up to find Romeo dead beside her. When she realizes what has happened, Juliet takes Romeo's dagger*** and kills herself.

*Friar: a man in a Roman Catholic order
**Sleeping potion: a liquid that makes you sleep
***Dagger: a kind of knife

B. Answer the questions in complete sentences. For some questions, you must think of your own answer.

1. What would have happened if Romeo and Juliet hadn't fallen in love?

   If they hadn't fallen in love, this story wouldn't have happened.

2. What would Romeo and Juliet have done if the friar hadn't married them?

   _____

3. What would Juliet have done if the friar had not given her the sleeping potion?

   _____

4. What would Romeo have done if he had received the friar's message?

   _____

5. What would have happened if Romeo had not taken the poison?

   _____

6. What would have happened if Juliet had not killed herself?

   _____

C. Complete the sentences about the story. Use *might have* or *could have* in your answers.

1. If Romeo had not met Juliet, he *might have married someone else.*

   _____

2. If Romeo and Juliet's families had not hated each other, _____

   _____

3. If Romeo's friends had not been in a fight, _____

   _____

4. If Juliet had not taken the sleeping potion, _____

   _____

5. If Juliet had not found Romeo's dagger, _____

   _____

6. If Juliet had woken up a little sooner, _____

   _____

D. What would you have done if you were Romeo? If you were Juliet?

1. If I were Juliet, I would have _____

   _____

2. If I were Romeo, I would have _____

   _____

3. If I were the friar, I would have _____

   _____

4. If I were Juliet's father, I would have _____

   _____

---

7 | Your Turn

Think of a past event in your life that could have been very different. Write three sentences about what would or would not have happened in your life if the event had been different.

Example:
If I hadn't graduated from high school, I wouldn't have gotten into college.

14d Conditional Sentences with *As If* and *As Though*

Form / Function

Tim: It looks **as if** someone has a sense of humor.
Sue: It also looks **as if** someone can't spell.

1. We use *as if* before a subject and a verb to say how someone or something seems. We can use *as though* instead of *as if*.

When *as if* or *as though* are followed by the simple present or *will/be going to,* the situation might be real.

> He looks **as if** he's cold. OR He looks **as though** he's cold.
> (He looks cold, but I don't know if he really is cold.)
> It looks **as if** it's going to snow. OR It looks **as though** it's going to snow.
> (The weather looks like it might snow, but I don't know if it really will snow.)

2. When we use *as if* or *as though* + a past tense verb to talk about the present, the situation is unreal or probably unreal.

> He's acting **as if** he **were** my father. (He definitely is not my father.)
> I felt **as though** I **had run** a marathon. (I definitely did not run a marathon.)

Careful speakers use *were* instead of *was* in unreal situations.

3. In informal English, we often use *like* instead of *as if* or *as though.* However, we use *as if* and *as though* in formal writing.

> He looks **like** he's cold.
> It looks **like** it's going to snow.

---

8 Practice

Read the descriptions. What do you think is going to happen? Use *as if, as though,* and *like.*

1. There are big black clouds in the sky.

   It looks as if it is going to rain.

2. Stan has a headache and a sore throat, and he keeps sneezing.

   He feels _____

3. My neighbors are shouting, and I can hear dishes breaking.

   It sounds _____

4. My brother applied for a new job, and they invited him to go for an interview in Seoul.

   It looks _____

5. My friend has just finished her exam, and she is smiling confidently.

   She looks _____

6. There is a lot of cheering and clapping coming from the office next door.

   It sounds _____

7. The classroom is empty. The tables are covered with paper plates and cups and pieces of leftover sandwiches.

It looks _____

8. Ron looked very unhappy this morning, and I heard him crying earlier.

It sounds _____

9	**Your Turn**

Look at the photo.
What do you think has happened?
What do you think is going to happen?

14e Conditional Sentences Without *If*

Had we **known** it would rain so much, we would have stayed home.

1. We can sometimes omit *if* and invert the auxiliaries *had, were,* or *should* and the subject in the *if* clause. This form is more common with *had* than with *were* or *should*.

   If I had known you were coming, I would have prepared some food.
   Had I known you were coming, I would have prepared some food.

   If I were you, I wouldn't go.
   Were I you, I wouldn't go.

   If I should see him, I'll give him the message.
   Should I see him, I'll give him the message.

Careful speakers use *were* instead of *was* in unreal situations.

2. We can sometimes imply (not say something directly) a real or unreal conditional. We use other words and phrases such as *if so, if not, otherwise, with,* or *without.*

	Implied Conditional	Conditional
otherwise	I didn't hear the phone; otherwise, I would have answered it.	If I had heard the phone, I would have answered it.
if so	This sounds like a good opportunity. If so, you should take it.	If you think it is a good opportunity, you should take it.
if not	I think that the earliest flight is at 8:00 A.M. If not, wait for the next one.	If the earliest flight is not at 8:00 A.M., wait for the next one.
without	Without your help, I couldn't have done this.	If you hadn't helped me, I couldn't have done this.
with	With your help, I will be able to do this.	If you help me, I will be able to do this.

10 Practice

A. Read Ms. Winters's letter of complaint about a product that she has bought.

Dear Mr. McMullen:

I am writing to complain about a kitchen mixer that I purchased in your store in December. It was a birthday present for my mother. The first time we tried to use it, it splashed tomato soup all over the kitchen walls!

(1) Had I known the mixer was faulty, I would never have bought it. **(2)** I'm sure that we would have enjoyed her birthday better without buying your mixer. **(3)** Had your mixer not been faulty, we would not have spent two hours that morning cleaning up the mess.

I would like a complete refund and some compensation for the damage to my kitchen. **(4)** Otherwise, I will take the matter to my lawyer. **(5)** Were our home not so far away, I would bring the mixer back personally.

(6) Should I need any kitchen appliances in the future, you can be sure I will not purchase them at your store!

Yours sincerely,

Susan Winters

Susan Winters

B. Rewrite the numbered sentences from the letter in 11A as conditional sentences using *if*.

1. <u>If I had known that the mixer was faulty, I would never have bought it.</u>

2. _____

   _____

3. _____

   _____

4. _____

   _____

5. _____

   _____

6. _____

   _____

11 What Do You Think?

Is Ms. Winters's letter of complaint an effective one? Why or why not?

12 Practice

A. Read the store's response to Ms. Winters.

Best Buy Appliances
1105 N. 6th St.
Tulsa, OK 74821

December 20, 20XX

Dear Ms. Winters:

I am writing to apologize for the faulty mixer that you purchased from our store in December.

(1) If we had known the mixer was faulty, we would never have sold this model in our store. **(2)** The sales assistant would have identified the fault if he had tried out the machine before selling it to you. **(3)** If we had not received this information from you, we would have continued selling faulty mixers to other customers. **(4)** If you wish to have a replacement mixer, we will send one out to you immediately. **(5)** If you do not wish to have a replacement, we can offer you a complete refund.

---

(6) If you were to have any further problems with the replacement mixer, please let us know immediately. **(7)** If you have any other questions, please do not hesitate to get in touch.

We hope you are satisfied with our service. Please shop with us again in the future.

Yours sincerely,

Andrew McMullen

Andrew McMullen

Customer Service Manager

B. Rewrite the sentences in 13A as conditional clauses without *if*. Start your sentences with words from the list.

had he   had we   should you   should you   were you   without

1. *Had we known that the mixer was faulty, we would never have sold this model in our store.*

2. _____

_____

3. _____

_____

4. _____

_____

5. _____

_____

6. _____

_____

7. _____

_____

13 │ Your Turn

Work with a partner. Write three past conditional sentences with *if*. Give them to your partner. Your partner will rewrite them as sentences without *if*.

Example:

If I'd known about downloading songs from the Internet for a dollar, I wouldn't have bought so many CDs.

Had I known . . .

14f Wishes About the Present, Future, and Past; *Hope*

I **wish** I **had chosen** another day for the picnic.

WISHES ABOUT THE PRESENT AND FUTURE

MAIN CLAUSE			NOUN CLAUSE		
Subject	*Wish*	(*That*)	Subject	Verb	
I	wish		I	**had**	a car.
He	wishes		he	**were**	here.
We	wish		you	**could come.**	
You	wish	(that)	she	**would stop**	complaining.
They	wish		you	**would come**	with me tomorrow.

1. For wishes referring to the present or the future, we use *wish* in the simple present + a noun clause with a simple past verb or *would/could* + a base verb.

   I **wish** you**'d come** with me.   (I want you to come with me, but I don't think you will.)

   I **wish** I **could leave** now.   (I can't leave now.)

2. The use of *that* in a wish clause is optional. We often omit it.

3. Careful speakers use *were* instead of *was* in unreal situations.

WISHES ABOUT THE PAST

MAIN CLAUSE			NOUN CLAUSE		
Subject	*Wish*	(*That*)	Subject	Past Perfect Tense Verb	
I	wish		I	**had gone**	with you.
He	wishes	(that)	we	**had come**	earlier.
She	wished		she	**had booked**	her flight earlier.

1. We use *wish* + the simple past or *would/could* + a base verb to say that we would like something to be different in the present and future.

   > I **wish** I **had** a car. (I do not have a car.)
   > He **wishes** he **could play** the guitar. (He cannot play the guitar.)

2. We use *would* after *wish* to express future action that we want to happen.

   > I **wish** you**'d come** with me to the doctor. I'm scared to go by myself.
   > I **wish** the situation **would change** soon.

3. We can also use *would* after *wish* when we want something to stop happening, or we want something to change, but it probably won't.

   > I **wish** she **would stop** complaining!
   > I **wish** people **wouldn't pick** the flowers.

4. We use *wish* + the past perfect tense to express regret that something happened or did not happen in the past.

   > He **wishes** he **had asked** her about it. (He did not ask her about it.)
   > I **wish** I **hadn't gone** to bed so late. (I did go to bed late.)

5. We use *wish* to express a desire for an unreal situation, but we use *hope* to express a desire for a possible real situation. Note the different tenses that follow.

   After *wish,* the simple past shows the unreal situation. After *hope,* the simple present or future shows that the situation is possible. We use the simple past to talk about hopes for the past.

   | Unreal Situation: | I wish I **had** more time. (I don't have more time.) |
   | Possible Situation: | I hope I **have** more time. OR I hope I**'ll have** more time. (Maybe I will have more time. I hope so.) |

   | Unreal Situation: | I wish the children **had slept** enough last night. (They didn't sleep enough.) |
   | Possible Situation: | I hope the children **slept** enough last night. (Maybe they slept enough. I hope so.) |

14 Practice

A. For many reasons, Oscar isn't very happy. Write wishes for Oscar that will make him happy.

1. Oscar isn't rich. *He wishes he was/were rich.*

2. His life isn't exciting. _____

3. His apartment is small. _____

4. He feels tired. _____

5. He doesn't have any friends. _____

6. He can't play the guitar. _____

B. Here's what happened to Oscar last week. Write Oscar's wishes after each event.

1. His car broke down. *He wishes his car hadn't broken down.*

2. He ate all the food in his refrigerator. _____

3. He didn't pay his phone bill last month. _____

4. He spent all the money on his credit card. _____

5. He was late for work and got fired. _____

6. He couldn't find another job. _____

15 Your Turn

1. Write five things you wish were different about your life right now.

2. Write five things you wish you hadn't done last weekend.

Example:
I wish I didn't have to do so much homework.
I wish I hadn't spent so much time at my computer.

_____

_____

_____

_____

_____

14g Conditional Sentences with *If Only*

If only I **were** bigger.

1. *If only* has the same meaning as *wish* or *hope,* but it is more emphatic. We use *if only* in conversation and in informal writing.

2. When we use a simple present after *if only,* we hope that something may become real in the present or future.

    If only I **get** the news today. (I really hope that I get the news.)
    If only my boss **is not** in the office today! (I really hope that he won't be in the office.)

3. We use the simple past form after *if only* when we wish for something that is unreal in the present.

    If only he **trusted** me. (He doesn't trust me, and I wish he did.)
    If only I **were** ready for this test. (I'm not ready for it, and I wish I were.)
    If only we **knew** his address. (We don't know his address, but I wish we did.)

    Remember, careful speakers use *were* instead of *was* in unreal situations.

4. We use *if only* + past perfect when we wish something had happened differently in the past.

    If only I **had explained** the situation to him. (I wish I had explained the situation to him, but I didn't.)

16 Practice

Write wishes for Linda using _if only_.

1. Linda isn't athletic.

She thinks, "_If only I were athletic._   "

2. She isn't rich.

She thinks, "   "

3. She doesn't have much free time.

"   "

4. She has to work very hard.

"   "

5. She can't sing or dance.

"   "

6. She can't drive a car.

"   "

7. She doesn't have a boyfriend.

"   "

8. She worries about her life all the time.

"   "

17 Your Turn

Write three regrets you have about your life. Write sentences starting with _if only_. Share with a partner. Your partner will try to guess why you regret them.

Example:
You: If only I had learned to drive!
Your partner: Is that because you wish you didn't have to take the bus every day?

REVIEW

1 Review (14a–14c, 14e–14f)

Match the parts of the sentences.

__f__   **1.** If it snows,

a. otherwise, I would have told you it's sweet.

_____   **2.** Had I known you were hungry,

b. I would put on a sweater.

_____   **3.** Without your help,

c. I'd go to Australia.

_____   **4.** If you need company,

d. leave a message.

_____   **5.** I only wish

e. quit right now.

_____   **6.** I didn't taste it;

f. we can go skiing.

_____   **7.** If I don't answer the phone,

g. I would have made a sandwich.

_____   **8.** If I had more vacation days,

h. I'll go with you.

_____   **9.** If I were cold,

i. I hadn't bought those shoes.

_____   **10.** I hate my job. I wish I could

j. I couldn't have finished this job.

2 Review (14b–14d, 14f)

Complete the sentences with *if, as if, as though, if only, even if,* or *wish*.

Jim: I'm in trouble! My boss saw me playing golf

yesterday after I called the office to say I was sick.

Now he's acting _____ *as if* _____
                            1
I were a criminal.

Kelley: _____ you had checked
                       2
with me, I would have told you that he had

a golf game yesterday.

Jim: When I saw him, I felt _____ a truck had hit me. I

        _____ you'd come with me to his office.

Kelly: Oh no! _____ you gave me a million dollars, I wouldn't

        go into that office.

Jim: It's looks _____ things can't get worse. I _____

        I'd never called the office to say I was sick. I _____ I had a

        good excuse. I _____ I could change what happened.

        _____ I had gone to another golf course, he would never

        have seen me.

Kelly: You're acting _____ your choice of golf course was what

        you did wrong. _____ you hadn't called to say you were

        sick and then gone golfing, you wouldn't be in trouble! _____

        you play with fire, you get burned. _____ you took your

        work more seriously, you wouldn't be in trouble.

Jim: I know.

Kelly: Anyway, _____ I were you, I'd tell the truth from

        now on.

Jim: Yes, it looks _____ I'll have to change my ways.

Kelly: You sound _____ that were a bad thing. You know that

        you need to change _____ you want to keep your job.

Jim: I know. I know. I _____ you would stop talking about it.

        I've learned my lesson. But I still _____ I were rich so I

        wouldn't have to work at all!

Complete the sentences with the correct forms of the verbs in parentheses. If there are other words in parentheses, include them.

Well, I am here on vacation, and I'm miserable. I wish I (never, come)

___*had never come*___ to this place. It's really hot and humid. When I got off the
          1

plane, I felt as though I (walk) _____ into a steam bath.
                                        2

If I had known that it rains here everyday, I (not, come) _____.
                                                                      3

I wish I (research) _____ this place better. It's not the tourist
                              4

season. There's no one here and nothing to do. Did I mention the rain? If I (be)

_____ a duck, I (love) _____ it here. It
          5   **6**

pours. Then the sun comes out, hotter each time. If I (be) _____ a
                                                                        7

flower, I (die) _____. If there were a swimming pool here,
                        8

it (not, be) _____ so bad. Did I mention the heat? If you (have)
                    9

_____ ice in your drink, it (melt) _____ in
          10   **11**

five minutes. Did I mention the insects? Last night I saw a beetle as big as a cat. If I

(have) _____ a camera, I would have taken a picture. But of course,
                12

I've lost my camera. Did I mention the food? I've lost five pounds already. If I (eat)

_____ too much of this food, I feel terrible. Did I mention I hate
          13

this place? I (not, bring) _____ someone here if they (be)
                                    14

_____ my worst enemy. I wish I (leave) _____
          15   **16**

right now.

I didn't ask the travel agent about the weather here in June; otherwise, I (come)

_____ at a different time of year. I am sure you wish I (stop)
          17

_____ complaining. Well, you would be right, of course. I need to
          18

make the best of it. Nevertheless, if you (not, hear) _____ from me
                                                                      19

soon, (send) _____ a rescue team!
                    20

Review (14a, 14c, 14f–14g)

Find the errors in verb forms and correct them.

Anita: I wish you hadn't ~~take~~ *taken* me to this party. It's boring. I wish we could ~~have left~~ *leave*

right now.

Louis: Well, I wish you stopped telling me that. I wish we go to the movies instead.

But there's nothing we can do about it now.

Anita: If only you listen to me earlier.

Louis: If only I know you would be so difficult! You're acting as if this be all my fault!

Anita: Well, without your invitation, I won't be here.

Louis: OK, OK. If more people come, we leave, all right?

Anita: Then I wish a hundred people come through that door right now.

Louis: I wish I not tell Mark that I had the night off. If only I keep it to myself.

I usually work on Fridays. The truth is that when Mark first invited me to this

party, I said no. Then I felt as though I hurt his feelings. "I know you're

working," he said. "But I sure wish you come to my party." That's when I broke

down. I wish I'm not so softhearted. If someone ask me a favor, I can't refuse.

Anita: Well, that's what makes you such a nice person. If I don't like you so much, I

won't have come.

Louis: Thanks, Anita. If I see Mark, I tell him that we need to leave. If only we have a

good excuse. If we had a reason to leave, I feel so much better.

Anita: Never mind. He's your friend. Let's stay. If we're lucky, more people come soon.

Louis: Yes, that's right. And if it were early enough, we can go see a movie. And if

you're hungry, I buy you some popcorn.

Anita: That sounds great. I wish I don't say those things to you earlier. I'm sorry.

Without your friendship, my life is not the same.

Louis: Thank you, Anita. I feel the same way. Well, it look as though we were about to

get our wish. More people are starting to arrive. Let's say goodbye to Mark.

Write a persuasive essay about a global issue. When we write a persuasive essay, we try to make the reader agree with us. To do this, we give reasons for our point of view and support them with facts. See page 470 for general writing guidelines. See page 471 for information on writing an essay.

Step 1. Choose one of the following topics or one of your own. With a partner, think of two strong reasons for or against the topic.

1. eliminating nuclear weapons
2. reducing our dependence on oil
3. protecting endangered animals
4. the use of genetically modified foods

Step 2. Think of or research facts to support your reasons.

Step 3. Write your essay.

1. Write the body of your essay. Write a paragraph for each of your two reasons. State the reasons and support them with facts.
2. Write an introduction that includes a thesis statement. Your thesis statement should state your opinion and the two reasons for it. Here is an example. The thesis statement is in bold.

> Every minute, over one hundred acres of the world's rain forests is destroyed to make land for farms and industries. The wood from the forests is made into paper, cardboard, and plywood. Rain forests cover only about two percent of the surface of the earth, but about half the world's animals and plants live in them. **If we destroy our forests, we will not only destroy many of the world's animals and plants, but we will also threaten the livelihood of many of the native people who depend on the forests.**

3. Write a conclusion that restates the thesis statement and your reasons.
4. Write a title for your essay.

Step 4. Evaluate your essay.

Checklist

_____ Did you write an introduction that contains a thesis statement and a conclusion that restates your thesis statement and reasons?

_____ Did you present facts to support your reasons in the body?

_____ If you were another person reading your essay, would you be persuaded?

Step 5. Work with a partner or a teacher to edit your essay. Check spelling, vocabulary, and grammar.

Step 6. Write your final copy.

SELF-TEST

A **Choose the best answer, A, B, C, or D, to complete the sentence. Mark your answer by darkening the oval with the same letter.**

1. You wouldn't be so hungry if you _____ breakfast.

   A. had eaten   Ⓐ Ⓑ Ⓒ Ⓓ
   B. have been eaten
   C. would have eaten
   D. eaten

2. I'll see her at the meeting if she _____.

   A. came   Ⓐ Ⓑ Ⓒ Ⓓ
   B. come
   C. will come
   D. comes

3. I don't know what he _____ if he couldn't work there anymore.

   A. do   Ⓐ Ⓑ Ⓒ Ⓓ
   B. will do
   C. would do
   D. would have done

4. If you _____ warned us, we would have stayed at that hotel.

   A. wouldn't have   Ⓐ Ⓑ Ⓒ Ⓓ
   B. hadn't
   C. haven't
   D. didn't

5. If only I _____ his phone number, I would call him. Unfortunately, I never wrote it down.

   A. had known   Ⓐ Ⓑ Ⓒ Ⓓ
   B. know
   C. knew
   D. would have known

6. I don't know how to do this exercise. I wish I _____ the teacher about it.

   A. asked   Ⓐ Ⓑ Ⓒ Ⓓ
   B. had asked
   C. will ask
   D. would have asked

7. There are clouds in the sky. It looks _____ it is going to rain.

   A. like if   Ⓐ Ⓑ Ⓒ Ⓓ
   B. as if
   C. though
   D. though if

8. If I _____ you, I wouldn't quit your job.

   A. were   Ⓐ Ⓑ Ⓒ Ⓓ
   B. was
   C. will be
   D. had been

9. I'm really tired. I wish I _____ on vacation now.

   A. could go   Ⓐ Ⓑ Ⓒ Ⓓ
   B. can go
   C. go
   D. would have gone

10. If you _____ tired, you should rest.

    A. would be   Ⓐ Ⓑ Ⓒ Ⓓ
    B. are
    C. had been
    D. were

B Find the underlined word or phrase, A, B, C, or D, that is incorrect. Mark your answer by darkening the oval with the same letter.

1. Unless I <u>read</u> <u>the book</u>, I <u>will be</u> able
         A   B   C
   <u>to answer</u> the questions about it.
     D

   Ⓐ Ⓑ Ⓒ Ⓓ

2. I <u>could had</u> <u>finished</u> <u>if</u> I <u>had had</u>
      A   B   C   D
   more time.

   Ⓐ Ⓑ Ⓒ Ⓓ

3. I <u>would</u> <u>mail</u> the application now <u>if</u>
       A   B   C
   I <u>am</u> you.
     D

   Ⓐ Ⓑ Ⓒ Ⓓ

4. Tina <u>wishes</u> she <u>had</u> a better job and <u>can</u>
         A   B   C
   <u>get</u> a higher salary.
    D

   Ⓐ Ⓑ Ⓒ Ⓓ

5. When should you go to New York? If you

   <u>don't</u> <u>like</u> hot weather, the best time
     A   B
   <u>to go</u> <u>was</u> in May or June.
     C   D

   Ⓐ Ⓑ Ⓒ Ⓓ

6. I <u>wish</u> I <u>could taken</u> guitar lessons <u>when</u>
      A   B   C
   I <u>was</u> younger.
     D

   Ⓐ Ⓑ Ⓒ Ⓓ

7. <u>If</u> you <u>will</u> <u>mix</u> oil with water, the oil <u>sits</u>
    A   B   C   D
   on top.

   Ⓐ Ⓑ Ⓒ Ⓓ

8. <u>If only</u> Tom <u>told</u> us earlier, we
    A   B
   <u>wouldn't have</u> <u>gotten</u> an extra ticket
         C   D
   for him.

   Ⓐ Ⓑ Ⓒ Ⓓ

9. Where <u>you would</u> <u>go</u> <u>if</u> you <u>had</u> the
         A   B C   D
   opportunity?

   Ⓐ Ⓑ Ⓒ Ⓓ

10. I <u>could have</u> gone <u>for</u> a swim <u>if</u> I <u>brought</u>
       A   B   C   D
    my swimsuit with me.

    Ⓐ Ⓑ Ⓒ Ⓓ

APPENDICES

Appendix 1   Grammar Terms

Adjective
An adjective describes a noun or a pronoun.

My cat is very **intelligent**. He's **orange** and **white**.

Adverb
An adverb describes a verb, another adverb, or an adjective.

Joey speaks **slowly**. He **always** visits his father on Wednesdays.

His father cooks **extremely** well. His father is a **very** talented chef.

Article
An article comes before a noun. The definite article is *the*. The indefinite articles are *a* and *an*.

I read **an** online story and **a** magazine feature about celebrity lifestyles.

The online story was much more interesting than **the** magazine feature.

Auxiliary Verb
An auxiliary verb is found with a main verb. It is often called a "helping" verb.

Susan **can't** play in the game this weekend. **Does** Ruth play baseball?

Base Form

The base form of a verb has no tense. It has no endings (*–ed, –s,* or *–ing*).

> Jill didn't **see** the band. She should **see** them when they are in town.

Comparative

Comparative forms compare two things. They can compare people, places, or things.

> This orange is **sweeter than** that grapefruit.
> Working in a large city is **more stressful than** working in a small town.

Conjunction

A conjunction joins two or more sentences, adjectives, nouns, or prepositional phrases. Some conjunctions are *and, but,* and *or.*

> Kasey is efficient, **and** her work is excellent.
> Her apartment is small **but** comfortable.
> She works Wednesdays **and** Thursdays.

Contraction

A contraction is composed of two words put together with an apostrophe. Some letters are left out.

> Frank usually **doesn't** answer his phone.   (doesn't = does + not)
> **He's** really busy.   (he's = he + is)
> Does he know what time **we're** meeting?   (we're = we + are)

Imperative

An imperative gives a command or directions. It uses the base form of the verb, and it does not use the word *you.*

> **Go** to the corner and **turn** left.

Modal

A modal is a type of auxiliary verb. The modal auxiliaries are *can, could, may, might, must, shall, should, will,* and *would.*

> Elizabeth **will** act the lead role in the play next week.
> She **couldn't** go to the party last night because she had to practice her lines.
> She **may** be able to go to the party this weekend.

Noun

A noun is a person, an animal, a place, or a thing.

> My **brother** and **sister-in-law** live in **Pennsylvania**. They have three **cats**.

Object

An object is the noun or pronoun that receives the action of the verb.

> Georgie sent **a gift** for Johnny's birthday.
> Johnny thanked **her** for the gift.

Preposition

A preposition is a small connecting word that is followed by a noun or pronoun. Some are a*t, above, after, by, before, below, for, in, of, off, on, over, to, under, up,* and *with*.

> Every day, Jay drives Chris and Ally **to** school **in** the new car.
> **In** the afternoon, he waits **for** them **at** the bus stop.

Pronoun

A pronoun takes the place of a noun.

> Chris loves animals. **He** has two dogs and two cats.
> His pets are very friendly. **They** like to spend time with people.

Sentence

A sentence is a group of words that has a subject and a verb. It is complete by itself.

> Sentence: Brian works as a lawyer.
> Not a sentence: Works as a lawyer.

Subject

A subject is the noun or pronoun that does the action in the sentence.

> **Trisha** is from Canada.
> **She** writes poetry about nature.

Superlative

Superlative forms compare three or more people, places, or things.

> Jennifer is **the tallest** girl in the class.
> She is from Paris, which is **the most romantic** city in the world.

Tense

Tense tells when the action in a sentence happens.

Simple present	– The cat **eats** fish every morning.
Present progressive	– He **is eating** fish now.
Simple past	– He **ate** fish yesterday morning.
Past progressive	– He **was eating** when the doorbell rang.
Future with *be going to*	– He **is going to eat** fish tomorrow morning, too!
Future with *will*	– I think that he **will eat** the same thing next week.

Verb

A verb tells the action in a sentence.

> Melissa **plays** guitar in a band.
> She **loves** writing new songs.
> The band **has** four other members.

Appendix 2   Irregular Verbs

Base Form	Simple Past	Past Participle	Base Form	Simple Past	Past Participle
be	was, were	been	keep	kept	kept
become	became	become	know	knew	known
begin	began	begun	leave	left	left
bend	bent	bent	lend	lent	lent
bite	bit	bitten	lose	lost	lost
blow	blew	blown	make	made	made
break	broke	broken	meet	met	met
bring	brought	brought	pay	paid	paid
build	built	built	put	put	put
buy	bought	bought	read	read	read
catch	caught	caught	ride	rode	ridden
choose	chose	chosen	ring	rang	rung
come	came	come	run	ran	run
cost	cost	cost	say	said	said
cut	cut	cut	see	saw	seen
do	did	done	sell	sold	sold
draw	drew	drawn	send	sent	sent
drink	drank	drunk	shake	shook	shaken
drive	drove	driven	shut	shut	shut
eat	ate	eaten	sing	sang	sung
fall	fell	fallen	sit	sat	sat
feed	fed	fed	sleep	slept	slept
feel	felt	felt	speak	spoke	spoken
fight	fought	fought	spend	spent	spent
find	found	found	stand	stood	stood
fly	flew	flown	steal	stole	stolen
forget	forgot	forgotten	swim	swam	swum
get	got	gotten/got	take	took	taken
give	gave	given	teach	taught	taught
go	went	gone	tear	tore	torn
grow	grew	grown	tell	told	told
hang	hung	hung	think	thought	thought
have	had	had	throw	threw	thrown
hear	heard	heard	understand	understood	understood
hide	hid	hidden	wake up	woke up	woken up
hit	hit	hit	wear	wore	worn
hold	held	held	win	won	won
hurt	hurt	hurt	write	wrote	written

Appendix 3 Spelling Rules for Endings

Adding a Final –s to Nouns and Verbs

Rule	Example	-s
1. For most words, add –s without making any changes.	book bet save play	books bets saves plays
2. For words ending in a consonant + *y*, change the *y* to *i* and add –*es*.	study party	studies parties
3. For words ending in *ch, s, sh, x,* or *z*, add –*es*.	church class wash fix quiz	churches classes washes fixes quizzes
4. For words ending in *o*, sometimes add –*es* and sometimes add –*s*.	potato piano	potatoes pianos
5. For words ending in *f* or *lf*, change the *f* or *lf* to *v* and add –*es*. For words ending in *fe*, change the *f* to *v* and add –*s*.	loaf half life	loaves halves lives

Adding a Final *–ed*, *–er*, *–est*, and *–ing*

Rule	Example	-ed	-er	-est	-ing
1. For most words, add the ending without making any changes.	clean	cleaned	cleaner	cleanest	cleaning
2. For words ending in silent *e*, drop the *e* and add *–ed*, *–er*, or *–est*.	save like nice	saved liked	saver nicer	 nicest	saving liking
3. For words ending in a consonant + *y*, change the *y* to *i* and add the ending. Do not change or drop the *y* before adding *–ing*.	sunny happy study worry	 studied worried	sunnier happier	sunniest happiest	 studying worrying
4. For one-syllable words ending in one vowel and one consonant, double the final consonant, then add the ending. Do not double the last consonant if it is a *w, x,* or *y*.	hot run bat glow mix stay	 batted glowed mixed stayed	hotter runner batter	hottest	 running batting glowing mixing staying
5. For words of two or more syllables that end in one vowel and one consonant, double the final consonant if the final syllable is stressed.	begin refer occur permit	 referred occurred permitted	beginner		beginning referring occurring permitting
6. For words of two or more syllables that end in one vowel and one consonant, do NOT double the final consonant if the final syllable is NOT stressed.	enter happen develop	entered happened developed	developer		entering happening developing

Appendix 4   Forms of Verb Tenses

THE PRESENT TENSES

The Simple Present Tense

AFFIRMATIVE STATEMENTS		NEGATIVE STATEMENTS		
Subject	Verb or Verb + -s/-es	Subject	*Do Not/Does Not*	Base Verb
I/You/We They	**work.**	I/You/We/They	**do not** **don't**	**work.**
He/She/It	**works.**	He/She/It	**does not** **doesn't**	

YES/NO QUESTIONS			SHORT ANSWERS	
Do/Does	Subject	Base Verb	Yes,	No,
Do	I/you/we/they	**work?**	I/you/we/they **do.**	I/you/we/they **don't.**
Does	he/she/it		he/she/it **does.**	he/she/it **doesn't.**

WH- QUESTIONS				
	Subject (Wh- Word)			Verb
Wh- Word Is the Subject	**Who**			**lives** here?
	Which (computers)			**work** best?
	Wh- Word	*Do/Does*	Subject	Base Verb
Wh- Word Is Not the Subject	**What**	**do**	you	**do** on weekends?
	Where	**does**	she	**live?**
	When	**do**	the children	**go** to bed?
	How	**does**	this machine	**work?**
	Which (computers)	**do**	you	**prefer?**
	Why	**do**	I	**feel** happy?
	Who*	**do**	they	**admire?**

*In formal written English, the wh- word in this question would be *whom*.

The Present Progressive Tense

AFFIRMATIVE STATEMENTS			NEGATIVE STATEMENTS		
Subject	*Am/Is/Are*	Verb + *-ing*	Subject	*Am Not/Is Not/Are Not*	Verb + *-ing*
I	am 'm		I	am not 'm not is not	
He/She/It	is 's	**working** now.	He/She/It	's not isn't	**working** now.
			We/You	are not	
We/You/They	are 're		They	're not aren't	

YES/NO QUESTIONS			SHORT ANSWERS	
Am/Is/Are	Subject	Verb + *-ing*	Yes,	No,
Am	I		you **are.**	you**'re not/aren't.**
Are	you		I **am.**	I**'m not.**
Is	he/she/it	**working?**	he/she/it **is.**	he/she/it**'s not/isn't.**
	you		we **are.**	we**'re not/aren't.**
Are	we		you **are.**	you**'re not/aren't.**
	they		they **are.**	they**'re not/aren't.**

WH– QUESTIONS				
	Subject (Wh- Word)	*Is/Are*		Verb + *-ing*
Wh- Word Is the Subject	**Who**	**is**		**speaking**?
	What (events)	**are**		**happening**?
	Wh- Word	*Am/Is/Are*	Subject	Verb + *-ing*
Wh- Word Is Not the Subject	**What**	**are**	you	**doing** now?
	Where	**is**	he	**going**?
	When	**are**	the children	**going** to bed?
	How	**is**	your car	**running**?
	Which (movie)	**are**	we	**watching**?
	Why	**am**	I	**doing** your work?
	Who*	**am**	I	**driving** home?

*In formal written English, the wh- word in this question would be *whom*.

The Present Perfect Tense

AFFIRMATIVE STATEMENTS			NEGATIVE STATEMENTS		
Subject	*Have/Has*	Past Participle*	Subject	*Have Not/ Has not*	Past Participle
I/You We/They	**have** **'ve**	**worked.**	I/You We/They	**have not** **'ve not** **haven't**	**worked.**
He/She It	**has** **'s**		He/She/It	**has not** **'s not** **hasn't**	

YES/NO QUESTIONS			SHORT ANSWERS	
Have/Has	Subject	Past Participle	Yes,	No,
Have	I/you/we/they	**arrived?**	I/you/we/they **have.**	I/you/we/they**'ve not/haven't.**
Has	he/she/it		he/she/it **has.**	he/she/it**'s not/hasn't.**

WH- QUESTIONS				
	Subject (Wh- Word)		*Has*	Past Participle
Wh- Word Is the Subject	**Who**		**has/'s**	**finished?**
	Which (computers)		**have**	**broken** down?
	Wh- Word	*Have/Has*	Subject	Past Participle
Wh- Word Is Not the Subject	**What**	**have**	you	**decided** to do?
	Where	**has** **'s**	she	**traveled?**
	When	**have**	our teachers	**been** wrong?
	How	**have**	they	**succeeded?**
	Which (movie)	**have**	you	**chosen?**
	Why	**has** **'s**	he	**come?**
	Who*	**has** **'s**	she	**visited?**

*In formal written English, the wh- word in this question would be *whom*.

The Present Perfect Progressive Tense

AFFIRMATIVE STATEMENTS

Subject	*Have/Has*	*Been*	*Verb + -ing*
I/You/We/They	**have** **'ve**	**been**	**working.**
He/She/It	**has** **'s**		

NEGATIVE STATEMENTS

Subject	*Have Not/Has Not*	*Been*	*Verb + -ing*
I/You/We/They	**have not** **'ve not** **haven't**	**been**	**working.**
He/She/It	**has not** **'s not** **hasn't**		

YES/NO QUESTIONS				SHORT ANSWERS	
Have/Has	Subject	Been	Verb + -ing	Yes,	No,
Have	I/you/we/they	**been**	**working?**	I/you/we they **have.**	I/you/we/they**'ve not/haven't.**
Has	he/she/it			he/she/it **has.**	he/she/it**'s not/hasn't.**

WH- QUESTIONS

	Subject (Wh- Word)	*Have/Has*		*Been*	*Verb + -ing*
Wh- Word Is the Subject	**Who**	**has**		**been**	**trying** hard?
	Which (cars)	**have**			**breaking** down a lot?

	Wh- Word	*Have/Has*	Subject	*Been*	Verb + -ing
Wh- Word Is Not the Subject	**What**	**have**	you	**been**	**cooking?**
	Where	**has**	she		**living?**
	When	**have**	they		**planning** to visit us?
	How (long)	**have**	we		**waiting** for him?
	Which (book)	**have**	you		**reading?**
	Why	**has**	he		**eating** so much?
	Who*	**has**	she		**dating?**

*In formal written English, the wh- word in this question would be *whom*.

THE PAST TENSES

The Simple Past Tense

AFFIRMATIVE STATEMENTS		NEGATIVE STATEMENTS		
Subject	Past Form of Verb	Subject	*Did Not*	Base Verb
I/You/We/They He/She/It	**worked.**	I/You/We/They He/She/It	**did not** **didn't**	**work.**

YES/NO QUESTIONS			SHORT ANSWERS	
Did	Subject	Base Verb	Yes,	No,
Did	I/you/we/they he/she/it	**work?**	I/you/we/they he/she/it **did.**	I/you/we/they he/she/it **didn't.**

WH- QUESTIONS				
	Subject (Wh- Word)			Past Form of Verb
Wh- Word Is the Subject	**Who** **Which** (students)			**gave** you that ring? **passed** the test?
	Wh- Word	*Did*	Subject	Base Verb
Wh- Word Is Not the Subject	**What**		you	**decide** to do?
	Where		she	**go?**
	When		the children	**arrive?**
	How	did	he	**do** that?
	Which (movie)		you	**see** last night?
	Why		he	**come?**
	Who*		she	**visit?**

*In formal written English, the wh- word in this question would be *whom*.

The Past Progressive Tense

AFFIRMATIVE STATEMENTS			NEGATIVE STATEMENTS		
Subject	*Was/Were*	Verb + *-ing*	Subject	*Was/Were Not*	Verb + *-ing*
I/He/She/It	**was**	**working.**	I/He/She/It	**was not** **wasn't**	**working.**
We/You/They	**were**		We/You/They	**were not** **weren't**	

YES/NO QUESTIONS			SHORT ANSWERS	
Was/Were	Subject	Verb + *-ing*	Yes,	No,
Was	I		you **were.**	you **weren't.**
Were	you		I **was.**	I **wasn't.**
Was	he/she/it	**working?**	he/she/it **was.**	he/she/it **wasn't.**
Were	you		we **were.**	we**'re not/weren't.**
	we		you **were.**	you**'re not/weren't.**
	they		they **were.**	they**'re not/weren't.**

WH- QUESTIONS				
	Subject (Wh- Word)	*Was/Were*		Verb + *-ing*
Wh- Word Is the Subject	**Who**	**was**		**speaking?**
	What (events)	**were**		**happening?**
	Wh- Word	*Was/Were*	Subject	Verb + *-ing*
Wh- Word Is Not the Subject	**What**	**were**	you	**doing** at 10:00?
	Where	**was**	he	**going?**
	When	**were**	the children	**going** to bed?
	How	**was**	your car	**running?**
	Which (movie)	**were**	we	**watching?**
	Why	**was**	she	**doing** your work?
	Who*	**was**	I	**helping?**

*In formal written English, the wh- word in this question would be *whom*.

The Past Perfect Tense

AFFIRMATIVE STATEMENTS			NEGATIVE STATEMENTS		
Subject	*Had*	Past Participle	Subject	*Had Not*	Past Participle
I/You/We/They He/She/It	**had** **'d**	**worked.**	I/You/We/They He/She/It	**had not** **'d not** **hadn't**	**worked.**

YES/NO QUESTIONS			SHORT ANSWERS	
Had	Subject	Past Participle	Yes,	No,
Had	I/you/we/they he/she/it	**arrived?**	I/you/we/they he/she/it **had.**	I/you we/they he/she/it**'d not/hadn't.**

WH- QUESTIONS				
	Subject (Wh- Word)	*Had*		Past Participle
Wh- Word Is the Subject	**Who**	**had**		**finished?**
	Which (computers)			**broken** down?
	Wh- Word	*Had*	Subject	Past Participle
Wh- Word Is Not the Subject	**What**	**had**	you	**decided** to do?
	Where		she	**traveled?**
	When		our teachers	**been** wrong?
	How		they	**succeeded?**
	Which (movie)		you	**chosen?**
	Why		he	**come?**
	Who*		she	**visited?**

*In formal written English, the wh- word in this question would be *whom*.

The Past Perfect Progressive Tense

AFFIRMATIVE STATEMENTS				NEGATIVE STATEMENTS			
Subject	*Had*	*Been*	Verb + *-ing*	Subject	*Had Not*	*Been*	Verb + *-ing*
I/You/We/They He/She/It	**had** **'d**	**been**	**working.**	I/You/We/They He/She/It	**had not** **hadn't** **'d not**	**been**	**working.**

YES/NO QUESTIONS				SHORT ANSWERS	
Had	Subject	*Been*	Verb + *-ing*	Yes,	No,
Had	I/you/we/they he/she/it	**been**	**working?**	I/you/we/they he/she/it **had.**	I/you/we/they he/she/it**'d not/hadn't.**

WH- QUESTIONS					
	Subject (Wh- Word)	*Had*		*Been*	Verb + *-ing*
Wh- Word Is the Subject	**Who**	**had**		**been**	**trying** hard?
	Which (cars)				**breaking** down a lot?
	Wh- Word	*Had*	Subject	*Been*	Verb + *-ing*
Wh- Word Is Not the Subject	**What**	**had**	you	**been**	**cooking?**
	Where		she		**living?**
	When		they		**planning** to visit us?
	How long		we		**waiting** for him?
	Which (book)		you		**reading?**
	Why		he		**eating** so much?
	Who*		she		**dating?**

*In formal written English, the wh- word in this question would be *whom*.

THE FUTURE TENSES

Be Going To + Base Verb

AFFIRMATIVE STATEMENTS			
Subject	*Am/Is/Are*	*Going To*	Base Verb
I	**am** **'m**	**going to**	**work.**
He/She/It	**is** **'s**		
We/You/They	**are** **'re**		

NEGATIVE STATEMENTS			
Subject	*Am Not/Is Not/Are Not*	*Going To*	Base Verb
I	**am not** **'m not**	**going to**	**work.**
He/She/It	**is not** **'s not** **isn't**		
We/You/They	**are not** **'re not** **aren't**		

YES/NO QUESTIONS				SHORT ANSWERS	
Am/Is/Are	Subject	*Going To*	Base Verb	Yes,	No,
Am	I			you **are.**	you**'re not/aren't.**
Are	you			I **am.**	I**'m not.**
Is	he/she/it	going to	work?	he/she/it **is.**	he/she/it**'s not/isn't.**
	you			we **are.**	we**'re not/aren't.**
Are	we			you **are.**	you**'re not/aren't.**
	they			they **are.**	they**'re not/aren't.**

WH- QUESTIONS					
	Subject (Wh- Word)	*Is/Are*		*Going To*	Base Verb
Wh- Word Is the Subject	**Who**	**is**		going to	**speak?**
	Which (musicians)	**are**			**play?**
	Wh- Word	*Am/Is/Are*	Subject	*Going To*	Base Verb
Wh- Word Is Not the Subject	**What**	**are**	you	going to	**do** next?
	Where	**am**	I		**sleep?**
	When	**are**	the children		**go** to bed?
	How	**is**	the story		**end?**
	Which (movie)	**are**	we		**watch?**
	Why	**is**	she		**come** late?
	Who*	**am**	I		**drive** home?

*In formal written English, the wh- word in this question would be *whom*.

Will + Base Verb

AFFIRMATIVE STATEMENTS			NEGATIVE STATEMENTS		
Subject	*Will*	Base Verb	Subject	*Will Not*	Base Verb
I			I		
He/She/It	will / **'ll**	**work.**	He/She/It	**will not** / **won't**	**work.**
We/You/They			We/You/They		

YES/NO QUESTIONS			SHORT ANSWERS	
Will	Subject	Base Verb	Yes,	No,
	I		you **will.**	you **won't.**
	you		I **will.**	I **won't.**
Will	he/she/it	**work** tomorrow?	he/she/it **will.**	he/she/it **won't.**
	you		we **will.**	we **won't.**
	we		you **will.**	you **won't.**
	they		they **will.**	they **won't.**

WH- QUESTIONS				
	Subject (Wh- Word)	*Will*		**Base Verb**
Wh- Word Is the Subject	**Who**	**will**		**help** me?
	What	**'ll**		**happen** next?
	Wh- Word	*Will*	**Subject**	**Base Verb**
Wh- Word Is Not the Subject	**What**	**will**	you	**do** next?
	Where		I	**sleep?**
	When		the children	**go** to bed?
	How		the story	**end?**
	Which (job)		she	**choose?**
	Why		we	**be** late?
	Who*		I	**see?**

*In formal written English, the wh- word in this question would be *whom*.

The Future Progressive Tense

AFFIRMATIVE STATEMENTS				NEGATIVE STATEMENTS			
Subject	*Will*	*Be*	Base Verb + *-ing*	Subject	*Will*	*Be*	Base Verb + *-ing*
I/You He/She/It We/They	**will** **'ll**	**be**	**working.**	I/You He/She/It We/They	**will not** **won't**	**be**	**working.**

YES/NO QUESTIONS				SHORT ANSWERS	
Will	Subject	*Be*	Base Verb + *-ing*	Yes,	No,
Will	I/you he/she/it we/they	**be**	**working** tomorrow?	I/you he/she/it **will.** we/they	I/you he/she/it **won't.** we/they

WH- QUESTIONS						
	Subject (Wh- Word)	*Will*	*Be*		*Be*	Base Verb
Wh- Word Is the Subject	**Who**	**will**	**be**			**helping** me?
	What	**'ll**				**happening** next?
	Wh- Word	*Will*		Subject	*Be*	Base Verb
Wh- Word Is Not the Subject	**What**			you		**doing** next?
	Where			I		**sleeping?**
	When			the children		**going** to bed?
	How	**will**		the story	**be**	**ending?**
	Which (job)			she		**choosing?**
	Why			we		**working** late?
	Who*			I		**seeing?**

*In formal written English, the wh- word in this question would be *whom*.

The Future Perfect Tense

AFFIRMATIVE STATEMENTS				NEGATIVE STATEMENTS			
Subject	*Will*	*Have*	Past Participle	Subject	*Will Not*	*Have*	Past Participle
I/You/We/They He/She/It	**will** **'ll**	**have**	**worked**	I/You/We/They He/She/It	**will not** **won't**	**have**	**worked.**

YES/NO QUESTIONS				SHORT ANSWERS	
Will	Subject	*Have*	Past Participle	Yes,	No,
Will	I/you/we/they he/she/it	have	**arrived?**	I/you/we/they/ he/she/it **will** **(have).**	I/you/we/they/ he/she/it **won't** **(have).**

The use of *have* in short answers is optional.

WH- QUESTIONS

	Subject (Wh- Word)	*Will*	*Have*		Past Participle
Wh- Word Is the Subject	**Who** **Which** (team)	**will**	**have**		**finished** by 5:00? **won** at the end of the game?

	Wh- Word	*Will*	Subject	*Have*	Past Participle
Wh- Word Is Not the Subject	**What**	**will**	you	**have**	**decided** to do?
	Where		she		**traveled?**
	When		they		**finished?**
	How		you		**completed** all of your work?
	Which (book)		he		**read?**
	Why		she		**read** that book?
	Who*		I		**visited?**

*In formal written English, the wh- word in this question would be *whom*.

The Future Perfect Progressive Tense

AFFIRMATIVE STATEMENTS				
Subject	*Will*	*Have*	*Been*	Verb + -ing
I/You/We/They He/She/It	**will** **'ll**	**have**	**been**	**working.**

NEGATIVE STATEMENTS				
Subject	*Will Not*	*Have*	*Been*	Verb + -ing
I/You/We/They He/She/It	**will not** **'ll not** **won't**	**have**	**been**	**working.**

YES/NO QUESTIONS					SHORT ANSWERS	
Will	Subject	*Have*	*Been*	Verb + -ing	Yes,	No,
Will	I/you/we/they he/she/it	**have**	**been**	**working?**	I/you/we/they he/she/it **will** **(have).**	I/you/we/they he/she/it **won't** **(have).**

The use of *have* in short answers is optional.

Appendix 5 Forms of Modals and Modal Phrases

MODALS

Simple Modals

AFFIRMATIVE AND NEGATIVE STATEMENTS		
Subject	Modal (Not)	Base Verb
I You He/She/It We They	can/cannot/can't could/could not/couldn't would/would not/wouldn't should/should not/shouldn't may/may not might/might not must/must not/mustn't	swim here.

YES/NO QUESTIONS			SHORT ANSWERS			
Modal	Subject	Base Verb	Yes,		No,	
Can Could Would Should May Must	I you he/she/it we they	swim here?	you I/we he/she/it you they	can. could. would. should. may must.	you I/we he/she/it you they	can't. couldn't. wouldn't. shouldn't. may not. mustn't.

WH- QUESTIONS				
	Subject (Wh- Word)	Modal		Base Verb
Wh- Word Is the Subject	Who Which (children)	can		speak Portuguese? swim?
	Wh- Word	Modal	Subject	Base Verb
Wh- Word Is Not the Subject	What	can	you	do to help us?
	Where	could	she	go?
	When	would	the children	take the test?
	How	should	he	work?
	Which (car)	may	you	buy?
	Why	might	he	leave early?
	Who*	must	they	pay?

*In formal written English, the wh- word in this question would be *whom*.

Progressive Modals

AFFIRMATIVE AND NEGATIVE STATEMENTS			
Subject	Modal	*Be*	Verb + *-ing*
I You He/She/It We They	can/cannot/can't could/could not/couldn't would/would not/wouldn't should/should not/shouldn't may/may not might/might not must/must not/mustn't	be	**working** at 9:00 tonight.

YES/NO QUESTIONS			SHORT ANSWERS			
Modal	Subject	*Be* + *-ing* Verb	Yes,		No,	
Can **Could** **Would** **Should** **Must**	I you he/she/it we they	**be working** at 9:00 tonight?	you I/we he/she/it you they	**can.** **could.** **would.** **should.** **must.**	you I/we he/she/it you they	**can't.** **couldn't.** **wouldn't.** **shouldn't.** **must.**

WH- QUESTIONS				
	Subject (Wh- Word)	Modal		*Be* + Verb *-ing*
Wh- Word Is the Subject	**Who** **Which** (children)	**could**		**be speaking** Greek? **be studying** now?
	Wh- Word	Modal	Subject	*Be* + Verb + *-ing*
Wh- Word Is Not the Subject	**What**	**can**	you	**be doing** to help us?
	Where	**could**	she	**be going?**
	When	**would**	the children	**be taking** the test?
	How	**should**	he	**be working?**
	Which (students)	**may**	you	**be talking** to?
	Why	**might**	he	**be leaving** early?
	Who*	**must**	they	**be driving** home?

*In formal written English, the wh- word in this question would be *whom*.

Prerfect Modals

AFFIRMATIVE AND NEGATIVE STATEMENTS			
Subject	Modal	*Have*	Past Participle
I You He/She/It We They	cannot/can't* could/could not/couldn't would/would not/wouldn't should/should not/shouldn't may/may not might/might not must/must not/mustn't	have	**arrived** by noon.

*We rarely use *can* in the perfect modal form in statements.

YES/NO QUESTIONS			SHORT ANSWERS			
Modal	Subject	*Have* + Past Participle	Yes,		No,	
Can **Could** **Would** **Should** **Must**	I you he/she/it we they	**have** **arrived** by noon?	you I/we he/she/it you they	**can (have).** **could (have).** **would (have).** **should (have).** **may (have).**	you I/we he/she/it you they	**can't (have).** **couldn't (have).** **wouldn't (have).** **shouldn't (have).** **mustn't (have).**

The use of *have* in short answers is optional.

WH– QUESTIONS				
	Subject (Wh- Word)	Modal		*Have* + Past Participle
Wh- Word Is the Subject	**Who** **Which** (children)	**could**		**have written** the letter? **have finished** their work?
	Wh- Word	Modal	Subject	*Have* + Past Participle
Wh- Word Is Not the Subject	**What** **Where** **When** **How** (hard) **Which** (teacher) **Why** **Who***	**can** **could** **would** **should** **must**	you she the children he you he they	**have done** to help us? **have gone?** **have taken** the test? **have worked?** **have talked** to? **have left** early? **have visited?**

*In formal written English, the wh- word would be *whom*.

Perfect Progressive Modals

AFFIRMATIVE AND NEGATIVE STATEMENTS			
Subject	Modal	*Have Been*	Verb + *-ing*
I You He/She/It We They	**cannot/can't***	**have been**	**working** at that time.
	could/could not/couldn't		
	would/would not/wouldn't		
	should/should not/shouldn't		
	may/may not		
	might/might not		
	must/must not/mustn't		

*We rarely use *can* in the perfect progressive modal form in affirmative statements, but we do use *can't* in this form.

YES/NO QUESTIONS			SHORT ANSWERS			
Modal	Subject	*Have + Been + -ing* Verb	Yes,		No,	
Can **Could** **Would** **Should** **Must**	I you he/she/it we they	**have been** **working** by then?	you I/we he/she/it you they	**can (have).** **could (have).** **would (have).** **should (have).** **may (have).**	you I/we he/she/it you they	**can't (have).** **couldn't (have).** **wouldn't (have).** **shouldn't (have).** **mustn't (have).**

The use of *have* in short answers is optional.

WH- QUESTIONS				
	Subject (Wh- Word)	Modal		*Have + Been* Verb + *-ing*
Wh- Word Is the Subject	**Who** **Which** (children)	**could**		**have been working** here? **have been watching** TV?
	Wh- Word	Modal	Subject	*Have + Been* Verb + *-ing*
Wh- Word Is Not the Subject	**What**	**can** **could** **would** **should** **must**	you	**have been listening** to?
	Where		she	**have been going?**
	When		the children	**have been taking** the test?
	How (hard)		he	**have been working?**
	Which (teacher)		you	**have been talking** to?
	Why		he	**have been leaving** early?
	Who*		they	**have been visiting?**

*In formal written English, the wh- word in this question would be *whom*.

MODAL PHRASES

Be Able To, Be Supposed To, and *Be Allowed To*

PRESENT AFFIRMATIVE AND NEGATIVE STATEMENTS			
Subject	*Am/Is/Are (Not)*	Modal Phrase	Base Verb
I	am/'m (not)	able to supposed to allowed to	leave early.
You	are/'re (not)		
He/She	is/'s (not)		
We	are/'re (not)		
They			

PRESENT YES/NO QUESTIONS				SHORT ANSWERS	
Am/Is/Are	Subject	Modal Phrase	Base Verb	Yes,	No,
Am	I	able to supposed to allowed to	leave early?	you **are**.	you're not/aren't.
Are	you			I **am**.	I'm not.
				we **are**.	we're not/aren't.
Is	he/she			he/she **is**.	he/she's not/isn't.
Are	we			you **are**.	you're not/aren't.
Are	they			they **are**.	they're not/aren't.

PRESENT WH– QUESTIONS					
	Subject (Wh-Word)	*Is/Are*	Modal Phrase	Base Verb	
Wh- Word Is the Subject	**Who**	**is**	**able to supposed to allowed to**	leave early?	
	Which (workers)	**are**			
	Wh- Word	*Am/Is/Are*	Subject	Modal Phrase	Base Verb
Wh- Word Is Not the Subject	**What**	**are**	you	**able to supposed to allowed to**	do?
	Where	**is**	she		swim?
	When	**are**	the students		relax?
	How (much)	**am**	I		earn?
	Which (ones)	**are**	they		take?
	Why	**is**	he		leave early?
	Who*	**are**	they		visit?

*In formal written English, the wh- word would be *whom*.

PAST AFFIRMATIVE AND NEGATIVE STATEMENTS

Subject	*Was/Were (Not)*	Modal Phrase	Base Verb
I	was/was not/wasn't		
You	were/were not/weren't	able to	
He/She/It	was/was not/wasn't	supposed to	leave early.
We	were/were not/weren't	allowed to	
They	were/were not/weren't		

PAST YES/NO QUESTIONS

Was/Were	Subject	Modal Phrase	Base Verb
Was	I		
Were	you	able to	
Was	he/she	supposed to	leave early?
Were	we	allowed to	
Were	they		

SHORT ANSWERS

Yes,		No,	
you	were.	you	weren't.
I	was.	I	wasn't.
we	were.	we	weren't.
he/she	was.	he/she	wasn't.
you	were.	you	weren't.
they	were.	they	weren't.

PAST WH– QUESTIONS

	Subject (Wh- Word)		*Was/Were*	Modal Phrase	Base Verb
Wh- Word Is the Subject	Who		was	able to supposed to allowed to	leave early?
	Which men		were		

	Wh- Word	*Was/Were*	Subject	Modal Phrase	Base Verb
Wh- Word Is Not the Subject	What	were	you		do?
	Where	was	she		swim?
	When	were	the students	able to	relax?
	How (much)	was	I	supposed to	spend?
	Which (ones)	were	they	allowed to	take?
	Why	was	he		leave early?
	Who*	were	they		visit?

*In formal written English, the wh- word would be *whom*.

FUTURE AFFIRMATIVE AND NEGATIVE STATEMENTS

Subject	Will (Not)	Be + Modal Phrase	Base Verb
I/You/We/They He/She/It	will 'll will not won't	be able to be supposed to be allowed to	leave early.

FUTURE YES/NO QUESTIONS / SHORT ANSWERS

Will	Subject	Be + Modal Phrase	Base Verb	Yes,	No,
Will	I	be able to be supposed to be allowed to	leave early?	you **will**.	you **won't**.
	you			I/we **will**.	I **won't**.
	he/she			he/she **will**.	he/she **won't**.
	we			you **will**.	you **won't**.
	they			they **will**.	they **won't**.

FUTURE WH– QUESTIONS

	Subject (Wh- Word)	Will	Be + Modal Phrase	Base Verb
Wh- Word Is the Subject	**Who** **Which** (men)	will	be able to be supposed to be allowed to	leave early?

	Wh- Word	Will	Subject	Be + Modal Phrase	Base Verb
Wh- Word Is Not the Subject	**What**	will	you	be able to be supposed to be allowed to	**do?**
	Where		she		**swim?**
	When		the students		**relax?**
	How (much)		I		**earn?**
	Which (ones)		they		**take?**
	Why		he		**leave** early?
	Who*		they		**visit?**

*In formal written English, the wh- word in this question would be *whom*.

HAVE TO

PRESENT, PAST, AND FUTURE AFFIRMATIVE STATEMENTS		
Subject	*Have/Has To* *Had To* *Will Have To*	Base Verb
I	have to had to will/'ll have to	
You	have to had to will/'ll have to	study.
He/She	has to had to will/'ll have to	
We	have to had to will/'ll have to	
They	have to had to will/'ll have to	

PAST, PRESENT, AND FUTURE YES/NO QUESTIONS				SHORT ANSWERS			
Do/Did/Will	Subject	*Have To*	Base Verb	Yes,		No,	
Do **Did** **Will**	I	have to	be early?	you you you	**do.** **did.** **will.**	you you you	**don't.** **didn't.** **won't.**
	you			I/we I/we I/we	**do.** **did.** **will.**	I/we I/we I/we	**don't.** **didn't.** **won't.**
	he/she			he/she he/she he/she	**does.** **did.** **will.**	he/she he/she he/she	**doesn't.** **didn't.** **won't.**
	we			you you you	**do.** **did.** **will.**	you you you	**don't.** **didn't.** **won't.**
	they			they they they	**do.** **did.** **will.**	they they they	**don't.** **didn't.** **won't**

PAST, PRESENT, AND FUTURE WH– QUESTIONS					
	Subject (Wh- Word)	*Have/Has To Had To Will Have To*			Base Verb
Wh- Word Is the Subject	**Who**	**has to/had to**			**leave?**
	Which (students)	**will have to**			**take** the test?
	Wh- Word	*Do/Did/Will*	Subject	*Have To*	Base Verb
Wh- Word Is Not the Subject	**What**	**will**	I		**do** to help you?
	Where	**does**	she		**go?**
	When	**did**	the boys		**take** the test?
	How (hard)	**does**	he	**have to**	**work?**
	Which (car)	**do**	you		**repair?**
	Why	**did**	he		**leave** early?
	Who*	**will**	they		**visit?**

*In formal written English, the wh- word in this question would be *whom*.

NOT HAVE TO

PRESENT		
Subject	*Not Have To*	Base Verb
I You	**do not/don't have to**	
He/She/It	**does not/doesn't have to**	**be** early.
We They	**do not/don't have to**	

PAST		
Subject	*Not Have To*	Base Verb
I You He/She/It We They	**didn't have to**	**be** early.

FUTURE		
Subject	*Will Not Have To*	Base Verb
I You He/She/It We They	**will not have to** **won't have to**	**be** early.

Ought To and *Had Better*

AFFIRMATIVE AND NEGATIVE STATEMENTS		
Subject	Modal Phrase (+ *Not*)	Base Verb
I/You/We/They He/She/It	**ought to** **ought not to** **had better** **'d better** **had better not** **'d better not**	**go** now.

YES/NO QUESTIONS*			SHORT ANSWERS			
Verb	Subject	*Better* + Base Verb	Yes,		No,	
Had	I you he/she we they	**better go** now?	you I/we he/she you they	**had.**	you I/we he/she you they	**hadn't.**

*Yes/no questions with *ought to* are rare. Example: **Ought** we **to** help them?

WH– QUESTIONS				
	Subject (Wh- Word)	Modal		Base Verb
Wh- Word Is the Subject	**Who** **Which** (student)	**ought to** **had better**		**leave** now? **take** the test?
	Wh- Word	*Ought/Had**	Subject	*To/Better* + Base Verb
Wh- Word Is Not the Subject	**What**	**ought**	I	**to do** to help you?
	Where	**had**	she	**better go?**
	When	**had**	the children	**better take** the test?
	How	**ought**	he	**to complete** the form?
	Which (car)	**had**	they	**better repair?**
	Why	**ought**	he	**to leave** early?
	Who**	**had**	she	**better talk to?**

**In formal written English, the wh- word would be *whom*.

Function	Coordinating Conjunctions		Subordinating Conjunctions	Transitional Phrases
	Simple	Complex		
	To Join Two Main Clauses	*To Join Two Main Clauses or Two Sentences*	*To Join a Main Clause and a Dependent Clause*	*Used Before a Noun or a Gerund Except as Noted Below*
Addition	and	also besides furthermore in addition moreover		
Comparison	and but	also likewise similarly	as just as	like/just like not only...but also
Contrast	but yet	despite the fact that however in contrast in spite of the fact that instead nevertheless nonetheless on the other hand	although though even though whereas while	despite in spite of
Time		after that finally first, second, etc. last meanwhile next since then soon (after) then	after as/so long as as soon as before by the time once since until when while	since the first, second, etc.
Reason	for	as a result consequently therefore	as because since so...that such...that	as a result of because of due to

Function	Coordinating Conjunctions		Subordinating Conjunctions	Transitional Phrases
	Simple	Complex		
	To Join Two Main Clauses	*To Join Two Main Clauses or Two Sentences*	*To Join a Main Clause and a Dependent Clause*	*Used Before a Noun or a Gerund Except as Noted Below*
Purpose			so that in order that	in order to (+ base verb)
Result	so	accordingly as a consequence as a result consequently therefore		the cause of the reason for
Condition	or (else)	otherwise	even if if if only in case only if unless whether or not	

Punctuation Guidelines for Conjunctions

1. Simple Coordinating Conjunctions

Main clause + , **conjunction** + main clause.

      Main Clause   **Main Clause**
We asked everyone in the office for help, **but** we had to do the job ourselves.

Many writers use *and, but,* and *yet* to begin a sentence, but some instructors do not accept this usage.

      Main Clause   **Main Clause**
We asked everyone in the office for help. **But** we had to do the job ourselves.

2. Complex Coordinating Conjunctions

ONE SENTENCE: Main clause + **; conjunction,** + main clause.

    We didn't have enough workers**; furthermore,** we didn't have enough time.

OR

TWO SENTENCES: Main clause + **. Conjunction,** + main clause.

    We didn't have enough workers**. Furthermore,** we didn't have enough time.

3. Subordinating Conjunctions

Main clause + **conjunction** + dependent clause.

    Stan cooks his own food **because** he wants to save money.

OR

Conjunction + dependent clause, + main clause.

    Because he wants to save money, Stan cooks his own food.

4. Punctuation of Transitional Phrases

Transitional phrases can come at the beginning, in the middle, or at the end of a sentence.

BEGINNING: **Transitional phrase,** + main clause.
               Because of the weather, we decided not to go to the beach.
MIDDLE: Start of main clause, + **transitional phrase,** + end of main clause.
               We decided, **because of the weather,** not to go to the beach.
END: Main clause + **transitional phrase.**
               We decided not to go to the beach **because of the weather.**

Appendix 7   Capitalization Rules

First words

1. Capitalize the first word of every sentence.

   They live in San Francisco.   **W**hat is her name?

2. Capitalize the first word of a quotation.

   She said, "**M**y name is Nancy."

Names

1. Capitalize names of people, including titles of address.

   Mr. **T**hompson   **A**lison **E**mmet   **M**ike **A**. **L**ee

2. Capitalize the word "I".

   Rose and **I** went to the market.

3. Capitalize nationalities, ethnic groups, and religions.

   Latino   **A**sian   **K**orean   **I**slam

4. Capitalize family words if they appear alone or with a name, but not if they have a possessive pronoun or article.

   He's at **A**unt Lucy's house.   vs.   He's at an **a**unt's house.

Places

1. Capitalize the names of countries, states, cities, and geographical areas.

   Tokyo   **M**exico   the **S**outh   **V**irginia

2. Capitalize the names of oceans, lakes, rivers, and mountains.

   the **P**acific **O**cean   **L**ake **O**ntario   **M**t. **E**verest

3. Capitalize the names of streets, schools, parks, and buildings.

   Central **P**ark   **M**ain **S**treet   the **E**mpire **S**tate **B**uilding

4. Don't capitalize directions if they aren't names of geographical areas.

   She lives **n**ortheast of Washington. We fly **s**outh during our flight.

Time words

1. Capitalize the names of days and months.

   Monday   **F**riday   **J**anuary   **S**eptember

2. Capitalize the names of holidays and historical events.

   Christmas   **I**ndependence **D**ay   **W**orld **W**ar I

3. Don't capitalize the names of seasons.

   spring   **s**ummer   **f**all   **w**inter

Titles

1. Capitalize the first word and all important words of titles of books, magazines, newspapers, and articles.

    *The **S**ound and the **F**ury*   *Time **O**ut*   *The **N**ew **Y**ork **T**imes*

2. Capitalize the first word and all important words of titles of films, plays, radio programs, and TV shows.

    ***S**tar **W**ars*   "**F**riends"   *Mid **S**ummer **N**ight's **D**ream*

3. Don't capitalize articles (*a, an, the*), conjunctions (*but, and, or*) and short prepositions (*of, with, in, on, for*) unless they are the first word of a title.

    *The **S**tory **o**f Cats*   *The **W**oman **i**n the **D**unes*

Appendix 8   Punctuation Rules

Period

1. Use a period at the end of a statement or command.

    I live in New York**.**   Open the door**.**

2. Use a period after most abbreviations.

    Ms**.**   Dr**.**   St**.**   U**.**S**.**

    Exceptions: NATO   UN   AIDS   IBM

3. Use a period after initials.

    Ms**.** K**.**L**.** Kim   F**.**C**.** Simmons

Question Mark

1. Use a question mark at the end of questions.

    Is he working tonight**?**   Where did they use to work**?**

2. In a direct quotation, the question mark goes before the quotation marks.

    Martha asked, "What's the name of the street**?**"

Exclamation Point

Use an exclamation point at the end of exclamatory sentences or phrases. They express surprise or strong emotion.

    Wow**!**   I got an A**!**

Comma

1. Use a comma to separate items in a series.

    John will have juice**,** coffee**,** and tea at the party.

2. Use a comma to separate adjectives that each modify the noun alone.
   Purrmaster is a smart, friendly cat. (*smart* and *friendly* cat)
3. Use a comma before a conjunction (*and, but, or, so*) that separates two independent clauses.
   The book is very funny, and the film is funny too.
   She was tired, but she didn't want to go to sleep.
4. Don't use a comma before a conjunction that separates a sentence from an incomplete sentence.
   I worked in a bakery at night and went to class during the day.
5. Use a comma after an introductory clause or phrase.
   After we hike the first part of the trail, we are going to rest.
6. Use a comma after *yes* and *no* in answers.
   Yes, that is my book.   No, I'm not.
7. Use a comma to separate quotations from the rest of a sentence. Don't use a comma if the quotation is a question and it is in the first part of the sentence.
   The student said, "I'm finished with the homework."
   "Are you really finished**?**" asked the student.

Apostrophe

1. Use apostrophes in contractions.
   don't (*do not*)   it's (*it is*)   he's (*he is*)   we're (*we are*)
2. Use apostrophes to show possession.
   Anne's book (the book belongs to Anne)

Quoted Speech

1. Use quotation marks to show the exact words that someone said.

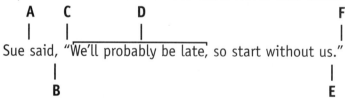

A. Mention the speaker and use a verb like *said*.
B. Put a comma after the verb.
C. Open the quotation marks (").
D. Write the quotation. Capitalize the first word.
E. End the quotation with a period, a question mark, or an exclamation point.
F. Close the quotation marks (").

Here are some other ways to write quotations.

PUT THE SPEAKER AT THE END.

"We'll probably be late, so start without us," **Sue said.**
(Notice the comma at the end of the quotation.)

PUT THE SPEAKER IN THE MIDDLE

"We'll probably be late," **Sue said,** "so start without us."
(Notice the commas before and after *Sue said,* and no capital letter for *so.* Also notice the two sets of quotation marks, one for each part of the quotation.)

When using this form, you must put the speaker in a natural break in the sentence.

INAPPROPRIATE BREAK: "We'll, Sue said, "be late, so start without us."

When a quotation is a question or an exclamation, put the quotation mark or the exclamation point after the quotation.

"Do you mind if we're late**?**" Sue asked.
(Use a question mark, not a comma, after the quotation, and use a period at the end, not a question mark.)
"Don't be late**!**" Sue said.
(Use an exclamation point after the quotation, not a comma.)

We can invert the speaker and the quotation verb (*say, exclaim,* etc).

Said Sue, "We'll probably be late, so start without us."
"We'll probably be late, so start without us," **said Sue.**
"We'll probably be late," **said Sue,** "so start without us."

2. Use quotation marks before and after titles of articles, songs, stories, and television shows. Periods and commas are usually placed before the end quotation marks, while question marks and exclamation points are placed after them. If the title is a question, the question mark is placed inside the quotation marks, and appropriate punctuation is placed at the end of the sentence.

Burt's favorite song is "Show Some Emotion" by Joan Armatrading.
He read an article called "Motivating Your Employees."
We read an interesting article called "How Do You Motivate Employees?".

Italics and Underlining
1. If you are writing on a computer, use italic type (*like this*) for books, newspapers, magazines, films, plays, and words from other languages.
   Have you ever read *Woman in the Dunes*?
   How do you say *buenos dias* in Chinese?
2. If you are writing by hand, underline the titles of books, newspapers, magazines, films, and plays.
   Have you ever read <u>Woman in the Dunes</u>?
   How do you say <u>buenos dias</u> in Chinese?

Appendix 9   Writing Basics

1. Sentence types

There are three types of sentences: declarative, interrogative, and exclamatory. Declarative sentences state facts and describe events, people, or things. We use a period at the end of these sentences. Interrogative sentences ask yes/no questions and wh- questions. We use a question mark at the end of these sentences. Exclamatory sentences express surprise or extreme emotion, such as joy or fear. We use an exclamation point at the end of these sentences.

2. Indenting

We indent the first line of a paragraph. Each paragraph expresses a new thought, and indenting helps to mark the beginning of this new thought.

3. Writing titles

The title should give the main idea of a piece of writing. It should be interesting. It goes at the top of the composition and is not a complete sentence. In a title, capitalize the first word and all of the important words.

4. Writing topic sentences

The topic sentence tells the reader the main idea of the paragraph. It is always a complete sentence with a subject and a verb. It is often the first sentence in a paragraph, but sometimes it is in another position in the paragraph.

5. Organizing ideas

Information can be organized in a paragraph in different ways. One common way is to begin with a general idea and work toward more specific information. Another way is to give the information in order of time using words like *before, after, as, when, while,* and *then*.

6. Connecting ideas

It is important to connect the ideas in a paragraph so that the paragraph has cohesion. Connectors and transitional words help make the writing clear, natural, and easy to read. Connectors and transitional words include *and, in addition, also, so, but, however, for example, such as, so ... that,* and *besides*.

7. The writing process

Success in writing generally follows these basic steps:

- ❖ Brainstorm ideas.
- ❖ Organize the ideas.
- ❖ Write a first draft of the piece.
- ❖ Evaluate and edit the piece for content and form.
- ❖ Rewrite the piece.

The Paragraph and the Essay

The Paragraph	The Essay
The Topic Sentence*	**The Introduction** A paragraph with general sentences leading to the thesis statement*
The Body Sentences that support the topic sentence	**The Body** Paragraphs that support the thesis statement
The Conclusion A concluding sentence	**The Conclusion** A paragraph that restates the thesis statement and adds a final thought

*The topic sentence states what the paragraph is about. The thesis statement states what the essay will prove or explain.

Sample Student Paragraph

Too Much Television is Harmful to Children

Topic Sentence

    Watching too much television is harmful to children because it can take time away from studying, harm their personalities, and make them inactive. First, television takes away time from children's studies. They may not do their homework or study for tests enough. Second, their personalities can be affected by excess violence on some programs. They may get frightened or accept violence as something normal. Finally, sitting in front of the television for hours is not healthy for a child. They should be playing with friends or doing sports instead of watching the action on a screen. It is clear that, watching too much television can be harmful to children, and parents should control the amount of time children watch television and the programs they watch.

Body

Conclusion

Sample Student Essay

Essay Organization		Paragraph Organization
	Too Much Television is Harmful to Children	
Introduction *Thesis Statement*	Watching television has become a normal activity for most children in our culture today. They watch television when they are home in the morning, in the afternoon, and in the evening. There are some excellent programs for children, but many parents feel that watching too much television is not good for them. Watching too much television can be harmful to children in three ways: It can take time away from studying, it can harm their personalities, and it can make them inactive.	Topic Sentence Body Conclusion
Body	First of all, watching too much television takes time away from studying. Instead of doing their homework, children prefer to watch television. This can affect their performance at school. They may get lower grades because they haven't done their homework or prepared sufficiently for a test. They may feel tired or sleepy in class because they have stayed up to watch a late movie. They never have time to read a book, and as a result their reading skills in general are poor.	Topic Sentence Body Conclusion
	Second, some programs on television may affect their personalities. There is a lot of violence on television, especially in police stories. This may affect some children. They may get frightened and have nightmares, or they may think violence is a normal part of life and may hurt themselves or others. They often see movie stars and sports stars that look glamorous and lead glamorous lives and may want to copy them. These effects of television are not good for children's development.	Topic Sentence Body Conclusion
	Finally, sitting in front of a television set for hours every day is not healthy for children. Instead of playing with other children, and interacting with them, they become inactive. They just look at the television screen and usually eat snacks while watching television. They watch sports on television but don't play the sports themselves.	Topic Sentence Body Conclusion
Conclusion *Restatement of Thesis* *Final Thought*	In conclusion, if children watch too much television, it may affect their studies at school and their health by making them inactive and unsocial. Furthermore, if they watch the wrong kinds of programs their personalities may be affected. Therefore, parents should control the amount of time children spend in front of the television and the programs they are watching.	Topic Sentence Body Conclusion

Index

Noun clauses; *That* clauses
Commas, 12, 30, 63, 181, 185, 301
    adjective clauses, 361, 362, 368
    adverb clauses, 383–85, 389–90, 394
    conditional sentences, 406
    coordinating conjunctions, 304–6
    noun clauses, 318
Complements, 295
Compound nouns, 97–100
Conditional sentences, 63–66
    as if/as though, 416–18
    implied, 418–21
    mixed, 412, 414–16
    real (present/future), 406–9
    unreal (past), 412–13, 415–16
    unreal (present/future), 409–11
Conjunctions, 301, 436, 463–65
    clause markers, 380–82
    coordinating, 304–6
    correlative, 307–8
Consequently, 384
Consonants, 133
Contractions, 3, 12–13, 36–37, 152–53, 436
    + *have,* 200
    be going to/will, 58–59, 70
    had, 159
    have got to, 155
    let us, 175
    may not/might not, 188–89
    must not, 195
    should have, 162
    would rather, 177–78
Coordinating conjunctions, 304–6
Correlative conjunctions, 307–8
Could/could not/couldn't, 150–53, 175–76, 180–92, 422–23
    adverb clauses, 387
    conditional sentences, 409–14
    passive/active voice, 219–20
    progressive forms of modals, 198–200, 202
Count/noncount nouns, 100–103, 106, 110–11, 130, 133–34, 138–41

D

-D/-ed, 11, 28, 36, 367, 439
Defining/nondefining adjective clauses, 361–64, 368
Definite/indefinite adjectives, articles, pronouns, 123, 130, 133–41, 268–70
Dependent/independent clauses, 63–66, 304, 384, 406
Direct/indirect questions, 321–26
Don't have to/doesn't have to, 157–59

E

Each of, 362
Each other, 131
Each/each (one), 110, 293

-Ed/-d, 11, 28, 36, 367, 440
Either...or/neither...nor, 293, 307–8
Enough, 270–73
-Es/-s, 2, 90–91, 93–96, 130, 439
Even if/even though, 389–93
Ever, 12, 15, 38
Every/every one of/every other, 4, 110, 131, 293
Everyone/everybody/everything, 123, 293
Expressions/words
    ability, 150–52, 181–82, 189
    deductions, 194–98
    expect/expectation, 60, 164, 232, 318
    necessity/lack of necessity, 154–55, 157, 220
    obligation, 154–55, 159
    permission, 150, 180–83
    possibility, 150, 187–92
    preference, 176–80
    purpose, 273–74, 387
    quantity, 103–4, 106–9, 362
    requests, 183–87, 215, 339
    suggestions, 174–76
    time, 297, 380–81

F

Feminine/masculine pronouns, 122
Few, 101–2, 106–9, 130
For, 14, 37, 78, 239, 244–45, 260–62
    + noun/indefinite pronoun, 269
    + object, 270–74
    coordinating conjunctions, 304–6
    subject-verb agreement, 295
Future conditional sentences, 63
Future in the past, 74
Future tenses, 70–73, 78–81, 188, 214, 448–52

G

Gender-specific pronouns, 122, 126
Gerunds, 174, 176–78, 184–85
    as objects of prepositions, 260–62
    parallel structure, 301–4, 307–8
    passive/active voice, 275–79
    perfect/simple, 275–79
    person +, 281–82
    as subjects/as objects, 256–59
    verbs +, 265–67, 279–80
Grammar terms, 436–37
Group nouns, 122, 131

H

H (silent), 133
Had better, 159–61, 219–20
Had to be, 220
Hardly, 104
Have to/have got to, 151, 154–59
He who, 407–8
He/she/him/her/his/hers, 120–23, 329–30, 336

Himself/herself, 128
How, 2–3, 12–13, 29, 37, 162
How about, 174–76
How long, 37
How many/how much, 12, 106, 212, 322
However, 389–90
Hyphens, 97–98

I

If, 63, 324–26, 391–93
    conditional sentences, 406–10, 412–14,
    418–21
If only, 425–26
If so/if not, 419
If you like, 175
Imperative sentences, 407, 436
In, 244–46, 260–62, 359
In addition to, 295
In case, 391–93
In order that, 387
In order to, 274
Indefinite/definite adjectives, articles, pronouns,
123, 130, 133–41, 268–70
Independent/dependent clauses, 63–66, 304,
384, 406
Indirect/direct questions, 321–26
Infinitives, 74, 176–78, 227
    adjectives +, 268–70
    enough +, 270–73
    indefinite pronouns +, 268–70
    not +, 336
    nouns +, 268–70
    parallel structure, 301–4
    passive/active voice, 275–79
    perfect/simple, 275–79
    of purpose, 273–74
    too +, 270–73
    verbs +, 263–67, 279–80
    verbs of perception +, 279–80
-Ing, 440
    verbs +, 3, 13, 29, 37, 46, 229, 395
        adjective phrases, 367–68
        future perfect progressive tense, 78
        future progressive tense, 70–73
        gerunds, 174, 256–59
        object + verb + *ing,* 279–80
        progressive forms of modals, 199–200
Inseparable phrasal verbs, 238–39
Into, 239
Intransitive/transitive verbs, 178, 213, 237–38
Introductory phrases, 276
Irregular verbs, 28–29, 438
Irregular/regular nouns, 90–93
Irregular/regular past participles, 367
Itself, 128

J

Just, 12, 15

L

Let/let us/let's, 174–76, 232
Like, 417–18
Little, 101–2, 106–9

M

Main clauses, 63–66, 79, 304, 318, 321–26
    adjective clauses and, 350, 353, 356, 361,
    362
    adverb clauses and, 383–84, 394–95
    conditional sentences, 406–7, 409–410,
    412–14
    wishes, 422–23
Main verbs, 150
Many/many of, 101–2, 106–9, 362
Masculine/feminine pronouns, 122
Maybe/may be, 60, 175, 188, 219–20
May/may not/might, 150–51, 180–83, 187–92,
199–200, 202, 387
    passive/active voice, 219–20
Me/myself, 120–21, 128, 281–82, 330, 336
Might/may/might be able to/might not,
150–52, 187–92, 198–200, 202, 232, 412
    passive/active voice, 219–20
Mine, 121
Modals, 149–209, 436, 453–62. See also
individual modal verbs
Most/most of, 293, 362
Motion verbs, 213
Much/much of, 101–2, 106–7, 109, 362
Must have been, 195, 198–100
Must/must not/mustn't, 150–51, 154–59,
194–200, 202, 219–22
My, 121, 134, 330

N

Need, 276
Neither...nor/either...or, 293, 307–8
Never, 4, 12, 15, 38, 104
Nevertheless, 389–90
No one/nobody/nothing, 123
No problem/no way, 184
Noncount/count nouns, 100–103, 106, 110–11,
130, 133–34, 138–41
Nondefining/defining adjective clauses, 361–64,
368
None of, 362
Nonprogressive verbs, 8–11
Nonrestrictive/restrictive clauses, 361
Nor, 301
Not have to/don't have to, 157–59
Not much, 107
Not only...but also, 307–8
Noun clauses, 318–26, 338–41, 422–23
Nouns, 436
    + infinitives, 268–70
    + prepositions, 245–47